# The Road from Decadence

The Road from Decadence

From Brothel to Cloister

Selected Letters of J. K. Huysmans

Selected, edited and translated by
BARBARA BEAUMONT

THE ATHLONE PRESS
London

First published 1989 by The Athlone Press Ltd
44 Bedford Row, London WC1R 4LY

© B. Beaumont 1989

British Library Cataloguing in Publication Data
Huysmans, J. K.
　The road from decadence : letters
　of J.K. Huysmans.
　1. Huysmans, J. K.—Biography
　I. Title　II. Beaumont, Barbara
　843'.8　　PQ2309.H4Z/

ISBN 0–485–11331–7

All rights reserved. No part of this publication may be reproduced, stored in a retrieval system, or transmitted in any form or by any means, electronic, mechanical, photocopying or otherwise, without prior permission in writing from the publisher.

Printed in Great Britain at the University Press, Cambridge

Make me know the way I should walk,
To you I lift up my soul.
                         Psalm 142

Contents

Introduction		1
Textual Note on the Letters		12
I	1876–84 Naturalism and Decadence	13
II	1885–92 Carbolic for the Soul	62
III	1893–98 The Call of the Cloister	125
IV	1898–1907 Ligugé and the Last Years	177
Notes on the Correspondents		237
Notes on the Text		245
Bibliography		265
Index		267

Introduction

The aim of this collection of letters of J. K. Huysmans is to throw light on the life and work of this man whose career swung from an esoteric expression of sensual delights to commentaries on the liturgy of the Roman Catholic Church; whose personal life oscillated from brothel to monastic cloister. The letters form the background to his literary works; as in a tapestry, the background has the primordial function of filling in the gaps but also, by its own detail and nuance of tone, of giving added relief to the artistic creations for which Huysmans is remembered.

There exists no published edition of the complete correspondence of Huysmans in French. Until recently, it would have been a more or less impossible undertaking, for this correspondence presents a formidable task to the would-be editor, both by its sheer volume, and the fact that much is still in private collections. A number of French scholars have produced editions, partial or complete, of his letters to a single correspondent.[1] But all Huysmans scholars owe an enormous debt of gratitude to the late Pierre Lambert, whose life's work it was to assemble or copy as much of the correspondence as he could. On his death in 1969, he left his archives (including forty-seven folio volumes of letters) to the Bibliothèque de l'Arsenal in Paris, where they are now available to researchers, although the cataloguing remains in a fairly rudimentary state. The two hundred letters in this present volume have been drawn from this Pierre Lambert collection of manuscripts, and also from the monastic archives of the Abbey of St Martin at Ligugé, where Huysmans settled towards the end of his life. A number of the letters are published here for the first time.[2]

The literary destiny of J. K. Huysmans is in fact curious. Although in his own lifetime he was overshadowed by the colossal figure of Émile Zola, his novels were very widely read and he was a prominent figure on the French literary scene, constantly hounded by gossip columnists, and nominated by Edmond de Goncourt in his will as president of the Académie Goncourt. In the 1880s and 90s he was much better known than the poets he sought to protect and encourage, notably Paul Verlaine and Stéphane Mallarmé, both of whom have since overtaken him in terms of fame and literary fortune. The influence of Huysmans' novel *A Rebours* (usually translated as *Against Nature*), published in 1884, was enormous. It brought him to the forefront of public attention, and its impact on the young writers of the last two decades of the nineteenth century should not be underestimated. The work was well known in England also, and the name of its hero, Des Esseintes, became synonymous with everything ultra-refined or debauched, as can be judged from the reaction of horrified delight when Oscar Wilde's character Dorian Gray discovers *A Rebours*, which also has a historical value as a compendium of *fin-de-siècle* taste. Even Huysmans' hefty last novel, *L'Oblat*, which is little read these days, sold forty thousand copies in its first year. There has, however, been something of a revival of interest in his work in France in recent years; a number of significant studies have appeared and his novels are being republished in attractive critical editions.[3]

The life of J. K. Huysmans too is a subject worthy of study: by what stages and by what means did he progress from a nihilistic pessimism *à la* Schopenhauer, via occultism and Satanism, to a confident faith in a merciful God which enabled him to accept, and even transcend, the suffering and intense pain of the cancer that carried him off at the age of fifty-nine?

As far as possible, the letters in this volume have been selected and arranged so as to form a fairly continuous narrative of Huysmans' life, and a sustained commentary on his artistic career. They fall into two categories: those letters that highlight a significant aspect of Huysmans' thinking or a crucial moment in his life, and are of interest regardless of the correspondent to whom they are addressed; then those letters to well-known figures – Émile Zola, Paul Valéry or Odilon Redon – that are interesting also because of the light they throw on Huysmans' relationship with his contemporaries in the artistic world, as well as his opinion of their works. Not surprisingly, it is often in his letters to the less well known, his closest friends, that the more intimate side of Huysmans emerges. In this respect, his correspondence with Arij Prins, a Dutch candle manufacturer and aspiring writer, is particularly valuable. More letters to him than to any other single correspondent figure in this selection; this is in part to provide a unifying thread, as this correspondence covers the greater part of the period under consideration here, and also because Huysmans was obviously at ease in this relationship and spoke freely about whatever was on his mind, whether it be venereal disease, his latest novel or the state of his soul. On the other hand, in some of his letters to well-known literary figures such as Edmond de Goncourt or aspiring writers such as André Gide, we see a much more self-conscious Huysmans, striking something of a pose.

As in all correspondence, the personality and temperament of the writer soon emerge; familiar phrases recur, betraying mood. In the case of Huysmans, we get a picture of a nervous man, whose anxiety brought on frequent bouts of bad health: neuralgia, digestive disorders, headaches; who suffered from an ongoing state of *ennui*: 'Nothing new here' is his constant refrain, even in letters that run to several pages of description of recent events. We see too an isolated man, one who never formed an intimate and long-standing relationship. Friends he had in plenty, but they tended to come and go with the different phases of his life. Huysmans never married, and seems never to have seriously considered doing so; family life and children are remarkably absent from his novels. Like their author, his characters are largely solitaries, who struggle with various troublesome relationships. And like most people, Huysmans enjoyed a good moan: variously about his health, his publisher, the low taste of the French reading public or women who sing in church. Frequent also are his lamentations on the subject of the weather: he could not bear the sun or any degree of heat. In this respect he saw himself as a true child of the Netherlands of his ancestors, having a marked preference for the grey, overcast skies of the north.

Huysmans' commitment to art and literature was the major driving force in his life, and his letters leave us in little doubt on this point. He shared something of Flaubert's desire to pursue and express beauty; but unlike the author of *Madame Bovary*, he saw beauty also as an essential ingredient in the spiritual life; after his conversion in 1892, he sought in religion and its artistic expression the same aesthetic qualities he had previously pursued in secular art. Indeed the correspondence of Huysmans embraces a very wide range of subject matter, for besides his literary activity, he was also an art critic of considerable repute; he relied on journalism to supplement his income and commented frequently on the state of the press in his day. After 1892 much space in his leters is devoted to reflections on the state of the Church in France under the Third Republic; and we encounter too his opinions on the Dreyfus case, America and modernism, which he abhorred. Taken as a whole, this correspondence constitutes an important documentary source for many aspects of French intellectual life in the last years of the nineteenth century.

Linguistically, too, the letters are not without interest; as for the Symbolist generation that was to follow, language was one of Huysmans' great delights. He loved outlandish and colourful expressions, and would readily resort to a neologism if the conventional resources of French failed to provide the nuance he required. In some of the early letters, there is all the preciosity of the debutant writer, seeking to impress with lavish accounts of his literary and sexual prowess. In 1877, for example, he wrote to the Belgian poet Théodore Hannon, who was on holiday at the seaside:

> Has she [the sea] donned her emerald and sky blue dresses, exuded her incomparable saltiness, that smell of an unwashed woman? ... Ah, but we are supposed to be being chaste, wearing baggy trousers to disguise the ardour of our virility ... Céard and I will anoint ourselves with camphor, swallow bromide and water lilies, stuff ourselves with purslane and lettuce leaves. To make up for it, I shall have to let off a loud fart in my novel, which I shall dedicate to virgins embittered by chastity and seminarians worn down by desire.[4]

Patterns of imagery recur; there are many centred on the Deity, even in the days when specifically religious thoughts were far from his conscious mind. God emerges variously as divine pharmacist, cabinet-maker, supreme artist. The notion of the confessional had its appeal too. In general the visual image was immensely important to Huysmans. On his father's side, he came from generations of painters and graphic artists in the Netherlands; Huysmans himself was a first-generation immigrant in France. He undoubtedly had a painter's way of looking at reality, and the essential parallelism between the crafts of writer and painter is a theme of his correspondence. One can imagine that Huysmans readily concurred with the sentiments expressed in a letter he received from Théodore Hannon: '[Literature and painting] are both excellent girls, two sisters who get on perfectly well, without the least jealousy ... That explains my thirst for colour, and the trouble I take with the palette of my style.'[5] He once described himself as a curious mixture of Parisian aesthete and Dutch painter; he was proud of his Flemish forebears, although he himself spoke no Dutch and had very little contact with his surviving family in Holland. He retained throughout his life a taste for Flemish painting, and as a young man showed interest in the work of contemporary Belgian writers such as Emile Verhaeren and Camille Lemonnier who evoked their native Flanders in their poems and short stories.

Huysmans and the Impressionists
In 1879, Huysmans launched the first of a series of attacks on 'official' art in France; that is, the style of the Academy, the kind of picture that was exhibited each year at the 'Salon'. Since the eighteenth century, the preference in such circles had remained for history painting, mythological or religious subjects and portraits, the work of artists such as Bastien Le Page or Puvis de Chavannes. These painters worked essentially indoors; their pictures were the result of intellectual activity within the studio rather than direct observation of life and nature out of doors.

Alongside these official Salons there grew up also, from 1880 onwards, an 'Exposition des Indépendants', the initiative of painters whose work had been refused for the other exhibition as being too modern, too outrageous. Huysmans was to write articles in the Parisian press on both the official Salons and the Indépendants' Exhibition for 1880–82. He never held back from giving full rein to his invective and heaping ridicule on the fashionable painters of the day, most of whom have in fact fallen into obscurity since Huysmans' time. The work of Vollon, for example, he described as 'unhealthy, with syrupy tones and the dullness of molasses'. Indeed, Huysmans can be seen as directly instrumental in the change in public taste. Those who exhibited at the 'Exposition des Indépendants' were, by and large, the Impressionists, now almost universal favourites but at the time virtually to a man struggling and poverty stricken, their work ridiculed and misunderstood. Huysmans was to be their first serious champion. His relationship with this group of painters has been well summed up by Robert Baldick, who writes: 'he had identified himself with their cause to a degree unusual and probably unique in the history of art criticism.'[6] His family background had given him an intuitive feel for painting, and this natural tendency had been developed by regular visits to the Louvre since early youth; this, combined with the verve and fluency of his prose style, made of Huysmans an art critic of outstanding talent – but of course it also made him enemies in the artistic establishment.

Huysmans, who was at this time a disciple of Émile Zola and himself a naturalist novelist, admired the daring of the Impressionists, who cast aside convention and sought in their work to portray modern life in its everyday context; the washerwomen of Degas and the factory chimneys of Raffaëlli filled him with delight. These painters took their canvas and easel outdoors; they took account of the effect of light in modifying colour and outline; they used the full range of colours on the palette in new and unexpected combinations. Because he had a profound understanding of the painter's craft, Huysmans' appreciation of the Impressionists was based on sound technical knowledge and thus had added weight. In 1879 he singled out Manet, who had managed to find his way into the Salon, and praised him alone amongst the exhibitors for his 'open-air' technique and original use of colour. The following year, the Indépendants' Exhibition gave him ample opportunity to further the cause of those he admired. His particular favourites were Gauguin, Monet, Pissarro and especially Degas. This latter he esteemed as a man of rare genius and a painter of striking originality.

There were those who accused Huysmans of simply promoting the work of his friends; but in fact it was more usually the case that the friendship with the painter came after Huysmans had written some favourable article on his work – the result of a letter of thanks, for example. His support for the Impressionists was all the more convincing as he did not hold back from negative comment, where he judged it to be necessary. If he considered that Manet, for example, had exhibited no new pictures of worth in a particular year, he would say so.

It is interesting that in this early stage of his own literary career, alongside his devotion to the Impressionists, Huysmans should also greatly admire the work of Gustave Moreau and Odilon Redon, whose paintings were significantly different from those of Degas and Raffaëlli. Both Moreau and Redon sought to go beyond nature, venturing forth from observation of reality into the domain of dreams. They were blazing a trail in the realms of painting that Huysmans was later to seek to parallel in the world of the novel.

Huysmans' Artistic Credo
Huysmans began his career as a writer under the banner of naturalism, the literary theory of Émile Zola, who sought to bring scientific principles and method to the business of writing novels; the novel would in this way acquire an extra, sociological dimension, the character assuming the value

of a case-study. The philosophical groundwork for this new approach is to be found in the determinism of Hippolyte Taine,[7] for whom race, social class and historical context were the crucial formative factors in human nature. Zola sought to give literary expression to these ideas in his huge Rougon-Macquart novel cycle whose full title is *Histoire naturelle et sociale d'une famille sous le Second Empire*. Such an ambitious and new undertaking inspired great admiration in the young Huysmans, who saw Zola as bringing 'new vigour, audacity and breadth of vision'[8] to the realist tradition in the French novel as practised by Balzac, Flaubert and the Goncourts. Indeed in 1877, in the wake of controversy surrounding the publication of *L'Assommoir*, Zola's novel of alcoholism and human degradation, Huysmans undertook a vigorous defence of his master's literary theories in a pamphlet entitled *Émile Zola et L'Assommoir*. Here the disciple maintains: 'Society has two faces; we show those two faces; we use every colour on the palette, the black as well as the blue.' That he should express his view on the art of the novelist in terms of imagery drawn from painting was highly appropriate, for this defence of naturalism in the domain of the written word was the prelude to his equally vigorous defence of the Impressionists.

In 1891, Huysmans received a letter from the novelist Louis de Robert expressing surprise that he had apparently abandoned naturalism in his more recent work, and enquiring about his current thinking in matters of literary aesthetics. Huysmans replied that he felt that he could not go on producing the same kind of work indefinitely, that evolution was necessary in the career of an artist. He referred the enquirer to the opening chapter of his novel *Là-Bas* which had come out earlier that year and which, he added, 'is basically a summary of what I think about art'.

This chapter takes the form of a dialogue between Durtal, the loosely autobiographical hero of all Huysmans' later novels, and his friend Des Hermies, in which they take apart naturalism as a literary theory, assessing its advantages, but mostly its disadvantages. Des Hermies sets the ball rolling with the provocative statement: 'It's not its lavatorial vocabulary that I reproach naturalism with, nor its outer coating of coarse style, it is rather the trashiness of its ideas that I hold against it, that it is the incarnation of materialism in literature and has glorified artistic democracy!' Such an approach, he maintains, imposes a straitjacket on literature, and eliminates a whole dimension of human experience. He accuses the naturalists of wanting to confine the novel to the 'wash houses of the flesh', rejecting the supersensible, denying the value of dreams, failing even to understand that 'interest begins in art where the senses cease to function'. Zola, for his part, explored the domain below the belt, his work being 'a truss for sentimental hernias'.

Durtal, Huysmans' voice, replies that he too feels repelled by all this materialism but that at the same time one must not underestimate the invaluable service rendered to art by the naturalists, who finally succeeded in ousting the sub-human puppets of Romanticism, furthering the development of language, and conveying genuine emotion in their works. But, retorts Des Hermies, these people actually *like* the age in which they live; yes, adds Durtal, whereas neither Flaubert nor de Goncourt could bear the contemporary world.

Zola is given credit for being a great landscape painter and manipulator of crowds, whereas others of his school, notably Rosny,[9] are guilty of 'descriptive incontinence', writing three or four hundred pages whilst having nothing to say. After the departure of his friend, Durtal continues his reflections alone, wondering what the way forward might be. He realizes that he has been struggling with thoughts such as those expressed by Des Hermies for some time: the theories of naturalism, which he had considered unshakeable, were disintegrating, collapsing about his ears. But, he wonders, what can the novel become, if it is not to return to the stuff and nonsense of the Romantics, to the tearful little stories of George Sand? Durtal feels that he must guard against throwing out the baby with the bathwater; the good aspects of naturalism must be retained: its documentary truthfulness, its accuracy in detail, together with the full and lively language of realism. But, in addition to all this, water needs to be drawn up from the depths of the human soul; mystery cannot simply be explained away by nervous illness. The novel must learn to cater for, as indeed does life, the body *and* the soul, to concern itself with their interaction, their harmony and their conflicts. One should continue to follow the path marked out by Zola on the ground, but at the same time trace another, parallel course in the air, a route leading to the above and beyond, a more complete form of naturalism: a spiritual naturalism. The only person Durtal can see who comes anywhere near what he has in mind is Dostoevsky, but, he reflects, this Russian is more of an evangelical socialist than a disciple of realism. In France, he laments, there are two camps: the liberals, who refine and water down naturalism, and the decadents, who reject all structure and setting, and under the pretext of giving expression to their souls, write gibberish in a telegraphic style. And so, Durtal reflects, the literary scene is in a mess; there is a need for a spiritual dimension, but those who feel this need are floundering amidst spiritism and occultism.

True to the essential dualism of his artistic sensibility, Durtal/Huysmans now switches from literature to painting, highlighting the one with an example and insight drawn from the other. He realizes that the Primitives had succeeded in achieving with the brush the effects he sought to convey with the pen. He remembers how those medieval German and Flemish painters had conveyed, within the detail of a realistic setting, the fullness of holy souls. They achieved a transformation of matter in a flight away from the senses, towards an infinite horizon. Durtal recalls a visit to the museum at Kassel in Germany the previous year, and his reaction there to a painting by Matthias Grünewald of the crucifixion.[10] Here the sufferings of Christ on the cross are portrayed in stark horror: the flesh torn apart by the nails, the congealed blood on the waterlogged flesh of the feet. How far, he muses, is this blood- and tear-stained Calvary from all those debonnaire Golgothas patronized by the Church since the Renaissance. Grünewald was the most outrageous of realists, but there was an extra, transforming dimension to this picture: a superhuman expression that illuminates the distortion of the flesh. Surveying the literary scene, Durtal can find no verbal equivalent to Grünewald's painting. Perhaps certain pages by the mystic Anne Emmerich[11] on the Passion of Christ came somewhere near. Then he realizes with a start that if he follows this line of thought to its logical conclusion, he will arrive at the Catholicism of the Middle Ages, at mystic naturalism. Durtal has a moment of hesitation; he draws back a little, wondering if he is ready for such a venture. But the future course of Huysmans' own career reveals that this logical conclusion was indeed pursued in his later work, in novels such as *La Cathédrale* and *L'Oblat*.

Huysmans and the Novel Form
Huysmans' letters trace the evolution in his own relationship with the novel as a literary genre. We have seen him beginning his career as a faithful disciple of Zola, and in his first ten years as a published writer he produced four naturalist novels: *Marthe, Les Sœurs Vatard, En Ménage* and *A Vau l'Eau*. In these works, he protrayed in a documentary spirit scenes of working-class and bourgeois domestic life. But unlike Zola, Huysmans already revealed an interest in the unusual case, the exceptional character, rather than seeking simply to re-create typicality amongst peasants, pork butchers or bankers. The potential of this latter kind of material came to strike him as essentially limited and fundamentally boring. He longed to stretch his wings with something out of the ordinary. *A Rebours* was to provide him with that challenge. Des Esseintes' quest for esoteric experiences is as far removed as possible from the slice-of-life approach to novel writing. This is a novel with only one character, where the artificial reigns supreme. Des Esseintes' dining room, for example, is a mock-up of a cabin on board ship; an inner structure allows water to be pumped around and be visible through portholes, but unlike the sea, the colour of this water can be changed at whim by various additives, and the fish that swim in it are, of course, all mechanical, not real. A book where the experiences of the senses took precedence over the events of everyday life was bound to indicate to Zola that his disciple was now questioning naturalism as a formula for the novel. Huysmans' rate of literary production slowed down rather at this point in the mid-1880s, as he sought a new perspective, a new approach to his art.

With *En Rade* of 1887 he tried to keep a foot in both camps, so to speak. The book oscillates between naturalism and supernaturalism; it is 'a pair of trousers with badly matched legs' as he admitted in a letter to Zola. The naturalist part presents Huysmans' impressions of country life and the brutish nature of an unidealized peasantry. Interspersed with this narrative are three long accounts of dreams, in an attempt to combine the conscious and subconscious dimensions of human experience.

From 1891 and the publication of *Là-Bas* onwards, all Huysmans' fictional works form a loosely autobiographical cycle centred on Durtal; the fictional element becomes progressively diminished between Durtal's first ventures into occult circles in *Là-Bas* and the concluding volume of the series, *L'Oblat* of 1903. Huysmans was clearly becoming more interested in fact than in fiction; he wanted to write about such things as the symbolism of medieval ecclesiastical architecture, which he did exquisitely well in *La Cathédrale*. But he was a novelist by training, geared to reaching a wide reading public, having access where the works of the specialist historian could not reach. And so he continued to coat the pill with sugar, to use his own phrase, although one has to admit that the coating is remarkably thin in parts and the artistic unity of his work inevitably suffers. *L'Oblat*, for example, which has as its *raison d'être* the deepening of the religious quest of Durtal, provides as a non-fictional bonus a fairly detailed history of the phenomenon of oblation in the Order of St Benedict, and this can be seen as integral to the novel's purpose. But besides this, there are excrescences for which it is difficult to find any artistic justification – for example, lengthy descriptions of paintings in the museum at Dijon – that contribute little to the fabric of the novel. On the other hand, this digressionary technique does at times provide us with some wonderful set pieces, virtuoso descriptions, such as those of the statuary of Chartres cathedral, where Huysmans the stylist emerges in full control of his art.

One feels that by the turn of the century Huysmans had virtually given up on the novel form; indeed, he produced no more fiction after *L'Oblat*. And so, paradoxically, he who had, as early as the mid-1880s, pointed the way forward for future pioneers of the novel such as James Joyce and Marcel Proust had either not known how to develop, or had lost interest in developing further those tentative steps he took with Des Esseintes in *A Rebours* towards the stream-of-consciousness approach to novel writing. A shift in Huysmans' own perspective on life seems the most likely explanation for this situation. The direction of his life changed radically after his conversion, which brought with it a shift in priorities. He was now far more interested in content than in form; the aesthetic, which still held pride of place in his artistic canon, was now to be combined with a moral and didactic purpose.

Church and State in France 1892–1907
At the time of Huysmans' conversion in 1892, relations between the Catholic Church in France and the Third Republic (in power since the Franco–Prussian War of 1870–1) were already strained. The Catholic parties had always been staunch supporters of the monarchy, and the new regime feared that this right-wing opposition might take advantage of the democratic process to secure a parliamentary majority and then proceed to change the constitution, returning France to a monarchy. This it was determined to avoid at all costs, and so embarked on a programme of

repressive measures designed to limit the influence of the Church, not only in the specific field of politics, but across the whole range of the Church's activities. (At the end of 1891, for example, the government banned pilgrimages; the archbishop of Aix-en-Provence, who ventured to protest, was put on trial and fined.)

In February 1892 Pope Leo XIII – who, despite his age, was not lacking in wisdom and perspicacity – issued a would-be conciliatory encyclical, urging French Catholics to accept the established government in their country. This, however, had the unfortunate effect of dividing the Catholic opposition between those who toed the Vatican line and rallied to the cause of the secular State, and those who held out against it. This division was to prove a fatal weakness in the coming years, as the Catholics failed to present a united front to the onslaught from anticlerical elements in the government. This lack of unity was a constant source of frustration to Huysmans, who lamented cynically that the Catholics deserved the harsh treatment they were to receive in the coming decade.

By the mid-1890s, the composition of the French government had taken a radical turn, and in 1896 the Cabinet included no fewer than nine Freemasons, traditional enemies of Catholicism, including Émile Combes as Minister for Religious Affairs. One of his first acts was to introduce a tax on religious orders and congregations, although Masonic lodges were to be exempt.

The Dreyfus case further fragmented the Catholics, as indeed it split the whole French nation. One of the essential things at stake in this affair was the honour and integrity of the army, and it was this that had made a majority of Catholics take sides against Dreyfus, a Jew and supposed traitor. The whole business was immensely complex, with much evidence suppressed, and the divide was by no means simply between pro-Church and anticlerical factions. The attitude of French Catholics towards the army at this time is well summed up by Professor McManners:

> To those who believed that France had betrayed its mission as 'the eldest daughter of the Chruch' and saw the Republic falling a prey to Freemasons and Jews, the army stood as the one uncontaminated institution. The officer corps of the Second Empire had been continued intact into the Republic, and as a conservative group, had been strengthened by the influx of young men of Catholic and Royalist families.[12]

When Waldeck-Rousseau became prime minister in 1899 (at the time of Huysmans' move to Ligugé and his plans to end his days in the shadow of the monastery), he began an attack on the religious orders. Feeling confident after the débâcle of the Dreyfus affair, the government no longer concerned itself with conciliation and tackled the Church head on. The teaching function of religious had always been a source of resentment; now over three thousand Church schools were closed, despite riots in Brittany and elsewhere. The represssive measures were aimed particularly at religious, for they seemed to be outside the control and supervision of the State, having no roots in secular society, living apart and looking towards Rome for leadership. Hence the Republic considered monks and nuns to constitute a threat. The law of 1 July 1901 required religious congregations to apply to parliament for authorization. If this was refused, their property was to be auctioned and their members dispersed. Many religious, including the Benedictines at Ligugé, now went into voluntary exile abroad, knowing that they had no chance of receiving government authorization. Indeed, on one day alone, eighty-one congregations of nuns were abolished with a single vote in the chamber of deputies.

As Combes succeeded Waldeck-Rousseau as prime minister, the battle became even more acrimonious. On the question of Church schools he declared: 'Liberty of education is not one of those essential rights which are inseparable from the person of the citizen . . . it is a concern of the social power, which has the right to regulate its usage.'[13] There were unfortunate changes on the Catholic side too. The new Pope Pius X did not pursue the same policies as his predecessor in social matters but, more significantly, he appointed Cardinal Merry Del Val to liaise with the French government; this latter's brashness and undiplomatic remarks did much to hasten the final separation of Church and State in France. The leaking of a document written by Merry Del Val in 1904 put this fragile relationship in jeopardy, and a Law of Separation was indeed voted by the chamber on 3 July 1905. There was no consultation with the Church in the preparation of this legislation, which came into force in December 1906, a few months before Huysmans' death. Church buildings and property were taken over by the State, this latter having already secured the right to appoint bishops without consultation; payment of clergy salaries ceased, and local mayors acquired rights of inspection. It was to take the upheaval of the First World War to stem the tide of bitterness in the relationship between Church and State in France.

Textual Note on the Letters

The letters in this collection are reproduced in entirety with one or two exceptions, where only extracts were available for consultation; this is indicated in the text. Huysmans' use of punctuation was erratic, especially his predilection for dashes; in the translations, punctuation has been standardized in accordance with English usage, but some dashes are retained as a reflection of a quirk of style in the original. He signed his letters in a variety of ways, varying initials and spelling of his name according to his correspondent. For example, in his letters to Arij Prins he uses a Dutch spelling of his name; this feature has been retained. All the letters are written from Paris unless otherwise indicated.

I acknowledge a debt of gratitude to the scholarship of the late Robert Baldick in his excellent biography of Huysmans, to the late Dom. P. Minard OSB, archivist of the abbey of Ligugé, and to my husband, who transcribed many of the manuscripts consulted.

I
1876–84
Naturalism and Decadence[1]

Huysmans was twenty-eight in 1876, and had already been employed as a civil servant for ten years. He had obtained his post as a sixth-grade clerk after successfully taking the baccalaureate examinations in 1866. His schooldays had been far from happy. His father, Godfried Huysmans, a lithographer and native of Breda, had died when Georges (as the man we know as Joris-Karl was baptized) was only eight years old. Within the year his mother remarried to Monsieur Og, who was to become a partner in the bookbinding business on the ground floor of the family home at 11 rue de Sèvres. The young Huysmans was now to feel starved of affection, seeing his two half-sisters preferred to himself and being sent to a Dotheboys Hall-type boarding school, virtually within walking distance of home. When he began his job at the Ministry, he had also planned to study law part-time at the University of Paris, but he did not persevere with his studies for more than a year, although he passed the necessary exams. He was becoming more and more drawn into the life of the Latin Quarter, and as he admitted, he preferred to spend his money on women than on faculty fees.

He was also beginning to write. His first volume was published initially at his own expense, but it sold sufficiently well for the publisher to run a second edition, this time at his expense. This was *Le Drageoir aux épices* of 1874, a collection of prose poems very much in the style of Baudelaire, who had been dead for some seven years. The subjects are mixed: some are evocations of working-class life in Paris; some show a taste for the exotic, Japanese geisha girls; others are still lifes, revealing the painterly dimension of Huysmans' artistic make-up.

1876 was also the year in which he met Zola. It was literally a case of the struggling debutant on the literary scene daring to go and knock on the door of a famous and controversial novelist in order to pay his respects, and offer the master copies of his own work. Huysmans was soon admitted to Zola's circle of intimates. Indeed, the latter found it useful to have such admiring young writers at his beck and call; in this way he could farm out much of the documentary research needed for the novels of his panoramic Rougon-Macquart cycle. Huysmans became a frequent visitor at Médan, the property that Zola, with fortune in the ascendant, bought just outside Paris. He was to be one of the writers who contributed to the volume of stories *Les Soirées de Médan*, under Zola's patronage.

He became an active participant in the Parisian literary scene; he frequented Flaubert's Sunday afternoon salons, and the Goncourts' famous 'grenier'. Huysmans was also drawn to the company of poets and felt that he had a great deal in common with Mallarmé, Verlaine and Villiers de l'Isle-Adam, who figure amongst his correspondents. During this early period, he was also in regular contact with a number of young Belgian artists. Huysmans' maternal grandparents had lived near Brussels, and in his childhood he had spent a number of holidays in Belgium. But in the summer of 1876, he was to set off for the Belgian capital on literary business. Knowing that his first full-length novel, *Marthe, histoire d'une fille*, a strictly unsentimental treatment of love and prostitution, risked problems with the French censorship, he determined to find a publisher in Brussels, where regulations were less severe. It was during this stay that he met the poet Théodore Hannon and the critic Camille Lemonnier, with whom he was to exchange letters regularly for a number of years.

Huysmans' approach to fiction has been described as naturalism at its most sordid in this first phase of his career. Indeed, none of the characters in his first four novels achieves anything approaching happiness, and the conditions of their lives are drab and depressing. His second work, *Les Sœurs Vatard*, set in a small bookbinding firm, reflects an aspect of Parisian working-class life that Huysmans knew well from personal experience. On the death of his mother it was he who had to take on managerial responsibility for the modest family business in the rue de Sèvres. He continued to live over the shop for many years; the business provided the raw material for his fictional bookbinders.

En Ménage of 1881 reflects the negative view of marriage that Huysmans was to retain all his life. It is the story of a young novelist for whom both wife and mistress prove a disappointment, failing to provide the material comfort and emotional security he had yearned for as a bachelor. Huysmans himself had had one disastrous attempt at cohabitation, with an actress who had given birth to another man's child before his very eyes one freezing winter night, when they had money for neither coal nor midwife. His subsequent preference was for prostitutes or mistresses who continued to live in their own apartments. Indeed those letters he wrote to friends, ostensibly to congratulate them on a forthcoming marriage, read more like dire warnings or commiserations than a participation in a happy occasion.

His next, much shorter work, *A Vau l'Eau*, contains a denunciation of the restaurant trade in Paris. Huysmans always feared for his delicate stomach when subjected to the adulterated – not to say putrescent – fare offered in the capital's hostelries. But it is also an expression of black pessimism; its civil servant hero seeks refuge in the maxims of Schopenhauer. Huysmans himself described this novel as a 'missal of petty misfortunes'; it is an expression of the potential for tragedy in the wretchedness of everyday life. In this sense, the hero Folantin is a prototype of Jean-Paul Sartre's character Roquentin.

The exploration of these various aspects of nineteenth-century French life engendered in their author a far-reaching disgust with the modern world and its values. This repugnance was such that he no longer wished to depress himself with the research necessary to re-create in his works naturalist portrayals of everyday life. He was now attracted rather by the unusual, the exceptional, the extreme; this fascination was to culminate in what has become known as the spirit of decadence, which was to find its expression in *A Rebours*, on which Huysmans worked in 1883–4. This work is generally acclaimed as the supreme literary expression of decadence, making of its author a herald of the Symbolist movement. This spirit of decadence expressed itself in a feeling of futility, coupled with rejection of any notion of moral or religious restraint. It sought refinement in the avoidance of the banal and the novelty of sense experience, going beyond the limits of the natural and venturing even into the domain of the perverted. Huysmans' hero, Des Esseintes, is the embodiment of this spirit in his efforts to conquer his profound *ennui* and his cult of the extraordinary. But his experiments with exotic pleasures, perfumes, furnishings, etc., all end in failure, leading only to illness and pessimism. By the end of the novel, Des Esseintes is beginning to look to the possibility of religion as a last resort.

But Huysmans had not yet travelled as far as his hero. He had long since abandoned the Catholic faith of his Dutch forebears and of his own childhood, and was by no means contemplating a return to the ecclesiastical fold at this stage. We see rather, following on from *A Rebours*, the beginnings of a fascination with the occult in various forms.

Huysmans was also active in the field of journalism during these years, and for his defence of his friends the Impressionist painters he himself suffered abuse and attack in the Parisian press. When, in 1883, he decided to collect into a volume his articles on the lamentable state of academic art and the merits of the new school of artists, his publisher considered the work (which Huysmans entitled *L'Art moderne*) too hot to handle. He delayed publication for a while, and then agreed to bring out a much emasculated version, greatly to its author's chagrin.

Throughout this period, Huysmans continued to earn his living at the Ministry of the Interior, where he found the work profoundly boring; he heartily resented this incursion into his time. But the office desk was to remain a necessary evil, for although his books enjoyed moderate success at this stage they did not bring in enough to live on, and any profits from the bookbinding business went towards supporting his orphaned half-sisters, for whom he assumed responsibility until their respective marriages. Huysmans' conditions of work at the Ministry would not strike us today as too onerous: his hours were from midday until 5.30 p.m., and so many of his letters to his friends were written during office hours and on Ministry letterhead that the job cannot have been so demanding, despite his incessant protests.

To THÉODORE HANNON

16 December 1876

Dear Sir and Colleague,

I heard that the article in *L'Artiste* on *Marthe* was by you. I thank you for those gallant lines you devoted to a poor girl thrown to the mercy of the French censorship.

You said it – I am a realist of the school of Goncourt, Zola and Flaubert etc. In Paris there is a small group of us convinced that the novel can no longer be a story that is more or less true, more or less dressed up, coated in fish paste like certain pills, to mask the taste. By realism we mean the patient study of reality, achieving an overall impression detail by detail, cruel ones if need be, trivial even, if that helps us to strike the right note. As you can see, we are far removed from the days of the novels of Dumas the elder.[2] Balzac was the first to blaze a trail; we follow him, as bravely as we can. As far as style is concerned, we are all more or less indebted to Gautier.[3] By observation and word colour, we hope to convey the ideas and incidents that haunt us.

This will explain why, dear sir, as we are determined not to select exceptions within character types, as Goncourt does for example, I did not wish to cast Marthe naked on to a zinc table top, with her stomach slit open, exposing the nervous and muscular system, like the pipes of an organ which can be exposed to view. The ending, which is not really an ending, is certainly much more true to reality than death, which is as worn out as an old drama or the hideously heavygoing works of the late Ponsard of the French Academy.[4]

But instead of discussing the greater or lesser variety of the subject matter, I should do well to applaud your good, fine prose style. Here in Paris it was a pleasure to see that there are courageous stylists like you and Lemonnier in Brussels as well.

I have asked M. Degeorge to let you have a copy of *Marthe* if you do not already have one. Moreover I hope to be able to speak with you at greater length than is possible by letter, should you come to Paris. I should be glad of your visit, if you were to have a few minutes to spare.

I assure you, my dear colleague, of my friendly feelings towards you.

Huysmans

To ÉMILE ZOLA

7 January 1877

Dear Sir and Master,

Marthe has been so stupidly attacked by the censorship and by certain newspapers, for the benefit of outraged morality, that your kind letter made me proud and pleased.

I have just read the latest instalment of *L'Assommoir*.[5] It is fine, oh but absolutely fine! Gervaise walking the streets in the mud, watching her shadow dancing, is admirable, and the refrain: 'Will you listen, sir' that keeps recurring is moving to the point of tears! I know of nothing more poignant than Gervaise and Coupeau meeting in the snow and going each on their way, without exchanging a word. But what is the point of telling you all this, telling you that the scene between the man with the golden beard and the starving woman is simply splendid? You will receive, if you have not already done so, praise more precious than mine; but all the same, I felt the need to tell you all this. Of all the superb scenes you have invented in your earlier novels, it is most certainly the most powerful and the most incomparably beautiful!

Excuse my scribbling and accept my thanks and the genuine assurance of my admiration.

Huysmans

To THÉODORE HANNON

7 April 1877

My Dear Poet,
You ask me if I have any information on what is being sent to the Salon this year – alas, no! Or very little: I know that Carolus Duran[6] is sending a portrait, that Vollon[7] is sending nothing, that Laurens[8] is sending 'Marceau's funeral' and Georges Sauvage 'Gauls'.[9] This ignorance is a result of the situation prevailing in Paris; as I was saying to Lemonnier in my last letter, Zola and I were kicked out of a literary dining club of which we were members, as these gentlemen found that we lowered the artistic tone; suffice it to say that the writers who make up this dining club are H. Malot, Mendès, T. Réveillon etc., in fact all our literary enemies.[10]

Our situation is the same as that of the painters. We have always supported the Impressionists, who have likewise been put beyond the pale of society, and no longer send anything to the Salon, knowing that they will be rejected; they have just opened a private exhibition of their works which contains pure marvels!

I have the unrivalled joy of being the particular *bête noire* of those good Parnassians,[11] since I slated those circus tumblers of the written word in my first article on Zola; they accuse me of bringing about the failure of the poverty-stricken, which is quite an admirable charge. It is all becoming eminently laughable.

I promise myself some more delicious moments when the Salon opens; I am sharpening my pen for cutting words, to pierce all those cream puffs and romantic or classical concertinas that will be spread before our eyes. What is more, I hope that we shall have the pleasure of going to the Salon together, as you will be in Paris then, and those ancient Greek efforts, portraits by Cabanel and women with white flowers, leaning on one elbow, had all better look out![12]

I am still working away at my novel,[13] alternating between anxiety and satisfaction; this one will be a rough lad and will make the balding bourgeois reach for an eye shade. And what about your volume of verse to give goose flesh to timorous souls! Is it finished? I hope that in Paris you will treat us, my friends and me, to a few vigorously turned sonnets, bursting with bright gleams!

Here the weather is indecent, my soul is full of blackness and I am stuffing mud into the heart of the heroine of my novel, Désirée, a bookbinding employee, a girl with squinty eyes and an amply filled-out bosom. This little lass is proving quite difficult to dress as she should be, without the least adornment. I think you will like certain passages in the aforementioned work, amongst them a wonderful gingerbread fair and a train that I have roll along with all the changes of disc, points, vibrations – it's modern! Damn it, it's modern!

In the meantime I must leave you, I should have done better to talk less nonsense and more of serious matters, but enough! That will be for another time! Désirée gives you a curtsey and her father shakes you by the hand.
Yours

Huysmans

To THÉODORE HANNON

20 April 1877

You should, my dear friend, tell the gentleman who edits *La Chronique* not to use up so much of his wit all at one go. It is an enormous waste of energy, but after all, one must not complain, for it is a joy to be attacked by fools, and the said gentleman most certainly falls into that category.

From that point of view, the Belgian press has no reason to be jealous of the French press, which is unspeakably rich in ineptitude. Céard,[14] who wrote to you, must have told you of the bitter-sweetness and the gall that Mendès vomits over us in his paper, on the subject of the unfortunate dinner that took place recently with Flaubert, Goncourt, Zola, Charpentier the publisher and us.[15] These Parnassians are really most curious, we take no notice of them, we treat their works with the most perfect and deserved disdain; we live quite apart from literary circles which, what is more, despise us as much as we despise them, and we cannot even have a quiet dinner, without someone making up a ridiculous menu and a load of foolish remarks that we are supposed to be making to each other!

It is true that what annoys these dear colleagues most is that they do not see us anywhere; our group has chosen to isolate itself, and does not frequent the beer houses and other literary haunts. For the most part we are fortunate enough not to have to earn our bread from journalism and be obliged to stir up the mud of this odious trade, such as it is plied – such things are unforgivable!

They would gladly call us the nobs of the literary rabble and the revolutionaries of literature, just as those unfortunate Impressionist painters are accused of stirring up revolution in painting; we are reputed to wish to overturn all finer feelings, such as the tears of love, patriotism, illusions concerning mistresses etc. We 'raise a high-flown corpse' (I have really no idea what *Le Gaulois* meant when it applied this nice expression to my book). But there you are.

I laughed until my sides ached when I read your *Courrier de Paris*. Well, you will get yourself put beyond the pale of Brussels society if you continue to set squibs like that off under their feet, because there must be very few of you in the van over there!

Meanwhile, nothing new, I am hacking away vigorously; I am still immersed in my novel and I am floundering about in some very simple situations, but in the end the chapters grow longer and lie down one beside the other. Only, damn it all, there are days when one gets stuck over a sentence, and the words to convey a splash of colour do not come; style is a hellish thing, and to think that all that is lost on the majority of readers, who do not give a damn for our fireworks and understand nothing of the sentences we work and rework!

Basically, as I was saying to Céard, we write for fourteen people, and it is not quite enough! And you know, between you and me, I think this state of affairs will continue for a long time yet. Others will benefit later, we will play the role of advance guard, we are firing the first shots from the bushes, and we get the full blast from the prudish press and from Lady Censorship, who pulls the ground from beneath our feet, as happened to me over *Marthe*.

Enough! I have run out of room; there is just enough to send you my friendly greetings and a warm handshake.

Huysmans

To THÉODORE HANNON

[24 April 1877]

My Dear Poet,

I have savoured the ignominious bouquet that some foolish creep felt obliged to send you on the subject of *L'Artiste*! This good soul must be about his devotions twice daily, drinking glasses of Bordeaux in those abbeys open-to-all-comers that line the little street by the barracks, not far from St Gudule, in the good city of Brussels in Brabant. May this perfect ass have the remaining twenty hairs plucked from his head by some caressing hand. I shall not protest, he does well, it is only natural. But that he should cry out against indecency, filth! Oh, no! These cold fish are a nuisance to us, after all! And to think that things are the same here, that none of what we write is understood, that that fool Bergerat makes out that I insulted T. Gautier, his father-in-law, in *L'Actualité belge*!![16] That all the romantics are using me for target practice, and that their anger is equalled only by my complete disdain of all of them!

In the meantime, to tell you the whole truth, we have problems – there is only Zola who supports us absolutely! Goncourt is an egoist who makes fun of us, and terrible as it is to admit it, Flaubert, acclaimed by Mendès and all the Parnassians, the man who wrote *Madame Bovary*, and who detests his own masterpiece and goes into ecstasy over his *La Tentation de Saint Antoine*, is more of an enemy than a friend![17] We spent the day at his place on Sunday and Céard and I came away more distressed and dejected than I can put into words. All of that is not much fun, as you see. Basically, Hugo is absolute master; our little group did not bow in homage to his latest *Légende des siècles*;[18] it has been noted, and everyone is against us. And what is more than sad is that these people all hate each other: Flaubert runs down Goncourt, Goncourt knocks Flaubert, both use Zola as a whipping-boy behind his back. What blessings! It makes one want to bolt one's door and stay at home!

Still, it looks as if that is the way it has always been, and that it is we who have been simpletons in believing great men to be incapable of baseness; so let us say no more about it.

I thank you for the reproductions for *Le Drageoir*.[19] One can take or leave many things in the said volume; I cut my teeth on that one, a hotchpotch of modern and medieval. Most certainly if the book were to come out now, I would cut out a good half of it – juvenilia! I have tasted sarsaparilla since then, and have been purged!

Mucous membranes and illusions! Brr! How things all fall about one's ears. I would not stir up all those medieval cast-offs again now!

You mention Rops, but damn it all, I have admired him for a long time![20] I know most of his work, including the erotic ones; there are some splendid things! This valiant engraver is a natrualist of immense talent! Damn it all, I should be very happy to meet him, if he were to be agreeable to it. One can only wish that all those French softies would get a bit of inspiration from him, instead of bothering us with their eighteenth-century insipidness and those modern works that smack of Hinduism.

Last but not least on that subject – we were supposed to be launching a journal entitled *Le Salon*. Those painters immediately refused to subscribe; the names of the editors, which they probably got to hear of, might have given them a vague idea of the naturalist campaign we were promising ourselves. We died a death before being born!

A return to relative calm here. *L'Assommoir* is sold out at every edition, but is progressing more calmly. The battles it sparked off have come to an end. Flaubert's short stories are unmodern for the most part, two out of three.²¹ Moreover they are gentle, but admirably written; there will be no controversy there. All we can do is wait.

I am still working, but am no longer inclined to hurry. I have learnt from a reliable source that as the censorship did not dare to attack Zola and Goncourt, they have decided to come down like a ton of bricks on the first young man to launch a novel that pulls no punches. Having landed in the *avant-garde*, I do not care to fall on my backside, so I would not mind if someone overtook me between now and when Désirée is finally wrenched from me. Come now, you are most fortunate! To be able to say whatever you like without risking prison and fines! What a depressing system we have here, and what an armoury our adversaries have against us, the guillotine always to hand!

Nothing besides all that: mud, rain, wind. Visited a painter who considers Gérôme a very great man;²² a battle naturally. On Saturday saw Stevens²³ at Montrosier's, director of the *Musée des Deux Mondes*, a paper which was in the van and which has, alas, just folded. Saw also pupils of that odious painter they call Cabanel. All these fine young men upset me, and when I am back home they make me want to respond to all their artistic and literary theories with works full of defiance.

Seen again also that fat brute of a publisher by the name of Dentu. He is more and more determined never to take a novel from me on the most curious pretext that I write in a language that does not amuse the readers of his books. That is quite possible! For after all, the Zaccones and Du Boisgobeys and the rest,²⁴ who are by the way atrociously afraid of us, have most certainly learnt that special language that charms the hearts of pork butchers and tripe merchants! We need re-educating. It was Dentu, moreover, who told me, when I offered him *Le Drageoir*: 'little things like that don't prove anything, there must be action'. And he asked me the meaning of half of the words I had used. It was high comedy, I beg you to believe it, all the more so as the explanations were interrupted on that day by the arrival of famous writers such as Paul Féval, Assolent and other nitwits of letters.²⁵ And the prodigious Dentu hurried up to them, shaking their hands, purring, billing and cooing, playing the simpleton and saying to me: 'I am all yours, young man'. I began to understand literature that day.

There! Hereupon my girl runs her fingers over you and gives you a friendly smile with her lips pursed and her hand on her heart; as for me, I am going to undress her a bit more, for the amazement of the reading public, and with my free hand I shake yours merrily.

Your most devoted

Huysmans

To CAMILLE LEMONNIER

[May 1877]

My Dear Colleague,

Firstly thank you for what you say you are sending me. Ah, on the subject of those articles, *La Vie littéraire* reproduced a part of the first one without even taking the trouble to say where they got it from; a fine case of plagiarism as you can see.

Now let us talk about Flaubert, if you are agreeable. I am going to have to tell you some monstrous and unlikely things, but they are unfortunately true. Flaubert, who is a wonderful genius, a great master, has never had his portrait drawn in his own home. It would be interesting to do it, if it were possible. But here is the problem – you will keep this to yourself, won't you – when this great writer is not holding his pen, he is as stupid as a pork butcher. Thus his friends hide the man in the dressing-gown and confine themselves to exalting the stylist as he deserves. You see the situation. I spent the day at his place on Sunday. I left there distraught and sadder than I can say. Zola admitted to me that it had made him completely ill the first few times, and that his wife had had to make him some herb tea when he got home. What is to be done in such conditions, portray him as he is, dressed half as a Turk and half as a monk? What would be the point? I think it would be better simply to review the book. Moreover I think that he, who lives quite apart from literary circles and sees only Zola, Goncourt, Daudet and his great friend Turgenev,[26] would be furious if one were to reveal the inside of his home. He is an excellent man, obliging, very affable, but he goes off the rails as soon as he talks about literature and art. It is overbearing, it is unheard of, but that is the way it is. Moreover that article on his work would be more than difficult. Flaubert does not like people to talk to him about *Madame Bovary*; for him *Salammbô*[27] and *La Tentation de Saint Antoine* are his favourite children. I admit to finding *Madame Bovary* superior from every point of view; I should feel obliged to say so, and I am sure that he would consider me a complete fool if I admitted it.

There is the situation. You can see that it is quite difficult. After all, one could get away with a simple literary article, giving deserved praise to *L'Éducation sentimentale* which, in my opinion, contains admirable pages that are too little known.[28] Needless to say he has a weak spot for this book which has had no success; what is more, that is stupidity on the part of the reading public. In any case, see what you think and tell me your opinion in all this.

As for the Salon, I will send you all the notes you like, but damn it all, you were supposed to come to Paris then. Have you abandoned that good idea? I shall see Céard in the next few days I think, and I will give him the message.

Nothing new apart from all that; I continue to be the *bête noire* of the Parnassians. I share this honour with Zola. All the band of Hugo-ites abhors us. It is becoming quite funny.

Have you received a letter from Montrosier informing you of the painful loss we suffered in the person of the *Musée des Deux Mondes*? The review is dead. What a majestic fool Bachelin is![29] He was always plotting; he wanted the thing to be very carefully written, so as to whet the appetite of artists, and at the same time lure the middle classes with his dreadful colour plates. Both camps fled. For my part I am very upset by it, for in spite of the ridiculous chastity of his notions, that paper did show advanced thinking, and that thanks to Montrosier, who really went to a lot of trouble to try and get it out of the rut.

As for *La République des lettres*, with which we are at daggers drawn, it is flapping only one wing at the moment; there is no money – Mendès is selling it for three sous instead of ten now. Symptomatic! It is true that as the whole of the present editorial staff is composed of reactionaries, its loss would not be something to weep over!

We are still waiting for Charpentier to make up his mind and found his great review. If the Zola faction gets the upper hand, we shall be the masters of this paper; if, on the other hand, the Daudet faction wins the day, we shall be in a very difficult situation, for he is as ill-disposed as is possible towards new writers. I shake you by the hand, for I have no more room.

Yours

Huysmans

To THÉODORE HANNON

18 May 1877

My Dear Hannon,

That was good news you had to tell: the king of Belgium is buying your pictures. Great! You are lucky to have intelligent rulers. We are completely dumbfounded: we are going to have another government that will be out to get us and the censorship of books will again be stricter than ever. How the devil shall we manage? You can see that politics is having an influence on literature at the moment, and that we are more than cross at the *coup d'état* that has just taken place.[30]

Ah, it was hard to get them to swallow *Nana*.[31] The truth is that the article was a bit highly spiced and that the theory about the silk stockings was really a bit much. What was simply admirable was the exquisite scene that took place. I should be grateful if you could send me two or three copies of that issue.

I might also ask you to let me place a few lines on a volume of verse that has just come out. This book is far from being a masterpiece, but it is Parisian and modern, and is not a product of the Hugo stable; it is intensely disliked by the Parnassians. Without quibbling over many points that our group does not like in this poem, I think it should have our support all the same.

If you agree, I will run off a few lines on this Parisian poem, which is called *Marcelle*.[32]

Nothing new apart from that. I have been completely out of sorts for the last week. Neuralgia has seized hold of me, and I spend my time with opium patches on my temples, quinine pills in my pockets, and I am doing no work! Still, I hope all that will come to an end and I shall be on my feet again soon.

We are still expecting you, and wishing that the unfortunate accident that keeps you in Brussels will come to an end. We welcome also the good news that *L'Artiste* is expanding. We will talk about it in Paris, a sad city at the moment, with alternating sun and rain.

There is what I had to tell you; I have no courage to laugh or to write any more, I am so naïve!

What sadness! Have you read *The Art of Being a Grandfather*?[33] I have picked out this admirable line:

'I, who am rendered quite stupid by a little child.'

I would never have dared to say it. What a load of clichés that book is: a sickly purée of moonlight and little petticoats. Basically it is the seventh time he has poured more water over the tea leaves of his early poems. Is it not distressing to see a man who had talent talking drivel and chewing bread and milk slops with his last two teeth? One has to say that if *La Légende des siècles* sold badly, this one is not selling at all, despite the clashing of cymbals and the fanfare of trombones in *Le Rappel*. It is symptomatic! Zola continues to be sold out while Hugo remains untouched in the shop windows.

Yours

Huysmans

To CAMILLE LEMONNIER

[May–June 1877]

My Dear Colleague,

I answer the letter you sent me this morning. Flaubert is just as I told you, an excellent man, helpful and most devoted to his friends, but one must not discuss questions of art, for he goes off the rails. It is a singular example of the difference that can exist between the writer and the man.

Add to that that he is an artist of conviction, so much taken up with his own art that he denies all others! I have heard him answer someone who was speaking to him about painting: 'Is there such a thing?' As for musicians, they are cabinet-makers, he says. But none of this detracts from his admirable talent as a writer. His literary theories, which vary, moreover, two or three times a day, would be a most prodigious hotchpotch if one could but follow any of them. For example, one of his favourite axioms, for he is always repeating it, is this: there is no such thing as ancient, there is no such thing as modern. What is there then? In short, we get our legs broken; it is certainly hard to imagine that this is the man who wrote *Madame Bovary*.

As for the article, I think you should simply pass in review his work until you arrive at *Trois Contes*, which I am about to read. I shall tackle it in a couple of days.

Now I come to your post scriptum. Do not hesitate, go ahead and accept the preface. What is more, if naturalism were to remain pitched on the sharp note we have given it, that would certainly lead to artistic narrowing. It does not matter if the preface attacks the troublemakers; one should never be wounded by a slating made in good faith. The best proof I can offer is that the one in *Le Gaulois* on *Marthe* made me want to meet its author. Fourcaud[34] spoke his mind straightforwardly and did well to do so! That is all I know.

So let things take their course! No one here will mind; in the first place, no criticism would be possible if we were constantly having to put corks on our pen-nibs!

This perpetual swinging of the censer by the Parnassians over the most wretched works by the most wretched among them seems to me stupid. What is more, my cutting words did not spare their feelings. Let others do likewise!

There in a nutshell is my opinion, which is certainly that of every artist: accept! Accept!

Apart from that, nothing new under the sad sun of the moment; we are becalmed. I am still working at my novel, which is limping along, getting caught up in the skirts of dancing girls, but picking itself up again nevertheless. I am staking everything on this one, and I shall have shivers down my spine when the moment of psychological truth comes and it is submitted for examination by the masters; basically I am full of apprehension. This damned French language is heavy to handle! And it is devilish hard to get it to produce the effects one dreams of!

The brochures were delivered to me yesterday by the Ministry of the Interior.[35] I thank you for sending them and giving pleasure to our friends here.

I hope to see you soon in Paris! Bring your volume of stories out quickly, so that we can savour it.

Huysmans

To CAMILLE LEMONNIER

[early July 1877]

My Dear Colleague,

Here then are the soldiery and the landscapery.[36] This Salon is really sickening; what a mess, made up of pearls crushed in crude oil. Oh happy man, in this torrid heat you are growing melons and roses! Here we are being baked, fried, grilled, but, in spite of everything, Paris still retains some of its charm; some corners are extraordinary when the sun is fierce. On one white-hot Sunday, Hannon, Céard and I went for a walk and we saw some quite amazing female forms. They were all languid and sweaty, their eyes were imploring and at times burning with a terribly indecent gleam. To say nothing of the young girls, girls on their fathers' arm! What joy for a naturalist to meet such prudishly wanton pretty faces!

Apart from that, nothing new, complete calm. Insults, however, continue to rain down on us from time to time. It would seem that there is a fool who has started a paper for the sole purpose of insulting us in every issue. That is where a lack of news leads! We are becoming gradually inured to it, and I shall end up not even bothering to answer.

Ah, why does the devil attack the Impressionists through the pen of old Babou?[37] *La Vie littéraire* did not cover itself in glory with that wretched article. These unfortunate painters are, in the current deluge of mediocrity, the only ones who are trying to do something. Yes, their work is incomplete but courageous. Let us support them, all the more so as there is amongst them a man with a significant talent, Degas. Along with Rops, he is the only one to have understood that the Parisian woman is so complex and so charming. Let us plait for him garlands of lovage and lemon verbena! For the most part, contemporary French painters are so unliterary and such nullities.

I am working at my novel without great enthusiasm. I am getting bogged down, and if I don't get arrested for this one, there is no justice in heaven. Needless to say, I am obliged to make innovations, my subject matter forces my hand. My heroines neigh furiously, poor souls that they are, torn apart by their excessively chlorotic and nervous disposition.

What about you? When shall we see the book you were telling us about? Is it finished or is it still under way? Have you abandoned it to chase caterpillars from your garden? Or does the publisher or printer have it? We are interested to know, let us have news of your newborn.

On Saturday I saw Montrosier, who is going to work for *L'Art*. He keeps asking me when the Rubens centenary will be. You are the only one who can help him there, when you write to him. In the meantime the poor *Musée des Deux Mondes* is being sold on the embankment for ten sous, colour plate included! What a comedown! What is more, Bachelin is in quite a bad way commercially, it would seem; he had asked me for a book, so there's an end to that. One publisher less, and there are so few of them!

There, my dear colleague, is all the nonsense I had to get off my chest. Along with it I send you a good shake of the hand.

    Yours

Huysmans

To ÉMILE ZOLA

[late July 1877]

I have been wanting to write to you for over a month, my dear Monsieur Zola, but then as I would have been ashamed to admit to you that I was doing nothing, I put off my letter for the day when I should (without a lie) be able to say: I am working. Now I am! Not very hard, but I am at it! I am very undecided, very out of tune, not at all sure if my novel is any good, sunk in the mud of a devil of a subject, which is so simple that it frightens me to death. Still!

The heat here is enough to kill us; it is weather for sleeping, not for working; and by way of extenuating circumstances, the two balls and chain – the Ministry and the business – that I drag around on my ankles have weighed more heavily than usual over these damned months, and in the evenings I was stultified by figures and accounts, quite incapable of putting two ideas or two words together. There is my confession – give me absolution. Lazy as I am, I have so far produced the equivalent in print of *Marthe* plus ten pages, but there is no action in it, no action! It is all bricks and mortar and chaff, as in foreign novels (the spicy ones); it is coming on gradually, I push it along, but the style is rather cowardly, the colours are blurred and there are no extraordinary or poignant happenings. Cynicism is the herb sauce that helps this fish go down. That is what it will be hard to make the censorship and the reading public swallow! I go into a sweat whenever I think about it.

But that is enough about me, let us talk about you. Céard told me joyfully that you and Mme Zola had got over the illness you had had. It appears that you also have been working hard, and so I lick my lips in anticipation. And the various views of Paris from the top of the Trocadéro, are they finished, are you pleased with them? Have you had time to think about the play for the Comédie française? What a lot of questions you will say, but damn it, all that interests us madly.

It comes back to me that that poor braggart Barbey[38] was violently distraught by the sound slating he received. Your pen pierced through the surface skin of his make-up and his stays and entered his flesh, it would seem. It was a good job well done. Thus he was paid back once and for all for the baseness he has poured out over talented men. I think that article has just been reprinted in *La Vie littéraire*.

I have not much news to give you, because I lead the most monotonous life imaginable. Maupassant is spending his life on the water, pretending to be a water nymph, rescuing the drowning, aiming for a medal for life-saving; but it seems to me that he is not working much, except with his arms. Céard as usual is still walking unspeakable distances from Vincennes to the centre of Paris and vice versa. I have no news of Hennique, Alexis is still at Étampes I think, and as for Mirbeau, he must be electioneering.[39] All this does not seem to me to be getting much literature under way for next winter!

Are you reading Daudet? In the last few days I have read a few column inches of *The Nabob*.[40] It gets more and more like Dickens. The English novelist's method, which consists in attributing human feelings to animals and inanimate objects and making them laugh or cry along with the characters, recurs constantly in *The Nabob*. Why the devil does he tangle up his long sentences with a string of whiches and thats, instead of breaking them up? It becomes so hard to swallow! But come, I do not think that that is the book to topple *L'Assommoir*. Another lost illusion for Daudet. On the subject of *L'Assommoir*, I believe I have heard the finest praise of it that ordinary people are capable of. The forewoman in the workshop had asked me for it; I lent it to her, and as I asked her opinion she replied: it's *too* true, I don't like that – I see it every day! This opinion, coming from a working woman who declares that it is absolutely true to life, and who wept bitterly at the death of Lalie, seems to me priceless; all the more as this woman has mixed with working people all her life. She found *La Curée*[41] simply gripping, it taught her about, as she says in her jargon, a world she does not know.

I take leave and wish you good health, fruitful labours and beg to be remembered to Mme Zola. Tell her I have not bought up the rue de Rennes,[42] despite the fact that they have some fine stuff at the moment, but expensive mind you! Copper and everything, a real paradise of junk. Have you found any curios where you are? Here it is hopeless, prices are getting so high. Even dubious pottery costs a fortune, so I fall back on engravings that are to be had for a good price.

But I must cease my chatter, sending my respects to Mme Zola and a good shake of the hand to you.

Your devoted

Huysmans

And little Ratty? Has he been up to any more pranks? If not, I squeeze his little paws.[43]

To THÉODORE HANNON

1 March 1878

My Dear Hannon,

I have received the two albums with the wonderful vermilion titles![44] We shall savour that this evening, Friday, as some friends in the trade are supposed to be coming to my place and we shall see what effect it produces. I will begin the preface on Sunday I hope, if I am not disturbed by my woman or some other importunate.

Have you got quotations of Parisian prices? They are very dear, damn it all; if you get Callewaert[45] to do your printing, which for your sake I hope you will, try not to get such commonplace ornamentation and end papers as

I had with *Marthe*! And stuff the volume with engravings. Sales will be virtually guaranteed if you have a publisher for bibliophiles.

Saw Zola yesterday – practically no one at his place, none of the Charpentiers; pouring rain into the bargain. We argued a good part of the evening, unable to agree (Maupassant, he and I!) on T. Gautier, whom he declares unreadable. Oh! That is as may be, the devil take it, but between you and me, Gautier's language was not without its uses when he was writing *Le Ventre de Paris*.[46] Also saw Goncourt on Wednesday, he is going to preface Gautier. So at last, in this artistic famine, we are going to have a book worth reading!

As for the weather! You cannot imagine the lake of mud we are wallowing in. This grey, dirty yellow puts death into my soul. Fortunately I have bought a square of pink Japanese silk, embroidered with birds and flowers, and I have stuck it to my door; that gives a little sun, and I shall drink in the gleaming red tones of your *Rhymes*. That will put me in good form.

News apart from that – none! A good and attentive shake of the hand from your

Huysmans

To CAMILLE LEMONNIER

[July 1878]

My Dear Colleague,

I have just tasted again the fine good work you wrote on poor Courbet.[47] The book is full of beautiful phrases that outline a profound idea and sum it up from top to bottom; it is seething with them! 'Courbet put his clog through the plate-glass window!' 'Michallon[48] and company tarted up nature as if she were an ageing dowager.' 'This plebeian spat on the Olympians.' And many more! And this fine accurate remark: 'He forgot to put the birds in his landscapes.' That is what can be called an artistically plaited garland to crown a great painter with. I thank you from the heart for the pleasure you gave me in sending me your good book, which I had read, disjointedly, naturally, in *L'Artiste*. If I had a criticism to make, it would be only that you did not cover the whole of Courbet, the Courbet of 'The Woman with the Parrot', 'The Two Lesbians', etc. But that is almost impossible, given that most of Courbet's pictures are scattered across France and are inaccessible.

As it stands, it is unquestionably the finest praise, restricted in scope as it is, that has yet been given to the apostle of realism. This evening I am taking to Zola the copy you sent me for him, and I advise you most strongly to send one to Charpentier, or via me, for he deals with realist and Impressionist paintings and will certainly be happy to read your sincere study.

Yesterday evening I reread your *Flemish and Walloon Tales*[49] – 'La

Bloentmenje' is an exquisite jewel and it has a regional flavour all of its own. It is an injustice of the age that your books are not proudly displayed by first-rate publishers; they have few to compare with yours. Anyway, the day will come when there will, I hope, be justice in the distribution of glory, although sometimes Zola's saying does not ring very true to me: there is no such thing as a book of talent that does not become famous.

Nothing very new here. As I wrote to Hannon, who is in purgatory with his leg and his throat, I am for my part going through a bad patch. I am hatching nothing worthwhile. Ah, if only the bourgeoisie were aware of the sufferings of artists, the sadness of long evenings where one bleeds over a sentence, they would be moved to pity! But rather no, it would give them joy, for it would bring to mind miseries they are sure never to experience. I would like to start on my first novel,[50] and the first scene is so difficult, so full, that I am torturing my brain to get the effects I envisage in it.

Well, perhaps it will come one fine evening. What an admirable set-up Zola's is, he knows nothing of these heart-rending struggles: three hours of work in the morning and that is all. It comes in a single burst, and barely needs touching up, no crossings out, all in one go! Damn it all, what!

Have you any news from Dentu? I have a friend who has a volume with him, it is the same thing as with Charpentier, total indifference as far as manuscripts are concerned, no curiosity, no consideration. He is, they tell me, as slow and as careless as the others are! What stress and rage such hounds hold in store for us! And to think that we have to pass through their clutches! That is where the job of breaking stones on the highway is preferable to ours; and then to think that Charpentier, without the least dissimulation, admits that a novel that is not recommended to him, and whose author he does not know, is a novel rejected in advance! How fundamentally sad all this is!

Anyway, when you return to the good city of Paris, you will perhaps get an answer from the fat man, the Padishah of letters at three francs a volume.

You can see that the news I have to tell is of little importance; we are living here in total monotony, especially me, who hardly ever goes out, leaving my lair only to visit my friends or rummage through bric-à-brac stalls. And so I am dreaming about those *Rubens Festivals* you announced.[51] Is that the volume Dentu has, or have you got it in portfolio? The title promises such a fleshy epic, with such Flemish rejoicing that I often think of it, especially when I have just come out of the Louvre and my eyes are full of the good paste of the old masters.

Keep us informed, and proffer your valiant hand which I shake most heartily, and come to Paris soon!

Yours

G. Huysmans

To ÉMILE ZOLA

8 August 1878

My Dear Master,
 I have received your letter and the Russian card you enclosed. I thank you most heartily for thinking of us in that way. We will tell the Russian[52] this evening that copy for September's issue [53] has arrived, and as you recommend, we will keep absolute silence on the question of finances.
 Ah, *Nana* sounds as if it is going to be marvellous.[54] It is hardly surprising. Keep at it! There's something to finish off romanticism and rouse grumblings from the prudish press!
 This evening, Céard and I are leaving Paris, which is smelling high. We are escaping by the night train to Belgium, in order to experience ecstasy before the Rubens, to down a few ample pints of local beer, and to walk through the swarming crooked alleyways of the port of Antwerp.
 We will be back in a week, however.
 Nothing new apart from that. I have begun a new novel.[55] As for *Les Sœurs Vatard*, they are lounging about at Mazereau's at Tours.
 I expect the proofs daily; I am constantly on the lookout for them.
 Lebarre[56] cheers me up by telling me that the said printer is so badly equipped that he cannot undertake two volumes at once. For the moment the space is occupied by a book by Mme Judith Gautier that Charpentier is having printed. When this Chinese nonsense is out of the way,[57] the two girls will be subjected to the ink rollers.
 We have not seen anyone lately; Hennique is rolling in the grass at St Quentin, Maupassant is playing at Neptune in the Seine and Charpentier is still not back in Paris.
 Thereupon I wish you good health, courage, and beg you to remember me to Mme Zola.
  In gratitude and devotion

Huysmans

I send a tweak on the nose to little Ratty.

To ÉMILE ZOLA

[September 1878]

My Dear Master,
 I spent yesterday evening reading the volume of your plays,[58] and it has quite raised my spirits. I was gripped by *Thérèse Raquin* as before.[59] Damn it all! The first act is so powerful in its presentation of character and plot – no strings, no tricks! It opens up vistas on the play in a striking manner. As for the second act, I was imagining the face of the good bourgeois, who comes

for a laugh or simply for a bit of emotion, sitting there peeling his oranges. It must grab him by the throat, knock him off his feet, and roll him into the third act, which sends him back out into the street alarmed and completely stunned. As a dramatic situation, as a rendering, and by its scale, it should create a proud stir on the stage, for the scene where the mother wags her finger is really first-rate. It is certainly a very vigorous and very fine play.

As for *Les Héritiers*,[60] their lack of success will always be a source of surprise to me. There are scenes of great comedy in it. The lunch is staggering and the third act should have filled the auditorium with laughter. There was a misunderstanding on the part of the public, and bad faith on the part of the journalists. You really ought to have that play put on again. I cannot believe that justice will not finally be done to it. Even admitting that there might be a battle, it could not be lost, that is unthinkable, otherwise one would totally despair.

I have got as far as *Bouton de rose* now,[61] and I will tell you sincerely the reactions it suggests in me. In all truthfulness I prefer the other two; but looking at it calmly now, whereas the actors only half see each other through the mist, there are scenes that you were right to call comic; while reading them I caught myself laughing: the scene between Ribailler and the young woman, where the good gentleman becomes amorous and loses his head, is really funny. Geoffroy acted it well all the same, but it did not come across as it did on the page. Now if I had an objection to raise, it would be on the subject of the end of Act III. The nocturnal happenings which seem sufficiently well explained to me: would this have been the case for the audience *listening* to it? Was it not a bit too brief, a bit discreet? Did you not count too much on the intelligence of the audience? With its own special perspective, the theatre needs to put people off course; it is a devil of a job to know where to be expansive and where concise. Perhaps that is the trouble, as in the admirable second act of *Raquin* too; the first scene, where the setting and characters are the same, only Camille's armchair is empty, was not understood straight away by the audience, who did not realize, as the curtain went up, that a year had gone by and that Camille had done a stint in the morgue. The explanation comes a few minutes later, it is true, but if it had been given straight away, perhaps the crowd would have understood the author's thinking immediately. What I am saying there is quite stupid, quite bourgeois, but perhaps not impracticable. Basically I am pleading against my own cause, for as I told you, I think it is superb as it is, and I believe in all conscience that when one has discovered scenes as gripping, such original effects, one can manipulate the theatre as one likes, rid it of the conventions in which it is thrashing about, infuse totally new blood into it.

What else can I tell you? That your prefaces are amazing and that the short one, added at the beginning, is of an insolence and plain speaking that delighted me, you know it as well as I do.

Saw Charpentier this morning; *Nana* continues to make admirable progress, you told him, and you are pleased with the first chapter. That book will be a proud argument in the naturalists' favour! The good old Hugo-ites will need to be ready.

Nothing new here; the articles have been sent to Boborykin. I am not having much fun at the moment, with neuralgia of the stomach and toothache. I am vaguely working. Type is finally being set for *Les Sœurs Vatard*. I await the proofs.

I think I shall have them when we all come in chorus to see you at Médan.

A thousand kind thoughts to Mme Zola, I beg you, and to you the best and most cordial handshake from your devoted

Huysmans

To THÉODORE HANNON

5 November 1878

My Fine Phosphorus Eater,

Well, that is the diet to which the abuse of *coitus* and the arts leads![62] Blisters for homos, lead colic for painters, neurosis and anaemia for writers!

That is the best of what the supreme judge has invented for his elect! He would have done better to keep quiet, that coleric Jehovah who is inundating us with rain and mist at the moment!

Saw Carton de Wiart in Paris on his rapid visit;[63] illness will be good for something, as you also will be coming to see us again in January. No news from Rops on the other hand; I still await him and the manuscript!

Nothing new, ah nothing! *Les Sœurs Vatard* are coming to an end. I have only one more sheet of proofs to check.

For the moment I am working hard on my new novel, despite formidable commercial problems and poverty which raises its implacable head!

It is enough to make one spit with disgust!

Quid? About *L'Artiste* – I have not received any copies of it for ages. Has it stopped, or is it the fault of the despatch women (who put the wrappers on)?

No news from Russia. Céard and I are in a rage. That rotter was supposed to send us some roubles, and nothing! A fine tale! We are dining with Zola this evening, Tuesday. We shall beg leave to give Russia a good telling off. Boborykin is a swine!

What about women? How do you manage to supply them with sperm, given the disastrous state of your nerves? Here I am in a lull, I do not proffer my tail to my young person, due to a lack of sperm. We are going downhill, ah, downhill.

Four o'clock! I shall clear out of the office and go and collect Céard from his, and from there on to dine at the *Bœuf nature*. So for the moment, a good shake of the hand, and I wish you good health plated with aluminium and iron, by Jove.

Huysmans

To ÉMILE ZOLA

19 May 1879

I have received your letter, my dear Zola, and I answer it. Yesterday I witnessed a private and ridiculous scene at *Le Voltaire*. First of all, it is impossible to tell you the stupefaction and disgust that my article inspired in them. Etiévant[64] throws his arms in the air and declares that in the whole of his journalistic career he has seen nothing like it. So yesterday, Sunday, I went to the editorial offices. I found Etiévant there, quaking in his shoes. He had just received your letter. He was walking up and down the room saying: M. Lafitte has still got money in the *R.F.*[65] and has many friends there, there is no alternative but to cross out that line. As Etiévant's pain intrigued me, I stayed; at that point, Lafitte came in and was given the letter. He paled at it and had me called into his office. I will not bother to recount the grotesque aspects of the scene: this man, of an American type, dry and stiff, speaking in telegraphic style, is losing his wits and his prestige. He begs me to set off for Médan to look for you, to talk you round, Etiévant and me. I ask it of you as a personal favour, he adds, and thereupon says that never would a great newspaper have dared to print violence such as mine. I tell him there is nothing I will not do for him, I will go to Médan, but as I share your opinion, although I try to put myself in his position, I do not see how I could be of help. Thereupon Etiévant brings in the rest of your article that they would have liked to cut even more, but I think they will not, they are so afraid. So the departure for Médan is put off, for as far as I could understand, they would have liked to ask you to cut *another line*. They took their decision.

Now something else. They no longer want Bourges's novel.[66] Lafitte makes out that the novel had, what is more, never been accepted. I maintained the opposite for all I was worth; I said that Marpon[67] thought it was good, that it was all agreed. They made out that this novel is obscene. They must have written to you about it.

Céard's article on Hugo has been turned down. They are going to let *Tragaldabas*[68] through, despite their heaving. Hennique and Alexis must have delivered some copy yesterday, but I do not know what answer they got.

I am going to try and hold out with the *Salon*; I probably will not stick it right to the end as it seems that my first article created a devil of a stir, and that *Le Temps* was bowled over by it (which I expected, what is more). I delivered the second yesterday. *Thanks to your stiff letter* it will get through, I think. But it is impossible to express the fear of these people, the pain they feel in printing such theories. Guillemet[69] has just written to me, the artists' camp is ablaze. Ah, I am glad that you are satisfied, because I do not give a damn for the opinion of the rest of them, and am concerned only to please you. I think the second one is better. I will send it to you if it does not get through.

That is where we are. they would like to turn us out like criminals, but they do not dare. Two letters like the one you wrote and we shall manage to hold on. *That was my overall impression of yesterday's scene.* We shall continue to follow your advice in every detail. I am going to see Hennique on purpose. Don't be afraid, it has been decided that the names of Ulbach, Véron, etc. should never be mentioned.[70] It is all agreed. What is more, I apply the same system to the Salon. I only attack the ringleaders vehemently.

I shall never manage to write to you today. I am in my office, where I am brought bundles of stupid work every three minutes. This is the third time I have taken up this disjointed letter. The important thing was to tell you the enormous power you wield with that newspaper. Ah! If only Lafitte would give us free rein, what fun we should have!

A thousand respectful greetings to Mme Zola, I beg you. We will catch the earliest possible train to come and have a chat with you; in the meantime I send you all the friendly gratitude of the young naturalists, who are being labelled ferocious beasts in that good newspaper.

Yours

Huysmans

You can be sure that we will speak the plain truth.

To EDMOND DE GONCOURT

[May 1879]

Dear Sir and Master,

I have just finished *Les Frères Zemganno*,[71] which you were kind enough to send me.

I find this book most extraordinary and very new. It strikes a highly original note and I do not think anyone has dared to face up to such difficulties before.

To produce a novel of such simple texture, while retaining interest, and to be profoundly moving while eliminating love, that eternal pivot in all works; to succeed in setting on its feet a novel virtually without a woman in it and yet which is haunting and gripping, is simply marvellous, and I am delighted to tell you that a wager I had always thought it impossible to carry off has now finally been won!

Without being able to analyse the book here, let me tell you of the leaps of joy it provoked. This novel's language, inverted language, pirouetting in places like the clowns, fixed and anchored to them like a shiny sequined vest, surprises and makes one submissive. One would have to go back to *Madame Gervaisais*[72] to find fleeting and intangible sensations captured in such a way. It is a sustained stroke of genius, executed with incomparable grace and ease. There are some really unique bits, the superb scene of the accident with the silence of the crowd after the great cry, the death of the mother is full of emotion, so charming, set in the landscape that she watches slipping away through the window, and Agoust the juggler, whom we see through the flying circles of his golden rings. And damn it, those things were virtually impossible to convey, and you have done it! Decidedly Gautier was right when he said that there is no such thing as the inexpressible. And I have quoted two or three chapters and there are twenty of them, the book is damn near full of others the equal of those!

As for the two brothers, they are charming and interesting and one likes them throughout the book. The fall causes real pain, one was wishing so hard for success! The veiled emotion which emanates from each page comes across. *Les Frères Zemganno* is a book to be reread often and with real pleasure, and I promise myself that happiness.

As for the advice on the literary rabble that the author of *La Fille Elisa*[73] kindly gave to us younger ones, we can only be grateful and tell you how happy we are that the Goncourt brothers, whom we so much admired and supported at the time when their great talent was still disputed, have been kind enough to repay in paternity the filial literary affection we bore them.

Accept, dear sir and master, the assurance of my respect and devotion.

Huysmans

To PAUL ALEXIS

[Autumn 1879][74]

My Dear Colleague,

I waited before answering your charming letter until I had received a few copies of *Marthe*.

My little daughter has just successfully passed the French customs post,[75] and I am now in a position to make you a present of her, if such would give you pleasure.

But let us talk about 'Lucie Pellegrin'[76] – it is good, absolutely so; no, without foolish or mawkish compliment! And I find superb the scenes where the women enter the open apartment, where Lucie spits blood into the flower-patterned bowl, where she drinks absinth, finally her death and the rescue of Miss.

I am taking the piece back to front as you see, but over and above the fine lifelike portrayals at the beginning you have written a page to be proud of at the end of the first part; the sympathy of the girls which progresses from the dog up to Lucie is a plucky find and well done; but what is the point of telling you all that, you knew well enough that I would like Lucie a lot! For like you, I want what is true to life, and I am weary of sentimental stupidities, and all those troubadours who celebrate lifeless women who have no vaginas or backsides! We want what is alive, and what do we care if the prudery of fools is enraged and they accuse us of immorality? Anyway, I don't know what immorality is, and I don't care!

Ah, you say you were in a melancholy mood when you left me the other evening. Well, you have no idea of the strange night that female dressed up as a soldier had in store for me.[77] Just think, those two wretched women that I carted about in a damned cab lived in a foul slum. When you went in it smelt of Brussels sprouts and dirty washing. And all you could hear was snoring on every side, the walls being simply laths. Added to that there was only one bed, and so as the pianist could get some rest, we had to put a mattress on the floor – it was pitiful. There were not even any sheets, such wretchedness! Basically, I found it more interesting than some luxurious haunt. And the girl was a good sort, well built with a strong back, quite fiery and sensual, so that the throbbing of her thighs compensated somewhat for my disgust at the lodgings. But, damn it all, in the morning the two girls were snoring with their mouths open and their bare feet showing; I fled at daybreak in a state of sadness. The slovenliness of such poverty was unspeakable.

There you are – when shall I be able to give you *Marthe*? Shall we fix an evening – apart from Saturday? I should like to shake you by the hand.

Your devoted

G. Huysmans

Oh, have you read the latest issue of *La Revue des lettres*? There is an admirable piece of Zola in it.[78] He has never produced anything so fine, and yet there are some damned good pages in his earlier novels!

To ÉMILE ZOLA

15 February 1880

My Dear Zola,

I have just left *Nana*, amazed. Good Lord! Read straight through like that the savour of it is increased tenfold. What a fine book, and a new book, absolutely new, both in your series and as regards everything ever written so far. In fact I do not think you have ever been as good-natured and your powers as unaffected and simple. You have taken the process to its logical conclusion, as you say, but all of that disappears in the flapping of a masterly wing, I assure you.

I am writing to you straight away, not having had time yet to take full stock of my admiration, but it is full of breathtaking chapters. How adorable the scene between Zizi and Nana in the country is! And the third-rate actors in the heavily laden atmosphere in the wings. Long live Coquelin! And the scenes at table and the races and the admirable scene where Muffat learns that he is a cuckold and the divine Satin, who makes me most uneasy, I must admit, just like good old Chouard, and all of it, by God, is superb.

You can be pleased with yourself, you know. There is every reason! We will talk about the book at greater leisure on Thursday I hope; I will simply say, after a first reading, how sound and how alive *Nana* is and I stress this wholeheartedly, so!

In haste I send you a warm handshake, my dear friend, and beg you to pay my respects to Mme Zola.

Your devoted

Huysmans

To ÉMILE ZOLA

15 June 1880

My Dear Zola,

I do not know how to thank you for the fine things you said about me.[79] If I had had a little time, I would have come and shaken you by the hand, but that hateful *Gaulois*, which forces me to castrate all my articles, is monopolizing my time with all the errands I have to do on its account.

But all that will soon be over, for I am impatient for a quiet life working on more interesting things.

On the subject of the *Croquis* again. You did me proud in defending 'The Armpit', which has been hellishly badly received on all sides. People are starting to take me for an erotomaniac who needs to take a shower under some camphorated mixture.

Maupassant is leaving, or has already left, I think, for the banks of the Seine for a long holiday. We continue to row in our respective ministerial galleys.[80] The monotony is unrelieved, though it is true that on Thursday we shall have the great joy (!) of lunching with that death's head in round spectacles, the amazing Boborykin.

Little interesting news, as you can see. I am tending towards hypochondria and your article livened me up, and so I thank you for it again, shaking both of your hands and begging to be remembered to Mme Zola.

Your devoted

Huysmans

To CAMILLE LEMONNIER

[December 1880]

My Dear Friend,

I will answer your kind enquiry. First of all, this is the situaiton as far as *La Comédie humaine* is concerned.

Zola proposed the following arrangement: to produce a firebrand of four pages in all, written only by the *Soirées de Médan* authors, paid for at the rate of three sous a line, the whole thing to be launched without publicity, and with only the thirty thousand francs put up by Maupon.

This idea was accepted by Céard, Alexis and Hennique and opposed violently by Maupassant and me.

The paper, deprived of liberty in such a way, would be worse than *Le Rappel*;[81] it would be a chapel of Parnassus, the exhuastion of the small editorial staff (to no financial advantage), the most total monotony.

These factors were not taken into account. In the circumstances, I have given in my notice as editor, wishing in no way to take on responsibility for a Latin-quarter rag, and to have to refuse copy from friends whom I had taken on for the purpose.

So the paper will come out in January, but without my being anything but a simple, very simple, editorial assistant.

Such a combination of circumstances has provoked this reaction in me: at the present time, when we should be setting up shop in the avénue de l'Opéra, we go selling knives in a doorway.

I regret this mess. We will probably fall flat on our faces and dishonour ourselves with a worthless rag.

So there we are. As for *Le Mâle*,[82] I am at your disposal as far as Charpentier is concerned. I will hand it over to him myself, I will badger him and get Hennique involved too. I hope that in that way we will carry the day with this strange creature, despite his prejudices and eternal hesitation. Write to me when you are ready, so that we can tune our instruments and set the game in motion, keeping as many aces in hand as possible.

As for my novel *En Ménage*, it is still at the printer's. Has been for three months!!! And I get proofs only sporadically. What a ramshackle place that publishing house is! And that is one of the better ones! I hope to be out at the end of January, if ever this misfortune makes up its mind to come to an end. Ill fortune flows forth at the moment, as you see. Nothing is going well.

So I await with impatience your book with Hetzel. Thank you for the kind journal. I accept the offer gladly, although I am disgusted with newspapers, since all this business with *La Comédie humaine*. Still, it will all be over in a while I hope.

I am in the midst of preparing notes for a novel I am thinking about.[83] If I do not have too many problems with the rag in question, to which copy is to be supplied virtually for the love of God, I will set about it seriously.

I send you, my dear friend, a good, cordial shake of the hand.
    Your devoted

Huysmans

To EDMOND DE GONCOURT

15 March 1881

My Dear Master,

What is adorable and exquisite from every point of view in these two volumes,[84] is the profound love for the house and the beautiful objects that fill it. Every page is impregnated with it. It is a delicious intimacy which is moving and provokes a gentle nervous shiver when one reads certain pages.

Yes, you can flatter yourself that you have accomplished a fearful and wonderful *tour de force*. And God knows what artistry, dexterity and flexibility were needed in order to alternate descriptions and memories, to make a break from the catalogues and then take them up again, so that one arrives fresh and perceptive, one's eye rested yet ever curious for the new wonders revealed in each room! I was literally stupefied by this arrangement of things and at the unaffected daring, the way you juggle with the difficulties, without us feeling for a single moment that it is an effort or wearisome.

Then, leaving the whole aside for a moment, there are chapters that are truly extraordinary: the tapestries that come to life in the glow of dying embers; the garden in bloom at each time of year; memories of print merchants, so lightly done that one can see the grimace on their faces, their nervous *tics*; all the profound emotion of the upper room and finally that exquisite and precious Japanese art, which is dismantled and explained, made visible, palpable, transformed into an evenly wrought goldsmithing of words, through the artist's wise alchemy.

More than a book of refined taste, it is a work of reference, stuffed full with unpublished and rare details. Japanese art has been done now. Hokusaī and Takeoka have been evoked as formerly Watteau, Chardin and Gavarni were. The trilogy is complete. You can be proud to have undertaken and accomplished such potent labours.

I thank you with all my heart for the kind word you were good enough to put in for me in the library of contemporary books. I was all the more pleased and touched, for if I had an ambition to write, it is to your books that I owe it. It was your novels that were the first to grip me, and it is to them that I always return in hours of sadness, for they alone exude the intimate melancholy of existence.

Please accept, dear master, the assurance of my respect and devotion.

Huysmans

To CAMILLE LEMONNIER

2 April 1881

My Dear Friend,
I managed to get your *Charnel Houses*[85] which had got lost at Charpentier's, where it had been hanging around for several days. What a mess in that hole, and no need to tell you that I read them, or rather reread them, for *Sédan*[86] I have as a bound volume in my bookcase, it is a friend I visit frequently. You took a hellishly dangerous risk in altering a book that was so alert, so alive. You brought it off, for you have made it more balanced, whilst not losing or reducing the fearful odour that emanates from it. It is a fine book, yes a fine book which, if there is any literary justice, will remain one of the most solid, most artistic and most painfully poignant of its period.

Moreover, I have already told you quite frankly of the admiration this volume inspired in me. It is very original, very individual, whatever sly remarks Cladel might make.[87] It is you, completely you and nothing but you.

The wonderful pages with the Emperor, the campaign, the inside of the town, none of it, damn it, is derivative. It is simply a thing felt and seen and rendered by an artist.

Unfortunately I have no papers at my fingertips at the moment. *La Réforme* died a death along with Menier of the chocolate factory; my *La Comédie humaine* was abortive, so I am without accommodation for the moment, and given the system of sensational reporting, politics, hatred for the written word, it is difficult enough to place one's work just now.

It is true that on the one hand it gives me time to work, which is perhaps better.

I am just now immersed in a volume on modern art, on the Indépendants. It is giving me a lot of trouble, but really it is to give me a break between *En Ménage* and the novel I am planning.

And you who are always hacking away, where are you up to? You must have lots of work on the go. Hannon wrote to me, I think, that you are supposed to be planning a book about Antwerp. That is a good idea and you can brush out a superb Flemish novel about it. If it is only a rumour, I hope you will turn it into a certainty. What a curious modern style you will have to produce for that adorable town!

On the subject of Hannon, I begin to despair that Rops will ever deliver the proofs of his etchings. He is caught up in a terrible mesh; it would be better to hurl the book on to the market without the pictures, and risk drowning as far as the bibliophiles are concerned. The life jacket for the poetry is too long in coming. What stupid times all the same, when everyone clamours after Bouvier,[88] and no one will buy a line of poetry! It is America taking us over, my poor friend. I can see more of it each day: utilitarianism is driving away furiously, and sad to say, democracy is like iodide that draws out the boils of human stupidity. Paris has been awful for some time; you must have been able to see the way things were going from the newspapers, what is more.

I should have started by thanking you for the kind letter you wrote me about my book.[89] Here no one understands a word of it. In the papers they are all yelling, the reading public as well; they are all on the wrong tack. It is cheering and yet lamentable at one and the same time; in short, it is stupid, that is the only word for it.

I await your visit in May impatiently. Damn it all, don't clear off again so quickly this time, as you did on other occasions, so that we can at least get together. In the meantime I send you a warm handshake.

Huysmans

To GUY DE MAUPASSANT

[March 1882]

My Dear Friend,

Thank you for your brilliant defence of *A Vau l'Eau* and thank you also for trying to screw a little sense into the wooden skull of Sir Cherbuliez,[90] one of my literary *bêtes noires*.

There is a very funny expression in your article: 'Folantin, Ulysses of the chophouses'. I let out peals of laughter, it is really funny, and accurate at the same time. You will most certainly have read the article signed by Nestor in *Le Gil Blas*. Who is Nestor? The father of Trousse-Cadet or Visalœil?[91] There is a most curious phrase of literary criticism in it: 'I am not interested in all that, for I eat well', etc. A real pearl eh? My poor friend, I am very much afraid that universal stupidity is getting worse by the day. I fear that just like potassium iodide, democracy will bring out the spots of human folly.

How right poor Flaubert was when he screamed at America, crassness, etc.

I cannot tell you anything interesting; I have spent a horrible week with neuralgia of worrying intensity, enough to make one bang one's head against the wall, alas! You know what it's like. I am better now, but I have a feeling of a frightful void in my head; out of doors I drift along like a drunkard. And to think that there is no cure – ah, damnable nerves!

With all this, I am not working, being absolutely incapable of stitching two ideas together for the moment. I am getting bored and anxious. I wish you just the opposite, my dear Maupassant; and in gratitude for your valiant article, I shake you by the hand.

Huysmans

As a consequence of these nervous upsets, my penis is amazing, a bit of old rag in my pants.

To THÉODORE HANNON

18 April 1882

My Dear Hannon,

Yes damn it, it is an age since I corresponded with you, and yet I chuckled singularly on reading your last epistle telling me of the shower of cold water administered by you to the cranium of the said Potvin![92] But since then I have had a string of bothers. My woman has been ill;[93] and so I have had all the comings and goings between her place and mine, all in all a succession of sentimental and financial trivia! You can imagine what it has been like.

Nunc, I see that L'Alouette is going to bring out the awaited second edition. That is good, only the longer he delays, the more he is reducing the chance of sales. That sort of thing needs to be put out while it is still warm. I am surprised that Zola has not written to you; it is true that now he has got this damned Médan place, we don't hear anything. I don't think he reads any books, for when you go there, there are stacks of them piled up on tables, their pages not yet deflowered by the paper knife. I will speak to him about it next time I see him, for he ought at least to read the books of people who defended him at the critical time.

Apart from all that, nothing new here. Life continues its monotonous way, its drizzle of sewage. We need to invent some new vice in order to amuse ourselves; unfortunately the canon of vices is even more limited than that of the virtues, so what is left? Sleep – but that is rather monotonous too. If you discover a means of preventing boredom, do let me know, so that I may take advantage of it. That would ease my burden.

With a warm handshake, yours

Huysmans

To HENRY KISTEMAECKERS

23 August 1882

My Dear M. Kistemaeckers,

I have just come back from the country,[94] where I went for a while to restore and tune up the keyboards of my nervous system, which was singularly strained, and found the erotic plays waiting at home.

Thank you, really, for it is one of the most light-hearted volumes I know; the footnotes and prefaces are a scream, and add to the jovial flavour of Tisserant and Glatigny's texts, for they are the strangest and most cheering of these erotics.

I do not know if the sun has died in Belgium as it has in Paris. Here ash has been heaped on it, as on garbage. It is just like London. If one buys one's clothes at Old England, reads Dickens and goes to drink port at the

Bodega, one can easily imagine that one is on a journey, visiting that diabolical city of industry sung by Taine and Amicus.[95]

Apart from these illusions that are to be had with little expense, nothing new here; the dead season for the book trade is in full swing. All the booksellers I see are twiddling their thumbs, waiting for business to pick up in the autumn.

What are the *Sonnets du doigt dedans*[96] that I see announced at the end of the plays with the initials T.H.? Would it be Hannon?

He must be locked up with deaf-mutes, given that I receive no more letters from him.

I must dash to lunch, but not without sending you a good shake of the hand.

G. Huysmans

To STÉPHANE MALLARMÉ

27 October 1882

My Dear Colleague,

I am at the moment trying to persuade into blossom a quite singular story;[97] roughly, this is its subject.

Out of disgust with American lifestyle, contempt for the aristocracy of wealth, the last representative of an illustrious family takes refuge in definitive solitude.

He is cultured, of the most refined delicacy. In his comfortable retreat, he seeks to replace monotonous, humdrum nature with artifice; he enjoys the writers of the exquisite and penetrating period of Roman decadence. I am using the word decadence so as to be intelligible; he even flings himself into the Latin of the Church, into the barbaric and delicious poems of Orientius, Veranius of Gévaudan, Baudonivia, etc., etc.[98] In French he is mad about Poe, Baudelaire, the second part of *La Faustin*. You can see what it is going to be like.

There is a sweet vengeance to be wrought on those old miseries who have never understood a thing in the penetrating language that we try to write. Now, amongst modern poets, he naturally adores Tristan Corbière,[99] Hannon, Verlaine. My intention is to include a few quotations from those refined souls of Art, from these delightful and disturbing poets. I have their works and it will be easy, but there lies the question and subject of this present epistle: I own chilling, forgotten pages by you that appeared in *La République des lettres* of which I kept back numbers, when we were working on it together. I also have a few lines that Mendès quoted in the same paper in the article on *Eglogus, L'Après-midi d'un faune*,[100] but that is the extent of my documents in verse and in prose.

Could you get hold of *Death of the Antepenultimate* for me,[101] which appeared in a review whose name I cannot find, although I have been looking everywhere, unsuccessfully, for months? And *L'Hérodiade*,[102] of which I shall have great need, for my hero will have in his home the admirable watercolour by Gustave Moreau,[103] as well as the stupefying dream creations of Odilon Redon, whose exhibition of superb drawings you must have seen in *Le Gaulois*. So I will quote from your *Hérodiade* whilst trying to describe Moreau's magic. I should also like, if it were feasible, to have more lines from the *Faune* than those that Mendès quoted. I have searched for this little volume of the goldsmith's art. But oh! I was told you had withdrawn it from the shops.

That is why, impossible as it is to get hold of your works, I am approaching you, my dear colleague. Forgive me, and believe the sincerity of my intentions.

With all good wishes, your devoted

Huysmans

To STÉPHANE MALLARMÉ

[November 1882]

My Dear Mallarmé,

As soon as I received your epistle, that is yesterday evening, I went to Redon's; there was no one there, but really I went only for form's sake, as I do not think he would fit the bill at all. His hatred for etching is extreme, he would like to illustrate books with lithographs, smooth and silky, as Gavarni used to. Then given the highly original nature of his talent, personally I think he can display it only in large format. Reductions of Redon, by whatever method, would, in my opinion, produce no good results. I must introduce you to him, for his great charcoal drawings would delight you, beyond a doubt.

Thank you for your offer to consult your dispersed works. Coppée[104] is willing to let me see Villiers' ex-review which contains your exquisite *Pipe*.[105] He also has the Parnassus volumes.

So I can profit from his kindness for my book, without having to trouble you further.

Ah! I chased all over Paris for the Moreaus. And now I have found them: i) at Baschet's on the boulevard Saint-Germain, amongst a consignment of masterpieces from the 1878 exhibition, I found a very fine and very large photo-engraving by Goupil[106] of Salome at three francs; it is worth noting; ii) at Art, in the avénue de l'Opéra, a very agreeable etching, a proof on China paper of 'The Apparition', that stupefying and adorable watercolour where Salome stands before the radiant head of St John the Baptist. Cost: ten francs. There are still some at five francs on Holland paper from the final run, but they convey less well the exquisite nature of this strange art.

For the moment, I am up to my neck in my awful story, which is causing me awful trouble, and a lot of research, especially into uncommon locutions. As a consolation, it will be understood by ten people and will be a flop, just like the *Croquis parisiens*, which are a model of that genre! For in order to move that book, it had to be sold at a discount, readers being at first so sluggish at putting their hands into their pockets for those pretty coins with which to purchase it. It is true that people are terrified of prose poems, even more than of poetry; the reading public is largely composed of people like Homais.[107]

Yours

Huysmans

To STÉPHANE MALLARMÉ

[November 1882]

My Dear Mallarmé,

Here is my remaining copy of *Croquis parisiens*, which is now sold out. I hope that some of the pieces in this book, in which, as in a hymn, I would have liked to celebrate the delicate glory of spicy subjects, will not displease you.

In any case, some of the etchings that adorn the inside of the volume will delight you, I have no doubt.

I went to Jouaust's, and by a rare stroke of luck, I got the last copy he had of *La Revue du monde nouveau* containing 'The Analaogical Demon'.[108]

So here I am, quite delighted, for thanks to you I shall be able to quote, amongst the preferred reading of my dilettante, verse and prose that savour of true and troubling sublimity. Thank you.

Yours

Huysmans

To EMILE VERHAEREN

[1883]

Dear Sir and Colleague,

I thank you for the *Flamandes*[109] that you were good enough to send me; I am sure you cannot imagine the pleasure I shall have in reading them, for I have found in them a life blood and colours reminiscent of Rubens that gripped me profoundly. Beyond a doubt, the notion of writing came to me when I would go after school to walk round the Louvre; leaving aside the other rooms, I used to stop in those housing the Flemish and Dutch schools. I have always admired the work of Teniers and Ostade[110]: and it is wonderful the way you have succeeded in conveying in the piece entitled 'Old Masters' the enormous joy, the feasting and the fetid odour of beer shops. This piece is really sound; and the one about the lads is not less so, where there is strangely vast and ferocious fornication.

It is a very special book, with its landscapes and rustic perfumes; it is a book of Flemish verse, which is no mean thing, and it is quite a rest from the poetry published in France, where we have constantly thrown at us the love of some sweet little thing, eternal summer, in rhymes that are perhaps perfect technically, but in poetry that is not a true reflection of the subject matter. And so I was surprised to find, contrary to expectations, a masculine savour and a vigour in colour that are out of the ordinary. If I had a criticism to make, it would not be a serious one; it would simply be that you use an alternating rhyme scheme in a rather unrelieved manner; but that is the pedantry of a German.

The real truth is that the old Dutchman in me, beneath the surface of the neurotic Parisian, was very moved, and that the unrepentant lover of fine painting was delighted; there is amongst them 'Kato', whose well-fleshed-out verses pursue me, the images are so clearly formed; that one keeps coming back to me, haunting me, as I scribble these few lines to you. You helped me to spend a good Sunday yesterday, far away from Paris, in deepest Flanders with your book.

Thank you, and permit me to give you a friendly shake of the hand.

Huysmans

To THÉODORE HANNON

[Spring 1883]

My Dear Hannnon,

Are you alive or dead? Was it an erotic shade that published *Mirliton priapique*, which I have not received?[111]

Quid?

Is the cult of the phallus so occupying your sixth finger that the other five cannot hold a pen?

Oh silent man, reassure J.K.

Have you read Villiers de l'Isle-Adam's *Contes cruels?*[112] If not, rush immediately to buy them, for it is a precious collection of black and often exquisite mystification.

I have just spent two awful months with neuralgia, this alternating winter and spring is crucifying me, and the old neurosis sets in; I am a singularly poor wretch, with pain in body and mind; I hope you are not in such a sorry state as old father Vatard.[113] Reassure me on this point.

All the same I am working, immersed in the depths of a very strange novel, vaguely clerical, a bit homosexual, the story of the end of a family devoured by memories of a religious childhood and nervous illness. A novel with only one character! I think it will be curious – all the more so, as it contains the ultimate refinement of everything: literature, Art, flowers, perfumes, furnishings, gem stones, etc.

Now it is your turn for the confessional.

And who is this Hoscheteyn in the rue de la Paille who publishes the books I receive? So Kistemaeckers has a rival in Belgium. Let me have some information on this subject.

And your next volume of verse that was supposed to be coming out with Kistemaeckers, what stage is it at?

Write, write!

You will be blessed by your

Huysmans

who raps your knuckles.

To THÉODORE HANNON

28 May 1883

My Dear Hannon,

I am shaking myself out of my frightful idleness in order to write to you; you ask for information concerning the effect produced by the art book.[114] That is quite a story. Charpentier, terrified, despite the cuts he had imposed on me on the subject of Henner etc.,[115] did not release it for sale! That is how it was; scared in advance of complaints from those attacked, and from his friends Gervex and B. Le Page, etc.,[116] he did not announce its publication, and finally admitted to Hennique that he preferred to lose money on it, rather than bring it out; in short, he stifled it the best he could. Unfortunately for him, the book found its way into the painters' hands all the same; thereupon general commotion in the studios. Booksellers, who were receiving requests for it, went and collected copies; in short, despite everything, the said book has exploded like a bomb in an oil depot, and has brought me a string of letters, quite badly written, but mostly stupid and with no spelling!

Whatever happens, from the point of view of sales, it will be almost zero in the circumstances; basically I don't care. It is a collection of articles. I want to express my opinion, to say amidst the cowardice and folly of French criticism what I believe to be the truth, and to be the first to put into writing the greatness of the personality of Degas! It is done. So everything has turned out for the best.

You complain in your letter, my good fellow, about the silence of the press concerning your volume of poetry; one thing is certain, that as time goes by, the newspapers are printing fewer and fewer reviews of works of art. We must be prepared for even greater silence from day to day. We have only enemies in the camp of the pen-pushers; they are giving up shouting through fear of drawing attention to us. As for the so-called friends of the press, I have had my opinion of them for a long time.

I received a letter from Kistemaeckers, who related in a few lines Lemonnier's disappointment at not getting the prize. What was he doing in there anyway, jockeying for position like a schoolboy? Do give me more details of this affair.

Here, complete moroseness. One sweats all night in this ignoble heat. Paris stinks of drains from one end to the other, and as a consolation, we have the official Salon of painting!

What a thrill! I am still working away at my novel on artificial and licentious mysticism, but progress is slow, this thing is so difficult to pull off, as it has only one character, in all!

And you? You must be breathing a sigh of relief now that *Le Pays* has come out:[117] you deserve a bit of a rest on a beach. When you have some free time, send me the news from Brussels, of Lemonnier, whose spider scrawl I have not seen for a long time. Something strange! Since we have been suffocating in this heat, the bit of old rag I have had in my pants these months has picked itself up, and here I am, fornicating away furiously. It must be the beginning of general paralysis, what else can it mean?

Yours

Huysmans

To GUY DE MAUPASSANT

[June 1883]

My Dear Friend,

What strikes me most in the composition of the *Contes de la Bécasse*[118] is the book's cruel irony, the nice, quiet, dirty dealings stirred up without the least comment, no taking of sides.

The story of Pierrot is delightful from this point of view. Basically it is true to life, where, out of greed for a few coppers, one brings about the death of one's neighbour. The man with the severed arm is equally amazing and opens up a perspective on the mentality of seamen and peasants. Another excellent one is 'Fear', that awful fear without object, when nerves give way for no reason, it is full of energy, very sound.

But one needs to take each of them in turn. 'That Swine Morin' is captured in so jovial a manner, and 'The Cockerel'. But I don't want to recount all your titles to you. I simply wanted, my dear friend, to thank you for your good wishes and send you a good shake of the hand.

Yours

Huysmans

To JEAN-FRANÇOIS RAFFAËLLI

[9 August 1883]

My Dear Raffaëlli,

Thank you for your kind letter and the copy of *Justice* that came with it. I am going to drop a line to Geffroy to thank him for having defended that unfortunate book *L'Art moderne*, which has not exactly had an easy time of things until now.

How are you in that little hollow, Le Tréport![119] I was there, or rather passed through there, five years ago. The sea seemed to me rather infantile, with a very short beach, dishonoured by repulsive gatherings of magistrates and bankers. I hope that socially it has gone downhill since then, that it has become more friendly, less stuck up. But the important thing is to drink in the air, to empty oneself of Paris, in order to sniff at other nasty smells, which is what I should love to do, if my minister of whom I despair would let me go, which I think is unlikely for the moment, alas!

As far as health is concerned, I am fine. There is a marked improvement, not really attributable to medical science, for I had ended up doing nothing. It is true that it has not been hot. That is the crucial thing for me now. Heat is without mercy for me. I have the nerves of a native of Greenland, and to think I have to live in France!

I am working hard, my amazing book is coming to an end, what clerical and sadistic neurosis there will be! Obviously everyone will think I have gone mad, in every respect. I shall be shouted down by the Catholics and attacked by all the rest. It might be amusing.

I see that you are working hard, my good Raffaëlli, and I am pleased. Your portrait of Clemenceau is a good thing,[120] for he is one of the few real characters of our age, and he has not yet been painted. It is an awful job to tackle, but you are capable of it, and of showing all those official daubers, those colour photographers, those guady disciples of Cabanel, what a portrait with skin underneath and something beyond is like. I really must go and see it when you are back at Asnières. It will cleanse my eyesight. Oh, my poor firend, if you could see what the modern art merchants have put in their shop windows for the summer season! No, it is unbelievable. It is enough to make one wonder what the brains of people who paint such things are made of. Evidently they have the brains of some inferior race, Tasmanians or South American Indians, all that is lowest in the animal kingdom.

Take your revenge, my dear Raffaëlli, bring back some fine seascapes too.

I don't have any fresh news from Paris to send you. Literature is becalmed, on account of the season. And as for what comes out at other times of the year!! But still, the city is void of all writing. There is only Goncourt left within its walls. Zola is near Quimper, on a bit of desert island, where he is working hard, so he writes, and he will not be back before October. Céard will be leaving any day, I think. Hennique has been

away for a long time. As for Maupassant, he continues to be never in Paris. It is a desert; I wish you better weather, for you must have rain and mud as we do here, with sunny spells and squally showers. I wish you good health, courage and success with your work, for lunchtime has arrived, and I have just the time to send you a shake of the hand.
Yours

G. Huijsmans

To GUSTAVE GEFFROY

[9 August 1883]

My Dear Colleague,
My friend Raffaëlli sent me this morning from Le Tréport the issue of *Justice* in which you were good enough to write about *L'Art moderne*.

I thank you wholeheartedly, my dear colleague, for all that you say about that unfortunate book, and for all that you did not say.

I thank you for having written that it is a sincere book; that is, in truth, its only merit, but with the present climate in art criticism, it might be useful for the unknowns; those who are attacked and in poverty are not sufficiently defended. The whole art world is on the side of the mediocre, the Laurens, the Bouguereaus, etc.,[121] and no one is for Degas! I tried to bring a bit of justice to bear in this book and I am really grateful to you for having said so.

The defect, or rather defects, of the book must have struck you. You were sufficiently indulgent not to point them out to me, but there are some that are not entirely my fault.

It is full of gaps, of things unexplained, there is a visible lack of linking, rough bits, but there you are! Emasculated by order of the publisher, this book had whole pages struck out at the proof stage. You can imagine the impossibility of joining it together. Things that should be completed by examples that have been completely suppressed. Everything concerning Henner and Cot was mercilessly slashed, and given the impossibility of finding in the streets of the capital two publishers willing to print this piece of wreckage that passes for an art book, I had to submit, and, what is more, sprinkle ash on my sentences here and there.

Forgive me for boring you with all this, but you showed such kind understanding for my book as it stands, that I wanted at least to offer my apologies to you for at least some of the mediocre things to be found in it.

I hope that Raffaëlli will introduce us one day when he gets back. I am just about rid of my damned nerve troubles and I hope to be able to go to Asnières without hitch.

Until then, I send you, dear colleague, my thanks and the assurance of my good wishes.
Yours

Huysmans

To LUCIEN DESCAVES

[January 1884]

My Dear Descaves,

Your letter soothed the old wound opened up by my bourgeois family, with whom I had to dine on New Year's Day. I was full of disgust when I came back to go to bed on Tuesday evening, and your epistle cheered and strengthened me, for, after all, it was a reminder of friendship and reassurance that, in the ignominious Americanization that surrounds us, there are still some people left who have not lost their souls and who are not preoccupied with piling up money in some ugly piece of furniture made by Fichet or suchlike.

I am very pleased that my art book found favour with you, for it has been found universally repulsive, without distinction of school or class. People saw it as a low pamphlet, a squib, an obscenity worthy of the madhouse. They might at least have admitted that the book defended the unknown and the spurned and that it attacked quite bravely those powerful Michets[122] who rule uncontested over the brutish clan of painters.

At least it was disinterested criticism and in good faith, sufficiently good faith to give its opinion on Courbet and Manet without hesitation. As for the writing of the book – ah, no one noticed anything. You are the first to have seen the truth of it. Yes, my dear Descaves, I wanted, besides the opinions in the book, to try and include prose poems, to write it as a novel, to bring together the descriptive method of the painter with that of the writer, in fact to give it, besides the critical ideas, a value as a personal book. And damn it all! Basically they do not find it any more curious or appetizing than Marius Vachon or Havard's work!![123]

There you are, that is what we who write carefully sifted books can expect, my good fellow, at a time when the Ohnets of this world reign supreme.[124]

I have at last finished *A Rebours*, which is now at Charpentier's. He is stupefied by it, but respectful, according to Zola, who has seen this noble publisher. I have only to be patient and await the proofs. For the moment I am going to try and write a story for good Kiste,[125] before tackling a new novel.

And you? Is the book you announced coming on? Do you have any time? Do you think you will be able to get any serious leave? If you put in a request, do let me know, for as I told you, I could always put in a word for you with the War Ministry, if the request gets as far as the offices.

In this hope, my dear Descaves, I send you a good shake of the hand.
    Yours

Huysmans

To ÉMILE ZOLA

[March 1884]

My Dear Zola,

This evening I have finished *La Joie de vivre*,[126] which I have been reading as a welcome panacea amidst the irritation of correcting proofs on which I am engaged.

I find in this book a note that you have touched on to a certain extent already, but which you have not, until now, rendered entire, whole and with such a particular accent: a note of painful tenderness. From this point of view the whole section following the death of Mme Chanteau is typically superb. And the death of the dog is one of your finest pages and stands out from all you have written. The childbirth is frightful and of a simplicity that amazes me, for that is what we all dream of. Pauline is well put together, but perhaps her soul is rather too angelically seraphic, given her coarse flesh. The spirit of sacrifice that possesses her can obviously occur, but all the same, the little girl of *Le Ventre de Paris* has become singularly celestial. As for Lazare, I find him a masterly study from the psychological point of view, but here there is a Schopenhauerian theory that I think is not quite exact. All the positive, consoling side of this doctrine, which is both anti-Romantic and anti-Werther, whatever you say, does not come across sufficiently, I find. Just think that it is the theory of resignation, absolutely the same as in *The Imitation of Jesus Christ*,[127] minus the future panacea, which is replaced by a spirit of patience, the decision to accept everything without complaint, by the consolation of waiting for death, which is considered as in religion as deliverance and not as fear. I know that you do not believe in pessimism, and that Bourdeau's preface to the *Pensées* of Schopenhauer[128] states that this extraordinary man was afraid of death; but the theory is more sublime, it rises above the man who did not apply his own ideas to himself. But given the impossibility for intelligent people to believe in Catholicism, these ideas are certainly the most comforting, the most logical, the most obvious there are. Basically, if one is not a pessimist, there remains only to be either a Christian or an anarchist; one of the three, if only you think about it.

But all that is beside the point. The truth is that you have conveyed a special note, not only in the *Rougon-Macquart* but in this present book, a gentle wrenching, a melancholy renunciation. Basically it is Pauline who is the true disciple of Schopenhauer, as you hinted with a smile, but it is true!

I am curious to see what the press will drop on to this book which is quite apart from all contemporary trends, and will be wounding to the foolish utilitarian mind; which way will they take it? The whole aspect of spiritual delicacy, by spiritual I don't mean that stupid adjective used by journalists, but the opposite of bodily (there are words that have become so debased that one hardly dare write them any longer!!), will obviously throw the commercially minded and peddlers of threepenny rags. Keep the stack of inanities, so that we can laugh over them together as we read them. In any case, you can tell yourself, my dear Zola, that you have brought off one of the most difficult *tours de force* possible, you have renewed your method, after producing a considerable volume of work, and have discovered a new corner in literature, that abomination where all springs seem definitively dried up. That is really something!

Until Thursday then, in the meantime I shake you by the hand.

Your devoted

Huysmans

who asks to be remembered to Mme Zola.

What a splendid, magnificently elevated episode is that of Pauline's period, after the marriage of Lazare and Louise.

To ÉMILE HENNEQUIN

[April 1884]

My Dear Friend,

I am at the moment plunged into the bitter proofs of my book. Now this *A Rebours* is cosmopolitan, written in all sorts of languages, Latin, French, even English.

I have a problem with the spelling of the following words in the plural:

lloyd
pudding
stout   do they need an s?
porter
porto

If I don't see you one of these evenings, it would be kind of you to send me a note.

Sorry for these stupid questions, and a good shake of the hand from your

G. Huysmans

To ÉMILE ZOLA

[May 1884]

Your letter, my dear Zola, is full of justified comment, that is undeniable. What you tell me, I told myself personally while writing that difficult book, where I consciously pared down dialogue and accepted the inevitable monotony. The truth is that, given the subject matter, I could not manage it any other way, despite the inevitable incoherence it entailed. I have been a victim of precision in this affair. It is true that I should have set the entire book in a dream, without retaining a single thread attaching it to the earth. Hence inevitable confusions and drifting. Yes, your perception is accurate, profoundly accurate: despite the exceptional linking in the structure of the chapters, latent defects remain. Thus the two modern literature chapters, separated by a weak *hors d'œuvre*, which you are good enough not to mention, are really too close together. They jolt despite the cushioning. But I could not arrange them any other way. I took trouble throughout the book, in a desire for perfect accuracy. I followed step by step Bouchut and Axenfeld's books on neurosis;[129] I did not dare to invert the stages of the illness, or move the accidents, thus I had to put at the end the changes in hearing, whereas they would have been better interspersed amongst other chapters, where they would have had a muffling and distancing effect. With this approach, I deprived myself of any progression in effects. With those Latin writers and G. Moreau I had given all the sharpness I could, it only remained for me to sustain the pitch. I was aware of it. I attempted this perilous leap which seduced me, despite the likelihood that I would break my back.

One sentence in your letter strikes me, it is this: 'As for the rest of us, we are to be obliged to the author for including us.' I believe you! If I had made Montesquiou[130] exactly Des Esseintes (he would have been too dull!), I would have expressed his unspeakable disgust with the whole of naturalism. I wanted to portray him as he is, but with greater accuracy and less narrowly. So I squarely took a stand, threw my own ideas out of the window and expressed ideas diametrically opposed to my own, which it could never occur to anyone to attribute to me, since I wrote the complete opposite in *L'Art moderne*. I declared that he preferred *La Tentation* to *L'Éducation*, *La Faustin* to *Germinie*, *La Faute de l'Abbé Mouret* to *L'Assommoir*.[131] That is all clear-cut, and this complete dichotomy with my own preferences allowed me to enunciate really sick ideas and celebrate the glory of Mallarmé, which I thought was quite a joke![132]

Basically, you see, it was a book not to write, because it was much too difficult with this floating character such as I had conceived him, Christian and homosexual, impotent and incredulous, a disciple of Schopenhauer through reason, a Catholic through atavism, returning nevertheless to a Christ who is not even Catholic but Byzantine, and fearing death as a consequence of his early education, exacerbated by solitude. In its very concept it was too complex and too diffuse. I do not expect much response from the press, because the article would be too difficult to write. They would not know how to untangle those tousled locks, it would take a hell of a large-toothed comb. From letters I receive and rumours I hear, I am aware of a general outcry! I have trodden on everyone's corns; the Catholics are exasperated; others accuse me of being a clerical in disguise. But I am nothing, damn it all! The romantics are outraged at the attacks on Hugo and Gautier, on Leconte de Lisle;[133] the naturalists at the book's hatred of what is modern! Basically there is emerging amongst the sceptics the idea of a great mystification, which, I think, is coming closer to the truth. All in all, I had this crazy book in my head, I released it and there is an end to it! Ah yes! It took too much of my time and aggravated my own personal neurosis too much. I have returned to work on a long short story,[134] which is simple and calm, and I have made a start on my novel about the siege of Paris; it is a change from the excesses of my nightmare of refinement pushed to madness.

I see that for your part you are working and working hard. You tell me that you have given up trying to see clearly into your work. Ah, I am not anxious on your account, for you are the most balanced writer I know. It will all fall quietly into place, with the linchpin linking all the chapters and holding them firmly together. I wish I could say as much about *La Faim*[135] which is tormenting me greatly, on account of the very simplicity of the context. I am splashing about for the moment, but from time to time, I seem to see a bit of light in the plan of it.

Thank you, my dear Zola, for your kind letter; don't forget to remember me to Mme Zola, and accept an affectionate handshake.

Huysmans

To LÉON BLOY

[June 1884]

Truly you have a way of giving breadth to subjects, of extending them into infinity, and this I admire, my dear Bloy. Your 'Représailles du sphinx' is superb,[136] with a perspective of an elevation unknown – oh yes – to today's critics.

Need I tell you the gratification my vanity felt in being so magnificently praised? You can believe it. For a man who has been used all his life to receiving only a cup brimming over with insanities or insults, to feel one's poor work loved and explained by someone other than oneself becomes a sensation of happiness that penetrates to the very sickness of one's nerves.

And then this article was a timely consolation. Yesterday morning, dragged off to Vaugirard by a family obligation, I came back to the Odéon via the rue de Vaugirard. For no specific reason, I was feeling really low. I looked in Maupon's and Heurtaut's windows. My book was no longer there. It was definitively dead, while swinish impurities, full of life, filled the displays. It is all very well to be quite confident about despising the reading public, but it is painful all the same, and whatever we do, my poor friend, we shall suffer cruelly all our lives from this denial of justice, to which we are both particularly attached, I think.

Well, I bought *Le Chat noir* and went and read it on a bench in the Luxembourg gardens, and reading it at that moment, it seemed a magnificent funeral oration pronounced over the corpse of the poor book, dead with no more dignity than a dog. This image haunted me and I told myself that at least it will not have gone off all alone into eternal oblivion, without a great voice having raised itself to make it known and to give it absolution.

And so I thank you with all my heart for the splendid Catholic funeral which you alone gave it.

Only it is with melancholy that I think of the virulent attacks on poor Mallarmé and Verlaine that you slipped in. That was not very fair. I leave literary matters aside, but think, my dear Bloy, that these are men crushed in the service of art, unknown to the public, that they have never had any success, will probably die unknown, having not even been able to find a publisher, while so many low poets, with the souls of cretins, triumph! Really from this point of view alone, they are worthy of your mercy. They have always been in the dust, why kick a man when he is down? No, in the world of art there are enough cads standing squarely on their feet; strike these unworthy idols with the strength of your arm, and spare the poor artists abandoned by everyone, even if you do not at all care for their work.

You have no pity. Nevertheless, how exceptional a temperament such as yours is in the modern Boston that this dreadful Paris has become!

Thank you again for the delicious consolations you gave me, and I convey, my dear friend, a warm shake of the hand via this icy white paper.

Yours

Huysmans

To ÉMILE HENNEQUIN

11 July 1884

Thank you, my dear friend, for the mythological information, I shall put it to good use on my return from the country where, cataclysms notwithstanding, I am going tomorrow, Saturday. For the nth time I am ging to try and drink in tranquillizing air in real countryside, and I am afraid that it will be no more successful than on previous occasions.

I am most probably going to be very bored after two days, and dream of artificial obscenities in the meadows. I am going to try and concoct my work on Moreau in the windpipe of my brain. Basically Nature is an excellent way of making me like the work of man. At the seaside four years ago, I wanted to work and all I managed to give birth to was 'The Armpit' in the *Croquis parisiens*.

Still, I shall be back from Jutigny on 7 August and will take up my old ways again.

Did you read in yesterday's *Radical* Pinard's article in which he talks about your study of me?

I have a piece by Verlaine that is tempting – a mixture of exquisite drunkenness, brutality and homosexual caresses. He is quite at ease with me, and his use of hiatus captivated me (figuratively speaking, of course!!!).[137] All in all, he is quite out of the ordinary, despite the fact that he rambles on obsessively whenever he talks about the countryside where he lives. He admitted to me that were he up to it, work alone could save him from his blessed prick.

No, I assure you, he is very fine, practising enlightened sadism, obscure but tolerant mysticism, affable and persistent drunkenness.

Long live *Sagesse*, oh Hennequin![138]

Thereupon I wish you good health and a little bit of joy, if such is possible during my absence. Ah, I also wish you that obscene epitome of low types from the south that we had the misfortune to meet last Tuesday week!

Yours

Huysmans

To STÉPHANE MALLARMÉ

11 July 1884

Thank you, my dear Mallarmé, for your mythological information; I shall try to untangle these tousled myths once I am back in Paris, for tomorrow I leave for a genuine village; I shall stay there for about three weeks, unless boredom grows too great, for appreciation of the countryside is not very well developed in me, and I have always dreamt of art and artifice when faced with a vast horizon. In short, I am going in search of air laced with opium for my nerves which still torment me, and I should like to calm them down a bit before stretching them on Moreau.

I hope to see you on my return, in the meantime let me at least delegate to my pen a good shake of the hand.

Yours

J. K. Huysmans

To ÉMILE ZOLA

Jutigny, 20 July 1884

My Dear Zola,

I am writing to you from the depths of remote countryside where I am living surrounded by peasants.

I wanted to come and see you before my departure, but as I told you at the funeral of Céard's father, I was without an accountant[139] and driven out of my mind by accounts, of which I understand nothing. Finally chance took a hand; three days before my holiday, I found the right man, Nardin, Charpentier's former employee who was without a situation. He is nice, knows the job well, and at my place will have all the time he wants to write poetry.

And so I fastened my bags and left as soon as he had got into things, and on the twelfth I landed at Jutigny where there awaited me a peasant's hut imitating the décor of the Adrets inn, with a large fireplace, exposed beams and sideboards with big iron hinges. I am now settled in and tasting the pleasure of doing nothing at all, chatting with the peasants, who are really interesting in these parts. Basically I am missing Paris a bit, for I don't understand the countryside, but it is doing me good, and I am poulticing my nerves for Paris. I am taking potions of fresh air, which are sometimes boring and bitter to swallow, but curative.

And you, my dear Zola, are you still in Médan? I am writing to you on the off chance – what is all this talk of a decoration that was rife in the Parisian papers before my departure?[140] I was to have been informed in this rustic hole where I am and where no journalism penetrates, if your nomination had gone through. I have received nothing, and so nothing has happened.

I saw Céard the day before I left; he did not have any information about it either.

And what about the coal mine?[141] Is it coming on? You are fortunate, nevertheless, in being able to work regularly as you do! For my part I am doing nothing, I am just taking notes on the amazing people around me. They are worth it. I went with one of them to buy a calf at Bray-sur-Seine, oh what an operation! It lasts a good hour, all washed down with white wine. It starts with insults all round and then agreement is reached on the calf that had been chosen in the first place! How wily and how stupid they are at one and the same time!

I shall be back in Paris on 6 August, when I return to the office. If you are still in Médan, I will try to come and see you on the first Sunday; for with all the snags there have been, it is ages since I caught the train out west to Villennes.

Until then, my dear friend, I beg you to give my kind regards to Mme Zola and receive a good shake of the hand from your devoted

Huysmans

To CAMILLE LEMONNIER

Autumn 1884[142]

My Dear Friend,

I ardently regretted not seeing you during your stay in Paris. At five o'clock last Monday, I received a letter from M. Destrée inviting me to go and meet you that same evening at ten o'clock at the Café de la Paix. This letter arrived too late for me to be able to liberate myself from my evening engagements. Moreover, M. Destrée put no address on his missive, so that I could not write and ask for another appointment.

Tell all that to M. Destrée, to whom I long since owe thanks for some very fine and very sound articles that he devoted to *A Rebours*, and tell him also not to forget me when he comes back to the capital.

Something else now. I have just finished *L'Hystérique*,[143] my impression is that as far as style is concerned, it is one of your best books. It is beautiful in its simplicity and is genuinely masculine. There are those scenes of adoration wafting up to fill the vaulting of the church roof amidst flashes of light from the tabernacle – really superb. Then intimate corners that I find charming, such as the pious women devouring those sweetmeats so nicely. The background surprises me more. I find the book solidly constructed and incomparably skilful with décors that are identical and yet renewed. Only is Humility a hysteric?[144] Scientifically not, I think. The nuns in the Cadière case and in that of Urbain Grandier certainly were,[145] but they were not mystics, true ecstatics. They were simply nymphomaniacs, helped by *non-seraphic* visions and by taking belladonna and datura, as we now know. Nothing like that here, you have taken a Lateau[146] or better a Sister Hemmerich [*sic*], the most complete example of a stigmatist. Now these are not hysterics, they are mad for Christ with a mystical folly, and they are too much that way for the flesh to have any hold on them.

I know that you can retort that Humility is inert, stultified, dominated by Orléa's magnetism, submitting to rape unconsciously. Yes, but that makes her even less of a hysteric.

But this is the quibbling of a German. The important thing was to produce a masculine book and you have done that, and I congratulate you on it my dear friend, by sending you a good shake of the hand.

Yours

Huysmans

To JULES DESTRÉE

22 November 1884

My Dear Colleague,

I thank you most sincerely for all the battles you have so willingly engaged in on behalf of *A Rebours*. Your chronicle on the book is of a surprising lucidity, given that it has met with total incomprehension on the part of the press. One portion of the press has supported it, another accused it of being Catholic and some papers brandished the word 'anarchy'. Good Lord! But I am none of these things, I am a naturalist, that is to say I work from documents and write as well as I know how. Perhaps I am different from the other writers grouped under this epithet, which basically does not mean very much, in that I do not care for the period in which I live, and that from time to time I seek an escape route into the 'beyond'. But after all, as you have said with absolute accuracy, *A Rebours* is a work of precision. I spent more than eight months taking notes, I defy a perfumer or a Latinist to catch me out from a documentary point of view, and the type of character represented by Des Esseintes does exist, albeit on a smaller scale and less odd.

As for the schism between Zola and me that they have shouted from the housetops, that is stupidity. We often have a friendly argument amongst ourselves about matters on which we differ completely, but we are old friends from the days before *L'Assommoir* and I consider him to have great talent that will stand up to the provocations of the press.

But then when it comes to basics, naturalism, romanticism, etc., what does it all boil down to? The truth is that some people are talented and some are not. Barbey d'Aurevilly, who is worlds removed from me, wrote *L'Ensorcelée* and *Les Diaboliques*,[147] which I admire greatly. And he, like Zola, like all of us, has a perfect contempt for his lordship Ohnet, whatever his opinions might be.

I am particularly grateful to you for having picked that up in your article and poured scorn on that insidious and absurd way of seeking to destroy one book with another by someone else.

Thank you and I mean it, my dear colleague. Allow me to shake you affectionately by the hand.

G. Huijsmans

II
1885–92
Carbolic for the Soul[1]

In the summer of 1885, Huysmans rented the dilapidated Château de Lourps in the countryside to the south-east of Paris. This he considered to be Des Esseintes' ancestral home. He took with him on this unconventional, and by all accounts uncomfortable, holiday his mistress Anna Meunier and her two young daughters, Antonine and Blanche (Huysmans was not their father). He had known this working girl from the provinces since the early 1870s, and although the affair was to continue for some twenty years, they never set up house together, rather spending weekends and occasional holidays in each other's company. This Château de Lourps experience was to provide the raw material for the novel Huysmans worked on in the following year: *En Rade*, an unflattering portrayal of the peasantry in which he sought to demolish the idealized myth of country life; here the harvesters' sheaves are not golden yellow, but 'dirty rust coloured'.

In the second half of the 1880s Huysmans became involved with a number of different groups in the rich patchwork of Parisian life. On the literary front, he was friend and admirer of the poets who were to be known later as the Symbolists. He particularly admired Paul Verlaine and Jules Laforgue, both of whom died before their work received any kind of recognition, and Stéphane Mallarmé, who was rapidly emerging as the idol of a whole generation. Huysmans had been amongst the very first to be convinced of the exceptional genius of Mallarmé and the freshness of his approach to the French language. Although he continued to write letters of congratulation to Zola on the appearance of each new novel, it is clear from those addressed to other correspondents that Huysmans felt himself to be drifting ever further away from his former master, finding that he now had little in common with his sociological approach to novel writing.

An aspect of Huysmans' life in Paris during these years that cannot be ignored is his sexuality. The comfortable arrangement with Anna Meunier was by no means sufficient to satisfy his strong appetite in this domain. Together with his friends, he was ever seeking out new establishments with girls who would give themselves up to the most perverted of practices. He also explored the homosexual underworld, although he was not personally attracted in this way. It is his new Dutch friend, Arij Prins, who becomes Huysmans' confidant as far as his sexual exploits are concerned; the letters of these years contain many explicit accounts.

He also flirted for a while with the fringes of the Royalist cause, but it is doubtful whether Huysmans ever took completely seriously Naundorff's claim to the French throne as Prince Louis-Charles de Bourbon, son of the supposed Louis XVII. This cause depended largely on mysterious revelations and prophecies, and attracted a number of occultists and visionaries. Huysmans was to become more and more drawn into such circles in the late 1880s. He now acknowledged his disappointment with the philosophy of Schopenhauer, and embarked on a spiritual quest starting virtually from the premise: 'In the incomprehensible abomination of life, there simply cannot be nothing at all.'[2] This search took him first of all, not surprisingly after his earlier attraction to the decadent, to a dabbling in the black arts and a fascination with the power of evil. The second half of the nineteenth century saw in France a great proliferation of occult sects and pseudo-religions.

In the circle of Barbey d'Aurevilly, Huysmans met Sâr Joséphin Péladan, a colourful character on the Parisian scene, noted for his silver waistcoat and generally eccentric style of dress. Despite his humble beginnings as a bank clerk, he claimed descent from the ancient three magi of Chaldaea, and liked to be addressed as 'magus'. The Rosicrucian Order had been revived in Paris by the Marquis Stanislas de Guaïta, who was a morphine addict. Huysmans' correspondent Oswald Wirth was a member of this sect. But one of the best-known names in the history of occultism in France is that of Pierre-Eugène-Michel Vintras, who claimed to be a reincarnation of the prophet Elijah. He died in 1875, before Huysmans became drawn into this scene, but his self-styled successor, Joseph-Antoine Boullan, was to have an enormous influence on the novelist over a number of years.

Despite having been warned against Boullan as a Satanist by several people, Huysmans sought him out and paid his first visit to his centre of operations in Lyons in 1890, in order to thank him in person for all the documentation he had supplied by post for his novel *Là-Bas*, in which he sought to demonstrate the reality of a power for evil in contemporary France. It is quite amazing that Huysmans never saw through Boullan until he read his personal confession after the latter's death in 1893. He was in fact completely duped. Boullan's story is indeed horrific: he had been ordained as a priest of the Roman Catholic Church, but his ambition, his weakness for women and the attraction of the sacrilegious gave an unconventional turn to his career. He founded, together with a Sr Adèle Chevalier, a Society for the Reparation of Souls, which was little more than a front for their illicit love affair, which culminated in ritual murder during mass of the child borne him by Sr Adèle. He also acted as spiritual director to various communities of nuns; whilst supposedly instructing them on how to achieve intimacy with the souls of saints he took practical, physical demonstration to its ultimate. After various complaints, Boullan was examined by the ecclesiastical authorities in Paris and Rome, imprisoned and defrocked. And so he set up as a 'freelance' priest in Lyons.

Huysmans was fascinated by the exorcisms and attacks on evil spirits that he saw at the house in Lyons, by the sight of Boullan in ecclesiastical vestments waving hosts and celebrating the sacrifice of the glory of Melchisedek. Even after his own reconciliation with the Church of Rome, Huysmans continued to see Boullan and his Lyons circle. Unfortunately none of his letters to this strange man survives, for as soon as he heard of Boullan's death, he hurried off to Lyons to retrieve his correspondence and destroy it. It was then that he learnt the full and awful truth about the man he had admired.

Huysmans undoubtedly saw sufficient in the way of occult practices to become fully convinced that evil forces exist and exert a powerful influence. We know that he attended séances and witnessed Boullan's heretical celebrations, but it seems unlikely that he had direct experience of the worst kind of sacrilegious practice, although he sought out all the documentation he could get hold of on such subjects.

So Huysmans now found himself perched on the edge of the clerical world; many of the occultists were former priests, and they aped the ritual of the official Church. This unlikely and devious path was to be the one that would lead Huysmans eventually back to Catholicism. In his letters of the period immediately following the publication of *Là-Bas* in 1891, there emerges his fascination with true mysticism, which he described as the 'art' of the Catholic Church, 'an immense unexplored field of strange and complex spiritual activity. And these things are more interesting – to me at least – than all the psychological studies of *femmes du monde* and fishwives.'[3] To date Huysmans had experienced only the dark side of spiritual life, but by a process of deduction he arrived at the realization that if these evil forces are indeed a reality, must not the opposite, the force for good, the Deity, be equally real, if one but knew how to approach Him?

This secret yearning to know God brought Huysmans face to face with his own lifestyle. How could he reconcile these vague religious stirrings within himself with his taste for women and the pleasures of the flesh? How could he dare, given his past life, to venture back to the bosom of Mother Church? He began nevertheless to frequent the churches of the capital and was frequently moved by the liturgy, especially at offices in convent chapels and at benediction of the Blessed Sacrament. In his embarrassment he would tell his friends that he was simply collecting material for his next book, but to himself he had to admit that he was struggling with the desire to break with his former style of life and make a new beginning. He was haunted by a feeling of uncleanness, for at the same time he continued to be a client of Parisian brothels.

Huysmans' disgust with himself was compounded by a general disgust with the world at large. He found the political situation in France eminently depressing during these years. Although the Third Republic managed to survive as a regime, times were turbulent with frequent changes of government amidst an atmosphere of bitterness created by repeated scandals arising from corruption.

So he was faced with the problem of how to recover the lost faith of childhood, to be reconciled with God and reintegrated into the Church of Rome. Ironically, Berthe Courrière was to be instrumental in this process. Ironically because this flamboyant character, the mistress of Remy de Gourmont and twice certified insane, had also been responsible for Huysmans' initiation into the occult arts. Séances were frequent in her apartment. But she also knew Fr Arthur Mugnier, second curate of the parish of St Thomas Aquinas. This priest was a remarkable man, not so much for the profundity of his spiritual insights, but rather for the role he played as a link between the literary and artistic milieu and the Church in Paris over a number of decades. Himself interested in the arts, he became guide, friend and confessor to many society figures, including the circle of Marcel Proust. Berthe Courrière introduced Huysmans to Fr Mugnier in the sacristy at St Thomas Aquinas at the end of May 1891. They were to meet frequently during the following twelve months. In the summer of 1891, Huysmans went on a visit to the Carthusian monastery, La Grande Chartreuse, and the shrine of the Blessed Virgin at La Salette in the French Alps, but this pilgrimage he made in the company of Boullan still.

Fr Mugnier realized that Huysmans' was a case requiring strong medicine, of a kind he would be unable to supply himself in a Parisian parish. In order for him to return to the sacramental life of the Church, it was necessary for him to make confession of his sins to a priest, and this was psychologically the most daunting prospect for Huysmans. Despite what was to be a lifelong friendship for the novelist, Fr Mugnier was never his confessor in the sacramental sense; the medicine he now prescribed was that the would-be penitent should make a retreat at the Cistercian monastery at Igny near Rheims. Huysmans bravely followed this advice and set off in the summer of 1892. His first impressions of monastic life are vividly recorded in his letters, but it is to the later autobiographical novel *En Route* that we must look for an account of the events that brought him back into communion with the Church. On his first attempt, he was unable to go through with the celebration of the sacrament of penance, but on 13 July he made his confession to the prior of the abbey and received absolution. He received Holy Communion at mass the following morning. The account in *En Route* is moving and beautiful as Huysmans compares his confessor to a swan rising from a lake, with arms outstretched in his long white cowl as he gave his blessing. Huysmans found a form of peace at last, and had at the same time given the Parisian newspapers ample material for their gossip columns.

To ÉMILE ZOLA

[March 1885]

My Dear Zola,

I spent all day yesterday, Sunday, devouring *Germinal*.[4] I emerge somewhat bemused from this reading, haunted by the prodigious carcass of the book, written with an iron grip. What strikes me above all, and appears to me to be quite the most superior aspect of the book, is the underground landscape and the geographical situation; there are naked plains, a few sugar-beet plants and troubled skies that seize hold of one with melancholy of a terrible intensity, and dominating everything, a magnficent landscape of furnace chimneys, a grandiose view of Montsou by night, and a descent into the shaft, in the midst of blackness, that you alone have succeeded in transforming into a colour, revealing a power to convey things that is really unique at the present time.

Then the gusts that make the immense timbering of this epic mine quake, tempests of wind and fire, the final collapse of Le Voreux,[5] with the fine image of the machine struggling against death, and the chimney sinking down, devoured in one gulp, will remain unforgettable. That was my first thought this morning on waking. I felt a sort of uneasy stupefaction. All this black atmosphere run through with a fury of fornication had been haunting me since the day before, and thinking about it again, at one night's remove, in less immediate focus, I could see the spectre hanging over that wretched place, the terrible image you evoke of Capital, the unknown god, in a tabernacle, like a Hindu idol; you have built it up superbly with just a few phrases.

All the same – you who want cheerful things! Despite the enormous jollity that could be cast into this succession of miseries by the expanse of bosom spread throughout the pages and the sight of that enormous backside that confronts us from time to time, it exudes a damned sadness, not that I am complaining, even the wretched horses stumbling in the water and blackness are oppressive; it is a lament of Darkness, a *lamma sabactani*[6] of hunger; and love, spread thinly in this book, is also enough to make one shed tears of sadness, poor Catherine's especially, she is truly charming in her resignation and innocent lack of modesty.

All in all, you have acheived what you wanted, to show us the life of a mine, leaving an unforgettable image in our brain. You can be pleased, for you have brought off this *tour de force*. Like the market,[7] the mine stands before us, brought to life with a soul of its own and a special body. You can flatter yourself on having a strong back and damned good fists.

I shall see you soon, my dear Zola; as always, I send you, via this scrap of paper, a good shake of the hand.

Yours

Huysmans

To JULES DESTRÉE

3 June 1885

My Dear Destrée,

This morning I retrieved the fine book,[8] which you were good enough to send me, from the Ministry of the Interior, where it had been sent by that useful institution, the Customs and Excise Department.

I really do not know how to thank you. There are some superb plates by the good Luyken in it: 'The Plagues of Egypt', rain of fire and extraordinary beasties.[9] What a singular artist he is all the same, and to think that in France even his name is unknown! While a load of old scratchers and oil daubers are famous!

This book has given me real pleasure, as you can imagine, but I am depriving you of it, and that takes the edge off my joy.

However, one day I should be the owner of a marvellous collection of Luykens that belongs to an uncle of mine in The Hague; I hope to give the books and engravings back to you when I come into the inheritance.

How fortunate you are not to be in Paris at the moment! The funeral of Victor Hugo was terrible.[10] Imagine Paris divided in two, the left bank, where I am, completely cut off from the right bank, no mail, no newspapers, nothing . . . Then they came down from Courtille in an apotheosis; it was like a working-class wedding, with guzzling of sausage and sucking of wine bottles everywhere, on top of the urinals, on ladders, in the trees. It was a real blowout, embellished with yelling of the Marseillaise and dancing as at a fairground. In melancholy vein, I thought of the funeral of poor Flaubert, where we were only a handful of nobodies,[11] and of Baudelaire's where there were just a few friends.

It is true that they did not titillate the testicles of democracy, and there was nothing familiar or patriarchal about them!

And how many of those in the interminable funeral procession had read good old Hugo, *Les Misérables* or extracts from *Les Travailleurs de la mer*, surely four at the most, from government ministers down to the corporation of galoshes-makers, lightning-conductor manufacturers and pork butchers, all of whom were officially represented in the cortège, behind the pauper's hearse. But come, glory is certainly a fine thing! A fine *mardi gras* for the cemetery!

But what! Your ears must have been ringing with news of follies in Paris for the last week, thanks to the press.

I am sending this letter to Charleroi, to the address indicated on the parcel, asking them to forward it, for I do not have your address in Brussels. I think it will reach you all the same.

Think of me when you come to Paris, and until then, my dear Destrée, accept my thanks and a cordial shake of the hand.

    Your devoted

G. Huysmans

To JULES DESTRÉE

12 June 1885

My Dear Friend,

I have read *La Réforme*, which you were good enough to send me. It gave a good push and shove to those abominable dye merchants who fill up the glasshouses of the art business. That little visiting card left by Puvis[12] at the mortuary put me in a good mood, that was good. One cannot denounce too much those cowardly daubers who awarded the medal of honour to Bouguereau!![13]

As for *La Jeune Belgique*, I do not receive it and in vain have I searched for it at the Odéon so as to be able to read your article. If you have a spare copy, you would be doing a kind deed in sending it to me.

La Revue indépendante has croaked in stupid circumstances, ousted by a journal that is now also defunct![14]

It is all over, there is not even one young magazine in Paris any more.

I was on the point of taking on *La Revue indépendante* with Caze,[15] but then there is really nothing one can do. It would be a complete waste of money. In France magazines are impracticable, unless you are *La Revue des Deux Mondes* or *Le Correspondant*. Nothing can be done except by capitalists intent on losing money in the business.

Apart from that, nothing new here; not a single interesting book coming out, not a single article, just a smooth blanket of mute stupidity. The Hugo business has calmed down, however. The press has dried its crocodile tears. The murderer Pel has become the next craze,[16] but we lack an Edgar Poe to get the facts straight.

I am going to lunch, and so I leave you, but not without a good shake of your hand.

G. Huysmans

To LÉON BLOY AND GEORGES LANDRY

Lourps, 26 Agust 1885

What I am up to, my dear friends, is that I am doing well and doing badly, both from a romantic and naturalist point of view.

I have taken over the defunct château de Lourps, a château of fine appearance, with a dovecote, former moat and two hundred bedrooms. The park, torn apart and bought up bit by bit by the peasants, is still delightful, returned to its natural state, with flowers growing haphazardly, full of delightful paths through the woods for leisurely walks, a beautiful dream of sunlit verdure, an orgy of ivy eating into the blue pines, a debauchery of doves and swallows in the eaves of the château of the Marquis de Saint-Phale, which is abandoned, ruined, divided up, exquisite with its vaults of times gone by, its trellises, its door giving on to the church, which is invaded by lichen and inhabited by crows.

There is the romantic aspect; I am greatly savouring this place, dreaming away in the lonely and secluded gardens, spending tranquil hours on the lawns where occasional traces of former flowerbeds can be made out.

As for the naturalist aspect, that is different. It is like being shipwrecked!!! One is further away from everything than if one were on an island distant from any continent. In order to get bread, one has to put a basket at the bottom of the immense and noble drive, decimated, alas, by devious felling. The baker leaves a loaf that we go and collect in the evening; even if we pay extra, the butcher will not scale the hill on which I am perched. And as for wine, I had to take a barrel, being unable to procure wine by the litre.

What is more, of the two hundred rooms in the château, five or six are habitable, the others are in a state of dilapidation or are inhabited by the birds. And the furnishings are in a sorry state. Impossible to find chairs in any quantity; you cannot imagine the savagery of these parts!

The question of eatables gets out of all proportion, and more seriously, the financial situation is becoming simply terrifying. Twenty-franc coins disappear at a frightening pace, we have to buy in everything, from the crockery to the bread. Things are likely to take a turn for the worse.

In short, the naturalist aspect is purely purgative! Added to that, in such an isolated situation, nothing closes properly, neither windows nor doors; we are surrounded by woods; the bourgeois are afraid at night in this barracks of a place, which is haunted, according to local gossip.

That is the state of our merrymaking, a delicate balance between peace and aggravation! Basically I come down on the side of peace, for the air is a marvellous tonic, and my spirit is calmed as nowhere else.

And you and Bloy? I think of him constantly. What is he up to? Is he busy with the religious rubbish of widow Lebel-Bouasse?[17] Is he managing to keep afloat in the liquid sewage of this abominable existence? I want him to come here, for only the sovereign bromide of the countryside could pacify him and enable him to recover from the awful shocks he has borne. I am wondering how to arrange it. The food is nothing, with skilful combinations we could manage something! It is the question of sleeping that is the most difficult. I am going to try and find at least a straw mattress and some sheets – I think I shall manage it – but blankets and a pillow are impossible! Couldn't he make a little bundle if he came? What is more, I am going to another village tomorrow, to see if I cannot find more resources in this connection. The inn that we mentioned is too far, too inconvenient, it is possible only if one sleeps at the château, as habitable rooms exist.

I should like to see you also, my dear Landry, for this ruined castle would delight you, I am sure; think about it, for one night, we could always manage. it is only a question of being willing.

Apart from all that, I am vomiting mentally on humanity; the newspapers

I receive stir up my fury and whip up my mind! Oh Bloy! I am full of rage, ready to spew buckets with you on contemporary swinishness, we could spend some fine days together. Despite the pecuniary cesspit into which we have been plunged by a diabolical providence, like pieces of bread dipped into a boiled egg, it would be, nevertheless, a few seconds' respite, a temporary but real life raft, a break from the preoccupations of that great crassness, and for you, my good Landry, from the voracious ignominy of Hayem.[18]

Let me have news of d'Aurevilly and Miss Read;[19] tell me if some happy event has not occurred in the monotony of your bleak existence; if since I left, oh impure Landry, murky delights have not taken you by surprise on Saturdays, the day devoted to the delights of amorous pursuit.

Write to me, my dear friends, I hope for news from you of whom I think when the hours I should like to share with you are good. It will be soon, won't it?

J. K. Huysmans

Anna, Joséphine and Tonine ask me to send you a kiss, which I do.[20]

To ARNOLD GOFFIN

[August 1885]

My Dear Colleague,

Your pretty volume[21] on silky, Japanese paper has reached me at Des Esseintes' castle, where I have taken refuge in order to forget Paris a little, as well as the newspapers, a whole string of artistic iniquities and the faecal abomination of electoral registers which is just beginning.

Alone in an old ruined building in an abandoned park like Le Paradou, I savoured on the grass *Le Journal d'André*, which I had read previously in extracts.

This diary underlined again a thought that preoccupies me. Where is modern literature heading? Classic and romantic have been buried, and it is unthinkable to exhume these literary relics; naturalism is moribund, and what is more, its field of enquiry is, in the very nature of things, extremely restricted. The supernatural dimension will be exhausted no less quickly; moreover, discipleship is impossible in this domain. Verlaine is bound to remain isolated in his way of expressing nuances. Dostoevsky and Edgar Poe could not possibly leave any progeny. There is nothing other than M. Ohnet, whose impoverished works satisfy the great rabble of readers.

And I am very much afraid, given contemporary crassness, the general artistic insensitivity, the guaranteed success of the commonplace and the unwritten word, that literature, which is of no use to the pleasures of the age, would be confined to that: a bit of Ohnet and Delpit in prose, a bit of Déroulède in verse,[22] and that will suffice for generations to come.

There is only one consolation in all this. There will continue to be forty of us and we shall write for each other. *Le Journal d'André* which came out in such a small edition revived that idea in me, and I am grateful to you both for the dedication, and for what you sent me.

So write to me, my dear colleague, about your literary plans. Given the artistic ideas you expressed in *Le Journal d'André*, you are already marked out to serve as stable litter for blockheads, and that interests me and endears you to me, for the daily life of an artist in Belgium is in the same category as Paris, as far as repeated woundings are concerned.

Farewell, I must leave you, for the visit of the postman to whom I am going to give this letter is imminent. I have just time to send you a good shake of the hand.

Your most devoted

J. K. Huysmans

To JULES DESTRÉE

27 September 1885

But oh yes, my dear Destrée, the Comte de Lautréamont[23] is talented with a fine madness. That singular book with its comic lyricism, a bloody rage reminiscent of the Marquis de Sade, and amidst a load of sentences put together like four pennyworth, a few that burst with magnificent sonority!

I await an article on this book with impatience, I hope you will have found some information concerning the life of this strange fellow, who has created his hymn of homosexuality with such fine phrases. It is also true that it contains some nightmares *à la* Redon. The screwing of the female shark by the man is stupefying,[24] and there is a disembowelling, liver and heart, through a vagina that is quite appetizing.

Thank you for having sent me these songs. They are in fact worth reading – what the devil could a man who has written such terrible dreams do for a living?

I am pleased that you are thinking of doing something on Luyken; there is a real need for it, you know. As far as information about him is concerned, I put all I had into *A Rebours*, except for this, which is good, as you will see.

It appears that Luyken made a great many licentious engravings. When mysticism hit him like a truncheon blow on the head, he went round the publishers and had them destroyed, but the more he tried to get rid of them, the more the publishers had them run off. There must still be some in existence. Bear that in mind in your researches.

Moreover, there is a book by him which bears his portrait as frontispiece, an extraordinary mug! Alas, I do not have the title of this book, it is a small one! I saw the book in Holland, but since then . . .

Nothing new here, the sky is overcast, rain; it has not made up its mind to be really cold yet, a grubby twilight in the middle of the day. It oozes with boredom and I am fed up; add to that that there is nothing for us coming into the bookshops. A heap of Ohnets on the horizon; everywhere is full of politics and every wall is daubed with posters for the special issue of *Le Petit Journal*.

I must go to a lunch appointment; I leave you, but not without sending you a good shake of the hand.
Your

G. Huysmans

Ah, and when will you come to Paris again?

To JULES LAFORGUE

28 September 1885

My Dear Colleague,

As soon as I had read *Les Complaintes*[25] that you were good enough to send me, I went to Vanier to get your address.[26] You were at Koblenz, he told me, but we were going to be travelling, so I do not know how to get my letter to you. I gather from correspondence I have seen in *Lutèce* that you should be in Paris at the moment. Vanier should know your exact address, so I am sending by his good offices this epistle, which I hope you will receive.

Yes, I wanted to tell you that this book, *Les Complaintes*, took a very insidious hold on me, with its horizons disappearing into the mist, its evocative epithets, opening up dream-provoking vistas, its curiously composite verbs, its strangely rhyming verse, with plurals embracing singulars. There are pieces such as 'La Complainte d'un autre dimanche', a lament of convalescence, where one comes across that delicious line: 'I am pleased with the pattern on my blue blanket'; 'La Complainte des pianos' and of the good moon, and many more that are truly effective lullabies from the beyond, a subtle music that haunts you once the book is closed. And I have said nothing of the prose piece, genuine impressionism in a prose poem, full of finds, and containing that melancholy sentence that one goes over and over in one's mind: 'How sad are the goods trains in the rain'!

It was a splendid feast for Des Esseintes; what a singular thing though! When I wrote that chapter on modern profane literature in *A Rebours* and I praised Corbière, Verlaine and Mallarmé, I thought I was writing for myself, and did not suspect that a whole movement was getting under way in that direction. The press judged that I was indulging in mystification and wanted to shock the middle classes. As yet no one has penetrated the intimate depths of this chapter, despite the fact that I explained Mallarmé, the most abstruse of these poets, so as to make him almost clear. Today I laugh when I see the effrontery of the press faced with these poems that simply stupefy them. I hope that some Claretie[27] or other will suddenly discover Verlaine!

The day I went in search of your address, Vanier told me that you had replaced Pigeon in the affections of the Empress of all the Prussias.[28] That sparked off my imagination, and I tried to picture you, as you must be having to read Ohnet's rubbish or Dumas the younger, but, when quietly on your own, rhyming away at your *Complaintes* in such advanced language.

You must have experienced pure and extreme joy in the perfect achievement of some of them – the one about the pianos for example.

And when is *L'Imitation de Notre-Dame de la lune* to be?[29]

Thank you my dear colleague, and allow me to shake you by the hand.
    Your devoted

                                                                        Huysmans

To JULES DESTRÉE

                                                                17 December 1885

My Dear Friend,
    As you requested, I am sending a few details on Redon. He is a big lad, very gentle, very shy, very well behaved – you wouldn't take him for a painter at first. In short he has the face of a monk with black, penetrating eyes. He has been married for years, he lives as well as he can, but mostly not too well, at 76 rue de Rennes, a stone's throw from me.

He is at a loss in the current climate. He has in his studio some extraordinary drawings, infinitely superior to those in his albums. One needs to have seen them to get an idea of just how far the art of dreams can go.

One evening, Mallarmé and I, leafing through his folders, were left gaping at strange primitives that he was reworking in a nightmarish manner.

As for sales! Oh! No one takes any notice of him. Since *A Rebours*, however, a movement in his favour has emerged amongst the young. Happily people took notice of me – and – I have come across an admirer of *A Rebours* who went from Italy to Paris, to Redon's, to buy 'Melancholy' which I wrote about in the said book and in *L'Art moderne*.

It is appropriate to give the name of this man who bought a Redon! – He is a Bonaparte, Count Primoli.

I have seen him, he is quite *compos mentis*.

To sum up, it seems to me that, despite everything, Redon has had no luck. Help out, my dear Destrée, by writing articles on him whenever you can.

The twenty-four albums that have been sold have been scattered to the four winds, God knows where! I have not even been able to get one, Redon no longer having a single one. So I do not think there is any hope of finding one.

And of the twenty-four, I think he gave at least fifteen away!

I have been working on your behalf; when your book of short stories is finished, I will try nevertheless to infiltrate it with Stock and Tresse, with whom I have signed a contract for all my books. I do not know if he will take it, he will read it at least; perhaps I will persuade him by promising that you will give him a novel later.

For the moment he has been warned.

I send you, my dear Destrée, a good shake of the hand.

Your

G. Huysmans

To ARIJ PRINS

[March 1886]

My Dear Colleague,

Alas, I have no very interesting information to convey concerning my genesis as a novelist.

What is a fact, however, is that I came to know myself as a writer at the Louvre, through looking at pictures of the Dutch school. It seemed to me that the same thing needed to be conveyed with the pen. In that period there was no question of naturalism or of any other label, and when I wrote *Marthe*, it seemed so monstrous that, despite the manifest chastity of the book, the government should forbid the poor girl's entry into France, although she had appeared in Brussels.

My ideas have barely changed since, except, that is, for an understanding of the underside of realism, of a pessimistic philosophy followed through in all my books, sustaining them, so to speak, with a common idea, which marks a contrast with naturalism in the strict sense, which limits itself to recording, without drawing any conclusions.

Bascially in any case, I have drawn back from all labels. In any genre there are those who have talent, and those who have none; that is all there is to it. I greatly admire Barbey d'Aurevilly and Villiers de l'Isle-Adam who are personal friends of mine, but none the less out-and-out romantics.

You can add to that an immense difference between Zola's ideas and mine, for example. He likes his period and celebrates it. I abhor it, and yet we manage to describe the same things. If one looks into the matter, he is, all things considered, a materialist. I am not; basically I am in favour of the art of dreams as much as of the art of reality; and if I launched Raffaëlli as a painter, I did as much for his counterpart Odilon Redon.

All that lacks clarity, but we would need to talk, not write, to explain it all, or it would run to several volumes of a treatise on aesthetics.

You speak of Boborykin. He has hatched thousands of books, he is a very low sort of Russian Claretie. One day he gave me a novel of his translated by his wife to give to Charpentier. Hennique and I read it and were left amazed at the empty stupidity of the book. Courrière, who knows Russian literature well and has written a book on it published by Charpentier, speaks of him vaguely as a Russian Dumas, churning out anything at all. It is obviously true. Boborykin claims to be very *avant-garde* in Paris, stuffing himself with notes on everyone and everything, saying he is an optimistic naturalist, and according to the information already referred to, supported by the opinion of Turgenev whom I consulted about him one day, he does nothing more than piss out verbiage, void of ideas and style.

As for our poor Caze, he is as bad as can be at the present moment,[30] almost gone, dead perhaps as I write. Yesterday the doctors attempted an operation that failed; the poor fellow, and his wife has a weak chest and two young children!

What folly he committed to no avail! And that through childish vanity.

I am literally devastated by this business, which explains the lack of gaiety emanating from this letter.

I send you, my dear colleague, a good shake of the hand.

Your

Huijsmans

To ODILON REDON

28 June 1886

My Dear Redon,

Unfortunately, 'L'Empreinte' was not for me, but for a Dutch writer, Arij Prins, who is enthusiastic about you, and determined to put himself out on your behalf in Holland and in Hamburg, where he lives.

Moreover he intends, as soon as he is more in funds, to commission me to buy up from you all the drawings he can.

He is a very strange, very devoted lad, very determined; you will see that there will be a genuine outlet there for articles and sales, for he is going to exhibit 'L'Empreinte' at the Hamburg Art Circle and try to develop a taste for your work there.

Apart from all that, nothing new here – sun – and you know my hatred for that celestial lout, who roasts my lodgings and renders me stupid, covering me with sweat and depriving me of what little appetite I have.

I see on the other hand that Mme Redon and your child are doing well. Your absence and your silence were worrying me somewhat; I feared complications. But ah, all is well!

At the moment there is an exhibition in the rue de Sèze, what a shame you aren't here. There are some mediocre Raffaëllis, but some Dutch tulip fields by Claude Monet that are stupefying!

A real feast for the eyes!

I shall see you soon, shall I not, my dear Redon; greetings to the little man, and all good wishes to Mme Redon. Drink in the fresh air! For in Paris you will fast – true monastic abstinence from clean air.

Yours

Huysmans

To ARIJ PRINS

11 August 1886

Ah, such fine news: on the one hand I have a stomach upset and on the other, neuralgia. How inferior this human machine is, compared to man-made machines. They can be decoked, unscrewed, oiled and parts replaced. Decidedly, nature is not a very wonderful thing.

You cannot imagine, my dear friend, what the weather has been like here these last few days; the wind was like a blast of hot air from an oven. I thought I was going to die. How I long for winter! Yes, I really do.

Received the plates of the Bièvre that Kloos was kind enough to run off for me.[31] It is really good of him. Your newspaper affair will have a happy ending as long as you are not financially involved, for I have no faith in the newspaper business, unless you put in 700,000 [francs] and then, with advertising, you can obviously try anything.

As far as binding is concerned, wait, my dear Prins; that creature Bellefond will not deliver your books or mine in less than two or three months. He is a hard case on whom nothing has any effect; it is better to go elsewhere, unless armed with unshakeable patience. And where else is there to go? The rest are no better than clog-makers.

As far as Villiers and Bloy are concerned, this is how things stand:

Villiers, by a stroke of luck, is managing to live. Stock finally accepted a book by him and discounted bills from another publisher and made him an advance of two hundred [francs]; he has placed an article with *La Revue illustrée*. So for the moment he is opulent, and not in urgent need of money.

As for Bloy, this month he would literally have died of hunger if it hadn't been for Villiers and me. At the moment he is begging; he tries to pick up five francs in Paris, goes home and works until the five francs run out – after which, he starts collecting again, and God knows the reputation this is getting him amongst writers who are not as good as he is! But his skull is formed in such a way as to be always full of hope. All the same, I would have thrown myself into the Seine long since if I'd been in his place! For it is no life to be shut in at home from morning to evening, with nothing to eat but coffee and bread. And he is not always fortunate enough to have that.

If you could, as you intimated, send him a few coppers, don't take too long over it, for the need is devilish pressing.

I saw him with Villiers on Sunday. Villiers had brought little Totor, who played with Tonine, my woman's little one.[32] It was quite an intimate gathering of us poor cripples with fatherless or motherless children. I thought of my virtuous family in Holland, those solemn bourgeois with private incomes, and married with all pomp and ceremony. But all the same, it was nice, and we spoke of you, envying Hamburg, which we thought must be misty, while at my place, we were roasting as in a big rustic oven.

That is the only news from Paris, my dear Prins. I have tried to place a volume of verse by Caze – no need to tell you that I accepted this thankless task for the sake of his wife. The result was zero, as I expected, moreover. No one being interested in losing money.

His wife is not pleased. But damn it all, I cannot do the impossible. I am getting myself laughed at, and that is bad enough.

As for the Rowlandson, they are rare and are worth a minimum of 1,500 francs when one comes to light.[33]

I send you, my dear friend, greetings from my woman and handshakes from everyone.

G. Huijsmans

To ARIJ PRINS

6 September 1886

Let me scribble these few lines, my dear Prins, from my office where I am between two administrative affairs, of which the stupidity and lack of interest are disconcerting.

Thank you for the cigars, they have an aroma like Malmsey wine, smoke such as is not to be savoured in this country, where the vainglory of that old fool called Chevreul is celebrated![34]

For this man in fact discovered nothing. He is one hundred years old – and that is all – what a stupid country France is, and what a population of halfwits we have!

As for news, yesterday I went to that hospitable house where we made a stop one evening. I rediscovered there the two girls that we honoured with the caresses of our members. I went upstairs again with the little fortune-teller, a gipsy type, that I had had before, and despite the prodigious heat, I devoured her parts. It was very good! On this point, I am not bothered that oral sex is spreading in this way. It would have been quite surprising if the Prussians didn't know this art before any of us – only they bring hypocrisy to bear! Like everyone else, what's more. It is the same in Paris, which is full of old swine of serious demeanour who vomit with digust over our books, declaring them indecent, and who indulge in these exercises with their tongues every evening. What a fine thing decorum is!

By a stroke of good fortune without parallel in years, that awful Bellefond has made up his mind to do the bindings in less than six or seven months.

My woman had to tie up the bindings with string and arrange things so that they don't arrive broken. So you are going to get them. They are not bad. I recommend a surprising dedication by old Barbey d'Aurevilly in *Les Diaboliques*.[35]

Nothing apart from this nonsense. We are dying from the heat, and on top of that I caught a prodigious cold in a draught, and that makes my head fuddled.

I am wonderfully out of form. I am dozing in my office armchair in front of my work; it is all I can manage to hold a pen to scribble these lines and proffer my hand.

Yours

G. Huijsmans

To ARIJ PRINS

20 November 1886

My Dear Friend,

I have been wanting to write to you for an enormously long time, but then the truth is that I am very unsettled; on the one hand I am annoyed at the Ministry, where everything is upside down and being reorganized from top to bottom. I am fighting to be appointed deputy head, but there are outside rivals who have backers and although I have every right to it, there is a good chance I shall be turned down – and it's no joke, for if I miss out, I shall have to carry on until the end of my days just to make ends meet.

On the other hand, I have that damned novel on my hands,[36] it has started in *La Revue indépendante* which you will receive, and promptly I hope. It's funny, everyone here is exasperated by this book which basically seeks to play a double role – a portion of real life on the one hand, and a portion of dream on the other. So the naturalists are exasperated by the dream aspect and the idealists by the naturalism of my peasants.

It's worse than with *A Rebours*, I have everyone against me. The novelty of it frightens them. What fun! I hear people say: 'but one bit doesn't follow on from the other'! Or, 'it's a very bumpy ride'; damn it, I know it's a rough ride because that is how I wanted it. Even Goncourt is amazed at it! As for Zola, he finds my peasants very good, but the apparition of Esther, the naked woman that you will see in the second chapter, monstrous. On the other hand, Villiers is delighted and is learning the apparition of Esther by heart, so are Mallarmé and Bloy. As for d'Aurevilly, he understands nothing of it, neither the peasants nor the dreams.

Damn it all, what a hotchpotch of opinions!

As for Bloy, the situation is indescribable. With his book completely printed and ready to come out, Stock, in a panic, surrounded by threats from the press, refuses to put it on sale, preferring to lose two thousand [francs] than to chance his arm.[37] It was like a great blow on the head to Bloy, and he is very upset and is running feverishly all over Paris as if impaled; he has hunted out a newsagent and won him over. And the book is being reprinted at the present moment and is going to come out!

It is truly amazing, the life of this man, who what is more is still dying of hunger, while he awaits success and his millions . . .

As for Villiers, he is going to work for the *Gil Blas*, I think. He has already placed an article with them. If it could last, he would be saved, for that way he would have nine hundred [francs] a month.

I hear that Redon is arriving in Paris in a few days' time and is going to settle here again for good. I will speak to him about the business of the exhibition.

Thank you in advance for the delectable cheese that you announce. We will eat it with all due recollection and your recommendations for opening it will be carried out to the letter by the good lady who will be in charge of it.

Nothing new apart from that – other than that I am still rheumatic and neuralgic. I've seen loads of doctors. There is nothing to be done. It is part of my make-up apparently. This revelation quite delights me!

On the woman front, complete calm, nothing. In my district, there are no *very* good women. The best are still where we went. And then I cannot bring myself to sleep with my own, having slept with her too much before, when she was young. In this way I am becoming chaste, for want of good opportunities.

Then after all, it is perhaps for the best, for every time I have myself sucked, I pay for it with a headache the following day.

There, my good Prins, is all the news.

Yours

G. Huijsmans

So you have moved house!

To CAMILLE LEMONNIER

[March 1887]

I must at least acknowledge receipt, my dear friend, of the new edition of *Le Mort*, to which you have added some curious and substantial stories.

Le Mort, on rereading, retains the fullness I remembered, and the odour of criminal effluent that had seduced me!

I did not write to you sooner, my dear Lemonnier, because I was horribly caught up with work. Under pressure to finish my novel *En Rade* in haste, driven into a corner by *La Revue indépendante*, I could not keep them waiting.

I have just written those felicitous words: the end!
You know what that means!!

It is the only really good literary moment in one's life, I believe, given that, the very next day, disgust with what one has written sets in. But still, there has been at least one minute of happiness.

Are we then destined never to see each other? When you come to Paris, would it not be possible to arrange things in advance and meet?

We must look into it. Do come, my dear friend, it would give pleasure to your devoted

G. Huysmans

To ARIJ PRINS

[28 March 1887]

Thank you, my dear friend, for the translation you sent me. My affairs over there are in a mess. My family is turning into a classic family of the Atreus type.[38] But at the moment I do not wish to act, on account of an aunt there, who is the only good woman in all this racket.

Moreover she is angry with my damned cousins the lawyers, who are trying to swindle her.

I am waiting for detailed letters from her before deciding to act in one way or the other. So we shall see. What fine blackguards these Catholics are!

Here the Indépendants' exhibition has opened. Not brilliant: Seurat, Signac, Dubois Pillet, young Pissarro, some curious things, but spoilt by this pointillist mania.[39] Everything served up in the same sauce. Coloured fleas. I shall make no bones about it in *La Revue indépendante*.

This will be my break with all of them, but in all fairness, I cannot let myself pass for a muggins and conceal the lack of enthusiasm that this method of painting inspires in me. Some fine Redons on the other hand, but without innovation.

As for the Dutch pottery, I am somewhat embarrassed, as I will not be able to do any articles about it for two months, for the official Salon is opening and will take all of my allotted column space; for me to be able to do something about it, there would need to be no topical subjects about.

What is more, they have announced an exhibition of real Impressionists soon, Monet and Renoir in Georges Petit's galleries.

But in any case let the Bernard Palissy of Flanders know, so that he won't get impatient.

En Rade is being printed by Stock. I think we shall make it for 1 May. What is more, *A Vau l'Eau* is probably going to be reprinted in a luxury edition, a very short run, by the publisher Piaget, who claims to have subscriptions for this volume, which will not be put on open sale.

It will be printed only on Japanese paper; an edition of three hundred, for bibliophiles.

To tell you the truth, the rush I am in with all these proofs coming at me from all sides, errands, articles, is unheard of. Especially as on top of all that, Zola is in Paris and devours evenings I could well use.

Like you, I sleep quite badly, but I am dosing myself up thoroughly with bromide, as I am still stricken with facial neuralgia that has sprung up again, with all these worries.

I see that you also are working hard. I congratulate you, for I still believe that it is the best thing we have, despite the pressure and those exhausting battles with blank paper.

Don't read my last two chapters in *La Revue*. They have been castrated, *La Revue* not daring to reproduce intact a bullish erection. It was the same as with my calving scene. Decidedly I will not have novels appear in magazines any more. It is too troublesome. Pieces that have been pillaged on account of prudery are no longer valid.

Nothing new apart from all that. Bloy is getting ready to start a book. Villiers is bringing out his *Tribulat Bonhomet* with Stock at the same time as me.[40] We are still busy hacking away. The factory is in full swing.

And as for me, hereupon I am going to bed, but not without sending you, dear Prins, a very genuine shake of the hand.

G. Huijsmans

To ÉMILE ZOLA

2 June 1887

My Dear Friend,

Thank you for your kind letter about *En Rade*. I am very pleased to see that the book did not displease you. As for your opinion on the ill-matched legs of this pair of trousers, one real, one up in the clouds, it is, alas, mine also! Your comments are absolutely justified. My approach was by way of a preconceived idea, a division fixed in advance: day, reality; night, dream. And note that given this idea, I would have done infinitely better to apply it quite systematically, and write alternating chapters, one of reality, one of dream. It would not have been any better, and it would not have avoided the bumpiness, but still it would have been preferable to these three great devils of chapters that seem rather haphazard.

The truth is that I saw clearly into this state of affairs only once the book was printed, and that proves to me that if I could manage to put into practice an old idea, that of keeping a book that is written in a drawer for a year, it would gain by it. It is certain that if *A Rebours* had not come out, I would have arranged it differently, and it would have been an improvement. *En Rade* also, for I would have left the subject in the midst of the countryside.

But it is quite stupid, I am always amazed when I have finished a book and at the same time am in foolish haste to think no more about it by getting it printed. It is one burden less.

I see, my dear Zola, that you have had some problems with *La Terre*,[41] and that you are going to be obliged to give them double helpings.

I have read the first instalments in *Le Gil Blas*, contrary to my custom, it exasperates me so much to read pages that are so hacked about; I find your Beauce superb,[42] with a sad grandeur, really beautiful, and as yet you have only skimmed the surface. Your sower has a wide sweep, and your bull is of a healthy and really daring realism. I am not anxious about the rest, subjects of this scale are your domain and you have the robust fists necessary to handle them.

Here in Paris, nothing; two Sundays ago I went to Goncourt's. It was dull and without colour, full of drips from the tap of that awful Rosny. Nothing very significant was said there. For the moment I am neuralging[43] and am bored. The warm, heavy dampness these days does not suit me.

And Mme Zola? I hope she is at last free of her migraines. Give her my greetings and receive, my dear friend, a good shake of the hand.

Huysmans

Good God! How stupid can Brunetière get![44] Have you read his article on Baudelaire! I received *Renée* this morning,[45] as I was leaving for my office. I shall see what it is like when I read it. I saw your preface in *Le Figaro*, which is one in the eye for the fools who turned the play down.

To PAUL VERLAINE

20 July 1887

My Dear Verlaine,

Thank you for sending me the new edition of *Romances sans Paroles*. I have again reread this admirable book, which enchants me, and is your greatest poetic work, after *Sagesse*.[46]

I know, my dear friend, that you have taken a singular beating from life, your health is affected, and perhaps you suffer too from the literary injustice of which you are a victim, in these days when the Jews' alley and Chicago reign supreme! And so I should have liked to come and shake you by the hand one day, but I am myself riveted to the spot by ignoble bonds – my nauseating office which slaughters time, and on the other hand I am scarcely any better than you, worn down by nervous pain, devoured by neuralgia, and still so ill at ease.

In place of an effective handshake, let me at least assure you, my dear Verlaine, on this bit of paper, of my sympathetic feelings for the greatness of your talent and of my real friendship.

J. K. Huysmans

To ÉMILE ZOLA

[November 1887]

My Dear Zola,

I have just finished *La Terre*, which I read a little at a time, savouring each bit. The overall impression I have gained from this first reading is one of undeniable greatness. The framework of landscape is superb; through your eyes we see the melancholy Beauce, flat, stretching into infinity, from one end of the book to the other. We are there, and in no other province, it is really very good; I find the sea of corn where the little church tower finally disappears one of the most solid pages you have written. As for your peasants, they are quite simply wonderful. The slow extermination of old Fouan by his children is sustained step by step, and achieves at the end a good effect of horror with the Buteaus.

And despite all the calculated cruelty in the book, I find for my part that enormous gaiety emanates from it. The two births are surprisingly joyful, the child's head pumping away and the vet are real fun. And what about M. Charles? Isn't it wonderful when Elodie declares that she knows all about her father's profession and proposes to restore the family fortunes? Moreover, I feel joy when M. Charles appears. Your fellow is valiantly well portrayed!

I find, what is more, irresistible gaiety in the fart scene. This sudden prudery on the part of the press and fashionable people is ludicrous! For Holland and Belgium are full of pictures by Breughel the Elder with people farting and shitting themselves. Everybody laughs at them. And so what?

But I would add that no picture has the fine appearance of your Jesus Christ calling out 'Come in' and the father answering 'Here I am'! Page 316 of *La Terre* shows the anger of the good old drunkard enraged at his daughter's lack of respect; this scene is surprising and of an audacity such as I have seen nowhere else or in any other period. And those good journalists who, in their usual foolishness or rather hypocrisy, would have hastened to reproach you with not being true to life if you had not included these absolutely genuine details of country life.

All in all, I find that the mechanism of the book gives an impression of substance and enormous scale, things that nobody bothers about at the present time.

Are you settled in Paris again, or in transit between Paris and Médan? I'll still send this letter to you in the rue de Boulogne, and I enclose all my good wishes to Mme Zola and a good shake of the hand to you, my dear friend.

Yours

Huysmans

To JULES DESTRÉE

30 November 1887

My Dear Friend,

I received your kind epistle with *La Wallonie*.[47] And first of all, I thank your brother for the dedication he made of his piece about rain and for sending his little poems, and I also read your notes on Cologne, which are very good; the last page on the anonymous Florentine is most striking. If you continue these notes, please be good enough to send me copies, as they interest me greatly.

You ask me where one can get hold of the poems of Mallarmé. They are not to be had, but I am sending them with this letter. They came out in 1876 in *La République des lettres*, and were reprinted, the best ones at least, in *Le Chat noir* in 1886. I had bought two copies of it, which means I can send you one; as you will see, they are superb, their strange language is clear and incisive.

Ah – I pity you in your gastralgia![48] I know what it is like – I have permanent neuralgia, but at the moment I have finally found salvation in the drug antipyrine. I am immersed in an enormous job in preparation for my novel about the fringes of the clerical world and the cause of King Charles XI (Naundorff).[49] You cannot imagine the reading I have had to do, hagiography, alchemy, Matteï's medicine;[50] the history of the later Roman Empire, stacks of brochures and newspapers on the survival of Louis XVII. I am exhausted by it. Now I have to put it all together, and get down to work.

I sweat at the thought of it – but if I could bring it off, it would be a curious book, set in an uncharted world, a book with some very strange flights of the imagination and some atrocious realities – the whole lot to be acclaimed as a flop, a huge flop, as far as the reading public is concerned.

Have you read Bourget's *Mensonges*?[51] He reels off analytical commonplaces, served up in a style that resembles beef broth. I have also read that great contraption *La Terre*. As always, the framework is gigantic, and the characters are peasants or bourgeois, according to circumstance.

All in all, that is not for the likes of us, these days. Sometimes I get frightened at seeing how far removed I am from everybody else's opinion, even in the literary world, where they vaunt Daudet as if he really existed in artistic terms!

The five of them are quite stupid,[52] they attack Zola wrongly and reproach him with being commercially minded, and what about Daudet with his *Tarascon sur les Alpes* [sic]![53] A shameful thing! But these fine young people who talk about justice are all vassals of that man from the south, whom they can hardly admire, but whom they support.[54]

All the same, how superior an artist Villiers is to all of these, and Verlaine! Even Goncourt pretends to be ignorant of these writers' work!

It is true to say that all this matters not, for the country is moving more and more towards the antipodes of art. It will soon care as little for Daudet as for Villiers – and what a fine vaudeville act we have at the moment, with those left-wing cretins wanting Grévy to stay in power!⁵⁵

Have you ever seen anything like it? The middle classes are decidedly ripe for a great bleeding. Is it possible to combine greater ineptitude and greater cowardice, to have such low instincts, and such a love of lucre! Perhaps Bloy is right in vociferating cataclysmic prophecies.

And what about the glory of Boulanger?⁵⁶ A strange mystery! I am afraid that a second and terrible routing by Prussia is drawing close. This time it will be decisive.

My dear friend, I wish a bit of peace for you and yours, and amidst all these turds that are flying around, the possibility of getting on with your books without too much distraction.

Many thanks to your brother, yours

Huysmans

To MAURICE DE FLEURY

Paris (alas!) 27 February 1888

The exams successful, the perspective of a few days of ardent pleasure, that is great, my dear Fleury.⁵⁷ And I envy you most sincerely, for I see no slice of happiness marked up on the slate for me in the near future.

When, in this ignominious tunnel in which we are groping around, one finds a temporary stopping place that is dry and disinfected, it is grounds for crying for joy and intoning hosannahs to the glory of the incommensurate blackguard who reigns in the Heavens, and pours the murkiest of sewage over the sore heads of clean folk!

Tell yourself that, so as to savour all the better the beneficial drops that the celestial Pharmacist is mixing with your potion. Forget Ste Périne,⁵⁸ all the underhand dealings, and drink in slowly the exquisite mixture!

Here, nothing, snow, wind and thaw – and caramel pudding in which weary boots squelch. My Choubersky stove is moribund, kept going only by brotherly care, hours of convalescence, that prevent me from going to bed when I get back late. Such a rosy perspective. Life is all lemon and mauve, imperious injunctions to Bloy to be cheerful – middling success – pricks in the ascendant! Filth!

Concerning (to use office jargon) the honourable young gentleman who worships the arts, I shall send you a *Drageoir* with a dedication plate next Friday. Try to bleed this man to the benefit of the Satyr of hyperbole of the rue Blomet, with whom I dined last Sunday, which was deadly.⁵⁹ Le Toboso was at his place, behaving like the good lass who persists in the belief that Russia has amputated yards(!) off her poor bloke's love tap. Outside in the street it was freezing hard enough to crack the paving stones.

It was good to be with friends, facing a red-hot grill, and on it a bullock that had surely revolted, but was, I think, well done.

Villiers is still in Brussels, where I fear he is lapping up too much beer. No news except for an incoherent, drunken letter in reply to Bloy.

Have seen Guiches also, the rampart of the Lot, the curse of the Ghetto, the incisor of May, the Vassiliev of that Jew's purse.[60] He is bored, but, like us, working. Seen Zola also – I'll rake over the ashes of our conversation: 'I'm writing a rather silly book on mysticism and the embroidery trade! *La Revue illustrée* is paying me 20,000 francs cash in advance.'

Also learnt of the sentimental reconciliation, the fooling around of those two whores Daudet and Mirbeau, through the good offices of Adolphe Poe and Edgar Thiers,[61] that channel of fantasy of the centre left, the grocer who keeps his imagination just in check, Sir Hervieu;[62] these two tarts felt each other and licked each other. The printer's plates they have where their hearts should be quivered, I assure you!

All the same, to be able to drop dead in one's own corner, to spew up what remains of one's soul in one's own lavatory! Far from this wretchedness, this shame – ah, yes, indeed.

And a good, true and generous shake of the hand for you, my dear friend

Huysmans

To PAUL VERLAINE

[12 March 1888]

I thank you truly, my dear friend, for your affectionate letter, and also for the promise that we shall see each other towards the end of the month, when you are out of Broussais.[63]

That is a must! If only to give vent to our bile, at the expense of the indecent bourgeois of our acquaintance, for you and I are more or less in the same boat, as far as family deviousness and close affection are concerned.

And then it seems to me that in this colossal Empire of Crassness in which we live, there are a few of us lost souls who believe in art, and we should stick together, for otherwise there is no one we can get on with.

What a singular epoch all the same!

I swear I await *Amours* with devilish impatience,[64] and I am genuinely proud that you were good enough to dedicate a piece to me. Drop me a line as soon as you are free, and we will dine together, commiserating over our wounds.

Your devoted

Huysmans

To ÉMILE ZOLA

26 July 1888

My Dear Zola,

I do not know at all, either by sight or even by name, this Poujet you tell me about.[65] As for Verlaine, that is another matter. I saw him in atrocious poverty a few months ago, when he was discharged from the Broussais hospital. I intervened at that time, together with Savine,[66] who had a manuscript of his and is a good man, and I got him an advance. he lived on that and on the little money that was owing to him that was paid. Then he has recently placed some poems with *Le Figaro* and I know he has received another payment; then yesterday, Wednesday, I gave him a little money. So I don't really understand this subscription, which would have been more justified two months ago. Verlaine is very unhappy, that is undeniable; without a penny, that is certain; but he is a little in credit at his lodgings, even in credit for food, he told me so himself.

That is the truth of the situation, such as I know it at least. I would not wish to dissuade you from helping a genuine artist in distress, a little or a lot through his own fault, for money melts away I know not where as soon as he has any. Do what you judge to be helpful. I would add that he did not say a word to me about this subscription yesterday, and that Poujet did not approach me, so none of it seems very clear-cut to me.

I am going to surprise you my dear friend, for can you imagine this strange transformation: a stay-at-home turned traveller? That is me, I am leaving next Tuesday by the night express for Hamburg, Lübeck and the Baltic! Oh! I am sick in advance at the thought of such an undertaking! The truth is that with my eyes that are still dubious, I need a change of air, and that I have a good friend in Hamburg,[67] and that I shall go and see the paintings of the Primitives in Cologne, Berlin and Dresden during the month's leave I have managed to extract, like a recalcitrant molar, from my damned office. I hope to see you when I get back from these distant regions, if you yourself have not wandered off to some remote beach.

I have finished *L'Immortel*.[68] I despise this book completely. It has no stature, no bravado, no depth of character, just a façade of nougat, and such impoverished language! The style of a factory owner with white gloves on! These pages are written in warm, thermal mud. It is the long-winded story of a pleasant and prudent artisan.

Apart from all that, I have nothing very new to tell you, other than the weather: the sun is playing hide-and-seek and this steady rain pleases me, as a nervous person, exasperated by heat.

I send you, my dear friend, a genuine shake of the hand, together with all my respectful greetings to Mme Zola.

Your

Huysmans

To LÉON BLOY

Hamburg, 16 August 1888

My Dear Friend,

I am back from the Baltic, a sea of grey and lilac under a vast, grey sky. I felt dreamy there, and that restored my intellect a little. Then I visited an adorable town, Lübeck, unsullied by modern filth, its old houses and churches intact. There is one church that contains admirable woodcarvings, Primitives and a dance of death with one or two very curious details.

So I am back in the fold for two days, for the day after tomorrow I leave the haven of Hamburg for a life in hotels. By an ingenious combination of circular itineraries, I shall travel across the whole of Germany, second class, wtih optional stopovers, for sixty francs. With the enormous distances I shall devour, it would cost me at least two hundred francs in France!

I see that things are not working out for you: that was to be foreseen, moreover, and all that in a temperature of thirty degrees! Alas, I pity you and am apprehensive about returning to Paris in such weather. Here the sun is behind the clouds, always sleepy, kind to people like me who hate it. The evenings are glacial; in order to survive, I am obliged to do as the natives of Hamburg do, wear flannel vests and drink gin.

What can I tell you? I am calm, but as if having been through a mill, exhausted by railways, running around in ports and docks. I am making masses of notes, I shall bring back enough to fill a volume. I am living most of all amongst the ordinary people; the middle classes of this town being, like ours, not given to intimacy. In the bookshop windows: *L'Immortel*, Ohnet and Maupassant, they are the three French writers read by the middle classes. I have not even seen anything by Zola.

I have got to know an acrobat, and in the evenings, over a cigar, Prins and I make her take all her clothes off and perform. It is all quite decent, we don't touch her; it is even paternal, and good for the notes. She is rather thin and brings to mind the contortions in the German Primitives.

Seen and sampled the brothels: there are some of a luxury unheard of, and genuine. Others, for sailors, are interesting. I have also studied the interior of the Stock Exchange. There are traders there worth over forty million. A certain kind of person. I keep a good stock of venom in store to spew up on them. All in all, my friend, I drift through the old streets, I drink it in with my eyes, and work three full hours a day at my notes. I have some curious material for sketches of Hamburg. I am not wasting my time, as you see. My only worries are of a financial nature, for in spite of a very low cost of living, money goes; here it is half Paris prices if one eats, obviously not in luxurious places, but excellent ones; but I have expenses for photography that are ruinous, yet indispensable for my book.

I am falling asleep on my feet, my friend, which will explain the interest of this epistle; I am dead, having covered miles in this enormous town.

Prins and I combine resources to send you a pittance, a drop in the ocean to nourish a luckless creature born under a funereal star. Have you seen Baron Ernouf?[69] Do you think you will find some sort of job? You won't get one in literature, the worthless Kahn is once again proof of that, alas![70] That hardly surprises me. He and Dujardin are incapable of paying;[71] what is more, if they had said yes and taken your manuscript, you would have had so much trouble and so many wasted journeys for a few coppers! Hervieu is paid, but he is the only one there who is.

Greetings to Guiches. I will drop him a line when I have a bit of time and am less weary; I am going to bed, but not before sending you, from Prins and myself, a cordial shake of the hand.

Yours

Huysmans

Don't write to me, because I don't know where I shall be, in which hotel, from Saturday onwards. Prins does not know the towns we are going to any more than I do; we are taking pot luck, and it will not be possible to have letters forwarded from Hamburg.

To ARIJ PRINS

8 September 1888

My Dear Friend,

Anna is setting off with a little box containing a mantilla, latest Paris fashion, for Mme Schmidt;[72] she is going to send it parcel rate, by post. You will find in the said parcel the volume by Alexis that the wretched binder finally made up his mind to finish, as well as my books. As for the mantilla, beg Mme Schmidt to accept this little gift with good grace and simplicity, as a humble reminder of her kind and gracious care. Here everyone envies you her; the Professor groans at not being so gently looked after,[73] so do I!

As for what's new, I have discovered a new source of bother I could have done without since I've been back. In Hamburg I told you about the strange Catholic woman,[74] who, after *A Rebours*, wanted at all costs to be screwed by me.

Having consumed in foolish exploits what remained of her fortune, and having become more eccentric than ever, she sent me her maid one morning, bearing a letter and a picture by Hawkins,[75] an English painter, rather like Bastien Le Page, who is liked here. She claimed to be in the most dire poverty and begged me to buy her picture for a hundred francs.

There was only one thing to do, to leave her her picture, and, as I had in fact slept with her in the period of her opulence, without there ever being a question of money between us, to give her fifty francs in order to have a bit of peace.

Which I did, and so my friend, I got a demented letter telling me that men of letters such as Maupassant had robbed her, that in her poverty they had bought her Renaissance armchairs for a hundred francs etc., that I was the only decent one, and that she was praying to God for me, and that she begged me to accept a little cross containing earth from the Holy Sepulchre etc., etc.

I gave no sign of life; the maid comes once again telling me that her mistress wishes to see me one last time, that she asks for a last rendez-vous. There's the rub. Fearing that she might come here, I decided to write that I would go to her house on Monday, adding decisive phrases concerning the absolute end of our relationship. But I foresee difficulties with a fanatic of that kind. On Monday evening I shall find myself obliged to park my poor tail, and be subjected to the great game of tears and anguish. Ah, decidedly it is a mistake not to go to bed exclusively with tarts whom one pays by the night. Otherwise there is nothing but trouble.

I will keep you informed as to how things end with this mad woman, whose flesh – what is more – no longer interests me.

Bloy is in the money. He has just got a booklet[76] accepted by Savine the publisher, his trio of excommunicates: d'Aurevilly, Hello,[77] Verlaine. It is bringing in a few coppers. No news of Villiers, nor of Verlaine. I saw Fleury,[78] who in his capacity as doctor is caring for the poor angel. He has diarrhoea, but is recovering, unfortunately for everyone I think.

As for M. d'Aurevilly, he is going sadly downhill, no longer speaks, is off his head; it is evidently the end. That show-off Daudet has gone to care for his aches and pains at Le Malou, which means Goncourt has come back to Auteuil.

But I am not supposed to know, and I shall dispense with going there for a while, being weary in advance of all the fuss they are preparing.

There now, no offence to your woman, but I miss the roundness of Ulrike and the perfect ambrosia of her thighs. I am not having any trouble on that front at the moment. Decidedly only brothels are genuine: at least one is done with it afterwards.

Greetings to your brother when you see him; and to you, my dear friend, a good old shake of the hand.

    Your

G. Huijsmans

To STÉPHANE MALLARMÉ

15 March 1889

Dear Friend,

It is agreed, I can manage ten francs a month,[79] which will by no means bleed me to death.

Arrange things for the best, my good Mallarmé, so that our poor friend is not pained.

I am starting to get better, but what dross is this rooming house of flesh, in which we are immured by I know not whom!

Yours

J. K. Huysmans

To EDMOND DE GONCOURT

17 March 1889

My Dear Master,

I thank you most sincerely for your fine and kind letter. Ah yes indeed! The hostelry of flesh in which we lodge our wretched selves is badly run. The architect/doctors who repair it are quite ignorant fools!

I am still dragging myself about, despite the torrents of milk I am consuming; things are not too bad in the morning, but once eight o'clock in the evening comes round, the spring unwinds itself and I hasten to bed. Then I am not free from anxiety if I go out. It is mainly nervous, but ridiculous enough to make one weep.

All this is to say that I dare not go as far as the Faubourg Saint-Martin. So I am returning the ticket to you, for you must be short of them. Needless to add, I trust, that I wish *La Patrie en danger*[80] may, in the full blaze of success, galvanize the apathetic slumbers of people stultified by Sardou and the like.[81] Despite the assiduousness of blackguard journalists in attacking you, I believe nevertheless that like *Germinie*,[82] it will be a fine success.

The first Sunday that I am not taken up with purges, baths or errands to the practitioner, I shall go to Auteuil, for I should be very happy to shake you by the hand other than on paper. I send you, my dear master, together with all my good wishes for success, the assurance of my respect and devotion.

Huysmans

To CHARLES MORICE

[May 1889]

My Dear Colleague,

I find *La Littérature de tout à l'heure*[83] infinitely curious, full of specious insights, very accurate observations and fortunate expressions; for example: 'the exact reproduction of nature would be a useless sin' and that charming word that you like, 'vigil'. And the exquisite page on music.

May I praise you, ah yes, for having finally toppled Loti,[84] and told a few home truths to the solemn clowns adored by the crowd, but on the whole, I find there are too many old pals in this parade, which I think includes useless people, and not enough of Laforgue.

What you say about Trachsel and Jean Court makes me dream;[85] this latter's novel could be very curious. I shall look out for the publication of the album and the book.

Now above all, in two places there is a theory whose meaning escapes me, once on the subject of Poe, I think, and the second occasion *à propos* of Banville,[86] where you say that joy is the true characteristic of art. I am sure that in commentaries in some future book you will explain what you mean by joy, but, all the same, I am not convinced that it is not suffering that is the only decent thing that exists on this earth and in art.

Moreover I find the last part a little disconcerting. It seems to me shrouded in mist and, what is more, sprinkled with aphorisms, like dangerous rocks: 'a work should never be laboured over'. That is a question of temperament. Hugo did not labour, but what about Baudelaire, what about Flaubert! What does it matter? Only the result counts.

But I am quibbling over nothing, and I would certainly do better to say, which is true, that the whole constitutes the most lively and most valuable portrait that we have of the literature of this century. It was a considerable undertaking, and you have brought it off well, with some personal insights and artistic phrases.

Let me thank you, my dear Morice, for those pages you wrote about me, and which might make me proud, and let me add to it a good shake of the hand.

Yours

Huysmans

To STÉPHANE MALLARMÉ

5 July 1889

Dear Friend,

I enclose the wretched prebend for our poor Villiers.

Guiches has seen Robin,[87] and alas we have learnt what incurable and diabolical ill he is suffering from.

Decidedly the Almighty dispenses horrors and a salary of special suffering to artists.

For which, it seems, we must praise Him.

Yours truly, my dear Mallarmé.

J. K. Huysmans

To STÉPHANE MALLARMÉ

[5 August 1889]

My Dear Mallarmé,

Villiers is not dead, thanks be to God – let this note reassure you immediately – but it is undeniable that he is weakening and that it is time we exerted ourselves for the sake of the child.[87]

I put pressure on Marie[88] in such a way that except for two certificates she has to get copies of in Paris, she is in possession of all the documents necessary for a marriage – but... but... Villiers will talk about this marriage only when time will have run out, all the more as, even if we get exemption from banns, a lapse of at least ten days is always needed for a single publication.

We will never do it. So I think we must make all haste, that is to get Totor legitimized, for this has not been done. Without that, we are lost and can count on neither the artists' orphanage, nor an allowance from the Ministry of Education.

The extreme difficulty lies in telling that to Villiers, who will worry. I have already hedged about the question four or five times and have been brought to a halt by the anxious look I see setting in.

Marie tells me that you have informed her about the orphanage question, etc. So couldn't you tell her that Roujon[89] has spoken to you about it again, but that it is essential for legitimization to take place?

What do you think of all this? Would there be any means of seeing you when you come to Paris?

Yours

Huysmans

To REMY DE GOURMONT

27 August 1889

What can I tell you, my dear colleague, in response to your request for information, other than that poor Villiers was carried, in our care, to the Batignolles cemetery. We made the ceremony modest, but quite heraldic. It was tainted by a certain Marras, a friend of Mendès, who felt the need to create publicity for himself by pronouncing vain words at the graveside.

Still! For the moment, in my capacity as executor of his will, which I share with Mallarmé, who is away, I am under siege from publishers who want to bring out Villiers' books without delay; a real flock of cormorants swooping down on a corpse!

At Villiers' place, papers are in an unbelievable mess. I wonder how I shall manage to bring out *Axël*, which he has left with many things in the course of being changed, on a mountain of proofs . . .

Huysmans

[full text not available]

To ROBERT DU PONTAVICE DE HEUSSEY

21 April 1892[90]

Dear Sir and Colleague,

You are not unknown to me. I have read your pages on Villiers in *L'Hermine*; our friend spoke to me of you several times, if my memory does not deceive me. So when Landry told me of your proposed book, I knew I was dealing with a friend, only his appearance was unknown to me.

I loved Villiers dearly, and like you, I find myself, especially on evenings when I have been exposed to sterile gossip, haunted by the memory of the writer who was, for certain, along with Barbey d'Aurevilly, the most amazing conversationalist of our time.

I met him years ago, in 1876, at *La République des lettres*, for which we were both writing, and at the house of Catulle Mendès, director of that review. Then different friendships and differing tastes in lifestyle separated us. After *A Rebours* I met up with him again; from that time on, far removed from the boulevards, we struck up relations. He would come and dine with me on Sundays with his child, little Totor. For all who saw him, such occasions were unforgettable festivities! Villiers, who was wary, legitimately on his guard as soon as he noted men of letters about, no longer stammering as he used to as soon as he felt he had gone too far, and feeling himself to be amongst tried and tested friends and admirers, protected from intellectual larceny and treachery, would let go and talk with enthusiasm about his life, giving way at one and the same time to lyricism, realism, irony and madness.

On this subject, I remember a 14 July when he came to dine at Montrouge at the house of Lucien Descaves's father. After the meal, he went to the piano, and, lost to the world, sang in his chill, broken voice pieces from Wagner into which he inserted barrack-room choruses, linking them all together with strident laughter, crazy jokes, strange verses.

What is more, no one had more than him the gift for raising the level of farce, of making it leap into the beyond with surprised fear. His brain was always fired with a heady brew. How many times have I seen him, just out of bed, barely awake, in full swing as on those evenings when, after coffee, he would tell us specious stories, inimitable tales.

Then our meetings became fewer, illness kept him prostrate, shivering in bed. Weary of Paris, he moved to Nogent and the state of his health became worse. Dr Robin recognized cancer, kept the truth from him by admitting to a dilation of the stomach, and fortunately Villiers believed him. One day when he was worse he complained to me about the house he was living in, which was in effect as icy as a water tank, bereft of sunlight and almost decayed with damp; he wanted to leave and said he needed nurses to prop him up in bed and turn him over. I spoke to him of the Brothers of St John of God in the rue Oudinot in Paris; two days later I received a letter from him informing me that he had installed himself in their house, thanks to Coppée, who had acted as go-between with the director to obtain really generous financial terms. I found him happy with the move there, convinced that he would soon recover, making thousands of plans, proposing to give up the alehouses of the boulevards and work in a quiet corner in peace, far from journalists.

He who all his life had been so unhappy, so poor, now found himself relatively comfortable. He was no longer obsessed by the worry about money. Mallarmé, who was a most sincere and attentive friend to him, had discreetly opened a subscription, and for my part, I had available quite a considerable sum that the devoted Francis Poictevin had made over to me.

Villiers started to talk again about *Axël*, which had remained on the stocks; he wanted to rework the play, cutting out those theories that seemed too unorthodox from a Catholic point of view, then suddenly he fell silent. Perhaps for the first time, the gift of dreams, which allowed him to forget in a fairyland of his brain the violent tribulations of life, failed him. He saw life as it is, understood that ignoble reality was finally going to take its revenge; and then his long martyrdom began.

His stomach ceased to function, he lost strength. His thinness was staggering, a golden straw colour crept over his features; in his fleshless face the eyes lived on, frightening, sounding to the depths of one's soul as soon as one entered the room. Despite the efforts of Mme Méry Laurent,[91] a friend who made a fuss of him, looking after him and bringing him good wine and substantial meat, Villiers could not eat; death was close at hand.

It was then that took place the episode that brings tears of sadness to one's eyes: his marriage. For many reasons that he did not reveal, Villiers was hesitant, secretive, unresponsive when timidly, after a good many preparatory remarks, we spoke to him of his little boy, inviting him, in order to legitimize him, to marry the mother with whom he had been living for some time. Pressurized by the argument that after his death the Ministry of Education could grant a pension to a child bearing his name, Villiers ended by agreeing, but when it came to fixing the day, getting the papers together, he strung us along, asking a few moments' respite, raising objections, in the end building around himself such a wall of silence that we had to keep quiet. The friends who were visiting him then, Mme Méry Laurent, Stéphane Mallarmé, Léon Dierx,[92] Gustave Guiches and I no longer knew what wiles to use to persuade him. He was weakening by the hour; we came to fear that he would die even before we could assemble the documents necessary for his marriage. One morning, sick with worry, I had the idea of speaking to the chaplain of the brothers of St John of God, a Franciscan from the Holy Land, Reverend Father Sylvestre. He was a gentle and compassionate monk, who had already eased Barbey d'Aurevilly's passage out of this life. I reminded him of the wretched story, which he knew, because he had heard Villiers' confession and given him communion.

He answered simply: 'Come, wait for me here; I'll go up and have a little word with him.' Five minutes later he came out of the room, Villiers consented to marry straight away.

It was becoming urgent; it was difficult to get hold of the documents spread around various distant town halls. Of the few who remained faithful to him, for all his café and journalist friends had naturally abandoned him, there remained in Paris only Léon Dierx, who was confined to an office all day long, Gustave Guiches and I. It was summer; Mallarmé, who was ill, had gone off to the country. Mme Méry Laurent was taking the waters. It was a chaotic hunt for documents. Guiches, M. de Malherbe, a messenger at Quantin's bookshop who was to be a witness for the woman, showed willing, and the three of us succeeded in supplying the documents on the very day the union was to be celebrated. We were much helped in all this by a clerk at the town hall of the seventh arrondissement, M. Raoul Deniau, an admirer of Villiers, who ironed out a number of difficulties we had come up against.

The marriage took place in his bedroom. Here I hesitate to reveal the whole truth; but you will make what use you will of this letter and will judge whether, amongst the absolutely exact information I am supplying you with, to fill out the material for your book, this ought to be made public; and on the whole I think it should, for when it is a quesiton of the suffering of a man such as Villiers, it is worth telling!

When it came to the signing of the registers, the woman declared that she was unable to write. There was a dreadful silence. Villiers was going through the agonies of death, his eyes closed. Ah, he was spared nothing; he had his fill of humiliation, was soaked in bitterness. And as we looked at each other, devastated, the woman added: 'I can put a cross, like I did for my first husband.' We held her hand to help her trace out the mark. After the ceremony, the four witnesses, Mallarmé, Dierx, M. de Malherbe and I partook of a little champagne that Villiers wanted at all costs to have served to us; and, in his turn, Fr Sylvestre came for the religious ceremony.

It was then that we got a chance really to appreciate the soul of this priest. Villiers' wife used to visit the patient during the day. Although her situation was an irregular one, the brothers of St John of God closed their eyes to this divergence from their rule, but naturally her visits came to an end with the daylight. She had to leave as soon as night fell. It was heartbreaking for the poor creature, who feared he would die in the night, alone.

After blessing their marriage, Fr Sylvestre said rather hurriedly: 'Although women are not allowed to spend the night here, I have arranged things so that, now you are married, you won't be separated any more.' This monk had thought to give that final joy to the dying man. Villiers' eyes filled with tears; he made a gesture, then fell back, exhausted, almost fainting with fatigue. We left.

I went to see him the next day, and every day that followed. He could no longer speak; he would gently shake your hand, and would look at you with eyes so full of resignation, yet so sad! The day before his death, he had received the last sacraments and remained absorbed, his emaciated face was now hollow, and there was a whistling in this throat. I saw that the end was near. Shattered, I had to hurry away, for it was late and they were shutting up the house.

The next morning, a ring at the door got me out of bed. I said to myself: Villiers is dead; that was it, his wife collapsed in tears on a chair in my house.

What is there to add now? It is better to be silent and not to speak of the literary vultures who descended on his corpse, of the reporters who had come each morning, awaiting his death in order to get an article; they could now make their money and save themselves the journey. And what use either to speak of the funeral where, in the beating rain, Mallarmé, Dierx and I, who were the chief mourners, sheltered as best we could under our umbrellas the poor boy who did not seem to realize that he had just lost his father. One word further, though, on the subject of this funeral at which Fr Sylvestre was good enough to preside, in the church of St Francis Xavier: as our resources had come to an end, Gustave Guiches and I went to *Le Figaro* and Magnard offered us straight away, with unforgettable good grace, the money necessary to bury our friend decently.

Others will give you now, dear sir and colleague, more complete information about his life; they will fill out the details of the phases of this disorientated existence, ruined by his perhaps unique poverty, so extreme was it at times that he had neither food nor shelter, and was penniless. I limit myself to narrating the painful episodes that preceded his death; in your book you have told of his beginnings, I am relating his end.

It remains, dear sir and colleague, to wish good fortune to your book. I do so with all my heart. May it arouse a vague regret for the injustice done to Villiers by the reading public, who remained so resolutely ignorant of his talent before his death.

Yours

J. K. Huysmans

To ODILON REDON

[15 September 1889]

My Dear Friend,

I found your kind letter on my return and I thank you for it.

Yes, I am just back from Brittany, where I savoured the melancholy of those interminable heathlands, a carpet of gorse and heather. It is really beautiful, and the caves of Morgat are marvellous – but again nature is beaten by art, for the cave in Hugo's *Les Travailleurs de la mer* is even more splendid!

I have also been in Vendée, at Tittaiges, where, for the sake of my novel, I went to immerse myself in the atmosphere of the frightful Maréchal de Rais, alias Blue Beard.[93] His crimes have been filling the countryside with terror ever since the Middle Ages.

The ruins of his castle are wonderful, and each dungeon one opens still contains the bones of children whom he raped and murdered whilst invoking the Devil!

It is superb!

Returning to Paris is unfortunately atrocious. My poor old Villiers' affairs are getting into a frightful state. I am threatened and hounded by a publisher on account of *Axël*. There are parts missing, it is the most awful mess!! The firm of Quantin is refusing to wait any longer to bring the book out.

I am surrounded by volumes of proofs – two books of Villiers' to get ready, and mine that is at the printer's – a relief!

I see, my dear friend, that for your part you and Mme Redon have had a worrying time! But it is all over, isn't it?

What about work? Think, oh Redon, about those drawings in colour – think about that – for it was really good, and new.

And savour the fresh air. Here it is pestilential and filthy – the streets are full of provincials, dragging confused-looking wives and weeping children. All this with their noses in the air, looking up to the skyline to read the street names. One feels the need for a massacre.

But what are they all after, these people?

There was a crowd of them at the Louvre yesterday; they smelt of damp dog, polluting the paintings with their breath. One of them, bald and obese, was explaining the subjects of the pictures to his abominable wife, done up Gods knows how, and she, rolling her liquid rubber eyeballs, her hands on her belly, mumbles: 'Them's old, them pictures, old, old.'

Massacres!

And in this sweet hope, I shall go to bed, but not without sending all my best wishes to you and to Mme Redon.

　　Yours

　　　　　　　　　　　　　　　　　　　　　　　　　J. K. Huysmans

To PAUL VERLAINE

　　　　　　　　　　　　　　　　　　　　　　　27 September 1889

My Dear Friend,

With pleasure I see that your leg is gaining strength. The relics of St Ganymede the Ancient are perhaps omnipotent,[94] for it seems to me that it would be only fair to drag this ephebe out of the pagan world and bring him into the bosom of a religion which has survived, despite the ignominy of the faithful.

As for the printer who gives credit whom you ask about, it seems difficult, or at least one would have to be a friend of one of his collaborators. And I know not a one! So, I cannot help you on that front; you know it is always very risky to bring out a book at one's own expense. One usually runs into a load of disappointments and problems. And it is especially difficult to recover one's costs. Still, you will see!

Nothing new since my return. I have gone back to that dreadful office that stifles my life, which will explain why, being free only in the evenings, it is difficult for me to see you in the *h*official establishment where you are lodging.[95]

There is at least one respect in which you are to be envied in being shut up: that of not seeing the city overrun with foreigners displaying their vulgar wealth, and the English. It is enough to make one vomit at the moment; what frightful tides of humanity foreign spermatozoa produce: comic and podgy. It is unbelievable.

The tortures of the Holy Office certainly had their uses!

I shall see you soon my dear Verlaine.

　　Yours

　　　　　　　　　　　　　　　　　　　　　　　　　　　Huysmans

To OSWALD WIRTH

2 February 1890

Dear Sir,
In connection with a book I am writing, I need certain information on the modern practise of Satanism. The Reverend Canon Roca,[96] who is in the Pyrenees at the moment, expressly requests that I do not contact Fr Boullan directly, as he considers him dangerous, and he authorizes me to use his name in asking you for a meeting at which I could talk to you about this Satanist, with whom you had dealings at the same time as himself.

Huysmans

[full text not availabe]

To ARIJ PRINS

19 February 1890

It is a long time since I wrote to you, my dear friend, but I am so rushed off my feet with this novel,[97] that I do not have a minute free. I am in regular correspondence with that sacrilegious priest who invokes succubi in Lyons.[98] He sends me documents on Satanism in our times; it is curious. I shall probably go and see him in the Easter holidays.

I hope to use all this to produce a book that will embarrass our foolish contemporaries, for it emerges from certified documents that black masses have continued to be said since the Middle Ages. In the seventeenth century, a certain Fr Guibourt celebrated it on the stomach of Mme de Montespan, and it is still going on today; there are sympathizers who indulge in sacrilege throughout Europe and even in America, where the poet Longfellow was head of a sect.

All that gets rather involved with sodomy, as you can imagine. In this connection I have made a few more sorties into the world of these 'pearls', but despite everything, I do not find these moustachioed types seductive. Ah, if only your skater....![99] But he is already sufficiently perverted, from what you tell me.

Seen Zola recently; things are a bit cold between us. He can sniff out what my book will be like, and senses that it will not do naturalism much good. The truth is that we no longer have anything to say to each other. He believes in positivism and materialism, in what is modern, and I have had enough of all that.

It is awkward when a relationship gets on the defensive and neither wants to finish it.

Seen also the amazing Poictevin between two trips. He is very anxious about my contacts with Satanism and is going to pray for my soul at Notre-Dame!

Finally some less cheerful news: poor Orsat has lost his sister recently. He is left with a nephew on his hands; that's an end to his quiet life.

Axël by poor Villiers has been a terrible flop here. It is bad, one has to admit, but still, all the same, the general contempt is excessive. I no longer see his wife, who is dragging Totor around the houses of the rich in order to beg. She ended up accusing Mallarmé and me of being thieves, because we would not give her straight away the small sum that remained. She is in the clutches of a defrocked priest, who has invented some hair cream and would evidently have liked some money to launch his product! I have withdrawn from all that. We got for her an allowance of six hundred francs a year from the Ministry of Education. She won't put Totor in a school. I am weary of all these discussions and wasting of time.

What a good thing it is to be in charge of other people's affairs!

Have you received *Les Sataniques*?[100]

I have not seen Bailly lately.[101] What about Ebeling??[102] I am afraid he will have to pay for his beer-swilling nights, and I am afraid you too will have problems on account of it.

Yours

G. Huijsmans

To ARIJ PRINS

15 June 1890

My Dear Friend,

Concerning the information you request about the Countess, I hardly have any.[103] She is not married, lives like a bachelor in a strange dwelling, and is certainly sleeping with that de Gourmont who did all my research for me at the Bibliothèque Nationale on diabolism from the fifteenth century to the present day.

She is an extremely shady character, pleasant, plays the cithern very well!! An instrument that has been done away with, lost! I am wary of her, although I see a lot of her, for she is an abominable intriguer. I wouldn't want to screw her for anything in the world, one really cannot tell what it might lead to. But her jewels are not bad, bearing in mind that she looked me straight in the eyes and said: 'I am good-looking enough to be able to wear them.'

As for my book, I am working hard at it, terribly hard, but I am in despair. The warp is too close, the slotting together of Gilles de Rais and Satanism in our day is very simple, it does it all by itself. But ... but ... the frightening aspect is the grey tone of this book. It all consists of conversation and dialogue. There are times when it takes on the appearance of theatre, and there is no way of doing it differently!! It has not got the gleam of my other books at all; it is dull and cold. I have moments when I am discouraged by it.

I do hope that this book, which is all episodic, will achieve a strange and curious whole, but that will be a question of chance, for nothing is less sure!

Oh documentation! There is so much of it in this book, that there is no way I can turn it into art!

They have got a cheek, those young people over there with their Zola and Barrès![104] What foolishness, and they have just said that the Middle Ages are easier to do than modern times, how stupid can you get! Yes, you are right, Hamburg would have been superb in that period. If you have all the documents in the library, it would be worth doing. A fifteenth-century port. That would not be bad!

I wrote to you that the horrible Bloy is married – *but not to the mother of his little boy*. He *dropped* them! He has married a woman of repulsive ugliness, some sort of school-teacher.[105] He doubtless hopes that she will earn the bread! He has quite a fine soul, as you see!

I will shortly send you *La Bièvre* in an edition with reproductions of all the engravings from the Carnavalet of it.[106] It is ugly but accurate. I found a mad publisher who got quite carried away by this volume. It will come out about the twentieth of this month, I think.

Your littler skater sometimes makes me dream. I should prefer him to the Countess. All the more so as he seems ripe for carnal sin. Come my friend, a little courage, deflower the mouth of Sodom!

The Professor would neigh at it for sure!

Greetings from him, from my woman who is still ill, and for you, dear Prins, a good shake of the hand.

G. Huijsmans

To ARIJ PRINS

24 July 1890

My Dear Friend,

You give me sad news of your love life: your gonorrhoea. *A propos*, do you know how we successfully treat it in Paris, without injections, and without relapse? I have myself followed this treatment, which is excellent.

Drink as much as you can of a herbal tea made from pine buds. You simply pour boiling water on to the buds and let it cool. This increases the flow, and then when you have had a really good flow, buckets of it, you take sandalwood capsules for a few days, and that's an end to it. The essential is to pee for all you are worth beforehand, let it run like a river. That's the secret. Then the pus is no longer green, like gamboge. It's all over very quickly and is a real cure.

I can see the feigned indignation on the part of your woman and Frau Schmidt!! But they know very well that one can catch this ridiculous and painful disease without having gone in for debauchery!

Anything new here? Nothing. The literary scene is enough to make one spew; Maupassant and Bourget are becoming more and more nonentities; but that satisfies our reading public very well, as Kolff, with his rehashing of Zola, will perhaps suffice for the Israëls and other devotees of Millet![107]

I am still hacking away. My infamous priest is exquisite. He is working prodigiously on my behalf, providing me with the most stupefying information about Satanism in our time.

On this point, I have been condemned to death by the Rosicrucians, one of the recent Satanic sects founded in France!!! In magic any secret revealed is lost, and they are trying to stop my book coming out. Needless to say that, despite the sympathetic magic and poisonings aimed at my person, I am quite well! Fr Boullan, it is true, maintains he is defending me against them. It is quite laughable.

All things considered, I am no longer going off to Honfleur in October to Poictevin's, who is just about mad at the moment, but to Lyons to my priest. I shall see unheard-of things there. There is a woman who is a *voyante* in the household,[108] and birds of prey that indicate by their call and their flight the attacks directed against the priest and against me.

You can see, it is well worth my going to these people, who are summoning me with loud cries. It is, my friend, the Middle Ages in full swing, plus the religion of the Holy Spirit, of the Paraclete, the religion of Joachim of Fiore,[109] the Middle Ages in action; that is something to dream about these days!

Ah, all the same, I have some unique and stunning documents for my book.

If you have received *La Bièvre*, tear out that abject watercolour at the beginning. What an arse that publisher is! There was no way I could persuade him not to put that filth in the book.

What taste!

At the moment there are some shady articles coming out in *Le Figaro*, signed by Fleury, who is completely under Zola's tutelage, and in which I am manifestly being got at, albeit in veiled terms.

Zola has no idea of what awaits him in my book. I shall be more frank about things.

My book will also have in its favour that it will be the final dismantling of that crumbling mound known as naturalism!

Greetings from the Professor. An affectionate good day to Frau Schmidt and your woman. I wish a cure for your poor penis, and a good shake of the hand, dear friend.

G. Huijsmans

To GEORGES LANDRY

Lyons, 11 October 1890

Dear Friend,

I shall be back tomorrow, Sunday. I am getting today's express – with the ticket which should, according to a telegram yesterday, reach me this morning.

So try and come to dinner tomorrow. Boullan is not a Satanist – that is for certain – but he is the most extraordinary miracle worker in existence! I have been cosseted by these good people in a way I could not have expected. I have also seen singular things, and to think that there are people who deny the existence of the mysterious!

Yours, on the hop,

Huysmans

To EDMOND DE GONCOURT

[October 1890]

My Dear Master,

It was really a good read.[110] If you knew the despair I have fallen into as far as reading is concerned. All I am doing is rereading things. All the great mechanized industrial products, such as Zola's, and pots of warm glue such as Bourget's, exhaust me. There is not twopennyworth of art in all that.

And so I swear to you that it was a real joy for me to taste such elixirs, where there is not a single sentence that is not profoundly artistic. Gautier's is much too stolid and void of any soul.[111] It is a mirror image and nothing more. Your memoirs are vibrant and formulate in fine sentences the only authentic philosophy of this age. There are unforgettable pages in it – and what a portrait of Louis Blanc,[112] the only revealing one. And Renan,[113] that admirable cad, that one is really good!

What is certain is that I spent yesterday evening by my fireside, and as I finished the book, I saw the whole awful epoch pass before my eyes, I relived it with you. It disturbed me greatly, but how beautiful these evocations are, under your direction!

Thank you both for the contents and for the book itself, which we are going to have covered in cape hide.

I am still wretched with the flu, but I hope to be sufficiently on my feet on Sunday to be able to come and thank you in person.

I send you, my dear master, every assurance of my respectful devotion.

Huysmans

To JULES DESTRÉE

12 December 1890

My Dear Friend,

You ask what I am up to. Alas, nothing for the moment! I have finished my book on Satanism, which is enormous (five hundred tightly packed pages!). I hope to come out in the first few months of next year. I expect nothing from it, I shall be accused of mystification or madness, and no one will believe that the strangest documents in this book were given to me by a priest, the last exorcist to be in possession of the secrets of the Middle Ages.

But basically, it is all the same to me; I am resigned, knowing that the reading public and the press like only badly put together books, whose documentation is worthless, false or falsified, as all Zola's are; he doesn't check them, and doesn't give a damn.

On that subject, have you read, in *Le Gil Blas*, the beginning of his novel on *Money*[114] The vulgarity of the writing and the crassness of it! I, who defended him so stoutly after *L'Assommoir*, heave at the mass-produced art he is churning out now, whether it be for the academy, as in *Le Rêve*, or for the lower classes, as in *La Bête humaine*.

Decidely, it is unfortunate to sell so well; one ends up abandoning all art – he, Daudet, Maupassant, Bourget, what examples!

Apart from that, nothing new here. Literature is mediocre; twenty-five novels come out every day, and, in this mass, nothing worthwhile. This overproduction is frightening, and drowns everything. Ah, how right they are, those who bring out their books for their friends, privately, not polluting themselves with the heady prostitution of paying customers.

I see that you are working hard and that is good. I await with impatience your transpositions of Primitives. That is a good idea you have there. They contained the whole of art, supernaturalism, which is the only true and great art. The only true formula, sought after by Rogier van der Weyden, Metsys. Grünewald,[115] absolute realism combined with flights of the soul, which is what materialistic naturalism has failed to understand – and has expired on account of it, despite all its useful service.

I haven't seen Redon lately, but here is his new address: 40 rue d'Assas. The last time I saw him, and that was some time ago, he and his wife were well, full of adoration for the product of their nocturnal frolics. He is very sweat, moreover.

I must leave you, as my wretched office work is arriving, but I shake you by the hand.

Yours,

Huysmans

To HENRY GIRARD

2 January 1891

Dear Friend,

Let me first of all thank you for your greetings and send you mine, which will perhaps be granted, for you and your brother, together with my good wishes for excellent health for your grandmother.

Now next Sunday, Landry is supposed to be coming with me in the afternoon to vespers at La Glacière convent. After that, we intend to dine in the rue de la Huchette, and thereafter, to go and pay a little visit to the hard-up whores of the place Maub'[116] and those interesting ladies of the Château Rouge, to whom I promised oranges for the New Year.

So, if you happened to be free, perhaps you could join us at half-past five at the café du Soleil d'Or, the one on the corner of the boulevard and the quai St Michel, and we could all dine together early, if you don't mind.

What do you think? Is it possible, given the demands of that dirty Jew, your director?

Yours,

Huysmans

I have just received a note from Niort, from good old Boucher.

To GUSTAVE BOUCHER

15 January 1891

My Dear Friend,

I am profiting from a free moment between two bundles of proofs to send you a bit of an epistle. I know that you are thoroughly bored, cooped up in the provinces. And indeed I can quite imagine that it must be no joke. Here it is hardly any better. The office, proofs, what dregs!

Girard must have related the terrible episode of the Château Rouge; my guide, Debray, was beaten half senseless, the waiter, who had his throat cut, died yesterday at the Hôtel Dieu; Trolliet attacked the murderers with a lead-weighted cane, killing one of them. A real massacre! And it is still going on. Mémèche,[117] who had been let out of Saint-Lazare a few days previously, arrived at the brothel like a fury out of hell. She cried out that the first one to lay a finger on me would have her to deal with, and to start with, she half killed Tache-de-Vin, who was the cause of all this havoc. You can imagine that I am lying low, and despite the invitations conveyed by Mémèche to go and see her again, I am managing without. I was lucky not to have been murdered one night previously when things were hotting up, and that's quite enough.

But what sadness! We had found a charming establishment, different from all the others, and it is collapsing under us! The truth is that Mémèche had declared that I was sleeping with her; I was known by the name of 'Antoinette's lover' and that's why they had put up with us for so long. Her departure for Saint Laz. spoilt everything. But she has a nerve, that one, saying that I sleep with her!!

Apart from these foolish tales, nothing else: the cold, general disgust, the daily infamy of the papers, and at Saint-Séverin they are singing worthless *Salutaris*.[118] So that is collapsing as well.

Yours

Huysmans

To GEORGES LANDRY

[18 January 1891]

My Little Father,

Blessings upon you. Your office book is perfect. It contains the *Salutaris*, *Vexilla Regis*, the *Stabat*, which, in Latin, are valid from an artistic point of view. I won't mention the translation, which is worse than bad, unfaithful, inaccurate, which is more serious.

I checked all that this evening. If only, apart from the question of documentation and linguistics, it could cleanse somewhat my poor wavering soul.

But what sort of phenol, what sort of cupric solution would clean out the great collector where the filth of the flesh gurgles away?

It would take barrelfuls, a disinfecting thunderbolt, and what Milleriot[119] could operate a sufficiently formidable pump to extract the residual waters from the old drains?

There are no more celestial pump men to delight in such labours. So, my old brother, there is no reason for things to change. It is true that when there is so much . . .

Thank you also for this inane chatter, and all the best to you, my dear Landry.

J. K. Huysmans

To ANDRÉ GIDE

[March 1891]

Dear Sir and Colleague,

I have just finished *Le Cahier d'André Walter* that you were kind enough to send me.[120]

Amidst the hurly-burly of modern works, I was singularly taken with certain pages of this pale, quivering book about convalescence and the early stages of sickness of the soul.

There are some touches of perfection in it. The 'if you like, we'll pray together' and Emmanuelle's adorable reply. Then the page on telepathy between friends. And so many more, in such melancholy whispers. I am a bit cross with you over a note pointing something out, but which doesn't explain it, page 217, the last four lines! It would have been superb to dissect that.[121]

But what does it matter! As you wrote: fancy, rather than reality! Oh yes! And you used this formula to advantage in this oh-too-short work.

It is out of the ordinary, and quite unlike the abominable vulgarities that are being hurled at us by all the booksellers!

So you receive my sincere thanks for the pleasure you gave me, and let me assure you, my dear colleague, of my good wishes.

Yours

Huysmans

To AN UNKNOWN CORRESPONDENT

[early 1891]

Dear Sir,

It is in fact true that Dr Johannès[122] is Dr Boullan, who lives in Lyons, with M. Misme, the architect, 7 Rue de la Martinière.[123] He is a mystic of the wisest and most curious kind, preaching on the whole the dogmas of the early church of Lyons, of St Irenaeus and St Pothinus,[124] the coming of the Paraclete.

He had devoted himself to the cure of evil spells, but had to give up, for not being a doctor of medicine but of theology he had trouble with both medics and ecclesiastics.

Many stories have been told about him; he has been accused of black magic, etc. But I know the man sufficiently well to be able to affirm that they are absolutely false.

Moreover, if you have nothing better to do, you will find me at the Ministry of the Interior, 11 rue des Saussaies, every day from midday until five o'clock, and I will give you any information about him that you might find helpful.

Yours

Huysmans

To JEAN LORRAIN

[15 April 1891]

My Dear Friend,
 The truth is that I am not at all well. The showers were a failure and caused me horrible pain. Bromide in high dosage has a sterilizing effect – so? Well, I don't know, it's not very funny all the same. Could the miracle worker be right?
 I looked through all the recent numbers of *Le Courrier français* at the café this evening. Lorrain! Lorrain! You are committing sacrilege in a premeditated way that means that when you are up there, being led by angels in uniform before the Definitive Assizes, you will be condemned to the maximum sentence. Your guardian angel, dressed in black and wearing a magistrate's cap, will plead in vain. The archangels in their crimson and ermine will be merciless. They won't be able to cite the freshness of your soul – beware! Beware!
 One should not play around too much with all that, for who knows? Who knows?
 Personally, I renounce all Satanism. I am going to write a mystical book, and after my *St-Séverin*, which is a relaxation, simply an interlude, I shall take a bath in a sheep dip, I shall purge myself, and with a clean body I shall go to confession – after which I shall, I think, be in a state of candour which will permit me to vent my hysteria in a reversal, an 'A Rebours' of *Là-Bas*!
 But for that, I shall have to get my nerves back in order, otherwise I should be likely to go off the rails for good!
 Perhaps from the point of view of physical and spiritual health Alexis is right. Writing *Mme Mœuriots* must be very cosy![125] You don't get overheated doing that, and Maupassant's play[126] cannot have overstressed his bone marrow either!
 I looked through a slice of Bourget in *Le Gil Blas* today. He is writing like Nicolardot.[127] At least every detail of today's episode bore a resemblance to this late-lamented cad – ah, your ladyship!
 This evening I am reading *The Beauties of the Liturgy* by Fr Michel. It is a sedative, and not without interest. I fear, oh Satanist, that you do not read such pious works. Joking apart, you know, it is less boring than Zola.
 Goodbye for now dear friend; I am getting bored, being confined to quarters like a common criminal, on doctor's orders.
 Have pity on your old wreck.

                                              Huysmans

To ÉMILE EDWARDS

[17 May 1891]

Mr Dear Colleague,

It seems strange, yet good to see your kind and well-written article coming from so far away, and so I thank you for the article in *La Turquie* that you were good enough to send to me via Vallette.[128]

Yes, you were right in thinking that *Là-Bas* is causing an awful stir here, for it raises questions that are taboo and puts terror into people who had become complacent by reminding them of the abominations of Satanism, at a time when materialism seemed to be taking over everything.

You wonder also what I can write next after such a book, which following on from *A Rebours* prolongs the rising pitch. I shall try to produce the opposite of *Là-Bas* – a book full of the whiteness of pure and divine mysticism.

That might need an even sharper note, and I may fall flat on my face, but still I shall try. It will take quite two years to get it off the ground, for there is an immense amount of reading to be done, and it would mean living in a particular milieu.

Still, everything is so worn out, so down at heel in the modern novel, that one really must venture into elevated subjects, even if the result is failure

Thank you again, my dear colleague.

Yours

Huysmans

To ARIJ PRINS

23 May 1891

My Dear Friend,

I see that you are working hard and I congratulate you on it. You are fortunate to be immersed in the Middle Ages, for basically it is the only decent period that ever existed, and I miss the time when I was researching for my Gilles de Rais, which is finished. I have been bored since.

Là-Bas is still going strong and the press also; in this respect, Germany has been like a mother to me. It has produced a number of articles and the book has sold well there. Blessed be that country held in aversion by France!

What has been very funny here, is that the religious press could not keep quiet and spoke out. It is divided into two camps. One followed *L'Univers* and asked for proceedings against me, and covered me in filth in Christ's name; the other, on the contrary, is in step behind the Vatican publication *L'Observateur français*, and said that the book was Catholic and mystic, and that consequently there was no need to attack it. Finally, as the outcome of a polemic engaged between me in *L'Écho de Paris* and the newspaper *L'Éclair* on the subject of my priest from Lyons, the cardinal archbishop of Paris despatched someone to come and ask me for the names of the three priests I had designated as celebrating black masses in Paris itself at the present time. To which I replied that it was not up to me to do the archbishop's detective work, and refused to give the names.

It is all quite funny, as you can see. The truth is that I have brought out into the light again, even into fashion, Satanism, which had been done away with since the Middle Ages. There are no end of people asking me to take them to black masses!! And everyone is talking about it. Charcot [129] and the materialist school have come down on me, treating me as a mystic and madman; the occultists, who are much attacked in *Là-Bas*, are prancing about. And Zola, not at all pleased, is making all his little naturalists protest, and is crying out that the book is splendid but mad! That is the state of affairs. Stock, who has got hold of a good thing businesswise, is jubilant, and in Lyons, my *voyante*, Mother Thibault, is saying novenas to the Virgin for sales of the book not to slow down.

Basically this book does not interest me any more now; I am sick of hearing about it; it is the future that is occupying my attention. For the moment I am savouring the writings of St Teresa and Maria d'Agreida, of the great mystics.[130] It is all very beautiful. There is a magnificent white book to be written, provided one could bring it off. The difficulty is being in the required state of soul, but in all this I have seen such curious things, and into the bargain my soul has such hysterical tendencies, that I might find a retreat at La Chartreuse exasperating from that point of view;[131] and, what is more, to brush aside all this carnal filth, which tempts me not inconsiderably.

Everything is so negative, everything is so stupid that this refuge in faith would be a real haven!

But it is easier to say than to do. The unfortunate thing is that it all has to be done on one's own, for the priests are nearly all abject fools. My people in Lyons, despite being cracked, are much better all the same.

As for the boor,[132] he is still in Denmark, where he is giving – inept – lectures; I can read them in a low Parisian rag to which he sends them. Since he is no longer being directed, he is quite ignorant and quite stupid. All the same, I hope he doesn't descend on you again when he returns to France, coming back to disgust the few decent people there are in Paris.

Ebeling. Yes, I am afraid he will lose more, and a hundredfold of what he makes. Your Austrian woman sounds quite exciting. Won't you use your tongue a bit with her? That would be quite medieval, for after all, in those good days, dirty practices and piety got on well alongside each other.

And so I am going to lunch, but not without sending you, my dear Prins, a good shake of the hand.

G. Huijsmans

To EDMOND DE GONCOURT

[9 July 1891]

My Dear Master,

It is an age since I saw you, but I am busy tracking down documents, and as Sunday is the only day of the week when I am free in the daytime, with no office, I have had, on these supposed days of rest, to run after people and extricate material from them, that I now have to digest.

Polygraphs like the woman Sand were really fortunate; they didn't give a fig for documentation, and didn't waste whole days gathering it!

On Saturday evening, my holidays begin, and I am leaving for Lyons; I shall be back around 15 August, and if you are not away yourself, I shall come and see you as soon as I am back.

This scrap of an epistle has as its sole purpose to tell you that I have not forgotten you and that I remain, my dear master, your respectful and most devoted

Huysmans

To GEORGES LANDRY

Lyons, 26 July 1891

My Dear Friend,

Just a couple of lines, as I have no courage for writing. Shattered by the journey to La Sallette [sic] and La Chartreuse, I have arrived in Lyons reduced to a pulp.

I tried my hand at contemplative life in a cell, and it had the effect on me of a spiritual shower, a good tranquilliser. But I do not care for the mountains. As much as the sea interests me, I find these blocks barring the horizon suffocating. At La Sallette, nature is ferocious and stripped bare, even trees will not grow there, the precipitous drops one is constantly skirting along goat tracks are unfathomable. It is curious and terrifying, but one drinks in the impression in a moment, and then boredom sets in. The cells are the only good thing about a monastery.

As for La Chartreuse, it is very overated.[133] Except for the night office, it is mediocre, modern! Even the landscape, which receives so much acclaim, seems like an enlarged reproduction of the Vaux de Cernay.[134] A real disillusionment! And then one could say a lot about the monks themselves. The Middle Ages no longer exist, not there nor anywhere else. Fr Mugnier was right in telling me that I would be disillusioned.

I hope that Anna is in good health; I am sending her a note this morning. Thank you for looking after her. Here at Boullan's, we have some most curious female diviners and somnambulists, who have told me some strange things about my life. Good old Mother Thibault makes a fuss of me and spoils me. Old man Misme is just a little gaga; but Boullan is more extraordinary than ever. I take leave of you, for I am falling asleep. Greetings to Orsat and to everyone, and a good handshake to you, dear friend.

                                                              Huysmans

To GUSTAVE BOUCHER

                                                   19 August 1891

My Dear Friend,
Back in the foul blockhouse of the rue des Saussaies, and weary to the point of sickness of the stupid inanity of these sedentary afternoons, I send you these few melancholy lines.

I see from your letters to our friend Girard that you are thoroughly bored. Perhaps my disgust will alleviate yours through spiritual homeopathy. I wish it would!

My travels were unusual, overturning preconceived ideas. La Chartreuse is a chophouse of the lowest kind, the brothers are shameful exploiters, even the landscape is overrated. They are only interested in money in that monastery! Before letting you sit down to table, they warn you that it costs 2 francs 50. The procurator, Dom Greysier, is a former quartermaster!! You can tell what mysticism there is in this monastery-cum-tavern!

They have grown rich from sales of their liqueur, and, like all rich orders, they have foundered. Fr Mugnier was right when he told me that I would experience the ultimate in disillusionment there, I did.

But, but, there is La Sallette [sic]. That is awesome, and the thought of it provokes a shudder.

Imagine a plateau rimmed with precipices, surrounded by even higher mountains, above which gleam the eternal snows. At La Sallette, vegetation will not grow: not a single tree, flowers die, birds are silent. It is rock and pumice stone, with a little grass, a dirty billiard table.

The sadness of this plateau, on which looms an ugly church and two monasteries, one for men, the other for women, is enough to make one weep. One walks up and down on the remaining free space, which is about as big as the place St-Sulpice. Vertigo and suffocation are all around. The sky is blocked by peaks, clouds pass through you. Below are frightful abysses, and one's head spins over them.

I don't know how I managed to climb these mountains for four hours, along goat tracks above these chasms; what I do know is that, shut up there for three days, I experienced a frightful malaise in body and soul.

I ended up staying in my cell and that was really good, for it is the one place where one can really take stock of oneself. I spent some very sweet hours there; better even than in the church; but outside of the cell, in this solitude, walking like a prisoner within a confined space, bordered by the void, literally finished me off.

It is a frightful place, perilous, leading straight to madness and despair.

In all, there were, besides about ten religious, seven men of whom four were priests, Boullan, old man Misme and me, plus about ten women who were put up by the nuns. As for the La Sallette Fathers, they are very agreeable, not at all exploiting, and very helpful in any case.

As for Lyons, it is unbelievable. There I visited sanctuaries to the Virgin in the homes of silk-weavers at Croix Rousse. What a town! At Boullan's, the strangest of follies reigns. We received a letter from Paris, some occultists sentenced us to death, and the battles lasted three days. It was like Wagram in the void![135] In his priestly vestments, with hosts in his hand, Boullan brought down his enemies, assisted by a somnambulist in a state of lucidity, and by Mother Thibault. And by me! I was responsible for seeing that the enemy did not cast little Laura (the somnabulist) into a state of catalepsy.

It was quite fine! But there was nothing to see, other than from time to time the famous sparrow hawks flapping at the windows, watched throughout the struggle by old Misme.

I have not yet gone mad, but I might as well be, there were sufficient grounds. Besides that, those people spend their time in prayer, and there is not one in which the Virgin is not invoked for dear Monsieur Huysmanes, as Boullan calls me.

I have also had experiences in that town with somnambulists and horoscope readers. They told me curious things; independently of each other they all predicted an equally strange future. But alas Mother Thibault, who is at the moment on a pilgrimage to Ste Baume, the cave of St Mary Magdalen, writes to me this morning that after a consultation with the saint, none of these predictions will come about.

Damn it all, I was to be rich!

Finally the fireworks have died down. I have returned to the office and am more bored than I can say. I try to console myself with mystic reading, with *The Interior Castle* by St Teresa and *The Inner Life of the Virgin* by good Fr Ollier,[136] but it does not stop me getting bored. After exemplary behaviour on my travels, once back in Paris I was taken with an itch for filth, and I have spent long periods inside Fernande's spicy incense-burner.

All that is very mediocre and not very proper, but it is very good, I must admit.

There, my friend, is an account of my stupid life since my departure. I hope that despite the horrible monotony of the provinces, yours is on a better course and less vain than mine. On Sundays, Girard and I talk about you and miss you greatly.

At Guérins, where we were last Sunday, Jacquemin,[137] seated before his mashed potato and spinach, invoked you for all he was worth.

Is there no chance of some stroke of good fortune bringing you back on business?

One must always hope for such things, since in fact none of us is in complete control of our lives. And sea bathing? That would be a comfort and at least bearable.

I take my leave for the post is going, but not without sending you, my dear friend, a good shake of the hand.

Yours

Huysmans

To ARIJ PRINS

30 September 1891

My Dear Friend,

You had not told me of the death of Frau Schmidt. Poor woman! I had pleasant memories of her.

I see that you are fornicating with an Austrian woman. That is good – provided that being just a stone's throw from you, her presence does not stop you working.

As far as filth is concerned, I have problems! I had discovered a girl whose depravity was first-rate; she had managed to get it into my blood and we had some fine times between us. Her delicious and terrifying anus haunted me. I devoured it without respite, and now some American swine has deprived me of her. He is carrying her off to run a bar in Cincinnati!

Damn! Since then other women seem insipid, even when using one's tongue. That particular flower is decidedly the only remaining pleasure; but, damn it, a little mauve and pink hole is necessary, and that is not to be found every day.

I have just spent an odious month in my office, doing a locum. Impossible to do my own work; I am nevertheless cooking up my next book in my head.[138] I should like to write the battle between piety and the flesh. A book where there will be both prostitution and convents, scenes of taking the veil, and of deflowering, music and the liturgy of La Sallette [sic] and strange corners of Paris.

I am meditating on all this, and it is simmering away. I hope something will emerge from this cookery.

Here the literary scene is in full disarray, a real mess, an army whose attacks never cease. I live more and more apart from all these cads; as for Zola, I no longer see him. He is working on a *patriotic* novel.[139] As you see, he has done it all now. And what is his faithful trusty Santen Kolff up to? Is the last admirer holding out?

Apart from all that, I am very bored; I hope things are not the same with you, and in that hope, I send you, my dear friend, a good shake of the hand.

Yours

G. Huijsmans

To LOUIS DE ROBERT AND EMILE LAPOIX

[November 1891]

Dear Sirs,

Let me first of all thank you for the literary affection which you and your friends have been good enough to show towards me. Such sentiments are so rarely showered on me, that I remain speechless. Now if I understand your letter, you rather miss the Huysmans of *A Vau l'Eau* and *En Ménage*, and you think, to be frank, that I have rather gone off the rails.

It is true. Yes, I believe naturalism to be dead and buried, if it continues in the way in which it is being enforced. The novel of the mediocre man, of the majority, of the average voter, an analysis of the man in the street seems to me to be finished. Flaubert achieved it in such a way in *L'Éducation sentimentale*, which is the one and only truly naturalist work – in the strict sense of the term – for Zola has only deviated, that after this masterpiece, we should keep quiet. Where have we got to? The novel of the centre left, sub-naturalist, worldy, for the ladies, Bourget – thugs, pimps, Méténier,[140] etc., etc. Haven't you had enough of that?

I think you cannot be so insatiable. There remain the exceptions, the rare cases, the extremes, away from the middle range of subjects. I think that is where one might find some newness. I have thought so for a long time, for *A Rebours* was an attempt in that direction.

And then all these points are not the real issue. There is something else. I believe that the question that needs to be answered is above all a question of the soul. Life in a novel is seen through a glass which tints everything, otherwise it is pure photography, if the personal vision of the author does not shape the environment and its inhabitants. Now it is in this respect that an evolution has slowly and imperceptibly taken place in me, but I believe that it can be traced in my books. Formerly I loved Schopenhauer – today I am disillusioned with him. I still appreciate the accuracy of his analysis, but the nihilism of his conclusions makes me uneasy. In the incomprehensible abomination that is our life, there cannot be nothing there at all. I have for the last year been frequenting convents, and in these places there are certainly souls who possess truths, probably certainties, only they are so exceptional, so much apart!

But so, you will tell me, that is Catholicism. Yes, or rather it is the art of Catholicism, the mystical. There one encounters extraordinary things about reality and life, frightening states of the soul, battles that the profane have no idea of, as in Satanism, which is as true to life as the love in *En Ménage* and in all the books, for *Là-Bas* is in fact naturalistic, if by this word you understand only its documentary veracity, the reality of its characters, and for me this is so, but in quite a different way from in *Les Sœurs Vatard*, for example.

In that area, the soul follows a special path that is unknown and immense, more interesting – for me at least – than all the psychology of wordly ladies or of fishwives.

But then, when it comes to basics, are there any theories? No. Alas, we do what we can! And if I don't lose my powers, if in a year or two I manage to produce, more or less badly, a book about the beyond, no less true to life than *A Vau l'Eau* in its own different way, will you be cross with me? The essential would be not to fail to pull off things that get more and more difficult. And that is what is discouraging, for one feels singularly little pride when the page one has dreamt of is written!

Have I made myself clear in all this? I doubt it. In fact I have done no more than elaborate on the first chapter of *Là-Bas*, which is basically a summary of what I think about art. So take that as the real answer to your letter. Accept that I cannot just mark time, or keep going over the same stuff, as so many do! To rewrite *En Ménage*? What would be the point? Moreover, isn't *L'Éducation sentimentale* superior by a hundred cubits to that book, which is consequently of no use?

To sum up, like you, I believe in exact documentation and in life, and I have no intention of straying from this path, but I am moving towards a beyond that is different from that of Zola, or even the Goncourts, towards states of the soul that are less well known, but I think interesting and disturbing. In the meantime, bear with me, and be assured, sir, of my best wishes to you and your friends.

Huysmans

Forgive all this disjointedness, but I am writing to you in haste, having no time to put my ideas in order.

To GUSTAVE BOUCHER

[January 1892]

My Dear Friend,
 On Friday (17th) a medium is supposed to be coming, possibly accompanied by a visionary. But that does not necessarily mean that we shall see anything. But if you are interested, come and see this disconcerting filth at eight o'clock, if they turn up.
    Yours

Huysmans

To ARIJ PRINS

30 March 1892

My Dear Friend,
 I am delighted to see that you are back on your feet. Here, health is mediocre, persistent nervous trouble, what a bore! Stock is just about insolvent. And sums of money mounting up with each new edition printed. My God, how stupid life is!

Here art is in a general state of confusion. Stimulated by *A Rebours*, *Certains*, *Là-Bas*, the younger generation is aspiring to mysticism, but what kind! They paint incompetent oddities, barely naïve, but claiming to be Primitives. In literature we have vaguely idiotic self-styled spiritualists. It is even more stupid than the old naturalism was. It is really sad to be helping a movement that could be decent, and to see it end up like this. But all these people lack ardour and faith, its spiritualism consists in knocking back beers and sucking women. You can imagine the effect that produces!

As far as the Redon albums you mentioned are concerned, they have been out of print for a long time, and if a copy were still to be found it would be very expensive. Redon, to whom I spoke about it, has only his own copy left. Trachsel, whom I told you about, has sold all his stock of strange watercolours and has nothing left at the moment. There are a few enthusiasts in Paris who snap up anything of that kind that is produced. Redon is earning quite a bit of money these days and his prices are rising.

Nothing new apart from that. I am not very well either. I have barely started my novel and am drowned in in-folios on mysticism and strange notes. Added to that, I have to go to a Trappist monastery, and that won't be much fun. No meat, no wine, only vegetables. Night offices as at La Chartreuse. I don't know if I shall be able to stick such a hard way of life for any length of time.

That will be in July or August. I shall try to go with a priest who is a friend of mine,[141] to alleviate the extreme solitude a little.

In any case, this book will take at least two years' work. As you see, it is not what one might call productive literature. But if we did not have such long works to write, what would become of us? We would die of boredom on this earth, for sure.

I have witnessed some curious experiences in spiritism and magic just recently. We are living in strange times, and the more I advance, the more proof I get that the Middle Ages were right in what they said about Satanism. *Là-Bas* is an understatement of the true situation. In Bruges, there is a Canon of the Precious Blood,[142] whom I used, it is true, for my Canon Docre, but he is far worse than mine. Unfortunately I got the best information after my book had come out.

Here, Paris is terrified of dynamite.[143] The bourgeois are shitting themselves; that is the only thing that cheers me up.

Yours, dear friend

G. Huijsmans

To FR ARTHUR MUGNIER

19 June 1892

Dear Father,
Given the lapse of time between now and 12 July, the date when I shall be free, I don't know whether you will have written to the Trappists yet.

In any case, I am sending you this little note to assure you of my desire to go there, and to make a break with the life I am leading.

Two weeks ago on Thursday, you saw me quite dumbfounded. I was trembling in fact at the idea of going and knocking on God's door, going myself to his house. Even now I am not very confident, but still, I am hoping. I have been struggling with myself for two years now. During that time, there has been a series of ups and downs, with my soul in a constant state of flux. I have been able to get the upper hand, at least I think so, but have found these struggles singularly painful. You who have always had Faith, if only you knew what it is like to get it back! In fact I am so weary, so truly disgusted with my life, that it is impossible for Him not to have mercy!

I would have been happy to see you, but I see from consulting *La Semaine religieuse* that you have a very busy week, with Benediction every evening. If you were to have a moment free in the one following, you would be rendering me a very real service in letting me know.

Receive, dear Father, the assurance of my respectful and very affectionate devotion.

Huysmans

To FR ARTHUR MUGNIER

29 June 1892

Thank you, dear Father, for the letter of introduction; I will call to see you on Friday, between a quarter- and half-past five.

I am not bothered about the chocolate,[144] as long as they have some prodigious bleach, exceptional solvents to clean me up once and for all!

Still, if anyone had told me, when I was writing *En Ménage*, that I should go to a Trappist monastery, I should have leapt in the air, and now it seems a little painful, but quite simple.

Which means I have been singularly stupid all these years!

I send you, dear Father, the assurance of my affectionate devotion.

Huysmans

To HENRIETTE MAILLAT

June 1892

My Dear Friend,

I enclose ten francs for you. It is absolutely impossible for me to do any more. Next month I have to pay for the removal, and three months' advance rent for the unfortunate woman who has just been turned out of the house where she lived, on account of her madness.[145]

That is a way of saying that I have been bled dry, on top of all the worry and aggravation.

I am going off to a Trappist monastery next month. In the solitude of the cell and in complete silence, I hope to find a little solace. For I have had as much as I can take of what people here call life!

I hope you may get out of the horrible situation you are in. That is the wish for you of your devoted

Huysmans

To FR ARTHUR MUGNIER

Igny, 15 July 1892

Dear Father,

I am keeping the promise I made to write to you. I have been with the Trappists from the twelfth, as we agreed.

I have come through the hardest moment of my life – confession. It is done, I have been liquidated – I received communion this morning at the abbot Dom Augustin's mass, and I am writing to you in the grips of an infinite sadness, the idea of absolute unworthiness, of a badly repaired soul, that has given all it could, but which needs to be propped up, and is vacillating in an immense melancholy, when it should be joyful to have made the break at last!

As confessor, I had the prior, a real saint, merciful and not narrow-minded!! But all the same, coward as I am, I wonder that I managed to come through this extraction. The forceps hurt me, but at last it is over.

The monastery is exquisite, luxurious! Yes, compared to La Salette, we are accommodated like princes, and then Fr Léon is exquisite; he has slackened the rules for me, allows me to smoke in the garden, gives me an egg and wine in the evenings. In short, I have never before in my life seen such souls. And there is a considerable sadness in the comparison I am obliged to make.

But all the same, the food situation is terrible. Fortunately, I did as you said, and brought a bit of meat and some chocolate, and with these I combat the weakness of my stomach in the evenings. On this point, admire this: in Paris, I manage to digest the diluted whitewash that passes for milk; here, I cannot, I have to abstain from it. I am so intoxicated that I cannot take real milk. Punishment for *A Rebours*! Everything has to be paid for, when you think about it!

All in all, I am perfectly happy, well looked after, and get on well with everybody. I am making notes on the book by Abbot Péchenard that you told me about, I pray, meditate, smoke, dream by the edge of the pool, walk up and down the tree-lined paths, and am taking a cure in silence and fresh air.

Unfortunately it is raining a lot, but the cell is not without charm.

I do not know where my letter will find you, probably near Sédan. I hope you find some sun and enjoyment in that military country!

I shall leave next Tuesday, probably, and push on as far as Rheims, to see the cathedral again, stay over in Paris for a day or two, and then off to spend a few weeks in Lyons.

Still, I have missed the national holiday, what a piece of luck! How sweet Trappist life is when one thinks about it!

What else can I tell you, except that it is to you that I owe all this? You have helped me so much in making the break! I don't know how to thank you. And to think I am obliged to be grateful to that unthinking creature, the gangplank from Limoges, who introduced me to you.[146]

I send you, dear Father, every assurance of my affectionate devotion.

Huysmans

To ARIJ PRINS

Lyons, 8 August 1892

My Dear Friend,

I am writing to you a few days before my return to Paris, so that you will not be worried if you chance to read the Paris papers.

I don't know how they got to hear about my departure for the monastery, but there has been an accumulation of inane gossip, ending with a denial by *Le Figaro*, saying that I had not been admitted as a monk, while other papers declared that I had renounced the world and forsaken all my friends for ever.

The truth in all this ridiculous and indiscreet confusion of news is that I left the Trappists two weeks ago, and have just spent a couple of days in Lyons with the Dr Johannès of *Là-Bas*.

Here in Lyons I am in possession of some most curious documents.

And what about the monastery, you say? It is a delightful and yet frightening place! Life there is more than hard. My soul has been shattered by it. One gets up at half-past two in the morning; perpetual silence; a dinner consisting of watery soup with oil added, an egg, a dish of vegetables with oil. No fish nor meat, nothing, but all the same, there are some exquisite moments. Anyone who talks abut mysticism without have experienced this life does not know what he is talking about, and I would add that anyone who has not witnessed Trappist prayer does not know what prayer is.

I kept very well there, and I found the monks austere, but they were as gentle with me as they could be.

But now that I have left there, I feel like a nocturnal bird let out into the light. I have come back from such a great distance, and I have been so quickly moulded into the religious life, that I stand dazed in the streets, missing the great monastic silence and the many offices. A strange thing! My stomach, which had adapted very well to abstinence, is rebelling now that I am eating meat again. There are a lot of good things about monastic life, and there one manages to penetrate the soul of the Middle Ages.

Zola declared that I was mad. Goncourt was not far from agreeing with him. For the Parisians, I have become an oddity. How uncomprehending they all are, and indeed I found amongst poor monks ideas of an elevation and breadth way beyond those of our representatives of art in France.

Not to mention that the former priest, healer of evil, with whom I am staying in Lyons, is much more intelligent and knowledgeable than all the Zolas in the world!

It is sad to say, but true, that it is away from literature itself that one must search for spirits and souls.

I have found a few curios in Lyons, but nothing very special; genuine items, moreover, are more expensive than in Paris.

I hope to see you soon, dear Prins.

Yours

G. Huijsmans

To GEORGES LANDRY

Lyons, 31 July 1892

My Dear Friend,

I should have written to you long since, if only to acknowledge receipt of Guy Valbor's book,[147] but I am suffering from the most amazing laziness. I still have cramp in my soul, and the idea of writing makes me run as far away as possible.

So I bugger about. Up very early, for the Trappists cured me of sleep, I smoke cigarettes on the banks of the Rhône, wander about the churches, take a glass of white wine to refresh myself like a good workman, and from there go and have lunch with the extraordinary Boullan.

After the victuals, we set to work, the two of us, on a most curious exchange of letters with superiors of convents, which he has in his possession. It contains stupefying demonic struggles and a high mysticism, which is really beautiful. I will bring the greater part of it back to Paris, when we have finished sorting it.

This Boullan is disconcerting. As a learned theologian, as a mystic and as an experienced confessor, he was incomparable. Why the devil did this man, who could long since have been a high-ranking ecclesiastic, have to sink into dubious Vintras-type visions!

There is also a correspondence with your former friend, the Reverend Tardif de Moidrey,[148] whom he had taken as teacher and guide. There are some very curious letters from this priest on his temptations, his life.

As you can see, our day is quite full; we break it with a walk and dinner. After which I go and read the papers in a café, and return to my hotel.

It is a bit complicated, but it has the effect of liniment. I really needed this poultice laced with laudanum by good old Mother Thibault, to heal my wounds. She is more and more caught up in visions, but is very worried, having received an order to go to Ste Baume at Christmas. But it is impossible to get up there in winter; so she declares that she does not know what she will do. Otherwise, she is always cheerful, and her usual good self.

The day after tomorrow, I am involved in a wedding!!! I am giving away the little somnambulist to a painter and decorator. All the clairvoyants of Lyons will be there. There will be no lack of atmosphere! On account of it, Boullan will break off the formidable thrashings he continues to inflict on himself on account of the Satanists. From time to time, we interrupt our work to win a battle . . . in the void.

It makes a diversion.

Ah, there is nothing run-of-the-mill here.

Did you read the stupid note in yesterday's *Le Figaro*, announcing that there had been a rumour rife on the boulevards that I was locked up in a Trappist monastery, and correcting it by announcing that I was in a religious house in Lyons? It is amazing all the same that they interfere in people's affairs like that!

Greetings to good Orsat, when you see him, and to Girard and to Boucher, if you come across either of them. And to Fr Mugnier, if he is back.

All the best to you, you old pagan.

Your chaste J.K.H.

To THE EDITOR OF *LE FIGARO*

Lyons, 5 August 1892

My Dear Colleague,

Allow me in my turn to rectify the news in *Le Figaro* which was itself a correction of the information given in several newspapers that I was locked up in a Trappist monastery, with the intention of never emerging.

You say that I am in Lyons, where I am resting a little in a religious house. I am indeed in Lyons, and I am gathering material for my future book, but I am neither living at, nor frequenting, nor indeed do I even know a religious house or convent in this town.

It is less interesting, but like an ordinary traveller, I am quite simply staying in a hotel.

I thank you in advance, my dear colleague.

Yours

Huysmans

To CHARLES RIVIÈRE

28 December 1892

Dear Sir,

This year is coming to a miry end, and its stench must have penetrated even into your solitude. The new year brings memories of the *sans-culottes*;[149] amid the disgust I feel, I turn my eyes towards the monastery, so quiet, and so much apart from these awful times, and I write these few lines to show you that life in Paris has not taken hold of me again so much that I forget the friends I saw too little of.

Perhaps you and Fr Léon might have thought some morning of the penitent who dropped like a meteorite into your isolation, and, in all charity, did you not wonder if he had gone under again?

Alas, he is evidently not of great worth, and has no reason to be very proud of himself; but after all, the bit of ground he has won over his habitual faults is thanks to you all. When in an awful situation, such as in the art world in Paris, and temptations become a real distraction, I have always managed to get the upper hand by referring myself back to the memory of the monastery and remembering the great goodness and the paternal and judicious advice of Fr Bernard. I have also learnt how to isolate myself, and to pray in an almost proper manner at home. In short, I have taken away with me from your monastery something resembling a powerful cordial of which a few drops suffice to set me on my feet again, as soon as I feel myself going under.

And so it is not without real tenderness, and in genuine gratitude, that I remember my retreat; I hope to tell you face to face one day perhaps, if good Fr Léon has been kind enough to forget my breaking of the rule, and agrees to have me again.

But in the meantime, dear sir, will you be my spokesman with the Very Reverend Fr Abbot, the Fr Prior, Fr Léon and the Fr Procurator, who was such a perfect travelling companion to me, and present in my name respectful greetings and humble good wishes.

As for you, dear sir, I think it is superfluous to add that I remain your grateful and devoted

Huysmans

If the architect is still at Igny, I should be grateful if you would remember me to him.

III
1893–98
The Call of the Cloister[1]

In the autumn of 1892, just as Huysmans had made his peace with God and the Church, the Panama scandal broke on the French political scene. In 1888, Ferdinand de Lesseps' canal-building enterprise had been in financial difficulties, and had obtained government authorization to issue loan stock, but this not without a considerable measure of bribery and corruption; those involved included the president's son-in-law. When the situation came to light, the Third Republic was in danger of definitive collapse, as its opponents took full advantage to bring the government into disrepute. The spring of 1893 was a period of crisis, followed by elections. The general atmosphere of no-confidence sparked off a number of terrorist incidents attributed to anarchists.

There was unhappiness and stress in Huysmans' personal life at this time also. His mistress, Anna Meunier, developed symtoms of madness that were to lead to her final paralysis and death. But Huysmans stood by her in her troubles, finally and reluctantly taking her himself to the asylum at Villejuif. He faithfully visited her there on Sundays until her death in 1895, although he found the atmosphere at Villejuif highly distressing.

All this conspired to make Huysmans begin seriously to think in terms of abandoning the world and seeking a definitive refuge inside the enclosure of some monastery. But in the meantime, he got on with the task of transposing his conversion into fictional form in the novel *En Route*, which he published in 1895. Here Durtal, the autobiographical hero of *Là-Bas*, reappears amidst an exultation in the artistic delights of the Roman Catholic patrimony. What he really wanted to do now was to write about his discovery of spiritual life, of the inspiration to be found in ecclesiastical architecture, music and liturgy. This he was to do at great length in *La Cathédrale*, which he finished in 1898; within the flimsiest of fictional fabrics, Huysmans now served up ever larger helpings of non-fiction in what he himself described as 'a vaguely novelish sauce'.[2]

He also felt unhappy with the state of the literary scene in Paris. Zola and Daudet he considered to be intellectual and artistic nullities, who continued to churn out repetitive banalities. Those whom he had admired were now dead, and without recognition: Verlaine, Laforgue, Villiers de l'Isle-Adam. Huysmans had a strong dislike for the younger generation of novelists: Bourget, Barrès, Gide.

After his conversion, Huysmans made a genuine and apparently successful attempt to live a celibate life. He confided to Fr Mugnier his reaction after having been dragged off to the Folies Bergères by friends one evening in 1897: '"Ah, the futility of all that" he cried at the sight of all those naked women, who did not even have good figures, he added, rejoicing in his chastity.'[3] Now in his mid-forties, he forsook the brothels and, as far as we know, had no more sexual involvement with women. But unfortunately for him he remained attractive to women, and was amorously pursued, virtually until his death. In the 1890s, he sought desperately to escape the clutches of a certain Countess Galoez, a fiery Spanish woman, whom Huysmans nicknamed La Sol. She apparently consulted him in connection with diabolical influences, on the strength of his reputation after the publication of *Là-Bas*. She vowed that she would seduce him; Huysmans, to his credit, was equally determined that she would not succeed, but he had no peace until he left Paris.

And so he began to explore various forms of monastic life, flirting with the idea of a vocation. He got to know a large number of monks, and visited religious houses the length and breadth of France. There would seem, however, to have been some misunderstandings on Huysmans' part, both as to the nature of religious life and the discernment of a vocation. His ideal of monastic life was imagined peace and quiet in a cell, where he could devote himself to artistic and literary pursuits *ad libitum*. To the glory of God, no doubt, but he was leaving out of consideration the fact that a monk owes first and foremost obedience to his abbot, and may engage in activities such as writing only if such is the latter's will, for the good of the community as a whole. If a monk/novelist were assigned instead to kitchen duties, he would have no right of appeal. Aesthetics undoubtedly played a considerable role in the spirituality of Huysmans. He could not have coped with the idea of devotion in sordid surroundings. In his view, the ideal monk was also something of an artist, in the service of God, the supreme artist.

There was also an element of seeking refuge from the world in his desire to embrace the religious life; as much, in fact, a running away from as an active running towards. Nevertheless, he persisted for a number of years in the genuine belief that God was calling him to monastic life, but his problem was that he could not make up his mind where! None of the many monasteries he visited lived up to his ideal, which probably indicated fairly clearly that the human overrode the divine in Huysmans' vocation. Those who are called usually either experience the call in relation to a specific place, or the call itself is so irresistible that place is of little importance. The 'shopping list' approach to a vocation as adopted by Huysmans, ticking off points at this monastery and that monastery (Saint-Maur de Glanfeuil was eliminated because the lavatories did not meet with his approval!), rarely works in practice.

Indeed, Huysmans was always quick to criticize, and showed relatively little tolerance of human weakness. Fr Mugnier once noted in his diary:

'The author of *En Route* sees with great clarity the faults and failings of his neighbours.'[4] And fond as he was of monks and abbots, he had very little time for the secular clergy, whom he was all too ready to dismiss as halfwits and fools whose ineptitude was directly responsible for the disaffection of large numbers of the faithful. Yet Huysmans' own experience ran counter to these frequently expressed opinions; he was greatly helped at the time of his conversion by Fr Mugnier, and enjoyed in the 1890s a very close relationship with Fr Gabriel Ferret. Fr Mugnier reflected rather sadly: 'Those monks are cut off and protected; we have to mix with the world and material things. We are to be pitied, and loved despite everything, so that we might become better... Groan at our failings, but don't set one section of Christianity up against the other.'[5]

The circumstances of Huysmans' meeting with Fr Ferret are amusing. He had been looking for a confessor and spiritual guide in Paris and had determined to take pot luck amongst the clergy at St-Sulpice, accepting whichever one of them he might encounter in the confessional on a particular Friday evening. He had secretly hoped, however, that it would not be a certain middle-aged curate of unprepossessing appearance. Providence of course willed that it should be, and the curate turned out to be Fr Ferret, who had been wanting to meet Huysmans for some time. From that moment they became close, almost inseparable, friends, and Huysmans greatly valued his spiritual direction until Fr Ferret died of cancer in 1898.

The death of Boullan in 1894 marked Huysmans' definitive break with occultism, although there were still those who doubted the sincerity of his conversion. There was notably an article in the Parisian press by a certain Fr Delfour, who maintained that if his conversion was indeed genuine, then he should formally repudiate all his earlier 'profane' works. Huysmans found all this quite distressing and would not repudiate his past, feeling that those works were a true expression of himself at the time he wrote them; he believed also that the evolution visible in his work as a whole was significant and that this, despite his unpromising beginnings, could be helpful to others embarked on a similar spiritual quest. But Huysmans was not without friends to come to his support; Dom Besse of Ligugé wrote a letter in which he unequivocally stated his personal conviction of the sincerity of the novelist's conversion.[6]

The climate of relations between Church and State in France was already uneasy in the 1890s, with anticlerical and Freemason factions in the ascendant. This made Huysmans' position at work difficult. As a prominent civil servant, his minister did not appreciate his publicly pro-Church position. He had serious fears that he might lose his job. But Huysmans' sense of identity as a Catholic is not an entirely simple matter. Although he returned to the practice of the faith in 1892, and remained constant in his religious observances until his death, his letters contain frequent denunciations of *the* Catholics, never *we* Catholics. It would seem that he had difficulty in identifying one hundred per cent with an institution that he perceived as less than perfect.

Huysmans was undoubtedly flattered by the interest and friendship shown to him by the abbot and abbess of the Benedictine abbeys at Solesmes. There had been a revival of the Benedictine order in France in the nineteenth century, after the ravages of the Terror of 1792; and the greatest flowering of liturgical renewal, liturgy always being the centre of Benedictine life, was at Solesmes. Dom Delatte apparently had genuine hopes that Huysmans might fix his stability there, but the latter found the resemblance to a military academy rather off-putting.

Meanwhile, life in Paris continued much as before: the routine of office, research for novels, and Sunday evening dinners with a group of friends in a modest restaurant in the rue de Grenelle. But Huysmans' dining companions now were fellow converts or catechumens: Georges Landry and Lucien Descaves, for example. As the decade progressed and his travels failed to reveal the monastery of his dreams, perhaps also as he increased in self-knowledge, he began to think more seriously about the idea of becoming a Benedictine oblate – that is, remaining a layman but acquiring a spiritual link with a specific religious community, through an act of personal consecration, made after a novitiate of one year. In this way, Huysmans thought he would have the best of both worlds: one foot in the monastic camp, while retaining his personal freedom and the right to write what and when he liked. As he explains in a long letter to Cécile, Abbess of Solesmes, Ligugé near Poitiers was the place he settled on for this new venture. And so, after thirty years' service, Huysmans retired from the Ministry in February 1898 and prepared to set off for the provinces, to begin a new life of tranquillity and devotion.

To ARIJ PRINS

[8 March 1893]

My Dear Friend,

I have received your letter, which stupefied me somewhat... and, all other considerations aside, I tell myself that if marriage is not repugnant to you, you are doing a good thing by marrying in such circumstances; better a penniless woman,[7] who is charitable and gentle, than a rich woman; moreover, in my opinion, it is a source of happiness not to marry a dowry, that is one of my own particular mystical ideas, but in which I believe absolutely. In marrying for the sake of marriage, you are then, I believe, on the only right path; and I am pleased, for I hope you will be given at least that small sum of happiness which it is permitted to hope for in this life.

What is more, we do not arrange our lives, we submit to them; it took the frightful misfortune[8] which has crushed you to bring about a happy change in your life, perhaps for the better; some people call it chance, others providence. I myself have been so well led along certain paths, in spite of myself, whereas the idea of vocation would have made me laugh when I was writing *Les Sœurs Vatard* or *En Ménage*, that I believe resolutely, absolutely in a providential intervention in the life of each one of us.

One needs to have gone through crises of soul such as I did for over a year, to be able to affirm with such complete certainty ideas that shock what is called modern science and the fine inventions of the new thinkers; but having wandered about for twenty years and more, one ends up, in the light of certain strange experiences that happen to one, seeing clearly and settling down in oneself, no longer remaining jostled and restless.

Keep me informed, and accept a shake of the hand from your devoted
G. Huijsmans

If you have any news, you can still write to me until the end of the month; I shall not be leaving for the Trappists until the last moment, that is for Holy Week, which I shall go and spend amongst the shadows of the cloister; and I shall come back to Paris on Easter Tuesday to take up again the useless yoke of this worldy existence.

To ARIJ PRINS

3 April 1893

My Dear Friend,

The more I think about what has happened to you,[9] having read your letter carefully, the more I believe you will get what you want in the end – absence is your trump card. It is certain that knowing you are far away, she will dream, and especially if she sees your family, she will have memories stirred up and will finally give in, weary of struggling against herself.

In this business you are lucky – really so – that she has no Catholic principles, for you would be irredeemably lost; she would not change peace and quiet for earthly uncertainties and submit to the necessarily indecent excitement of the flesh.

So I don't see your marriage as a lost cause; and your trump card is, I believe, being in Hamburg.

Oh no! We don't arrange our lives! And if it were all to fall through, you will have been useful to this good lass in helping her brother; that is something, and you acted very well in doing what you did – for her, for him and for yourself.

Nothing new here; I was not able to go to the Trappists owing to the collapse of the government.[10] I spent my so-called holidays partly at the office. It was most bothersome, for I really needed to go and re-immerse myself a little in monasatic austerity.

The further I get, the more I am convinced that that is where happiness lies. The mystics of the Middle Ages saw things aright. It is the only place where one gets a very clear impression of the distinction between body and soul, and where the joys of the latter seem infinite alongside those to be got from the ingestion of some tasty food or a few spasms.

Unfortunately I can do nothing about it; I still have my poor mad woman on my hands and should not decide on anything while she is still in this world. Then I still have five years to go at the office before my retirement and I have my book to write![11] Which is not inconsiderable!

I am disgusted at my work – and I have a strong desire to chuck everything on the fire, for what I am writing at the moment seems very mediocre!

I have lived for art – and – now that I am forty-five, I am aware of its nothingness, and the total vanity of what is called notoriety. This is a shallow and deceptive food, a nullity.

But to come back to your situation, I think there are no grounds for despair. Try to see that she visits your family often during your absence. I think that would be a good strategy. Basically, note that her hesitation is quite natural; the step to be taken is enormous – between the life she has chosen for herself and the one you offer her. All her ideals are to be thrown out of the window and she must try to assimilate others. Given that she has not said a definite *no* straight away, a resolute *no*, that means there is a breach in her ideals themselves, however small it may be. So there is hope, and with all my heart I wish that you may succeed, since in this way you will perhaps acquire the sum total of human happiness that can be hoped for.

Keep me informed, and a good shake of the hand to you, my dear Prins.
Yours

G. Huijsmans

To ARIJ PRINS

25 April 1893

My Dear Friend,

I have just received the copper Virgin that you were kind enough to send me. She is charming and shows religious feeling. Thank you for thinking of me.

It arrived at one of the most painful moments of my life, and to be thought of at such times is a comfort. I have had to have the unfortunate woman, whom you know, locked away in the mental asylum at Villejuif.

It was horrible. She is suffering from general paralysis, raving, but not so mad as not to know where she is and to suffer atrociously.

I went to see her yesterday, Sunday. I came away feeling sick. It is really awful. Imagine a room with two hundred mad women singing and crying. The unfortunate woman you have asked to see is led into this flock, around which nurses run like sheepdogs; she arrives, unsteady on her feet, bursts into tears, and begs you to take her away.

My heart breaks in advance when I think that on Sundays now I shall go and console this poor girl!

Life is decidedly terrible; and woman is the most powerful instrument of pain that is given to us, whoever she may be. Ah, I pity you, my dear friend; if you manage to get married, you will, I hope, be very happy, but basically, what a pity you ever set eyes on her whom you desire; at least you would have lived in peace. Still, it is to be hoped that possession, if it takes place, will compensate you for the present sadness.

Nothing apart from that; I am a bit disorientated by this awful time of psychiatric doctors, asylums, tears and shouting that I have had to go through.

When one's nerves are already in a bad way, it is frightful.

Thank you, my dear Prins, and all the best to you.

G. Huijsmans

To DR PAUL SÉRIEUX

15 May 1893

Dear Sir,

Thank you for your studies of sexual anomalies and of chronic delirium that you were good enough to send me. I read them with all the more interest, as certain of your observations, that are so clearly conveyed, provided me with the ending to certain stories of which I had seen only the beginning. For example, the observation of Thérèse M. and page 63 which is so sound on the three voices and chronic delirium.

Since *Là-Bas*, I have been wanting to write a book dealing no longer with black mysticism, but with white, so I have mixed quite a lot with religious, and especially with those known to be visionaries in such circles, and I have glimpsed some very singular cases. Only I think it is immensely difficult to define clearly the frail frontier that separates madness from reason in these people, for there are some admirable ones amongst them.

On that subject, I am in possession of the entire correspondence between a provincial convent of Carmelite nuns and their confessor.[12] It is disturbing.

I found your studies of disturbance in sexual gender no less interesting. Two years ago, with a view to a book which is unfortunately unwritable, for it would look as if one were digging up scandal, I was able to get an introduction into the frightful world of sodomy. Frightful! That is the word, and if demonic action were to exist, that is where it would be found. I believe they are just about all candidates for the madhouse, but stab wounds ensure that they die in hospitals rather than in mental asylums.

This is what is disconcerting; one could almost establish a law: that is, that true sodomites (I don't mean young lads who do it for money, but those who live only for this fixation) are physical giants. It seems that muscular strength develops this taste in men. Thus this army finds its recruits amongst the porters of the central market, butchers' boys, fairground strongmen. Those are the ones who are really enamoured of this vice and are, above all, the passive partners. All the bars around Les Halles are full of them. And what is frightening is that a man who has this vice cuts himself off voluntarily from the rest of the world. He lives apart. He eats, has his hair done, drinks in special establishments run by sodomites; his brain becomes even more given up to imbecility as his voice changes; imagine a Hercules with enormous arms, a bestial mouth, cackling like an old maid, putting on airs and graces in a loud voice that is shrill and husky! Is there any relation between the vocal cords and the genital organs? One might think so, if one observes that nearly all female singers are lesbians, especially contraltos.

If you get any patients at Villejuif who are members of these confraternities, try to get to know their past, if possible! You will find material for some very curious studies of the human soul,.

But you know more about that than I do, for in the field of medicine, you specialize in the really interesting areas.

Excuse this scrawl, dear sir; with thanks and devotion.

J.K.H.

To ANDRÉ GIDE

25 July 1893

My Dear Colleague,

I should not want, all the same, to pay you outlandish or stupid compliments by saying that *Le Voyage d'Urien*[13] is the only book to have appeared for ages, yet it is true.

It contains some superbly evocative pages written in the style of a fine artist. The minarets, the final plague during the journey on the Pathetic Ocean and the amazing seagulls on the Glacial Sea are irrefutable proof.

Ah, you know how to wind up the brain's capacity for fantasy!

Then the setting of these pictures is somewhat disconcerting – which is not displeasing. The ironic pride of this Narcissus, this Me, languid and preoccupied with valiant action, caught up in the 'seriousness of its mission', the whole thing going up in smoke, in a dream, and so strange in the serious – almost solemn – way in which you state it!

The framework of the book is superbly established: the illustrations are interesting and curious, conducive to dreams; those on page 36 and page 101 really disturbing.

For all this I sincerely thank you and M. Denis,[14] and I shake you by the hand, my dear colleague.

Huysmans

To ARIJ PRINS

8 September 1893

Dear Friend,

I write you a line in haste, for I am in a mad turmoil on account of a ridiculous story. I have just been decorated[15] as deputy head of the office – upon which the whole of the press spewed up, declaring that it was idiotic not to have decorated me as a man of letters – to the annoyance of my minister and making trouble for me. Added to that, stacks of letters, cards, in short a large dose of bother, which is not even compensated for by joy at the red ribbon, for which I don't give a damn.

I have been to spend a week with my good friends the Trappists and was perfectly happy there; monasteries are exquisite, for certain, and I understand why they flourished so in the Middle Ages. To be there or in Paris in a Ministry, where one is bored every day, in truth I prefer the silence of the cell, broken by the magnificence of the liturgical offices. Still!

I asked some experts about your curios. They all concur in declaring that you will be robbed as if by brigands in a wood, so don't commit yourself to trying to sell here, especially in the auction rooms, which are a real dive, at the mercy of what we call here 'the black gang'!

I am sorry about your Ebeling, who is really stupid; it is fortunate that he will not be your partner any more.

I leave you, dear Prins, but not without sending you a good shake of the hand.

G. Huijsmans

To ANDRÉ GIDE

[14 December 1893]

Thank you, my dear colleague, for your *Tentative amoureuse*,[16] so strangley elevated and shrouded in mist, with the weary knights that remind me of those of Albrecht Dürer, as they pass through the story, with its bored tone, and its own self-conscious weariness.

You know the secret of a simple epithet that becomes singularly mysterious by the way in which you place it: that is, the adjective 'important'. On a less intense note than *Le Voyage d'Urien* on the whole, there is the same ghostly brushing up against the fringes of life, and this game with the self, complementing your *Traité du Narcisse*;[17] it is about narcissism of the soul, spiritual contemplation of one's own navel. It would be dubious if it weren't written by you, who are a subtle and unusual artist.

And that is the only worthwhile consideration, and so I am grateful to you for having given me a taste of this highly personal and delicate essence. I thank you and remain, dear colleague,
     Your

J. K. Huysmans

To ARIJ PRINS

26 December 1893

My Dear Friend,

Thank you for the photograph,[18] and the card that came with it. The infamous and fateful year 1893 is coming to an end. In France, at least, it has been nothing but a heap of filth, so much so that it has made one sympathize with the anarchists throwing bombs in parliament, which is the rotting image of a country in the process of decomposition, with its reappointment of the brigands of Panama and Wilson,[19] making it evident that they are all rogues, and that no filth is too much for them.

I do not know what the new one will be like, in an old world that is cracking apart at the seams; Europe seems drastically undermined, as she heads into the sinister unknown; I hope there will at least be oases for some people, and especially for you, who are venturing on a new life.

The portrait conveys a pretty woman, gentle, charming, but gives no clue as to her soul, incomprehensible to me in its admirable, secular charity; I admire without understanding; but really I believe that in exceptional circumstances, there is a chance of happiness which is not to be found in more intelligible, more normal circumstances.

And that is what gives me pleasure, my dear Prins, for basically you are right; with the Dutch temperament, which I share, celibacy makes no sense unless in religious life, in a monastery. But there it is different, there are things that are independent of all will, impossible to guess at for those who have not experienced them. Apart from that, and the desire to end my days in a cell, it is quite certain that marriage is the only alternative, for all the rest is inferior. Cohabitation and mistresses make no sense, once one has reached a certain age. Marriage channels this filth, spiced with a touch of the human sublime, with a surging of the soul, which is the most elevated there is in the earthly domain.

So may the new year, which will see you married, be favourable to you! For you deserve it, and may gentle resting places be granted you in this badly run rooming house of life!

Nothing new here, except that I have discovered the most exquisite medieval cathedral there is, at Chartres, a blonde, slim church with blue eyes. The last effort of the Gothic style, emaciated, needing flesh and bone no more, desiring to be ethereal, to rise, like a soul, to heaven. A marvel with its blonde-coloured stone, its ancient stained glass, where strange figures emerge from a sapphire backgrouand. I am in love with this basilica where, what is more, the finest sculpted figures of the Middle Ages are to be found, and I can go there, for it is two hours from Paris by express. Nothing can convey the joy of this cathedral, where one can comprehend perfect mastery in a dream of stone. These journeys are exquisite; I am working quite hard, in less and less of a hurry to appear, since my book, announced by the press, is being asked for more and more. That disgusts me, and I won't come out until the end of 1894 at the earliest. And never, if I can help it, for this one has more soul than the others, and it is repugnant to me to open myself up in this way to the crassness of the reading public! Still!

Happy New Year, dear Prins; and may life be sweet for you and your wife; this is the true wish of your friend.

G. Huijsmans

To DOM BESSE

12 May 1894

Dear Reverend Father,

Boucher has passed on to me *The Benedictine Monk*[20] that you were good enough to send us, and I read with interest and profit of your monastic journey throughout the ages, which is so precisely and clearly summarized. It is history in its concetrated essence, and it also makes an excellent cordial for our time. If it were possible, the second part of your volume would make me love the order of St Benedict even more, for there you express ideas on the science of Faith and works related to its origins, and liturgy as practised even in churches that are separated from Rome; all this has great breadth and a fine balance.

And I am reminded of the evening when I had the pleasure of seeing you; we spoke of this current of mysticism which seems to be passing under our society unawares, as it lives its vices from day to day, heading we know not where.

I am indeed incoherent and timid, and am really amazed at some of the conversations I have had since our encounter with people one would not suspect of having any depth of Christianity, and who, on the subject of my proposed book, speak to me longingly of monastic life. It is quite possible that this comes in part from lassitude and disgust with life in general, but it is no less certain that this change of course in certain souls would not have happened ten years ago. And so one can think that the time will come when this influx will have to be channelled, otherwise it might be lost, and this is doubtless the weighty and magnificent task that will fall to the order of St Benedict, the only one that, while remaining impeccably monastic, is sufficiently enamoured of art, sufficiently intellectual and still close enough to the world to be able to influence it in a positive way by its example.

Perhaps it will once again have the job of saving the civilization of an old leaky universe. I even believe that at the present moment, if time were more favourable to monks, and if they had a monastery in Paris or nearby, they could cast their nets over the city by night, and the following day would find therein a plentiful catch of souls.

Something else: whilst foraging in booksellers, I found a little volume which I am sending you, thinking that your library, which is only just beginning, might not have it. It is the life of St Angela of Foligno,[21] written by herself. I have gone overboard for this book; there are pages, 93 and following, where it is really Our Lord speaking; it is admirable, but it is translated in a warm and sticky style, and what is more, it seems that whole passages have been removed (out of propriety).

But now, there is an element of gratitude in my love for St Angela. This book was good for me in painful moments. It helped me through terrible crises of soul and the unrelieved silence and solitude of the Trappist monastery. And certain passages in it stir up my soul less by what they contain than by the painful or exquisite memories they bring to the surface in me. In fact before becoming the saint she was, Angela of Foligno had sinned greatly, and it seems to me that the saint who has suffered the death and passion of his or her former faults will be more compassionate towards my wretchedness than pure virgins, such as St Gertrude,[22] or St Teresa, for example.

What else can I tell you, most Reverend Father? I hesitate to put your charity to the test by talking about myself, and inflicting upon you the burden of listening to my uninteresting lamentations. In any case, forgive the selfish side that, despite everything, seeks a little relief for itself in talking about its pain. But if you knew what it is like to be getting nowhere, to be not taking a single step forward! I am lacking in confidence in Him and in love. I am spending my life struggling against myself to go to communion, and what trouble I have getting the upper hand! Yes, it is complicated; I am obsessed by God, ready to pray to Him as much as He wants, I think only of Him. I can say that He harries me, torments me unceasingly – and all that stops at the altar rail. I have an absolute disinclination to present myself there, and I do not feel myself violently driven to it, by something outside of myself. I await I know not what, I live with perpetual procrastinations that oh, I reproach myself with. It is really very wretched not to have a simple soul. I have a real need of one, I assure you.

Forgive this scribble, extract from it at least, I beg you, my most respectful and devoted feelings.

J.K.H.

To ARIJ PRINS

14 May 1894

My Dear Friend,

I have so many difficulties, and so little time to resolve them, that as yet I have not found time to write to you.

Imagine the latest complication: my lout of a publisher is in the doldrums, threatened with bankruptcy, and he refuses to sell his business to a purchaser Descaves and I have found for him! He wants to carry on to the end, that is until he falls on his backside.

And to make my joy complete, my book is just about finished; and I do not know what course of action to determine on. But what can one expect of a publisher who is interested only in boxing, on account of which he recently had to spend two weeks in a darkened room with pieces of raw steak on his eyes, as a result of a memorable hiding dealt him by a Belgian champion whose challenge he accepted!!

What with that and the trouble with the anarchists, which means that I cannot get away from the Ministry, I do not at all know when I shall be free this year. I have to go to Lyons to put Boullan's affairs in order, and to the abbey of Saint-Wandrille, near Rouen, an old Benedictine abbey where I know the Father Abbot!

I will very probably not be able to get away from Paris in either August or perhaps September as well. I might go away in June or July, it will depend on my director and my boss, who have first choice, naturally, and the rest of us get only the leftovers.

I will write to you later on this subject, when my plans are fixed. If you come to Paris in July, I shall try to take June, so as to be back, but all that is still hypothetical, we shall see later on.

As I told you, my book is nearing its end. It is enormous, thicker than *Là-Bas*, which was copious enough.

I expect a general outcry; the Catholics are so stupid that they will all be as exasperated at this book as the Freemasons and freethinkers. Bascially it is written for a handful of monks. It is a visiting card that I shall send them before retiring to join them.

Nothing new apart from all that, except that I am bent double with work; this book has finished me off, and I am in great need of going away to the country.

I see that Ebeling really is a disastrous character. He should go into partnership with my Stock; the stupidity of all these people alarms me.

That is all for now, my dear friend. Greetings to your wife.

Yours

G. Huijsmans

To EDMOND DE GONCOURT

2 June 1894

Need I tell you, very dear master, that your 'Uffizi' are really admirable,[23] and reduce to despair those of us who aspire to render the visual impression of paintings with our pen.

For how much more do these short, these incisive notes conjure up an Italy that is particularly full of life and curiosities, captured in its artistic intimacy, than the whole of Gautier's volume,[24] so heavy and so dead, with lapidary sentences, unrelieved in tone.

And I would say the same of Taine's book,[25] that gentleman who never travelled without his compasses, and measured out art dogmatically. No, all those fine theories, rallied under the noble title of 'philosophy of art', will never convey the essence of the works of Orcagna, Botticelli, Memmi as you have done.

Then besides the paintings themselves, what exquisite portrayals, such as that of a certain Pierrot ploughing a field, and the terrifying, superb page on the murder of Rossi.[26]

This book was and will be a delectation, and I cannot understand why it has been so long in coming out.

And so I thank you with all my heart for having sent it to me, dear master.
    Your respected and devoted

Huysmans

To DOM BESSE

11 July 1894

Here I am back in Paris amidst the crowds, and I am still a bit like a drunken man, who does not really know where he is; the delightful antiphons of your vespers are ringing in my ears, and keep me company in the noisy streets. I carry a bit of Saint-Wandrille with me as I walk along the embankment. Then I remember my regret at not having seen you before I left ... But in the absence of a face-to-face goodbye and a filial handshake, let me tell you, and Very Reverend Fr Chamard,[27] in all innocence and without fuss, that I love you dearly and that I thank you with all my heart for all the kindness you showed towards me. You have really helped me to understand all the familiar affection and indulgent sweetness of the Benedictine family, of which the Trappists had given me no idea. But .. but what a contrast to find oneself in Paris again, in a hostile environment! Ah, Dom Chamard did me a bad turn with all his kindness. There is none of it here. And the contrast is so violent that it is painful. What else can I tell you, other than repeat the same thing, that I found your indulgent affection really moving.

Ah, do tell Very Reverend Dom Chamard and be assured of my gratitude and affection.

J.K.H.

To FR GABRIEL FERRET

11 September 1894

My Dear Father,

Your letter was really welcome; I see that you are somewhat recovered, and that is a relief, for I have hardly stopped thinking about you in this sad time you have been going through.

You ask me if I can manage to have a few days free at the end of the month; I hope so. My boss comes back on the 17th, that is next Monday, and I will see if I can take a couple of days before the end of the month; in that case we could go to Saint-Wandrille to see good Fr Chamard and all our friends in that monastery. It would be a sweet consolation. In the woods there is an old twelfth-century chapel dedicated to St Saturnin; I am sure you would find it charming.

I will write to you next week on this subject, when things are back to normal.

You cannot imagine, my dear friend, the horrible life I am leading. Imagine a frenzy for seven hours on end, papers to make you go off your head, telegrams every minute, ceaseless telephone calls, bailiffs coming to fetch me to go off to departmental heads or the minister. And all that in an office overloaded with work, with no will to work, yet burdened with responsibility and risking my position every day. I come away in the evening so exhausted that I can barely face eating before going to bed.

And what is worse is the obsessive nature of these annoyances; the soul is reduced to a state of idiocy, incapable of sweeping away the dross that haunts it. I sometimes go to church in the evenings. But alas, I rarely manage to be recollected. All these bothers spring back on me. I try in vain to chase them away; they return all the same to obsess me, prevent me from thinking, making my prayer nothing but vocal prayer.

Ah, it is really time for all this to come to an end. I can assure you that the Benedictine motto Pax! is hardly mine. Added to that, in times of prolonged and persistent trouble, disgusting thoughts nearly always come to one, and on top of everything else, one has to chase them away. One's soul is benumbed and under siege at one and the same time.

But it is all going to come to an end. I shall sweep it all away in a few days' time and take up a life that will be more or less calm. I am sending my book to the printer's and will have to work on it. Then once I am back from Saint-Wandrille, I shall try to take eight days of my holiday, and, however bad the weather may be, I shall go and see my old friends the Trappists. After being subjected to so much shameful and sterile gossip, I shall go and cure myself with silence in a cell.

All this cheers me up for the moment. Then at Saint-Wandrille and at Igny, with the help of the good monks, I shall build walls of prayer to hide behind when my book comes out. I shall have a lot of bother then, a general outcry from the press, and what is worse, more trouble at the Ministry.

Though it is true that I have found a little foreword that is quite crafty, and will prevent the government from taking measures against me. I will show it to you on your return. I don't say that the Ministry will not seek to pick a quarrel with me, but with that I defy it to dismiss me.

So there, my dear friend, is an account of quite dreary weeks, as you see. Added to that, there is not a single friend left in Paris, except for good old Landry; we share our melancholy over dinner on Sundays, when I leave the office. You can well imagine that we think of you, and shall be really pleased to see you again. I complain, and poor Landry gets no time off at all! And what a really good soul he has!

I thank you for having prayed for me at Paray. Alas, if it were human commerce, you would be duped! I do not say that I am not praying for you, but my prayers are of such poor quality that the Good Lord must cast them off like old rags! May He recognize the intention at least!

Affectionately and respectfully yours, my dear friend,

J. K. Huysmans

To JULIE THIBAULT

11 September 1894

My Dear Friend,

I am finally liberated from that stupid bondage which has been exasperating me for six weeks. I feel like a man who has been buried and has come to life again, and is going once more to busy himself with art and no longer with solemn futilities.

I have one awful responsibility less, and above all, it is a relief. I am drawing up plans to get leave on the grounds of overwork, and to get the end of this leave to coincide with the proofs of my book, which I am finally going to give to Stock.

I shall go and rest for a few days at Saint-Wandrille. My house in the rue de Sèvres has become a branch office of that abbey. There is a constant coming and going of monks. In short, I have finally committed myself to going there for three days at the end of the month with Fr Ferret of St-Sulpice, who is summoned there by one of the little monks whom he sent to the Benedictines earlier as a novice.

The journey will be less boring if there are two of us. After that, I shall head off to the Trappists, where the Father Abbot, who has taken a liking to me that I really don't understand, has sent a message telling me that he will *release* all the old monks who have been locked up in cells for twenty years and more from *their vow of silence*, because they are over a hundred years old, to allow me to chat with them and thus get a good idea of the Trappist soul.

As you see, all these saints are marvellously well disposed towards me; all this makes me all the more keen to become an oblate.

Still, I hope for I know not what after the publication of my book – some unexpected solution, divine help, something that will permit me not to languish for another four years in this abominable life as a layman, and finally to go and settle in a monastery.

I well know in advance, and from the monks I see at my house in Paris, that community life is not a bed of roses, but nothing could ever be as bad as the dazed anxiety of the last six weeks. That has steeled me against any regret of the world. Ah! Not to intercept telegrams all day long but to sing delicious plainchant melodies all day long, my mind is made up! Pray to God for that, my dear friend, for basically, it is the only haven I desire.

And you? And dear M. Misme? You have returned to pious Lyons and its quiet life. I hope that you are in good health, and have no news of that Freemason Wirth, for that is the best thing that could happen to you.

Embrace M. Misme, as I embrace you, and my affectionate regards to your sweet neighbours.

Your devoted

Huysmans

To FR GABRIEL FERRET

Igny, 9 November 1894

Dear Father,

Just a note from the depths of my solitude. It is total, for I have barely caught sight of M. Rivière, who has gone to organize some pilgrimage, and so I no longer open my mouth. This is a cure by silence in every sense.

From the spiritual point of view, I am in a state of numbness, which is not without its charms. I am exhausted by the ceaseless chapel routine; the Trappist timetable is no longer the same, since the congress at Tilburg a month ago. There are more liturgical celebrations.

I get up at about half-past three, to be in chapel by four. Imagine, they have no lights here. The offices take place in complete darkness; one feels like a blind man in the chapel, and it goes on for hours! It is sweet and sinister at one and the same time. I feel as if I am reciting the *De Profundis* over my own body.[28] All the same, the melancholy of these woods, of this damp stonework and this morning mist, is unspeakable. I received communion this morning in honour of my good St Denis the Areopagite,[29] whose feast day it was; it was just like communion in the catacombs, in the middle of the night, lit only by the sparse candles on the altar. It has put my soul to sleep, I no longer feel it at all, it is like an engine in neutral.

Physically I am not too bad, despite a stomach which is worse than mediocre, and which has a job to digest the warm, oily vegetables. I have unceasing and frightful fits of yawning, but all in all, it is bearable; the cold is the worst. It is just like at Saint-Wandrille, in a valley covered with fog in the morning, and adorned with ponds which make for constant dampness. Fortunately the weather has turned fine. In the afternoons, I do as old invalids do and warm my back in the sun as I doze by the pond.

So I have met up with my good Trappists again, but how ugly they have become! The new rules do away with their beards. They are all awful now. They are nevertheless saintly and helpful people, but Benedictine hospitality makes the Cistercians' seem muted and cold. One can even detect it in their plainchant. Here it is unrefined, in a raw state, dark, without any of those delightful antiphons that Fr George used to sing in his delicate little voice at Saint-Wandrille. Here it is the art of the crypt, and it smells of mildew. But there is only one thing that beats the Benedictines, that is the *Salve Regina* that they alone know how to sing.[30]

I am thinking of leaving on Friday for Rheims, where I shall spend the night and stay over on Saturday, to take notes on the cathedral and Saint Rémy. On Sunday I shall go to Laon to see the church, and return to Paris in the evening. So don't write to me, as I shall be able to see you as soon as I get back.

I have spoken of your business, and they are very willing to pray for your intention. I have also been building ramparts of prayer here for when my book comes out, so as to deflect the ministerial storm from my head. There are in this monastery some old saints whose intercessory power is certain.

I shall see you soon, dear Father; respectfully and cordially yours,

J. K. Huysmans

To JULES HURET

1 January 1895

My Dear Colleague,

Here is the information you were kind enough to ask for concerning my book.

Publicized, I know not why, with the title *Là-Haut*,[31] the book is in reality called *En Route*. It was supposed to come out with Tresse and Stock at the end of this month, but as the American novelist Edgar Saltus has just arrived in Paris in order to translate it, there is a chance that publication might be delayed until 15 February, if a deal were to be made, and the French and American publishers reach an agreement. Mr Saltus and his publisher would then have time to translate it and get it printed; the book is supposed to be put on sale in Paris and New York on the same day, in order to protect our rights.

As for the book itself, it is, in some sense, the counterpart of *Là-Bas*. Having done Satanism, black mysticism, I am now venturing into divine mysticism, white mysticism.

The plot of the novel is of the simplest; I have re-used the main character of *Là-Bas*, Durtal, whom I have undergo a conversion and send off to a Trappist monastery; in him, I have tried to note the episodes of a soul startled by grace, going from chapel to chapel, with an accompaniment of literature, mysticism, liturgy, plainchant, in that admirable artistic environment created by the Church.

The book is divided into two parts. The first takes place in Paris. Durtal, a refugee from satanism, having got rid of Mme Chantelouve,[32] wanders in solitude and disgust at everything amongst the churches, chapels and convents of the left bank, which is, in short, the religious district of Paris. Handled by a very exceptional old priest whom he has met, he ends up, after some horrible crises of soul, agreeing to be sent to the Trappists.

This part, which I have summed up drily in a sentence, and which the questionings of his soul will perhaps make interesting for some people, portrays the exquisite churches of St-Séverin, Notre-Dame des Victoires and St-Sulpice, the three churches in Paris of any interest, but for different reasons. It shows the inside of Carmelite and Poor Clare convents, describes a taking of the veil at the Benedictine sisters in the rue Monsieur, contains a résumé of the literature of mysticism: studies of St Teresa, St John of the Cross, St Angela, Madeldeine of Pazzi, etc.[33] It also deals with curiosities of liturgy and plainchant.

If one wanted, it could almost be a guidebook for art lovers who, leaving aside the pious idiosyncracies and little Catholic devotions of our time, would like to take stock of what remnants of the magnificent heritage of the Church are still to be heard, seen and read in Paris.

The second part takes place in a Trappist monastery. Durtal arrives at the monastery of Notre-Dame de l'Âme, which in reality is the abbey of Igny, near Fismes in the Marne, and there his conversion is completed, after diabolical crises that the monks cure him of. In this part, there is a detailed description of Trappist life, which has been so strangely travestied by all those people who have spoken or written about the customs of this order. I give it in minute detail and with strict accuracy; and I do the same for the monks I have known; they are portrayed from nature, only the names are changed; but however strange certain stories about Brother Siméon, the Cistercian swineherd, who is an admirable saint, might seem, I confirm that they are strictly true.

In a word, I have made nothing up, neither the daily timetable, which I copied out at Igny, nor the kinds of monk that I present.

There, very succinctly, is the book. At a time when everyone is talking about mysticism, without seeming to know very much about what it is, it seemed to me interesting to portray this science which has its laws, which can predict in advance most of the phenomena that take place in a soul when God is drawing it, and which follows spiritual operations as closely as physiology observes the different states of the body. I have tried to show and to explain that as best I could. It has cost me three years of work; I truly believe it not to be brilliant, but it was not easy.

When I add that if Durtal has a sincere affection for the family of St Benedict, he has a job to hide his aversion for the secular clergy, and in this volume he frankly abhors the unparallelled stupidity of clerics. I think I have revealed the major components of my book and exposed its mechanism to your gaze.

Excuse this scrawl, but it is New Year's Day, and I am writing in haste. Thank you for having thought of me, and all the best to you, dear colleague.

J. K. Huysmans

To FR HENRY MOELLER

[late 1894, early 1895]

Dear Father,

Our friend Buet[34] has passed on to me the letter you wrote him, and I thank you sincerely for all the affection towards me that it contains. Yes, it is true, after having dragged the sickness of my soul around all the clinics of the intellect, I ended up, with God's grace, going to the only hospital where they put you to bed and really look after you – the Church. One fine morning, in spite of myself I may say, and without any human spiritual support, I set off for a Trappist monastery, where I laundered my life, after going through some frightful crises of despair in those cloisters; I have tried to put all this, sincerely and without any embellishment, into my book *En Route*, which will be out at the end of January.

Perhaps it will interest you, for it deals with high mysticism, the admirable art of the Church, of convents, and it portrays some frightful struggles of the soul, amidst a liturgical setting.

I managed to make the Parisian reading public swallow the devil in *Là-Bas*; now it is a case of trying to get them to accept God. That is more difficult, but still, it remains to be seen.

Thank you once more, dear Father, for your kindness.

Respectfully yours,

Huysmans

To FR FÉLIX KLEIN

11 March 1895

Dear Father,

Let me first of all thank you for your penetrating and friendly article on *En Route*. It is a pleasure to see oneself understood in such a way, and it is sufficiently rare for me, that I owe you a real debt of gratitude for this boon.

I really must admit that you are also more charitable than I was; it is quite certain that it would have been better if those attacks were not in it.[35] But what could I do? Reflect that this book was basically written less for Catholics than for a section of the Parisian reading public, which at the present time is vacillating, waiting to be caught. There are people who are thinking things over, who would perhaps be not far off from returning to the Church, if they were not put off by that aspect of sentimental devotions, by sermons that they judge inadequate, by loads of things. So that they might listen to me, and so as not to lay myself open to counterattack, which would inevitably have happened if I had praised everything, I had to cut my losses. Do not forget either that I had to get a reading public that is full of mistrust to take in those essential theories on the contemplative life, to try to get them to understand the admirable art of the Church, and the radiant beauty of the monasteries; it was a frightening task! I had managed to evoke for them the spectre of the Devil in *Là-Bas*, but to try to interest them in believing in Our Lord, that was so difficult! All the more so, as hostile forces were involved.

I tell you all this in sincerity, Father, not to prove myself right, but by way of an apology for the flesh-eating epithets I used throughout the book.

Then, if only you knew, I have never been so unsure of myself, so discouraged as when writing this book. I felt myself crushed by the subject matter, so unequal to the task, and so frightfully anxious at having to speak about the Blessed Virgin. Ah, for that I should have found words of such candour and absolute love, but nothing came of it; that is what is wretched about this book. It is true that in order to achieve that, it would have been better not to have led for so long a life such as mine.

It was kind of you not to tell me about these woeful inadequacies, and for that too I thank you.

I beg you, Father, to accept the expression of my respect and devotion.

Huysmans

To FR FÉLIX KLEIN

[7 April 1895]

Dear Father,

I have just read your journey *Autour du dilettantisme* that you were good enough to send me.[36] Your criticism is so alert and penetrating, and it is a pleasure to see you go from Bourget to Barrès, stopping off at Anatole France.[37] I only regret that you did not mention an author – quite unknown, it is true – who, in the first place, is not without talent, but who is the epitome and worse of dilettantism, pride, egoism and the cult of the self: André Gide, author of a Treaty on 'Narcissism'! It is an extra strong dose of Barrès – if, that is, one can use the word strong to refer to those people who are lacking in that quality. I assure you that that man makes one love humility, and one has an overwhelming desire to have a good gossip with a hall porter when one emerges from what the author has to say about his 'g...reat soul', without the least trace of humour.

Shall I admit to you now that I was a bit surprised to see you reproaching Bourget with lewd portraits, whereas in literary circles he is on the contrary accused, when confronted with situations that are difficult to express, of writing them with an India rubber, to use the quite amusing phrase of a friend of Barbey d'Aurevilly. Poor Bourget – but he has never written any passionate pages. Moreover he defended himself well against that reproach in the letter you quote, which seems quite fair to me when he says that the unfortunate thing about Catholic writers has been a lack of daring in the portrayal of passion; that is why, because of this fear of situations and of words, we witness the monstrous phenomenon of all modern art having established itself, and developing, outside of the Church. She has only produced one talented novelist, d'Aurevilly, and he moreover was rejected on account of his motives. Ah, the fear of words! Look, Father, a sentence in *En Route* was found to be violent: 'foul liquid sewage, giving off gasses etc., etc.' And what if I had simply translated this sentence: *homo nihil est aliud quam sperma fetidum, saccus stercorum, cibus venerius*, and so it goes on![38] There would have been a general outcry. And that is by St Bernard!!

I am not sure, but it seems to me that the rigours of Jansenism[39] have left their mark on the Church, from that point of view.

But to come back to your interesting exploration of the land of the dilettantes, I admire your so courageous flaying of the cocoons of that grub who has set himself up beside the churches and whose name is: A. France.

That is true justice, and it was quite necessary for it to be done by a priest, in order to dispel all possible doubt, for there are so many people who find it charming that this writer singles out the *Fioretti*,[40] besmirching them at will, as he has just done, with the perfidious insinuations he inherited from Renan.

What can I tell you now about *En Route* that I have not already told you, other than to take advantage of this chance to thank you once again for having been kind enough to perceive the sincerity of the book and saying so, and for not having judged it more harshly!

Huysmans

P.S. It would also be only right for me to thank you for the indulgent sentence that you slipped in on the subject of page 250.

To FR JULES PACHEU S.J.

21 April 1895

Dear Reverend Father,

I have received the brochure that you were good enough to send me: *Idealism and Mysticism*, and I read it with real interest. Besides dealing with Mysticism, the sovereign science, it contains some very fine pages, such as the one on 'the Devil's hole' on the subject of Bunyan, and another on temptations undergone by poets, which provoked painful memories for me, reminding me how terrible such trials are; for I know them only too well, having endured them myself a few years ago.

Now a little note at the bottom of page 21 suggests a number of thoughts. You speak sympathetically about Verlaine; but from the very wording of this note, it would seem to emerge that you are not familiar with his work, and that you speak of him mainly from what Lemaître has said.[41]

If that were to be the case, would I dare to beg you, Reverend Father, you who love art and mysticism, to read *Sagesse* by Verlaine; I should be very surprised if you did not admire, besides the extraordinary poetic talent, that note of humble faith, virtually lost since the Middle Ages, which springs forth from almost every page of this book.

It takes the monstrous misunderstanding of Catholics in questions of art and their stubborn and instinctive hatred of mysticism for this admirable volume not to have been vaunted and cried from the house tops. It was a glorious and unique event for the Church; the only thing she could have set against the works of great talent produced by profane poets.

The Church, which in former times led everything, no longer leads anything now; these last years, the whole artistic world has functioned outside of and distant from her. You will admit that that is really sad. And was not this situation created by her sons who consider words as bearing the imprint of the Devil's seal, and art to be a sin? Instead of reading those debilitating little books of piety, they would do well to reread Odo of Cluny[42] and St Bernard; they would soon see if they were prudish and strait-laced, if they were afraid of ideas and of words. Are not the masculine candour and brutal frankness a tonic for souls that needs no additive ever since those times?

But, you will think, why is this man telling me all this? Since he knows that I love Mysticism and Art? The fact is that these observations do not have their *raison d'être* in your kind and attentive gift, but they came to me via a quite simple chain of thought, and so, naturally, I wrote them down. *A propos* of Verlaine, I remembered thoughts of a similar kind that came to me recently in the adorable cathedral of Chartres. Amongst the marvellous sculptures it houses is one representing the scene of the Circumcision. Well! Do you know what the clergy of Chartres have come up with? Out of prudishness(!!!) they have stuck a piece of paper to the stomach of Jesus! That's the limit!

Sorry for having inflicted this train of thought on you; take no notice of it, and be good enough to see in this letter only the sincere thanks of him to whom the spontaneous gift and reading of your brochure gave great pleasure.

Please accept, Reverend Father, this expression of my respect.

Huysmans

To CATHARINA L. M. ALBERDINGKTHIJM

6 May 1895

Dear Sir,[43]

You ask me if poor Durtal finally managed to silence himself and stop analysing himself. No; nothing is more difficult than not to listen to oneself, but we must, I think, make this sad faculty work for the greater good, or rather for the lesser evil. With the help of Our Lord, one can, by dint of reflections, direct one's steps towards that supreme virtue, humility. When one observes oneself closely, when one lets one's tongue go, one is forced to admit that one is a quite wretched creature; the best thought is immediately spoilt by a bad one. Do some good action, a charitable deed,, for example – it is quite rare for a certain feeling of vanity, of self-congratulation, not to creep in. It is very painful, for the more one analyses oneself, the more one notices it. I have suffered greatly from that. But truly, is it not salutary from one point of view? Is one not obliged to admit that one is incapable of any absolute cleanness of soul? By dint of realizing this wretchedness, one can, I believe, become less vile; that is what I personally would like to try and do at least.

Moreover it is the only antidote I know to the poison of analysis that you talk about. Ah! Blessed are the simple, like my Brother Siméon the Trappist! They are the privileged ones; they do not even know what analysis is, but then they have not suffered the rotting effect of literature for years on end. Still, I think there is no cause for despair; each one is led by a different way. With a little goodwill, everything falls into place, the Blessed Virgin is satisfied with so little.

All the best to you, sir, in Our Lord,

Huysmans

To ANDRÉ GIDE

19 May 1895

Dear Sir and Colleague,

I have just read the enigmatic *Paludes*[44] and it really interested me, as an ironical study of egotism, of impulsive thoughts and a mania for order; then the amusing hopping from one idea to another! There are some quite denigrating and some quite nice scenes at Angèle's, and from all this couldn't-care-less attitude of literature that contemplates its own navel, there emerge some very penetrating and artistic pages, that make a garland for the dainty spiritual dance that seems to bring movement to the lines of the book.

And so I am grateful to you, for allowing me to read it; it restores us after the coarse food served up to us by the bookshops, and I tell you so with a good shake of the hand.

Yours

Huysmans

To EDMOND DE GONCOURT

16 May 1895

My Dear Master,

I have just read your latest *Journal*,[45] which you were good enough to send me. It is penetrating, alive like its older brothers, with I know not what nuance of melancholy irony, more sensitive perhaps than in the earlier ones. As I close it, a regret comes that you did not give more of your impressions of that formidable cast-iron jamboree, the Exhibition.[46] What you do say about it is so extraordinary, expressed in such a definitive way, that I am almost cross with you for not having given us sooner this portrait that no one else, in any other book, has known how to convey.

You see, when one has discovered the meaning of Annam Theatre, and that admirable belly dance with little leaps of the navel, one can bring to life again all on one's own this surprising and unforgettable period.

Then what a feeling for cats you have, you know how to interpret their eyes. And I laugh, thinking about your note on convent cats, saying to myself that the nuns you mention would do well not to have castrated male cats, for the castrator's art has been lost, like everything else. There are no longer any paeans for tom cats, only real butchers who perform the operation badly, and then so many of them become obscene.

I used to have one, an enormous ginger one, that I had castrated. I had gone to a reputed specialist, who whipped off his testicles in the wink of an eye, replacing them with two smears of butter. He was a clumsy virtuoso, who sacrificed everything for effect; the result was that the creature spent its time in search of female clothing, and would trample it, roll it about and curl up on it, wearing itself out in these fruitless labours, which, moreover, ended in paralysis. It was at one and the same time pitiful and comic. You can well imagine a convent of nuns watching the silent mating of this poor creature!

On the subject of nuns, I believe there is a small error on page 279. In fact they are not Benedictines but Augustinians in the rue de la Santé.

But I am talking about the Exhibition and about cats, when I ought also to be talking about the attractive and accurate observations of colour, of the painting your book contains, and the feeling of relief one experiences at seeing your despisal of the hotchpotch of politics these days. That and so many other things, spread throughout these truthful pages.

Thank you also for sending me a handsome copy, and for the nice things you said about me in it, and for your opinion of *Là-Bas*, of which I am really proud.

I assure you, dear master, of my respect and devotion.
   Yours

Huysmans

To CATHARINA L. M. ALBERDINGKTHIJM

[20 May 1895]

Dear Sir,

It seems to me that you are going through a crisis that is singularly similar to the one I experienced a month before setting off for the Trappist monastery. It is a desire to run away, anywhere other than to the place where one should go. I endured an awful month like that, alone in Paris, with no spiritual help. I had arrived at a point of desperation through fear, I was positively in a panic. But I hope it will be for you as it was for me. When the moment comes, all these fears fade, perhaps it is necessary to exhaust all one's apprehensions; it is the waiting that is the worst; one's scruples keep going through the pockets of one's soul, and as one is incapable of thinking of anything else, life becomes unbearable; but you will see, the deed itself, at the moment you do it, will be a relief. But anyway, you can accept that God will support you, and that, from that moment on, what seems so hard to you will happen quite naturally.

As far as your little treasures are concerned, really I fail to understand you. Is it not God who is the supreme artist, who adores art? Why reproach yourself with this taste and wish to deprive yourself of it? It excludes neither charity nor duty. But the Middle Ages are full of saints who were mad about it! So do not trouble yourself about that, take a broader view. You tell me that you went on a retreat at Beuron,[47] and that you were unmoved there. If you were to go there tomorrow, perhaps you would be. I believe that it is necessary for one's soul to be in a state of neutrality, which is very hard, in order to be in tune with monastic life, and to be able to gloss over the human element, which is of necessity part of it. I have to admit now that the Benedictines are not very attractive from the point of view of pure saintliness; I have friends amongst them, I have spent a few weeks with them at Saint-Wandrille; it was quite different, too much so, from my little Trappist house.

Then souls have different needs. You, manifestly, are an active type; thus you are infinitely more suited to the apostolate than to the enclosed life; I on the contrary dream now only of a locked cell. Both kinds are necessary in religion; the one complements the other.

Ah, all is not a bed of roses when one spews up one's former life and returns to God. I know something about that, and human nature is so base that some evenings one comes to miss the former, easy life, the relationships that have been broken off. One feels alone and discouraged, bound by the new obligations. But is it not fair that it should be so? Is not expiation for the mess of one's life indispensable?

You asked me if I am not happier now. Yes and no. Yes, in the sense that I am less disgusted with myself; no, if I think of all the bothers, all the material and spiritual worries, that religion gives me. All in all, I am without any great sensible consolations, but, on the contrary, I feel myself being led;

I am convinced that I have to suffer this state of dryness, that it is necessary and just.

And basically, for nothing in the world would I take up my old life again. And then there are some delicious moments. At Chartres, in the ancient crypt, I experience masses at five o'clock in the morning where I am literally filled, where I am happy. It is more than one deserves.

The bad thing is to be lacking in trust and in love! Alas, alas, what can be done, other than to wait humbly for this state of affairs to cease? I have written to my good little convent at Fiancey,[48] and all the old saints there are going to try to help you, to make as gentle as possible the transition between your two lives. In July, moreover, I shall try to go and see them.

You ask me if my origins are Dutch. Yes, all my family come from Breda, and I lived there myself in my childhood. I still have many relations in Holland, at The Hague etc.; but I have so little to be thankful for in that direction that I have broken off all contact with them. They are Catholics, atrocious Pharisees, in love with money above all else. That is all there is to it.

Yes, if you could get me any information at all about good Lydwina,[49] you would be most useful to me. I have always dreamt of writing her life, when I am in my cell. She is such a rare and delicious saint!

Goodbye for now, dear sir. Do not get discouraged, pray a lot. The Lord is with you, you can be sure of that. The very idea of what you wish to do is proof of it. And once you are on the right road, why doubt any more?

Yours, in Our Lord,

Huysmans

To DR POL DEMADE

2 June 1895

I truly believe, my dear colleague, that your *Âme princesse*[50] should have ranked amongst the *Celestials* that d'Aurevilly dreamt of, but never wrote. It has a heroic conception that is worthy of him, but more than that, it is afire with the flames of Catholicism, that he would have stoked up less violently.

The most masterly pages of this book give me that impression: the one beginning *The Church prevents love*! They are superb, and contain a magnificent vehemence of soul. The whole story is curious – that is good – but those pages excel, and make even the delicate pages of *Double Amour* fade into the background.

How right you are to demand for Catholics the right to portray passion, life! But no work of art would be possible with the opposite system, and along with Barbey and Villiers, you have furnished palpable proof that art can evolve with just as much liberty when dealing with Catholic subjects as with modern profane subjects.

And so I thank you for enabling me to read *L'Histoire du Prince* and I take advantage of this opportunity to send you, my dear colleague, a most cordial shake of the hand.

Your devoted

Huysmans

To DR POL DEMADE

9 June 1895

Dear Sir and Colleague,

I thank you for your kind letter. You are right, a thousand times over, in thinking of making a study of the fathers and sacred writers from a realist point of view. For they all were realists from St Bernard up until gentle Angela of Foligno, of whom we have only translations that reduce her in stature. And what frankness we find with these saints! No one more than they spoke their mind to the clergy. Look at St Hildegarde or St Catherine of Siena:[51] they spoke sincerely, without being afraid of words! And what about the whole of Flemish art? Where not those Primitives highly exalted realists?

There would be quite a curious study to be done, and you would be doing a real service by undertaking it. Perhaps the Catholics would finally understand that they have drowned the magnificent art of the Church in a watered-down style.

As for the subject you ask me about, the way of the cross, it is crushing! Think about it, it is perhaps worth a try, but not at home; if one were in His home – but then one would need to have been through a process of purification in order to attempt it!

Later, if things work themselves out in my life, if God gives me sufficient protection to be able finally to follow my inclinations . . . we shall see. I am full of admiration for what God can do for a soul. I have received some divine letters from a Dutch man,[52] superior to any literature! This man, crushed by the certainty of God, has given all his goods to the poor, and he lives amongst them, washes them, feeds them and makes them say their prayers. He wept when he had to sell his collection of trinkets and books. He used to be afraid of himself and of other people. Now he is overwhelmed with joy. Each day he is the servant of fifty paupers. That's beautiful, isn't it?

Moreover, without suspecting it, this man writes admirable things. God comes across in his every word. To think that I have had the frightful humiliation of offering advice to such a soul and giving consolation! The roles are really ridiculously reversed.

I still don't know whether I shall go to Belgium this year, for I am obliged to go to the south on urgent business concerning the future with Him . . . Pray for me, that what a saintly woman wishes for me might succeed.[53]

Thank you for your friendship, I take it to heart, I assure you.

Yours cordially,

Huysmans

To G. RAMAEKERS

18 June 1895

My Dear Colleague,

I did indeed bring out a preface to Jules Bois' book on *Satanism and Magic*, although this book could not be less Catholic, and even expresses ideas which, I beg you to believe, I am far from sharing.

Moreover, I say so twice in my preface.

For me, the essential is this: to expose the sacrilegious inanities of the demoniacs, to shed light on a surface that is still hidden under a veil of darkness. Now if I had waited for a talented Catholic to tackle the subject – I began the task in *Là-Bas* – many years would have gone by, I believe. And time is short, for Satanism is profiting from the complacency which is guaranteed by the popular press, in order to rise up and gradually take a hold on everything.

I would add that in order to write a well-researched book on the Devil and magic, it needed a writer who was willing to spend three years in libraries, and to be of unquestionable literary integrity.

Bois fulfilled these two conditions; what is more, he is talented, and so his own ideas are not so important, if he is fighting the good fight with us. In all this, we are the snipers of an army that is making no advance; whose fault is it?

Do you not think that I would prefer to preface a book that was orthodox? But, I repeat, where is it?

Then I must admit that despite all his erroneous opinions, Jules Bois is a very honest lad, with a clean soul, and these days that is something to be encouraged!

That, my dear colleague, is the explanation of this preface that seems to be bothering you; I believe it is simple and truthful, as you can see.

Yours

Huysmans

To FR GABRIEL FERRET

[13 July 1895]

Dearest Friend,

I received your letter this morning and am answering it without delay; your excursion into the mountains sounds quite tiring to me, and I fear you will end up returning to us exhausted from all this running about. Fortunately I am keeping a good, restorative bottle for you when you are next in Paris, which we all hope will be as soon as possible.

As for me, I am not too bad for the moment. Boucher and I spent two days in Dijon, amongst the splendours of Burgundian art, and basically I have not changed, I am much more excited by a work of art than by nature itself. I prefer cathedrals even to the sea.

In Dijon, we went to confession and to communion in the chapel of the Black Virgin; then, although we were both very tired, we explored the museum and all the churches. What a fine artistic centre Dijon is!

Once back in Paris, I went straight away to Notre-Dame des Victoires. Ah, dear friend! If your journey does not go according to your wishes, it won't be my fault, for in all these places, and in the chapel at St-Sulpice, I have indeed prayed for you! But I see that the Virgin answers your prayer, that you are well and happy, and I thank her.

For my part, I have written to the Mother Superior at Fiancey. Although it was a very friendly letter, I could not stop myself giving her my opinion on that disgusting man Kneipp.[54] I did it quite outspokenly, but I hope she will not take offence. Basically I did not feel courageous enough to hide my thoughts from her. Perhaps our letters will make her think.

Poor Fiancey! I think melancholy thoughts about it on my terrace, as I contemplate rooftops by way of mountains, and forests of pipes in place of poplars.

Basically it was a stay full of gentleness, and I spent some unforgettable hours there with you. Better than ever before, I understood the joy of the canonical offices and the sweetness of communion. What a shame that one cannot choose such a monastery! It seems to me that one would not have turned out too badly there! Alas, all that is only a dream. the truth is that the monasteries are in a bad way.

On my return, I found a letter from Fr Parisot,[55] obviously not read by his abbot, a painful letter, and rather bitter about his order, which does not keep the promises it makes to postulants. I feel very awkward about answering it. That goes to show, in any case, that there is total chaos at Ligugé. No, you must not let little Arnaud go there;[56] for I am convinced that even a retreat in that place would be very bad for him. How could God protect such an order? Decidedly there is nothing to be done with it.

Ligugé, Fiancey – what wretchedness! Dear friend, what I want to tell you now is how fond I am of you and how much I thank the Blessed Virgin for letting me meet you. She does things in princely fashion! Ah, if She would complete Her merciful Goodness, and give us a little monastery. Perhaps She will agree to it. Her Son is so badly served. However, She could not ignore artistic volumes written for Her and to Her glory! There is so much work to be done in that direction; it seems to me that one can really count on divine aid for some work that is necessary and does not exist. To think that it is nearly four years since I went to the Trappists for the first time, and that a single day will not have gone by without my having been haunted by the desire for a monastery. what would be the point then, if it were all to come to nothing!

I thank you for getting the convents to pray, their prayers will be most useful to us.

Greetings from all the friends, and from Mother Thibault, who thanks you for the prayers and is also praying for you. As for me, I embrace you with all my heart, and remain dear friend, in filial devotion, your

Huysmans

To AUGUSTE LAUZET

5 January 1896.

My Dear Friend,

I was not without news of you, for I saw Robert from time to time on Sundays at the Benedictine convent in the rue Monsieur, but I am well pleased to learn from yourself that you are finally cured. You owe the Virgin a good candle! And you are working courageously, that is real and complete joy!

You ask what I am up to. As life has a limited range of felicity and disaster, I spent 1895 somewhere between these two extremes. *En Route* has been a prodigious success that I was hardly expecting, and for the first time I am experiencing sizeable print runs, for the book continues to sell as on its first day. My health, on the other hand, has been in a deplorable state: dyspepsia and frightful intestinal pains that have made me waste a year. I was supposed to go to the Benedictines at the centuries-old monastery of Saint-Maur, situated on an island in the Loire, and I have not yet been able to take refuge there, even though this would have been an important step for me, for I was in such a battered state. All I have been able to do is drag myself around cathedrals on little day trips: Amiens, Bourges, Tours, Poitiers, etc. For that is what I am up to.

It will take two or three years' work.[57] If I can only manage to do it, I will have given expression to the soul of the Church in its entirety: mysticism, symbolism, liturgy, literature, the arts of painting, sculpture, music and architecture. As you can imagine, it is a formidable task, and I hack away at it despairingly, collecting together material from all sources, taking Chartres cathedral as my model, for it is the most beautiful of all, the most intelligible, and grouping the others around it, and similarly for the symbolism of colours, I shall gather some of the Primitives around Fra Angelico, the most easily discernible and intelligible of all.

All this is a simple novel set in Chartres, with Durtal and Fr Gevrésin.[58]

On account of lack of space, and given the book's setting, I was unable to tackle in *En Route* the second part of the mystic tree: painting, sculpture and especially architecture, and all that is now the subject of my next book, which will complement mysticism, religious music and the literary art of the Church.

But that is not all. I need to revise the whole of medieval symbolism, symbolism of the forms of the Chruch, of the colours of paintings and of stained glass, etc.

Ah, there are the bare bones of it, dear friend, but when it comes to building up with black dots on white paper the great mass of the cathedrals, I sweat at the thought of it. Fortunately there is no hurry, and I don't give a damn about the press and the reading public.

Another piece of news: as you probably know, old Misme has died, and so I have taken in Mother Thibault, who had nowhere to go; fortunately I found a room on the same landing as myself. And we are living more or less together. She does the housekeeping and cooking. It has brought peace to us both, for me who am not well and need to work quietly, away from people, and for her, as the work is not arduous.

So there is the news, dear friend. I will give you less of people you know about. I know that Lorrain is finally cured, but I have not seen him for almost a year, any more than Bauer.[59] I have not really had the time. On the other hand, I have seen Le Cardonnel, who is studying for the priesthood in Rome.[60] I saw him together with an old abbess at a place where I had gone for a few days to be cosseted by little nuns. He is pleased, and is charming and gentle. Boucher is well, and so is Fr Mugnier, whom I saw recently.

You will doubtless have heard of the death of Dubus.[61] There were strange happenings there; he was genuinely possessed. I have not been able to forget him since one morning when he came to see me, a few days before his death. Poor creature!

Greetings to Mme Jacquemin,[62] and all the best to you, dear friend, with wishes for continued good health and the hope of seeing you in Paris again soon, even if only passing through, please?

Mother Thibault sends you affectionate greetings to which I add my own.
    Affectionately yours,

Huysmans

To MARC-ANDRÉ RAFFALOVICH

[1896]

Dear Sir,

The world of sodomy, your book,[63] your letter all reminded me of some frightening evenings I spent in those circles, into which I had been led by a talented boy,[64] whose deviant pleasures are a secret to no one. I spent a few days there, then they noticed that I was a fake, a phoney, and I managed to extricate myself, narrowly missing being beaten up.

It put me in mind of hell. Think about it: the man who has this vice voluntarily withdraws from commerce with ordinary men. He eats in restaurants, has his hair done, takes lodgings in establishments run by old sodomites. It is a life apart, in a constricted corner, a confraternity recognizable by the voice, the fixed gaze and affected singsong intonation they all have.

What is more, this vice is the only one that overrides class. The decent man and the rogue are equals, they converse naturally and without distinction of rank. This vice achieves what charity fails to, equality between people. Isn't that strange and disturbing?

But what a life it is for a decent lad such as my guide, devoured by this vice and permanently in danger of jealous stabbings!

One evening, in a bar in the rue des Vertus frequented by that milieu, where sixty-year-old queers, made up like old actors, operate behind a curtain, I saw a well-known theatrical type come in. He obviously had a lewd assignation in that meeting place. I have never seen anything so sinister. The man's face was livid, a sadness to make one weep, goaded on by his vice, as if pushed from behind, disgusted with himself, evidently struggling against himself, but carrying on all the same, with the collar of his coat turned up! When you have seen that, you can really thank Heaven for not having given you such tastes! And chastity seems to have an undeniable grandeur, and to be the only decent thing that exists. I know young men with souls of perfect whiteness, as are their bodies; these children have an aura, have something exquisite about them that those who 'know' a woman or a man will never have.

One really needs to have lived in these opposing worlds to have any notion that such people belong to the same race. Clothing can be misleading. Yet their bodies are the same, but that is where the soul, so much denigrated, emerges. It completely transforms everything.

What emerges clearly and distinctly, and it is that that is difficult to explain, is that it is amongst well-built, hefty men that this passion flourishes. The butchers of La Villette, fairground strongmen, the porters at Les Halles nearly all go in for this vice. Many of them are the active partner, but there are a lot of passives amongst them too.

The bars of the rue V. are the meeting places of this milieu, where one finds pell-mell along with the dockers, butchers' boys, slaughterers from the abattoir and weightlifters.

Contrary to received opinion and the ideas of Mlle de Lespinasse,[65] it is not to a weak constitution or delicate nerves that this passion is to be attributed. They are pure brutes, like those strong men who hate women the most and seek out big men too, for these people have a horror of pretty boys and weaklings.

Des Esseintes is an exception at that vice as at all of them; all in all, he is almost an unlikely sodomite, given his build; he is an amateur who would be singularly despised by this clan.

How can one explain how a big strong man who, one would think, would be attracted by a weak creature such as woman, on the contrary rejects her and seeks out his own kind? When I have asked them, these people have always answered: 'It's the smell: women's flesh is sickly, she has an ugly shape, etc.' In short, the phrase 'wholesome flesh' was used repeatedly of their own sex.

I give you these vague answers for what they might be worth, but what I guarantee is the genuineness of the taste of the colossus for other men.

Les Halles are the real hunting ground for deviant love and from that point of view, Zola's *Le Ventre de Paris*, which did not see beyond the food for sale, is really worthless and void of any serious study.

It seems, moreover, that the vocal organs have a special influence on these tendencies in women. Take singers, how many of them have a penchant for other women?

It is true that by an opposite effect, sodomy changes the voice, which becomes almost identical in all of them. After several days' study in that world, from nothing but the sound of the voice of people I did not know, I could infallibly predict their tastes. Do you not think there would be research to be done on the influence of one organ on another?

Yours

Huysmans

To DOM BESSE

26 January 1896

My Dear Father,

All of us here are glad to see that you are immersed in *The Benedictine Monk*.[66] Such a book, written by a monk, could render great service, if it were to be well launched and could reach the public. From that point of view, Liguge should make an agreement with a major religious publishing house in Paris, Tousselgue or Lecoffre, people who have agents in all countries, and the means to launch a book. That is a weakness with Benedictine publications, you don't see them anywhere, they bury themselves with inert and mute publishers.

The Benedictine Monk will be timely, against the diabolical hatred that is coming to the surface at the moment. It could be a defence of the magnificent monastic life, make it understood at last, at a time when Freemasonry is seeking to give the Church a blow on the head by persecuting the religious orders. There are going to be some hard times to get through, for certain. I personally know something about it since *En Route*, which marked me out as an enemy in the office. Still, we must hope that the storm will pass, and will not succeed in uprooting any order. But what an age we live in all the same!!

I am still immersed in my work, which at least permits me to live in another period, and to abstract myself a little from the chaos that surrounds me. Unfortunately the citadels of the spirit are fragile, and the enemy destroys them without great difficulty; and the whole of modern life floods in through the breach. That is when one really envies monastic life, the possibility of being recollected, taking on a long-term work in peace. In Paris it is impossible, there are distractions even in the churches. How far removed it all is from closed and cloistered chapels!

M. and G. are well.[67] In the students' chapel at St-Sulpice, Fr Ferret and they are trying to ensure a victory for plainchant, but he is having hardly any success; the other priests at St-Sulpice are hostile for the most part and the public even more so. One would need to take infinite precautions, use cunning and astuteness to get rid of this liking for operatic masses amongst such people.

Fortunately Fr Ferret is endowed with remarkable stubbornness, just like Fr Vigourel;[68] they will have a job to make him give up, but I feel sorry for him, for he will make enemies; all the more so, as the choirmaster and Widor,[69] the organist, who are greatly displeased at the hiding I did not spare them in *En Route*, are doing all they can to stop plainchant triumphing in their church. Boucher is well. He is still busy with the ethnography of Poitou, and hopes his efforts will be successful.

I am asked to convey many greetings to you from Fr Ferret. No news from Saint-Wandrille. But I think Fr Ferret has seen Dom Pothier[70] in Paris in the chapel where the prior found the two renegades.

That is all for now, dear Father; do not forget us in your prayers, and be assured of our respect and affection.

J. K. Huysmans

To CHAMBRY OF *LE GIL-BLAS*

[10 February 1896]

My Dear Colleague,

You ask me to let you know my opinion on the decision of the cardinal archbishop of Paris, who has forbidden women to sing in churches.

My opinion is quite simple. Mgr Richard is entirely right. Moreover he has done no more than revive the centuries-old proscriptions that forbade the use of female voices in consecrated places.

The Church has always excluded from her liturgical ceremonies those voices which, moreover, are impure, unless they belong to enclosed nuns. Faithful to St Paul's *mulieres in ecclesiis taceant*,[71] she has always disapproved of female histrionics in the temple. In former times she went even further, since St Leu[72] ordered that women may be admitted to the sanctuary only with their heads veiled, and St Soter[73] ruled that the deaconesses, who were well-born and rich, may not touch the chalice veil or even put incense in the thuribles.

That shows you the extent to which the Church has wished women to take no part in the practice of the liturgy.

Doubtless today the majority of priests no longer think that women should simply pray and keep quiet in church. They unbridle them themselves, organizing Marian months when they squash them up alongside a harmonium, and incite them to sing extraordinary hymns with the bellowing of a rutting deer. From there to allowing solos and having them accompanied on the organ is but one step, and it was taken long ago.

Let us add that the greater number of priests, who show crass ignorance in matters of art, let themselves be put upon by their choirmasters and organists. They have only one aim, to get their musical rubbish performed free of charge by a choir converted into an opera chorus, helped by an orchestra, embellished with solos by histrionic women.

And the priest is in ecstasy, while the musicians regret that the audience cannot applaud and shout *encore* as at a concert.

Mgr Richard judged that it was time to bring these grocers of the temple back to respect for their priesthood. He has done well, but while he was about it, His Eminence would have done well to take another measure as well, which would have been formally to ban all profane music, and to impose Gregorian chant in all the churches of his diocese.

Then he could have flattered himself on having done something really useful!

Yours etc.

Huysmans

To F. A. CAZALS

29 February 1896

My Dear Sir,

Amongst your alert and lively portraits which are, in a sense, the fixed landmarks of physiognomy in the amazing mobility of Verlaine's private life, there are two, above all, that hold my attention from differing points of view.

And face to face with one of them, I really appreciate your ability to create life in a few brush-strokes, and quite distant memories well up inside me.

I see Verlaine once more, just as you showed him, on the bench of a café, his head thrown back, his eyes closed. As far as I can remember, he had not been back in France long. A mutual friend, the good Robert Caze, had brought us together at his lodgings in the rue Rodier. Very few writers at that time knew *Sagesse*, which had been so carefully thrust to the back of a cupboard in a Catholic bookshop. For the author, I believe it was a bit of legitimate pleasure to hear the two of us speaking in admiration, which he felt to be genuine; and he let himself go, and all the affectionate side of the child and the good fellow in him gushed forth.

After dinner, we took him off to Villiers de l'Isle-Adam's, whom he had not seen for years. We ended up in Pousset's beer shop, with a series of outpourings that culminated in some of those stories that only Villiers knew how to tell. And I can see Verlaine in that pose that you have conveyed so well, watching his ebullient friends with his small eyes that revealed recollection, and waving his lock of hair with a shake of his head, moving back as if to take his distance, then raising his arms in the air and leaning his whole trunk over the table that divided them.

That is indeed the Verlaine of your sketch, accurate to a nuance; nevertheless you have perhaps made him more somnolent, but he was not listening to Villiers at the time.

The other portrait, the poet's head, in hospital against the background of a window whose bars formed a cross behind him, evokes the other side of this dual soul, so effusive in its religion and so tender; in a sense it sums up for me a symbol of Verlaine the solitary, Verlaine the mystic.

And it is really in this so simple composition that you were able to uncover the glorious effigy of the writer that the Catholics rejected, when they should have thanked Heaven for having given them a king among poets. What pharisees, what stupidity!

In your series, these two portraits of Verlaine seem to me to represent the cloudy and the bright weather of the seasons of his soul. Your other drawings link these two, and convey in such a lively manner differing episodes: the morose artist, almost anxious in the streets of London,[74] and the pensive poet, looking around as he walks leaning on his cane, or in his hospital clothes, surrounded by the painful spectacle of those crushed by life.

Yours, dear sir,

Huysmans

To ÉMILE ZOLA

14 May 1896

My Dear Friend,

Thank you for *Rome*,[75] which I have just finished. With the book closed, there rises before me, as I look for an evocative summing up, amidst the seething crowds that you alone can render, the extraordinary figure of Boccanera, who is the finest and proudest you have created, and who strikes such a clear contrast with the two extreme characters, the Italian Saccard, and Nani, whose attractive suppleness leaves its fragrant mark on the whole book. Your churches of Rome, from a descriptive point of view, and especially from the mystic point of view, are absolutely beautiful, with a discreet reminder of Gothic cathedrals. There is no point in telling you, is there, that I admire the great set pieces in the book, the scene of the papal reception, the ball, all the great gatherings; but I think that that is not the most unexpected part, the newest note in the book. It is rather, I believe, to be found in the great mass of ideas that it stirs up, this immense panorama of centuries passed under review with a dense and penetrating conciseness.

It is a book stuffed full with ideas, debatable perhaps, especially those at the end, but in the anaemia of our day, *Rome* is the proud product of your labours and a high flier!

If I had to sum up my impression, I would quite readily say – the similarity of the subject matter makes it appropriate – that it is the Zola of *La Curée*, with the added stature of a thinker, however worn and hackneyed that phrase may be.

And so I thank you, dear friend.

Yours

Huysmans

To CHARLES RIVIÈRE

28 May 1896

Dear M. Rivière,

I had been thinking of you constantly for a week, saying to myself: he had promised to come to Paris, and, like Sister Anne, I did not see anyone coming, when your letter arrived.

Alas! It proposes things that are beyond the bounds of possibility. I am confined to Paris by the ministry, where the holidays are beginning, and as my turn has not yet come, it is all the more difficult to get even a day off, as the others are not there, and we stand in for each other in turn.

I shall perhaps be free in the second half of July. I shall go to Solesmes, where Very Reverend Father Delatte is expecting me; if I were to have time, and were not feeling too bad – which, alas, is becoming a dream – perhaps I might push on to Igny, where I should be truly happy to spend a few days of recollection in good and healthy solitude.

I am still immersed in a huge work on medieval symbolism, cathedrals, all the old science of the Church, that it would perhaps be possible to bring to life again for the profane. Basically, the world is full of people who want nothing better than to admire, to walk in the right direciton, all that is needed is to catch them. Only this time, it is harder: plainchant and mysticism were more accessible to the masses than symbolism. Still, we shall see. In any case, I needed to complete *En Route*, which was unfinished, due to lack of space; three elements of religious art were missing: Primitive painting, medieval sculpture, cathedrals.

What else can I tell you? Other than that my soul is still mediocre, but well supported, I must admit, by so many devoted souls that the good Lord has given me at St-Sulpice and in Benedictine convents. They are my eternal good Samaritans! Only, you know what is frightening: to be so well protected and to continue to drag oneself along in a depressingly earth-bound way, without any real progress along the path one should be climbing up with resolute step. It is marking time on the spot; as St Teresa so rightly says, making no advance is a step backwards. Sometimes I reflect bitterly, for it is nearly five years now since I turned my life upside down; without merit, by a special grace, I have been able to live chastely and to keep on praying, but, but . . . nothing more. To sum it up, I go to communion only out of obedience. I am happy afterwards, yes, that is certain, but what dryness of soul beforehand, and what an effort! All in all, my seven or eight communions a year shatter me. Ah no, things are not brilliant, pray for me.

I should be very happy to see you, and I shall have to be in a bad way not to go and seek you out, if you don't come here. Will you offer my most respectful greetings to the very Reverend Father Abbot, to Fr Bernard, Fr Léon, and for yourself, dearest sir, the assurance of my affectionate deovition in Our Lord.

Yours

Huysmans

To ABBESS CÉCILE OF SOLESMES

16 October 1896

Dear Madam,

The little box is in Dom Thomas's hands, and you have made someone very happy, that was plain to see.

On the way back from Solesmes, I stopped off at Chartres, and there I was the inadequate, but at least faithful, missionary of your requests with Her. In return for this small service, may I remind you of the great promise you made me, in promising the prayers of your abbey.

I am in great need of them. How vain and empty Paris seems to me since I have been back! Decidedly one's heart takes root at Solesmes without one's suspecting it, the realization comes when one is no longer there.

The monastery of St Pierre was so paternal and so good to me that it is not without great melancholy that I think of it, now that I shall not be able to see it again for months.

And then I am haunted by the unforgettable matins at Ste Cécile. What a dream of faith and art they arouse.

I am immersed in your *Treatise on Prayer*[76] and am enchanted by its perfect lucidity. I shall try to set right in my next book that sentence that did not express my own opinion. As for the others,[77] I could not change their meaning without lying, consequently I am conscience-bound to retain them. This moreover is the opinion of all my friends, whom you would be sorry to upset.

Allow me to thank you once more for your kind welcome, and beg you to receive my respectful and devoted greetings in Our Lord.

J. K. Huysmans

Fr Ferret, to whom I have just given the book, thanks you for it, sends his greetings, and asks to be remembered in your prayers.

To DOM THOMASSON DE GOURNAY

20 October 1896

My Dear Father,

It is quite some time since I wrote to you – and how much has happened since! I am sending this letter to you in Bordeaux on the off chance, hoping that all the prayers for your return to health have been answered, and that my letter will doubtless be forwarded to Saint-Maur.

I am just back from Solesmes, where I spent some clement hours, enraptured by the Fathers' plainchant, and more especially by that of the Benedictine nuns, which remains unforgettable. We have no notion of that in Paris. In the rue Monsieur, it is a feminine warble. They know they are being listened to on the other side of the grille. At Ste Cécile, the voices seem seraphic and virile. At matins, some of the psalms have an incredible outburst of spirit, vying with the heavenly chorus. And then hovering over Solesmes is the admirable abbess. Her good grace towards me was really touching, and in chatting with her, I was able to ascertain that the soul of the great medieval abbesses lives on. She is profound and charming, extraordinary. At St Pierre, I ended up coming to appreciate the Fr Abbot too, who is singularly intelligent and really good. Lord, what a difference between such a handler of souls and the abbot of Ligugé whom I saw before!! I chatted very freely with him about this Solesmes business,[78] and I am very pleased to have been put in the picture and to have had the matter cleared up once and for all, concerning all the intrigue stirred up by bad monks. I was spoilt – by the good sisters, Doms Mocquereau, Mellet, Bourré, Olivieri! That is compensation for worldly relationships I assure you, and gives one a yearning for monastic life.

What is more, I was in luck – I was present at the taking of the cowl by two little lay brothers. It was very moving and very beautiful, and as I was there for the feast of the Dedication, I witnessed some splendid offices, and saw Dom Delatte officiating pontifically.

And what about you? Are you better, my dear Father? When you have a free moment, write to me on that matter. Fr Mugnier has just got an amazing promotion. He has leapt from being second curate at Notre-Dame des Champs to first curate at Ste Clotilde, the famous Parisian parish; so he is on the road to a bishopric. We are all very pleased for him.

Do not forget me in your prayers, my dear Father, and accept this affectionate expression of my respect.

Huysmans

I am still immersed in cathedrals; I really do not know how I shall cope with this crazy work.

To FR JULES PACHEU, S.J.

10 December 1896

Dear Father,

When I wrote to you about poor Verlaine, I said what I thought and still think, consequently I see no problem about your publishing the fragments of the letters you quoted in your affectionate missive. Make the great poet loved and forgive the man, who was weak, and that will be a truly good work.

As for *La Cathédrale* that you mention, it is a work of transition – of waiting, to be more accurate. I lead Durtal from the Trappists to Solesmes. All in all, it is simply a complement to *En Route*. In this latter volume, I was not able to include all the great symbolism of the Middle Ages, neither architecture nor painting. If I do this, I shall have just about covered all the admirable art of the Church; so this book is no more than that, Durtal settled in Chartres beside his cathedral, halfway to the monastery.

When it is finished, if God permits, Durtal will go away . . . and for good, to be with his friends the Benedictines – and then he might write the white book he has dreamt about so much.

The one about the cathedral is only grey. It won't upset the old prudery of the faithful, as it contains neither a woman nor carnal memories, nothing. But after all, whitewash from a cell wall is needed in order to write that white book – and a leather belt and a black scapular!

Yours

Huysmans

To Fr Jules Pacheu, S. J.

26 December 1896

My Dear Father,
   The title you announce does not seem a good one to me;[79] for without false modesty, in my soul and in my conscience, I believe that Verlaine was very superior in verse to what I might be in prose. So if there were a name that should be honoured in the title, it would be his. Why not this catchy title, let us spell it out: *From Dante to Verlaine*?[80] As for me, I am only a surrogate in all this. Note well, moreover, that there has been a great Catholic artist in our day, scorned by his own of course, but who was a fine prose writer, that is Barbey d'Aurevilly. In all fairness, that should be taken into account. Strange! But that man was the only one who saw things clearly in my case, after he had read *A Rebours* ... He wrote an article which contained these last prophetic words: 'There only remains for you to commit suicide or become a Catholic.'
   With the help of God, I adopted the second solution, or rather I did nothing at all, having been forcibly led to God, independently of my own will. I was evidently in need of cudgels, in order to overturn my life completely and to persevere in faith. If Father Delfour[81] had been through similar fear and anxiety, he would perhaps be less wary and show more good faith. Still, that is his affair.
   I am just back from Chartres, where I spent some delicious hours in the crypt, close to the Mother. All the rest is nought, compared to that!
   Affectionately yours, my dear Father,
   In Christo

Huysmans

To DOM THOMASSON DE GOURNAY

21 January 1897

My Dear Father,
   Firstly let me thank you for the excellent information on the properties attributed to certain plants, and now let me roughly explain the plan of the chapter on symbolic flora.
   The fundamental idea is this: a Benedictine liturgical garden, having a succession of flowers on account of their mystical associations or closeness to the scriptures or lives of the saints. And so would it not be admissible to follow the liturgy of the offices with that of plants, for them to be concurrent, to decorate altars with different arrangements according to the day and the feast, to link nature in its most exquisite aspect with religious ceremonies etc., etc.
   Once the principle is established, a vegetal transposition of certain ideas

is possible. Take the catechism, for example. I light upon the series of mortal sins and corresponding virtues, and set about transposing them; and I find them all in my floral version except for one sin: avarice! No possibility there; I cannot discover any plant interpreted in that way in the Middle Ages or now, whereas the others are easy.

It is the same for the four evangelists. Here I am obliged to have recourse to plants bearing their names in the Middle Ages. And so I discover: St Mark's herb, tamaesia, invoked for nervous illnesses; for St John I have heliotrope, for in a stained-glass window at St Rémy in Rheims, two stems of this flower are placed in his halo, to signify his gift of high inspiration. Difficulties begin with St Luke. Nothing in antiquity, but in her admirable visions, Sr Emmerich talks much of reseda in connection with this apostle. She links them, so that is all right; but St Matthew? Ah, nothing at all there.

Note that this more or less schematic outline is not as mad as it seems for, after all, the four evangelists are interpreted in the bestiary and also by gems. So why shouldn't they be by flowers?

All this is explained in my chapter, which must not exceed twenty pages: after a digression on purely medicinal plants, Albert the Great, Macer Florius, Walafried Strabo, the plants seen by Arthendorus in a dream, and the magical plants of St Hildegarde, I come to the construction of a vegetal church, following word for word the symbolism of Durand de Mende for the walls, turning the stones into flowers, or taking an unfinished chapel left as it is, and replacing the statues with flowers.[82]

In short, you see how far one can go along this path, without being completely mad.

It goes without saying that if there were a crypt, it would be constructed entirely with plants from the Old Testament. For this your information is perfect, for it completes what I had found out about cedars, olive trees, etc., and the amazing rhamnus, which was used to make Our Lord's crown of thorns, and of which it is said in the Book of Judges: '*Dixerunt omnia ligna ad rhamnum: veni et impera super nos.*'[83] Rohaut Fleury speaks about it interestingly in his *Instruments of the Passion*.

All in all, I am just about equipped now. In searching through the lives of the saints, I unearthed quite a few herbs connected with them or bearing their names; consequently they can be put in their chapels in place of painted or sculpted effigies if necessary. If in St Melito[84] you can discover a few plants with strange properties, unexpected meanings, dedicated to the Blessed Virgin or saints, that will suffice. I must quote that good bishop of Sardes a bit. But that is all. As I said, I have only twenty pages available in the book to align all these synonyms.

I forgot last time to tell you about Fr Mugnier. He has been appointed first curate at Ste Clotilde and is taking great strides towards a bishopric. Although he protests mildly, I think he would not be displeased at that purple flower. I hope for that; I have made him state before witnesses that the day he were made bishop, he would introduce Solesmes plainchant into his diocese. I would like it to happen at Chartres. Oh Lord, what a sweep with a clean broom that would be!

Be kind enough to pay my respectful homage to the Reverend Father Abbot, also all good wishes to Doms Mocquereau, Mellet, Bourré and to everyone, and affectionately yours, dear Father.

Huysmans

A curious plant for the chapel of Our Lady of the Seven Sorrows is the passionflower, which represents quite well all the instruments of the Passion, but I believe it did not exist in the Middle Ages!

To EDITH VALERIO

7 May 1897

Dear Madam,

The brief business relations we had on account of the terrible Quilter have not left the unpleasant memories you imagine,[85] and he is doubtless neither better nor worse than other directors of journals, for they all sink to the same level, within an inch or two.

And that is what makes placing your story in a publication here more or less impossible.

I find it interesting and very accurate in the notion that suicide depends on very little, a man passing by, a mere trifle; Hélène might not have killed herself, if the first impression of the wood had remained with her, but that is what magazines in Paris demand these days.

Anything like *La Revue indépendante*, where I could have got it accepted, no longer exists, properly speaking. The only one that comes near it, *La Revue blanche*, is a Jewish enterprise, and like the *Mercure de France*, these little businesses are strictly closed shops to those who don't belong and haven't invested any money in them.

Elsewhere, *La Revue des Deux Mondes*, *La Revue de Paris* and *La Nouvelle Revue* are in the hands of the students and lecturers of the École Normale Supérieure, our inveterate enemies, so there is not a single journal where one can place copy. It is quite simple: when one is not a member of a clique, everything is closed.

That is the exact state of the situation; and at the present moment, given the slump in the book trade, I do not see any prospect of change.

Provided you understand all this, and in accordance with your wishes, I am sending it to *Le Réveil* at the address given in your letter. Perhaps Belgium has some journals that are less clannish and more hospitable?

I have been without news of Villiers' child for some time now. The mother is unfortunately strange, and in a sense she has disappeared with him; the last news was saddening. The little one was very ill with old men's illnesses; there was talk of albuminuria and diabetes. Some of us got together then to have him sent to the country, but these plans did not suit the mother, and she has not been back since, and no one has been able to track down her address.

It is a sad story, I quite often wonder whether I did right to force poor Villiers into this marriage. The unfortunate thing is that this woman, who is completely uneducated and whose head has been somewhat turned, drags her new name about in a vague, begging sort of way. Still!

I see that you have traversed many countries since your stay in Paris. That still comes as a bit of a surprise to us stay-at-homes, but I wish you peace and good health in those remote territories, and you can be assured of my respect and devotion.

Huysmans

To DOM MICHEAU

23 November 1897

Dear Reverend Father,

It is me who is late in answering you, but if only you knew! I had to finish my great book *La Cathèdrale*, which is coming out at the end of January, and the research I did in Paris and at Solesmes to reconstitute the symbolism of the thirteenth century completely absorbed my time and energies. During the few days' break between finishing my book and its being sent to the printer's, I set off for Holland, to Schiedam, to seek out documents concerning St Lydwina, whose life I propose to write, as soon as I have a bit of free time. It was, alas, chaotic, and punctuated with great sorrow.

I have lost my poor friend whom you saw at Saint-Wandrille, Fr Ferret. I met him entirely through the will of Providence. Our lives were so intermingled that they made but one whole. And despite our besieging Him with prayers, Our Lord has called him back to Himself. He died as he lived, like a saint – but his loss is irreparable; I have felt singularly adrift ever since, and this at a time when I am experiencing terrible anguish in my soul.

Next year, I am retiring from the Ministry, where things are going badly, as I am considered to be pro-Church. And I shall have to make the awful decision.

For several years now, I have felt myself drawn towards monastic life, but now I am hesitating. I know what I want. Everyone discourages me; my new confessor, since the death of Ferret, does not know me well enough to be able to advise me. In short, I am eating my heart out, weary of living in Paris, far from God, despite everything, and desiring to come closer to Him; and then I draw back, seeing obstacles in the way, frightened at the poor state of my health. Added to that, I am passing through a period of dryness, my communions are as if dead, my prayers seem empty, in a word I am in complete darkness, without a light to show me the path to follow; and you, who know from experience how difficult it is to be sure of one's vocation, can judge for yourself the state of my poor soul, with all this being thrashed out in the midst of an over-busy life. Still, I tell myself, my book must come out first, and that perhaps I shall see things more clearly afterwards; then my pension qualification must reach its term at the Ministry, that gives me a bit more breathing space. Still there remains another frightful question: to which monastery should I go, supposing I were to make my mind up to it, and feel myself drawn to it. Those I know do not attract me at all, and that is another great cause of unrest for me. Despite the friends I have there, who are encouraging me to come, it seems to me that I have not found it yet. Ah, basically, how I would prefer it to be my little Trappist monastery at Igny, but after a week of their diet, I am prostrated. So I am obliged to put to one side the order I like best, by far; and the others, it is sad to say, are so full of bickering that one's soul would need to be singularly strong not to be troubled by it.

Still, I hope that God will finally enlighten me. Pray a little for that, dear Father, for I assure you that with all this questioning in my soul, I find very little happiness. I see that you have been to Ligugé and to Lourdes. This latter place is tempting, for if the horror of suffering is to be seen there, so too is the immense goodness of our gentle Mother.

I do not know the book you mention at all, but I will enquire at my bookseller's if there would be any means of getting hold of it. I will keep you informed of my researches.

I am sending you an *in memoriam* card for my poor Ferret.

That is all for now, dear Father; do not forget me in your prayers, and be assured of my respect and devotion.

J. K. Huysmans

To HENRI ALLAIS

31 January 1898

My Dear Friend,
 La Cathédrale is out this day, and I have myself put a nicely bound copy in the post addressed to you at la rampe Bouvreuil.

The article in *Le Figaro* is idiotic.[86] That 'Private Life of Huysmans' was written by a man *I have never seen* and who has never *been to my house*. It is a web of erroneous information supplied by a priest desperate for publicity.

It worries me on account of Solesmes. I do not at all know whether I shall enter there; I am flirting with the abbot; and my situation is now very difficult. In the meantime, I have no intention of entering straight away, as that fool Narfon maintains.

On Saturday I shall have an article, written by Descaves, put in *L'Écho de Paris*, to set the record straight.

Lord, who will deliver us from the busybodies of the press.

Cordially yours

Huysmans

To PAUL VALÉRY

10 March 1898

My Dear Friend,

When one can read it over in peace and quiet, the article[87] is very good, full of ingenious idea and sentences presenting the interesting medley of life; some are as if lit by a veiled lantern, whereas others shine forth with a fullness of light, and there are many finds, such as the souls of the blessed colouring in the sun. I assure you that you have no reason to worry. The article is out of the ordinary and is very good.

Thank you for all that, dear friend, and until the next time.

Your devoted

Huysmans

To CHARLES BRUN

13 April 1898

Dear Sir and Colleague,

I have found, in Stock's office, the article that you were good enough to write for the Lyons paper *France Libre* on *La Cathédrale*, and firstly I want to thank you for the goodwill that it contains, and the way in which it is expressed.

I thank you for having explained the book with such lucidity. It is evident that those who were expecting interesting states of soul on Durtal's part are disappointed, but such was not the purpose of the book. In *En Route*, basically there was mysticism and plainchant. I wished to complete the art of the Church: painting, sculpture, architecture, symbolism. If I had written a treatise on symbolism, no one would have read it. I have served it up in a vaguely novelish sauce, and it was a bit like the silver coating on pills that masks their repulsive appearance.

Fundamentally Durtal counts for nothing in the book, no more do his pastors. They are simply pawns in the game. Moreover I could not do it any other way than the way I have done, as I am full of dryness, and am thrashing about in the dark with my vocation. The freethinkers found it strange. That proves only one thing, that they know nothing of the very painful struggles that God makes souls pass through; but, one can only repeat, that was not the subject of the book. I am really grateful to you for having set things straight.

Basically, what a number of ecclesiastics find irritating is the language of my books. They reproach prayers that are not drawn up in the style they are accustomed to. What stupidity! And how formalistic and starchy they imagine God to be!

But here are a lot of useless sentences, when I simply wanted to thank you, sir, for your very kind and very wide-ranging article. Which I now do as I beg you to accept this expression of my good wishes.

Huysmans

To LÉON LECLAIRE

Saint-Maur de Glanfeuil
14 July 1898

My Dear Friend,

Your letter was handed to me just as I was leaving Solesmes. Here I am at Saint-Maur, a different kind of monastery, more intimate. Just the opposite of Solesmes, which has become much too flashy; things are dead here, in a tumbledown shack with no bog – I have to go a kilometre to find one – the monks are bent double, the chapel is horrible and the abbot is a man of the world. Ah, everything is collapsing about my ears, except Sol.[88] I have heard little Arnaud's confession. This visit to Solesmes opened one eye, he has just opened the other. It is unthinkable ever to live in that monastery!! The Virgin answers us all the same, and from now on I am convinced that there is nothing to be done at Saint-Maur either, that the Benedictine order will not get me.

It is better to have one's mind made up, and it is done. My life needs to take a different turn. Monasteries are fine in a dream but awful in reality! And one certainly works out one's salvation less well there than in the world. We must have a long chat about the abbot of Solesmes, who, like Sol, has sworn he will get me. I understand now his displeasure when I told him I was going to Saint-Maur. He suspected that I would get the truth out of the lad and learn of the web of intrigue that makes a hell of that monastery. Olivieri is the evil spirit of the place! I rather suspected that.

As for Mother Thibault, I wonder if I shan't turn her out of doors when I get back, and take Mother Giraud in her place.[89] It is true that this unfortunate woman is another one in the possession of Satan, but really I am surprised that the Devil is pulling all the stops out for me; it is quite an honour, I am not worth the trouble.

I am now going to launder myself with Fr Logerot;[90] the chapel is not very exciting, but still, from a religious point of view, one is no worse off here than at Solesmes.

All the same, Chartres, St-Séverin, Notre-Dame des Victoires all seem a long way off!

Let us moan no more in Paris, we are much better off there. Let this thought be a consolation to you!

The lad was full of joy to see me. They don't interfere with my seeing him. Poor thing! With what melancholy he said, telling me of his sufferings at Solesmes: 'If only they had loved me a bit! They could do anything with me, if they were good to me.'

I am still thinking of leaving here on Monday, going to Saint-Denis-sur-Loire, and returning to Paris on Wednesday at the latest. In which case I should see you on Thurdsay at St Germain l'Auxerrois; we shall have a lot to talk about, I assure you. Tell Mme Leclaire that the lad and I are saying litanies for her here. His blood is still boiling at the Sol story which they were foolish enough to tell him at Solesmes.

Greetings from him and from me; all for now.

Huysmans

To ABBESS CÉCILE OF SOLESMES

3 September 1898

Dear Madam,

Back from Ligugé, where I went to stay with a friend,[91] to avoid the intolerable heat in my lodgings in the fifth arrondissement in Paris, I read a letter from Solesmes, from Fr Mugnier, repeating, doubtless with some exaggeration, the displeasure felt at the Abbey of St Pierre over my stay at Ligugé; the letter contains this phrase, which was addressed to Father: 'When the Reverend Mother Abbess, who is in Brittany, hears of this, she will be most grieved.'

This has made me very unhappy. And so I am going to ask you something: let me confess to you, and you will judge. I swear to you before Our Lord that I am going to tell you the truth, the whole truth.

You know that for some years I have been tormented by a monastic vocation. It goes back a long way now, to the first time I left the Trappists. After that, I got to know, through a mutual friend, a Benedictine, the first one I met, Fr Besse, who was on the point of founding Saint-Wandrille. He attracted me there, and I would perhaps be an oblate there at the present moment, and have been so for some time now, if things had not collapsed in the wake of Fr Chamard's nomination. Fr Besse left for Silos, and my dream came down to earth with a bump.[92]

A few years later, I got to know Solesmes. When I went there, I was in the dark, certainly more so than in Saint-Wandrille days. Fr Ferret used to say to me: pray and wait for an answer. I did so, but did not know how to resolve matters, being attracted and repelled at one and the same time by the prospect of monastic life, not feeling the impulse I was hoping for. I assure you that I prayed a lot to obtain an answer, but it did not come.

Such was still my situation when I went to Solesmes this year. I was even more uncertain, more worried than ever, for now that I was no longer held back by the Ministry in Paris, I had to make up my mind, and alone, as my poor Ferret was no longer with us. I despairingly invoked the Blessed Virgin, who had given me such precise answers in less serious matters, and nothing came.

Once I was settled in at Solesmes, I felt a certain repulsion, without any tangible cause, for no specific reason, at the idea of entering this monastery. I tried to rationalize this impression that had no justification, but it proved itself more and more, so to speak, as I tried to combat it. Was it instinctive fear, a temptation? I could not tell. That was the stage I was at in my deliberations when, the day before I left for Saint-Maur, where I was going to see little Arnaud, the Father Abbot pressed me with a specific question and asked me when I would come.

Very embarrassed, I told him I did not know, to be honest, and that in any case there was one essential point to ascertain, knowing whether I had a vocation or not. He replied:

'Your reason tells you that monastic life is superior to all others, and that it assures your salvation. That should be sufficient for you to submit your will to your reason. Do that, and God will help you.'

This argument disturbed me, for it is of a far-reaching kind. It presupposes a generosity of soul that will withstand anything, a complete abandonment of self, an uncommon strength of will. In saying that, Dom Delatte was obviously reckoning on a toughened soul like his own, and had no idea of the debility of mine.

But the more I thought about it, the less convinced I was. It seemed to be putting the cart before the horse, God afterwards and not before; it was like throwing oneself into the water in order to force Him to rescue you. And then the good Lord had not led me along these paths; and they were in contradiction with what Fr Ferret had written to me on this point before his death.

A little light was dawning in my night now, and the idea that it was not at Solesmes that I should settle became clearer, and imposed itself above all others. It is impossible to analyse, but all these doubts faded away, and the certainty that I was not suited to monastic life affirmed itself.

I left for Saint-Maur. There, in spite of everything, I was afraid of having made a mistake, of being the plaything of illusions, and, not wanting to trust myself, I asked for confession. I was sent to Fr Logerot, who had clear insights into my situation, and gave me some very sound advice. I told him, as I am telling you, my sad business. He affirmed very decisively that I was right, and that the only practical solution he saw for me was to remain a layman, and to live in a monastery, or rather near one. And he quoted the example of M. Cartier to me.[93]

I left Saint-Maur reassured as far as my conscience was concerned, but in despair, because it was the end of everything.

From the spiritual point of view, I was going to fall once again into the void of Paris, rediscover the sadness of lack of direction, and again be subject to attack from a really diabolical Spanish woman, who has sworn to bring about my downfall.

From a material point of view, things were no less sad. My pension from the Ministry of the Interior and the little I have saved being insufficient to live on in Paris, I would have had to carry on the journalistic trade in perpetuity and live from my pen. And the history of St Lydwina put off until I know not when.

So I came back depressed. In the midst of all this, a friend, G. Boucher, who has been settled for a number of years at Ligugé, where he directs the review *Le Pays Poitevin*,, came to Paris and said: 'I have a spare room in the lodgings where I live. I put it at your disposal. Come and spend a few days with me and see Poitou, which you do not know.'

I was so at a loss, so fed up, that I accepted the offer and set off. At Ligugé I stayed with my friend, and was invited by Fr Besse, whom I met up with again, to dine at the abbey. The Father Abbot was very pleasant, and we did not at all talk about the Solesmes business.

My intention was to stay for a week, but the heat was becoming unbearable, and all the letters I was getting from friends in Paris urged me not to return; I stayed on there, and that is when the unexpected took a hand in things. One day, the secretary-general of the diocese, Canon Perret, who knew about my situation, said to me: 'There is a delightful plot of land, with a spring and centuries-old pine trees, not far from the station; it is for sale, you should buy it and build yourself a hovel there to end your days in peace.'

I had not thought of such a thing, and I was very confused. On reflection, I thought over again the idea I had had, but had always brushed aside, of living simply as a layman in the environs of a monastery, for, basically, I had dreamt of better things. And what Fr Logerot said came back to me. What would have been impossible at Solesmes which, apart from the abbey, is a hole, with no walks, no life, no easy transport to Paris, became quite possible at Ligugé, where the countryside is charming, full of woods, twenty minutes from a large town to which it is linked by numerous trains, and with the Bordeaux express one is in Paris in a few hours. And on top of that, I had the realization of my dream of monastic offices and my work carried on in peace.

The little money I had available, which, even invested in an annuity, would not have made up my pension to allow me to live in Paris, was enough to buy this bit of land and build a hut on it; so, poor in Paris on a pension of 3,000 francs, I was rich in Ligugé.

What is more, I barely had time to think it over, for Canon Perret concluded the deal on the spot and purchased the land on my behalf in Poitiers.

Such is the absolutely exact history of this affair. I wrote about it to Fr Thomasson from Ligugé itself. You see there is nothing that could imply, as people seem to think, any hostility towards Solesmes. All this happened without any premeditation, without any ulterior motives. I did not have the least idea, when I set off, that I would become a landowner in Ligugé, where, God knows, I had never intended to settle! All in all, things have sorted themselves out, at a time when I thought all was lost, through the intermediary of a priest who, moreover, is a friend of Solesmes. For my part, I am obliged to see a working-out of providence, an unexpected solution that extricates me from all my difficulties, that saves me from everything.

You will forgive me, won't you, for inflicting such a long epistle on you, but you have always been so good to me that the idea of upsetting you distresses me; and that is why I have bored you at such length with my petty affairs. I ask your forgiveness for this verbiage. Its only purpose is to tell you that were it to be in my power to be useful or agreeable to you, in Ligugé as in Paris, I should be most glad to oblige. I remain, in spite of everything, dear madam, your grateful and most respectfully devoted servant in Our Lord.

J. K. Huysmans

To PAUL VALÉRY

14 September 1898

My Dear Friend,

Before I leave this morning, I thank you, in a word, for the information you sent me concerning poor Mallarmé's funeral.[94] What a hotchpotch of people were there – I had read that in the press. D'Aurevilly, Villiers, Verlaine – all those who were precious to me in this age of crassness are dead. And he who was left is gone too. It is not without great sadness that, before withdrawing from the world, one witnesses the disappearance of the only decent artists for years.

But the worst is when there are children left who turn out badly, like poor Caze's. I do not believe I have ever spent such a sad evening as the one I spent, at the request of his barrister, preparing a letter to move the jury.

What is more, it had no success, for the unfortunate lad has just been sentenced to hard labour and deportation. No, in truth, it is time to be gone, and I wish I were already in my monastery.

Yours

Huysmans

IV
1898–1907
Ligugé and the Last Years[1]

The Benedictine abbey of St Martin at Ligugé is some five miles from Poitiers and is one of the oldest monastic foundations in the Western world, dating back to the time of St Martin and St Hilary in the fourth century. Although Huysmans did not move into his own new house at Ligugé until the summer of 1899, he spent a good deal of the preceding twelve months there, staying at first with his friend Boucher and later in rented accommodation. The newly built Maison Notre-Dame was, then, to be his retreat from the world, in the shadow of the monastery, and in 1899 the indications were that he would hope to remain there until the end of his days. But things were to turn out very differently.

Mention must be made at this stage of M. and Mme Leclaire, who were very much involved with Huysmans in this monastic venture. He had met them through Fr Ferret who had wanted that they should, after his death, become friends and brothers in a Christian family. At first sight, the Leclaires would seem an odd choice as companions for Huysmans: they were strictly non-intellectual, with a background in the drapery business. But the novelist was so fond of Fr Ferret that he was only too willing to take his advice, and at first all went well, especially as the Leclaires put money into the Ligugé project and dealt generally with all practical matters, leaving Huysmans free to get on with his writing. As the letters show, it had been hoped that this modest beginning might blossom into a Christian artistic community under the wing of the abbey. But that too was to come to nothing, and in fact the Leclaires themselves spent relatively little time actually in residence at Ligugé. Mme Leclaire seems to have been a rather nervous hypochondriac; but there is no doubt that Huysmans valued her husband Léon as a confidant during the last ten years of his life.

To his great consternation, Huysmans learnt that his works had been denounced to Rome, and that there was a chance that *En Route* and *La Cathédrale* might be placed on the Index. This distressed him because he felt that he was defending Catholicism against non-believers, seeking to present the attractive, artistic aspects of the Church to a materialistic world. The idea that the Church might reject his efforts he found hurtful, but in fact none of his works was ever placed on the Index, nor was he asked by the Vatican to make any changes to them. Despite his desire to be a submissive son of Mother Church, the whole notion of censorship remained abhorrent to Huysmans; he still bore the scars from the banning of his first novel, *Marthe*. His problems with the Index were probably no more than the result of personal jealousies, but the episode had one beneficial effect in that it led to his epistolary friendship with the Prioress of the Carmelite convent in Algiers, formerly a Princess Bibesco of the royal house of Romania, who, being well connected in ecclesiastical circles, offered to undertake Huysmans' defence with the Vatican. She was to be one of his regular correspondents during this last period of his life.

Whilst at Ligugé, he wrote a biography of Saint Lydwina; Huysmans was fascinated with the story of this obscure fourteenth-century Dutch woman, as she was an example of the phenomenon of the victim soul, one who expiates in his or her own suffering the sins of others. This time he made no pretence at a 'novelish sauce' and simply presented the facts and legends of Lydwina's life as he had been able to research them. He described the work in graphic terms to a friend: 'I have my hands covered in the pale putty of the life of St Lydwina'.[2] The product of these labours is in fact difficult to read, especially the early pages, stuffed full of names and dates, as Huysmans tries to present a vast panorama of European history in the fourteenth century as background to his story.

On the domestic political scene in France, the year of Huysmans' removal to Ligugé saw a further round in the notorious Dreyfus case. Controversy had been raging since 1896, when doubt was first cast on the justice of the sentence of Captain Dreyfus to deportation for life to Devil's Island for alleged military espionage. The matter was complicated by the fact that false evidence, claims and counterclaims were rife. Families were divided, friendships broken in the taking of sides in this affair that preoccupied French society for so long: Dreyfus was not finally pardoned until 1906. Huysmans now found himself diametrically opposed to his former master, Émile Zola, author of the famous article *J'accuse*, in defence of Dreyfus. Huysmans was decidedly *anti-dreyfusard*. Here, as elsewhere, he did not hide his anti-Semitism (Alfred Dreyfus was a Jew). This was in fact quite a current in French intellectual life at the turn of the century.

The battle between Church and State raged on, and the Law on Associations brought an abrupt end to Huysmans' monastic dream, as it meant that the community of monks was obliged to go into exile in 1901. But over the preceding two years his monastic ideal had suffered blows from other quarters also, and when it came to it, he was really quite glad for an excuse to return to Paris. He had found the provinces boring, and had never got over his disappointment with the human raw material of monastic life. He always expected monks to be more saintly than they actually were; he did not easily accept that they were struggling with the same defects of character of which he was himself a victim. He did, nevertheless, enter fully into the spirit of Benedictine liturgical life, attending the seven canonical offices daily in the abbey church. Even after his departure from Ligugé, he continued to recite the psalms of the Divine Office in private until his death; this was one of the commitments he made on becoming an oblate in the order of St Benedict. He began his year's novitiate in March 1900, and made his profession on the feast day of St Benedict, 21 March 1901. Nowhere in his extant correspondence does he make mention of this second and more important ceremony, although we know it took place from the documents preserved in the monastic archives at Ligugé. Even in a long letter to his close friend Georges Landry written the following day, the matter of his oblation is not referred to. Quite probably Huysmans felt by this stage that his becoming an oblate of this community was something of a waste of time, in a public sense at least, for he knew that the monks' days at Ligugé were strictly numbered. He no longer felt a very strong sense of identity with the community, but he went through with his act of oblation as a personal commitment to God, and in this sense he lived out his undertaking, remaining faithful in his devotions and reception of the sacraments until the end of his life. His relationship with the monks, however, was to be strained even further in the years to come.

The Benedictines left for Belgium in the autumn of 1901; Huysmans, for his part, had been offered cheap accommodation in Paris at another Benedictine house, the convent in the rue Monsieur. This he gladly accepted, although he was not happy there for long. It was now that his health started to be seriously troublesome, with an aggravation of what had been chronic neuralgia and toothache. He had to have a number of his teeth removed in a series of horrific operations.

Despite all this, he undertook further travels and embarked on another major novel. This was *L'Oblat*, which he finished in 1903. It is a thinly veiled reflection of his time at Ligugé: Durtal reappears in the setting of a fictional abbey in Burgundy. But to the initiated, the abbey of St Martin is easily discernible, and the abbot was not pleased at having the personal idiosyncracies of his monks made public. And it is perhaps surprising that Huysmans did not feel a greater sense of loyalty on this point, as these were in fact *his* brothers; he had asked to be admitted to their spiritual family, and had been so received in a solemn ceremony before the altar, not to mention the fact that Dom Besse had personally defended Huysmans when he had been under attack years earlier. But the novelist was to retain a fierce intellectual and artistic independence to the end; he remarked in one of his letters that he wrote only in order to tell the truth, and that his 'allegiance is not pledged to any party and never will be'.[3]

His travels took him first to Lourdes in the company of the Leclaires. There were elements that both attracted and repelled him at this shrine. The atmosphere of mystery at the grotto and the sense of intimacy with the Blessed Virgin in this place delighted him, but, as ever, he was to show himself an elitist, and was put off by the manifestation of a low taste in popular piety. These experiences were to find their expression in his book *Les Foules de Lourdes*.

Huysmans' interest in painting remained very much alive until the end of his life; a great enthusiasm of his last years stemmed from renewed contact with the religious painting of German and Flemish Primitives. He went on an extensive European tour with the intrepid Fr Mugnier in order to view these paintings, and his letters overflow with delight at the sublimity of his old favourite Matthias Grünewald's artistic sensibility. He was to produce a volume entitled *Trois Primitifs* in 1905.

Huysmans was not to be free of the attentions of female admirers even in his last illness. After his return from Ligugé, he was courted by an attractive young girl in her early twenties, Henriette du Fresnel, who had transposed her novelish infatuation with Durtal to his creator. The latter would have had ample opportunity to take advantage of her, but to his credit, Huysmans persevered in his commitment to chastity, and did all that he could to channel the girls emotional energies towards the religious life. And although Henriette remained faithful to him, visiting him in his final illness, she entered the Benedictine convent at Dourgne six weeks before his death; she spent the rest of her life there as an enclosed nun. Rather more innocently, a wealthy widow, a certain Mme Huc, sent Huysmans regular little parcels of gastronomic delicacies from her estate.

Neither did Huysmans abandon completely the Parisian literary scene. Edmond de Goncourt's will had nominated him as founding president of the Académie Goncourt, which was to have the annual responsibility for awarding the 'Prix Goncourt' to the best novel of the year. As Huysmans found amongst his fellow-academicians Alphonse Daudet, whom he had never liked personally nor respected artistically, tension was inevitable. All this meant that he had to continue to read large quantities of novels and keep in touch with literary controversy.

Huysmans had been a heavy smoker all his life, and it was to be cancer of the throat and mouth that finally carried him off at the age of fifty-nine. The last few years of his life gave him prolonged and intense experience of suffering. Even the pleasures of the table were denied him now, for he could barely eat. The inside of his mouth simply rotted away and collapsed. He tried to approach his suffering positively and from a religious point of view, seeing it as a stage in his own purification, as part of God's plan for him, to which he must acquiesce. He wrote to a friend: 'Take note that suffering is a pledge of divine love.' By November 1906, he realized that he would not recover and began to put his literary estate in order. Lucien Descaves was his secretary at this time, writing most of Huysmans' letters, and burning manuscripts on his instructions.

He was most keen that arrangements for his funeral should be properly dealt with (in contrast to Zola's, which had offended him greatly). He even drafted the invitations to his obsequies himself. He also sent to Chevetogne in Belgium, where the Ligugé community was in exile, for the monastic habit in which he was to be buried; this was his right as an oblate. Huysmans' death came peacefully on 12 May 1907; his old friend Fr Mugnier celebrated the requiem mass, which was attended by many of his artistic, literary and ecclesiastical friends.

To ARIJ PRINS

Ligugé, 19 September 1898

My Dear Friend,
Many things have happened since my last letter. The idea of becoming an oblate which I had abandoned has been taken up again, and carried through at the monastery of Ligugé, but in conditions different from those at Solesmes. I have just bought a piece of land, and am having a humble dwelling built near the monastery, which will allow me to be outside of the enclosure, and to retain a certain freedom in my comings and goings, not to mention that of my library, which remains intact; conceived in this way, oblation dispenses with the habit and leaves the oblate a layman.

Thus I am doing business with an architect from Poitiers who has come to erect my cell. I would add that the adjoining piece of land is attractive, with centuries-old pine trees and an exquisite spring of cold blue water.

If I were to invest my money, even in an annuity, I could not manage to live in Paris without practising journalism. I am spending my money on bricks and mortar, and with my pension of 3,000 francs, I am rich here, dropping the newspapers and working on my life of St Lydwina.

It is a different kind of investment. The Leclaires are going to do the same. They have bought the last remaining plot of land next to mine, and later, when they withdraw from the world, they will have something built as well.

That was unexpected, wasn't it?

The black spot is La Sol, whose arrival here I fear; those swinish newspapers have, in the last week, unearthed my departure and are recounting the most extraordinary things about me. Having returned from Fontarbie, La Sol is in Paris and thus, knowing that I am at Ligugé, is capable of anything. Who will rid me of that she-devil?

I am living quietly here with a friend, half at his house, and half in the monastery. The heat is bearable here, for we are surrounded by great woods and there is a little river that cools the air. If I had no articles to write, it would be perfect!

Ligugé is a sort of monastic village, belonging entirely to the abbey, which rules it in a way. All in all, I am laying the foundations for a little colony of Benedictine oblates. We shall see what comes of it with the help of Fr Besse, who is here. I shall give him the information you sent on homonyms.

I must leave you as it is time for the office to begin.
Write soon.
Yours,

G. Huijsmans

For the moment I can see no chance of finding a position as governess. I will try through Fr Mugnier, as he knows everyone in the Faubourg St

Germain, but those people are so stupid that they would not engage a Protestant for their children. As soon as I get back, I will speak to him about it and we will see. I hope to rouse the indignation of the Leclaires, who will come at the end of the month, when I give them your details on Clio!! I am returning to Paris about 12 October.

To ABBESS CÉCILE OF SOLESMES

Ligugé, 2 October 1898

Dear Madam,

First of all I thank you for not having doubted me, and then for having given me advice which I shall follow to the letter, for it is of the wisest, I can tell.

Moreover, I have already put it into practice, as soon as I returned to Ligugé, by closing my door and not having anything to do with the monastery, in order to have some peace. The example of an oblate living in the monastery itself, as M. Cartier did formerly at Solesmes, is proof enough.

So I take part in the offices and go home afterwards. As far as relations are concerned, I don't see myself having any there, and on the spiritual front, one is better off in Poitiers, where all the clergy are surprisingly open-minded, well-behaved and profess mystical ideas. And so my relations are more with Poitiers than Ligugé.

All in all I am, if I examine myself, happy in the belief I persist in that I have followed the will of the Good Lord, I know well enough that problems will be plentiful with the buildings I have to have put up, and that life will be turned completely upside down next year. But, but ... the rewards are so perfect.

If only you knew, there are some very special joys in Poitiers. Between two trains one can go and visit Notre-Dame la Grande,[4] at a time when one is quite alone with Her in the old church. I have begged Her to take the place of my good madonnas of Chartres, Notre-Dame des Victoires, Saint-Séverin, whom I shall perforce see less of when I am settled here. And I believe that the dear Lady of Poitou has accepted , for I spend moments of real sweetness in her sanctuary.

Basically, I still regret the monastery a bit. I thought about it for so many years, but I no longer experience those painful uncertainties that caused me so much suffering. What you are good enough to say to me on this subject confirms what Fr Logerot told me at Saint-Maur, it is the truth itself, and I am only surprised not to have seen the light sooner.

Something else: you have probably read in the press, which throws itself into some ingenious variations on this theme, that I have gone to Ligugé to found a colony of Christian artists. But for that, there would first of all need to be some Christian artists! And there aren't any! I have in fact often thought of this idea, which would perhaps permit a reawakening of somnolent religious art, but I cannot see any means, but none at all, of bringing it about. In any case, people who are telling such stories are singularly ahead of themselves, much water will have flowed under the bridge before I or anybody else puts them into practice.

Forgive me all this chatter, Madame, but I speak to you as to a spiritual mother of whom I am fond, I assure you. I simply wanted to show you my gratitude, and it is a strange way to set about it, submitting you to blows from my pen. Simply select from them, along with a little request for prayers, every assurance of my respectful and affectionate devotion in Our Lord.

In a few days I am returning to Paris until the spring.

J. K. Huysmans

To GEORGES LANDRY

Ligugé, 5 October 1898

Dear Friend,

Unless anything unexpected turns up, I am thinking of catching the train on Tuesday, so as to be in Paris by seven o'clock on the same day.

I have to come back to collect my pension certificate which has finally been cashed in, and to deal with all the necessary formalities, and to get my back pay from last February from the Ministry of Finance.

Mother Thibault is a lying old good-for-nothing. She reads everything in my house, and listens in, I am sure of it. She has quite simply gone through all my press cuttings that are not in sealed envelopes, and she has learnt from them what her supposed voices tell her.

In any case, they deceive her singularly when they announce that I am taking her with me. As for that, no, no! I want no diabolical influence in my new dwelling. Let her go and join forces with La Sol, who has not given up, and continues to burden me with passionate letters and vague threats, which I still do not answer, of course.

As for the d'Aurevilly business, it is possible, as long as I do not write the article directly. We shall have to find a way around it, as with little Esquirol's book, a general subject that I can deal with at the beginning and the end, whilst keeping the rest for the book. We'll talk about it. In any case, Miss Read can be sure that I will do all in my power to be agreeable to her, not to mention you, you old softy. I am scribbling these lines in haste. I have all the top clergy of Poitiers to dine this evening, and it is not easy to track down a few decent old bottles in the abbey or the village. I have been doing nothing but that since this morning. The plan will be finished on Thursday, and I hope that the foundation stone of the little monastery will be laid on Monday, before my departure.

It is all very strange, and I have not yet got used to the idea. I am a property owner in spite of myself. If I really did not believe that that Canon, who came into my life like a flash of lightning, as Ferret did previously, was an emanation from On High, I would tremble at having embarked on such an adventure. But good old Notre-Dame la Grande in Poitiers, with whom I am on good terms, will see to it all, I am quite sure.

Yes, dear friend, we talk to Her of you also, so that She may shed light on the situation; you will see, it will all work out.

Boucher sends you a thousand greetings. If you add all of mine as well, you will collapse under the weight.

Yours

J. K. Huysmans

To MOTHER BÉNIE DE JÉSUS

[December 1989]

Dear Reverend Mother,

How good of you to take an interest in my troubles, when you must have your own, which cannot be insignificant, being responsible for so many souls.

The truth in my affair is that I have aroused implacable hatred, less for having told the clergy a few home truths than for having taken sides in a struggle that does not look like coming to an end, involving the two monasteries at Solesmes; to sum it up, those who have denounced me are the same people who so violently attacked the abbess of Ste Cécile of Solesmes in Rome a few years ago. I defended her, because I am sure, besides her prodigious intelligence and incomparable open-mindedness, that she is a very saintly nun, and I am involved in the affair. Mgr Battandier, who is stirring things up against me in Rome, is in fact the one who was most relentless against the abbess.

The same with Cardinal Vannutelli, who, when he was in France recently, was asked to demand a rebuke from the Pope himself for Drumont [5] and me (we had both supported the same cause). His Holiness turned it down flat, but things can be done behind a Pope's back, and that is exactly what is happening.

I have this information from a reliable source. In the meantime, the bishop of Poitiers and the abbot of the monastery of Ligugé have written to Rome in my defence, unbeknown to me, and perhaps they will prevail, if they manage to find their way around the labyrinth of offices and the army of prelates that make up the Vatican.

As for me, I still believe that the wisest course is to commit everything to the hands of the Blessed Virgin. And then it would all be so stupid! *En Route* has brought about loads of conversions amongst Protestants. They use it in English translation for that very purpose in London. Here it has brought recruits to the Trappist monasteries. It would be a real triumph for the Devil, if it were to be struck down.

As for *La Cathédrale*, that book can be given to anyone to read. The only incriminating passage concerns the portrayal of the deadly sins in the cathedral porch. I supported the theory that the Church made a protest in this way, displaying an image of vice in order to inspire a horror of it.

If this theory is wrong, the people of the Middle Ages were a pack of fools, and the bishops and abbots of monasteries who built the cathedrals geriatrics who let themselves be hoodwinked and made fools of by architects and sculptors who laughed in their faces!

A likely story! Never have there been more intelligent and holy bishops and abbots than in those times! In any case, this idea is nothing to do with dogma in the opinion of all the theologians I know. They won't be able to do anything against *La Cathédrale*, despite the genuine or feigned fury it is arousing.

But I am ashamed to be boring you in this way. I prefer to tell you that as I was passing a bookshop in the rue Bonaparte the other day, I saw in the window a volume entitled *Le Carmel de la Vallée des Consuls* by Reiskiold. You can imagine that I snapped it up and have examined all the photoengravings of the place where you live.

Then, as everything happens together, I received a visit from an old friend, Dom Romain, Benedictine abbot of En Calcat, who says he knows you, and spoke so affectionately of your work! Decidedly, everybody knows everybody else in this life.

I have received a letter from Mme de Ste Foix.[6] The retreat you were kind enough to give her really did her a lot of good. One feels that she is more resigned, happier and closer to God. That was a real good deed.

Thank you for the holy picture; I shall place it in my book at the last verses of the last of the penitential psalms, which I cannot stop saying to God over and over, from morning till night, for it is so appropriate to my situation, to my desires, my problems: *notam fac viam in qua ambulem*.[7]

What divine literature the psalms are! They contain everything; the prophet foresaw all the different states of our souls, there is no need to invent anything else in order to speak to God! And the *Miserere*! These are in a sense the tonics and cordials for weak souls.

Thank you again, Reverend Mother, and please accept my renewed assurance of respect and devotion *in Christo*.

J. K. Huysmans

To MOTHER BÉNIE DE JÉSUS

25 December 1898

Very Reverend and Dearest Mother,

Our Lord has really given you a gift for consoling letters at the right moment, for I spent such a sad Christmas Eve at the Benedictine sisters'; alas, I was so little in communion with the joy of the liturgy, that I am quite at a loss. I am full of frightful blackness: judge for yourself. The day I bought, or was made to buy, a building plot at Ligugé, I came out of the solicitor's horrified at the thought of possessions, and ran to Notre-Dame la Grande. It seemed to me that it was Her wish. The arrival of friends from Paris, who came and bought other plots and offered to defray themselves all the expenses for a colony of oblates who would practise their artistic skills, seemed to me to be a proof of Our Mother's goodness.

There was only one difficulty outstanding: to find Catholic artists. Now I could see only one, a pure soul, an admirable and talented painter: Charles Dulac.[8] But he had been away in Italy for three years with the Franciscans at Assisi, and so I could not count on him.

I returned to Paris, and the Holy Father's statement on Benedictine oblation was published,[9] and at the same time, Dulac turned up and put himself at my disposal. I thanked the Blessed Virgin and had no more doubts. And now Dulac is dying!! While we were running about trying to get him admitted to the brothers of St John of God, the doctor, in view of the urgency of the situation, had him taken to the Beaujour hospital, and there is no hope.

The cornerstone of the building has been shattered. What does it mean? Evidently Our Lord always acts rightly, but it is terrible to be groping around and to lose a friend, just when one had found him again. Christmas became more like Holy Week last night. But you are right, and I reread your sweet embroidery and ask God to enlighten me.

I do not know how to thank you for all your goodness. This is the information I have since my last letter:

The letter was delivered into the very hands of the cardinal, Prefect of the Index. I enclose a copy of it.

So as you will see, it brings to His Eminence's attention the fact that I am the only person in Paris who defends Catholicism in the mass-circulation newspapers, and that consequently, if they hit out at me, all credibility is taken away, as well as any possibility I might have had for continuing to do a little good in the world I can reach, where the Catholic press is not read.

This argument may have carried some weight, for I have received from Poitiers a request to send with all urgency copies of my articles for despatch to Rome, which I have done.

What is more, I am going to bring out a book entitled *Pages catholiques*, extracts from my books that are suitable for Catholic circles, convents, everywhere. This volume will be prefaced by a long study by Fr Mugnier, head curate at Ste Clotilde, who wields great influence. And in this preamble, we will deal with the question of my earlier books. He will make all the necessary reservations, and I will approve.

It seems to me that, in this way, I shall have given satisfaction to the fierce pack of hounds that I have around my legs. It is true that they will invent something else, but I shan't budge.

Thank you for your prayers, and for those of your holy daughters. You see what need I have of them. Get them to pray for poor little Dulac as well, even though Heaven awaits that one. Barely twenty-nine years old! And now what shall I wish you in return for all your holy tonics, other than that your novitiate might prosper; that must be closer to your heart than anything else, and I ask God for it in the coming year with all my heart.

Dear Reverend Mother, please accept this assurance of my affectionate and respectful devotion.

J. K. Huysmans

enclosed/

To THE CARDINAL PREFECT OF THE INDEX

12 December 1898

Your Eminence,

There is a rumour in Paris that *La Cathédrale* and several others of my books have, as the result of denunciations made out of personal vengeance, been brought before the Sacred Congregation for the Index, as containing pages likely to offend Holy Church and the Papacy.

I do not know whether this rumour is well founded; but in any case, may I be permitted to assure your Eminence that nothing would be more painful to me than to have grieved the Church and the Sovereign Pontiff, whose humble and submissive son I am, and desire to remain.

If, then, there should be errors concerning dogma or ideas that could be deemed offensive to the Church and His Holiness in these works that have been accused, I am prepared to retract them and have them removed.

In that case, I would venture to ask your Eminence to be good enough to indicate the passages in question, so that I may set about rectifying them, taking into account any instructions given to me, or deleting them completely.

May I be permitted, your Eminence, to add this:

My book *En Route*, thanks be to God, who uses the most mediocre of instruments, has brought about a number of conversions, and has greatly helped recruitment to Trappist monasteries. These facts are publicly known. What is more, I am the only person in Paris at the present time who defends Catholicism in the mass-circulation newspapers that reach where the exclusively religious press cannot, by virtue of its limited sales and specialized subject matter.

If, then, I were to be attacked, a number of Catholics, who have returned to God by this intermediary, would be confused, and I would have lost all my credibility and power with the masses, amongst whom I have managed to do some good.

May your paternal solicitude permit me to protest with all my strength against the rumours that have been rife against me, concerning the sincerity of my conversion. These are abominable calumnies and odious lies. You can easily gain reassurance of my truthfulness by contacting, should you judge it appropiate, Reverend Fr Augustin, abbot of the Trappist monastery of Our Lady at Igny, where I was reconciled with Our Lord. The Very Reverend Benedictine abbots of Solesmes, Ligugé and En Calcat, who also know me, could if necessary provide you with information on this point.

In the hope that your Eminence will deign to consider my request, I beg you, etc. . . .

To ÉMILE BERNARD

15 February 1899

In haste
Dear Sir,

I received this morning *The Crucifixion* that you were good enough to send me and I hasten to let you know, so that you can be reassured, as to its safe arrival. It is very interesting in the way in which it uses nature in harmony with the terrible scene, and spares us repetition.

Nothing new, except that I still have problems with the Catholics, who have got the idea into their heads that I should renounce all my earlier books, and want me to write an open letter in the press to this effect.

Naturally, once again I tell them to go and get st. . . . But how they cling to their foolishness.

Between you and me, I fear I may have many problems of this kind at Ligugé – even though I shall be completely outside of the enclosure.

Thank you again, dear sir, and all the best to you.

Huysmans

To MOTHER BÉNIE DE JÉSUS

16 February 1899

Dear Reverend Mother,

If I did not answer your so welcome letter sooner, it was because I wanted to acquit myself of the little errand you gave me for the abbess of Solesmes.

It is done, and the gentle Benedictine, to whom I related all the trouble you had taken on my account, has written me a joyful letter on seeing me rescued from the claws of the censorship, and is going to send you her *Treatise on Prayer*, of which she has one last copy left.

It is a book of spiritual reading such as is rarely to be found these days. It contains an extraordinary range of quotations, and a particular page on reversing the Our Father, seeing it in relation to different stages of mystical experience, which seems to me a real find.

This poor Mother! What problems she too had with her book, at the time of the sad troubles at Solesmes, that you must know of. She emerged triumphant from it all, with the assurance that her book was unquestionably sound from a theological point of view; but the book was nevertheless hunted down by the most odious gossipmongers, and that is why I have spoken about it freely in *La Cathédrale*, at the request of the abbot in question.

The abbey of Ste Cécile is a marvel; this monastery is really flourishing, and she is adored by all her daughters. That is where one must go to experience the real art of plainchant. I remember a night that remains a sublime moment in my life. It was the day before the feast of the Dedication. I was at Solesmes, and the good Mother said to me: 'Come to matins, I will warn the portress.'

I went, and found in the dark church a little table beside the altar with a lamp, and the offices all prepared. The veil of the enclosure was drawn back, and the whole choir appeared before me, with the abbess at the back. And the singing was admirable, voices such as one hears no more; in this setting, the beauty of the liturgy seemed to me so striking that I wept in my little corner.

They are truly artists. There are amongst them also sisters who are reviving medieval illumination, as well as first-rate organists. It is art combined with the contemplative life. Added to that, there is in this monastery a mixture of the highest nobility with the simplest of women: the nieces of the emperor of Austria, the queen mother of Portugal, who is an oblate, and holy daughters of the bourgeoisie and the working class.

She is an admirable and most holy woman. My love and reverence for her know no bounds, and I am sure that she is fond of me too, for she has always bent over backwards to be pleasant and helpful to me: 'For my part, I am happy that you have given me an opportunity to show my respect and affection for the valiant prioress, and I am going to send her *On Prayer*. It is the last copy, or almost. I hope it will come out again later, considerably improved, and with some additions. It has great need of them.'

No so much as all that!

Nothing new here, apart from that, and apart from my permanent desire to get away from Paris; I spend my time dreaming of a life of offices, walks in the woods. By what trials will I have to pay for this vague, undeserved peace? I tremble rather at the thought; but it is in the hands of our good Mother, Notre-Dame la Grande at Poitiers, who is to take over from my sweet Madonna at Chartres and Paris, and will help me out, I am sure. The goodness of the Blessed Virgin is certainly an incomprehensible thing; but it is powerful and there for all to see; when one is an inveterate sinner, one is always a little afraid of the Father, even though one knows that He is singularly merciful, whereas Her one can approach without fear, knowing that She will intervene and set things aright. The Protestants must be blind not to see that!!

Dearest Mother, I assure you of my respectful and affectionate devotion in Our Lord.

J. K. Huysmans

To GEORGES LANDRY

Ligugé, [17 July 1899]

My Dear Friend,

The bookcases are finally in place, and the books in order. There is a lot more to do, and by dint of being impatient, we shall perhaps manage to settle in. We are inaugurating the bathroom today, and next week we are tackling the remaining bedrooms and beginning the colonnade outside.

We are finally sorting ourselves out a bit, and I have taken advantage of the fact to embark on liturgical life. It is very time-consuming, but very sweet; on Thursdays, Fr Besse comes and helps us to find our way around the mysteries of the monastic ordo, but once you have got the hang of it, this daily life of the Church celebrating her saints, who are all so different, is, in terms of piety and art, a pure joy.

Moreover, the old basilica of St Martin is exquisite and the monastic atmosphere is uninterrupted; the nuns who live near us have asked if they can cut through our garden to attend the offices, in order to avoid a climb, and so from my window I catch sight of white head-dresses nodding a greeting from behind the pine trees. While fingers run over rosary beads.

The heat is awful here during the day, but once the house is closed up it is cool, and in the evening the trees in the cloister are kind to us. I think of Paris, where people must be roasting, and those terrible airless evenings in the rue de Sévres.

Mme Leclaire still wants to have you here, and I cannot imagine it is impossible. You would only need to wangle a few days off, for I will take care of the train fare; so there is only the goodwill of the Yid to wish for. Is that impossible?

And then I shall end up dragging you out on to the bank once and for all, however unlikely that may seem to you. There are some very special things happening here, that may have an impact on you some day. I cannot tell you any more, as it is a plan that the Father Abbot has put to us, and we are studying it with him alone.

In the meantime, the best thing is to pray, and to say the last of the penitential psalms which, in its last verses, is quite in harmony with a desire to do the will of God.

Thank you for your visit to the rue de Sèvres. You can put down some fragrant closet his lordship Gide's literature. I have already read books by him;

it is sub-Barrès, and that is saying something; I find it simply odious, but it would be kind of you to send me *Durendal*,[10] which interests Fr Besse, I will pass it on to him.

Here the volume of corresponsence makes one despair; I don't answer letters, what is more. As for the boring ones, the maid dusts them very well, I must say. I am looked after like an Infanta threatened with kidnapping; Mme Leclaire is so vigilant that it would be difficult to take her by surprise; one has to admit that one of the triumphs of religion is to create family ties between certain people that are more solid than natural ones. She is really a big sister, so attentive in sparing me any bother, and such a perfect character! And he takes care of everything, deals with temporal affairs, so that one does not have to trouble about anything.

All that will evidently be paid for with trials in health or in some other way. But still, in the meantime, one can only thank Our Mother for Her goodness.

Greetings to Orsat and Daniel if you see them. I have written to Girard. Has Father left?

La Sol has written to Fr Besse. She is not giving up. Still, Father Abbot has been informed of the situation in order to counter any tittle-tattle. We have not seen the last of her. She is supposed to be returning to her husband in Spain, and the express stops in Poitiers. We shall be lucky if she doesn't come to Ligugé.

Huysmans

To ABBESS CÉCILE OF SOLESMES

Ligugé, 30 July 1899

Dear Madam,

How good you are to have thought of me, in sending me the new edition of the *Treatise on Prayer*. I spent all day yesterday and this afternoon locked up with it. As literary curiosity is not entirely dead in me, although it is weakening singularly, it amused me to look at the old edition and the epilogue to see how you have managed to rework and widen the whole, thus constructing in definitive form such a sound and wise book. The job of transposition and addition has been done with real ingenuity and lucidity. But you will smile at the futility of these remarks. What is of real interest, in fact, is the solid doctrine and the highly nutritious meat of this book. I rediscovered those pages I like so much on the Our Father taken in reverse, as well as the one on the Blessed Virgin, which I found delectable, needless to say, and another one too on our enemies and our protectors, revealing the experience of an extraordinary guide of souls. It is not possible that Satan, whose role in Scripture you have shown up so well, and unearthed the most secret of his traps, will not seek revenge, but it won't be the first time, and so I am not worried on your account.

I am at Ligugé, where I am living amidst a hubbub of hammering. Given the inconceivable indolence of the natives of Poitou, it takes months to get settled in; for the moment I am wandering about in an unfinished house, as a consequence of the folly of a fine fellow of an architect, who took it into his head, thinking to surprise me, to make a travesty of a little arcaded Romanesque passageway in front of the house, by converting it into a Moorish gallery!! The Alhambra of Poitou! So all these ridiculous bays had to be taken down. Unfortunately, in order to set this sad affair to rights, it has been necessary to put captials on the little columns, which is pretentious and rather ridiculous in such a modest dwelling, but it was a case of choosing the lesser of two evils, and so, to console myself, I have dedicated the pillars to those of the saints who are my closest friends: St Martin, St Francis of Assisi, St Radegonde,[11] St Lydwina, St Frances of Rome,[12] St Teresa, not forgetting St Joseph, and keeping the place of honour for Our Mother. And I had them represented quite outside the domain of archaeology, by the symbolism of flowers, helped along by heraldry.

Thus the Blessed Virgin is announced by a mystic rose, not a bad copy of a thirteenth-century picture, and surrounded with anemone leaves; St Joseph by the palm tree (*justus ut palmus florebit*)[13] and by the humility of hyssop; St Frances by the tower of mirrors and vine leaves, in memory of her miracle; St Radegonde by her coat of arms and laurel in memory of her miracle; St Lydwina by the coat of arms of her good native town of Schiedam and the roses carried by her angel; St Benedict by the raven and the oak, symbol of the vigour of his order, etc., etc. All this has been executed without genius, but sculpted in an honest manner by a fellow who was not a little perturbed by all this inventiveness.

So life here is not completely settled, but all the same it is infinitely sweet. I am with excellent people here, Christians such as one rarely meets with nowadays. That again is the doing of the good and holy Fr Ferret. He met the Leclaires, with whom I am living, in the confessional, as he did me, and from that moment on his one aim was to introduce me to them; I had always been surprised at his insistence that we should meet, but he evidently felt that he was close to death, and he did not want to leave me alone. On his deathbed he had them fetched in order to tell them that I was to be their brother, and despite the apparent divergence of our paths, he achieved what he wanted, to bring us together. I am very glad of it, for it is an admirable family that he has created.

I took your advice about keeping my door closed, and things are going well on account of it. I follow the offices, returning a call on Father Abbot when he pays me one, and that is as far as it goes. I do not see any problems ahead on that front. If there are to be any, they will most likely come from Poitiers, where the priests are very divided amongst themselves. Those are matters to keep one on one's guard, and that is my position.

The worst was that satanic Spanish woman, who managed to slide into my house between two removal men on the day of my departure. There was another scene to be gone through, but I finally managed to show her the door. A point to note: she had previously been to Bruges, to seek the aid of a dreadful demoniac priest, whom I portrayed in *Là-Bas* under the name of Canon Docre.[14] Moreover, we are obliged to conclude that the spells of this sorcerer and this unfortunate woman have no very amazing powers, since the result she obtained was zero.

But I am not without anxiety on account of this diabolical creature, who is put off by nothing, and I fear that on the way back to Spain to join her husband, she will come to Ligugé and try to create some sort of scandal. Anyway, as there is nothing I myself can do about it, I refer the matter to the Blessed Virgin, who will see me through as usual.

All in all, despite these little bothers, I am very pleased. I feel closer to Our Lord than in Paris. This life of masses, offices every day, more frequent confession and communion is very good for me. I am quite forgetting about Paris and the abominable intrigues going on there at the moment. All this sad business interests me only from the point of view of the Church and the religious orders. I have retained acquaintances in the Ministry of the Interior and I know that documents are being prepared on them. The report on Solesmes is favourable, and the Prefect is of the opinion that the monks should be left in peace. So there is nothing to fear for St Pierre, but the situation is not the same for the congregations in the diocese of Poitiers. The Prefect, Joliet, a Freemason, has made an abominable report on them, and especially on Ligugé. I have warned Mgr Pelgé to be ready for all eventualities. There is the question of the parish here; it has been left without an incumbent since the death of Fr Bouleau and it is worrying, for I know that the Department of Religious Affairs has a report asking for it to be taken away from the monks. I have also warned Father Abbot, but we can only wait. It is quite certain that the Dreyfus party is triumphant. From this point of view, there is everything to fear.

I have left *L'Écho de Paris* for the time being, in order to be able to work in peace.

It is a long time since I wrote to you; I hope the Dutch novice will stay, for I should be happy to know that you have in your house a compatriot of St Lydwina.

I assure you, dear Reverend Mother, of my devotion in Our Lord.

J. K. Huysmans

There is a curious person here from Solesmes, a Mme Godefroid[15] who makes the poor old church of St Martin reek with musk!

To ADOLPHE BERTHET

Ligugé, 9 November 1899

Dear Sir,

Thank you for thinking of me. I would have written to you long since if I had not had so much to do, with this endless getting settled in. But we finished it all a few days ago, except for the garden that we are working on. It is true that it will be no easy job. Besides the ordinary garden, I want to make a liturgical one, and, adjoining it, a ninth-century monastic walled garden for medicinal plants, as described by Abbot Walafried Strabo in his poem *Hortulus*.

Still, next spring, I shall see what this frenzied planting will produce.

You talk about the Vintras cult. I would need pages to deal with that question. The essence of it is given in *Là-Bas* and in *Les Petites Religions de Paris* by Jules Bois. The old gnosis keeps on cropping up, with the beatification of carnal instincts. There is still a pontiff in Lyons, a defrocked priest who is a legal clerk, I think; I have seen him, but I cannot think of his name. There are also the adepts, girls I have contact with, but they refuse to supply any information, being weary after all the trouble caused by Boullan; they, like old Thibault, operate *in camera*.

So it is difficult at the present time to know for certain what is going on in this sect. The pontiff of Paris is dead, and as far as disciples of Vintras are concerned, I know only one in that city, a woman who deals in poultry at Grenelle, but she dropped Mother Thibault, judging her to be compromising, and I do not know what has become of her.

But you are on an excellent track with Paray. Paray is, moreover, a most curious place. I recommend the 'Hiéron',[16] which is of a Catholicism of Péladan's kind: the Museum of Jesus-Host. The directors of this insanity are curious, you will get some idea from a brochure that they sell about their museum.

There is surely something to be done in that direction; follow the trail.

My life is very calm: walks, offices, work, few newspapers, liturgy lessons, superb ceremonies, and pure plainchant. It will all be spoilt next week by a trip to Paris for *Pages catholiques*. I do not feel any need to see that city again. My monastery and my books suffice. I do not think I shall stay there long.

And yet it is the rainy season here! The countryside is striped with streams of water and is full of shadows and intense melancholy! But the chapel is exquisite in the dark, and, in the house, stoves give out gusts of hot air, to combat the increasing dampness. We have had all sorts of problems here, but that is all nothing really; the important thing was to find a place to sit down, and so long as no angel of deception pulls it away from under us when we stand up, all will be well. In the meantime, we resolutely defy winter with eternally green cedars and pine trees before our eyes.

And to amuse myself, I hunt – books – by catalogue, and my library is growing ... growing ...

Mother Thibault is well, saying her offices in the village. So long as the parish priest leaves her alone!

That's all for now, dear sir.

Yours

Huysmans

To MOTHER BÉNIE DE JÉSUS

Ligugé, 22 December 1899

My Dear Mother,

I think of you often, for I am so fond of St Teresa and her daughters, and then, a little selfishly as well, I hope to avoid quite a few tribulations thanks to their prayers; and I have and shall have great need of them.

When life more or less settled down here, close to the monastery, I had such a feeling of peace that I took fright somewhat, finding myself too happy, incapable of gratitude, and telling myself, moreover, that human happiness in this life has no meaning. Then the problems I was expecting came, and from the only source one might expect.

From time immemorial, the Benedictines have served the ancient church of St Martin at Ligugé. The parish priest and curate were monks. The church was at one and the same time parish and monastic. Everything was fine like that, but suddenly everything has changed. The government withdrew the parish from the monks and imposed the appointment of a priest and curate whom nobody here wants. And for his part, the bishop, in order to give a little authority to this unfortunate priest, decided that, from now on, the monks could no longer hear the confessions of Ligugé people! So there was a general uproar. A sort of concordat was established between the diocese and the abbey as far as the church is concerned, to be used at certain times by the parish priest, and at others by the monks.

Pointless to tell you of the tensions caused by such a situation, the petty scandals if gives rise to. At the moment, the village is divided into three camps. The Freemasons who are behind this state of affairs, and are delighted and mark up the points scored; the village itself, made up of peasants who miss the monks, because the fees for burials and marriages have gone up; and the friends of the monastery, who refuse to have anything to do with the parish priest, and go to confession in Poitiers.

It is a storm in a teacup, but things can get worse, for the situation is being closely watched by the Prefect, who has only one wish, and that is to force the monks into leaving Ligugé; that is my great worry. If the legislation that is in preparation gets through, the abbey, which has survived until now under cover of a legally constituted company, will not be able to buy its way out any more, and will have to leave for Spain, where a house has been prepared for this purpose. And so can you see me in Ligugé without monks!!

I hope that Our Lord will intervene; unfortunately our Father Abbot is eighty, and is at the age when people become so fearful that everything frightens them; the prior is seventy-five and a little mad, so there is no counting on them being energetic in saving the monastery in case of danger.

Only if all of this misfortune can be avoided will my novitiate as an oblate begin next March; the clothing ceremony would take place on the feast day of St Joseph. And a year and a day later, according to the Rule,[17] I would make my profession on the feast of St Benedict.

In the meantime, I have managed to obtain from the bishop, given the special circumstances, that I should remain under Benedictine direction and make my confessions to my monastic director.

We have been cut off by snow just recently, and attending the offices has been a most praiseworthy act. It has meant getting to the church at night by means of a lantern, with snow up to mid-calf, and it is so cold in that church that I spent a week with my fingers numb from the cold; I could barely hold my book, and I don't know if it is not worse now that the thaw has come; one sinks down into it, and it is like walking through bowls of chocolate. We have finally taken to wearing carter's boots, and omnibus driver's hooded jackets; we laugh every time we look at ourselves.

I am alternating between the offices and working like fury on the fourteenth century; as St Lydwina was an expiatory vicitim, I needs must show, which has never been done, what it was she had to expiate. So I am preparing a panoramic picture of each European state at that time, of the lamentable state of schism and heresy, then on the other hand, the sum total of the virtues of the saints of this period. It is an enormous job, for the heresies have to be taken one at a time, the saints also.

I have read the speeches of your good bishop. Yes, a prelate who understands St Teresa as well as that and is so fond of her daughters is for sure a true bishop, and it is a real blessing for Algeria to have him. I was pleased at what he said about you. Your pastor is quite right, and he will certainly achieve happiness in thinking as he does!

Ours here is a bishop of lesser stature, but good, and a man of prayer. In this unfortunate Ligugé business, which causes him ceaseless trouble, his hand has been forced, and he gave in from fear that the resolute opposition of the Prefect, who is a Freemason, would only bring down still worse on our abbey.

So we and our monastery are much in need of prayer, dear Mother; I hope and I do believe that the Blessed Virgin will see us through; otherwise it would only remain for us to try and sell the house and emigrate to Belgium, to be near the monastery of Maredsous, where we have friends, and we would become oblates there; but it would be sad all the same. I prefer not to think about it, especially as Christmas is coming, and we shall have a wonderful night of offices in the old church. I immerse myself in the liturgy with a joy I could not describe.

Dearest Mother, let me assure you of my respect and filial devotion.

Your

J. K. Huysmans

To FR HENRY MOELLER

Ligugé, [14 February 1900]

My Dear Friend,

I have been wanting to write to you for a long time, but letters are more abundant here than in Paris, and the interviewers have followed me. The illusion of peace, away from it all, is nonexistent. You might have read in *Le Figaro* a strange interview with that great Panjandrum of journalists,[18] who punctuated my every sentence with oaths. A doddering old mystic! He doubtless thought he was being very sharp, but I do not give a damn for the kind of wit he attributes to me.

The truth is that I have no time to do anything. Besides being invaded by people and papers, I have the crazy research necessitated by *St Lydwina*, and I have the offices and the instruction I am receiving in the monastery. My novitiate is to begin on 19 March, and should, according to the Rule, as we know, last for a year and a day, after which I shall be professed as an oblate, that is to say on the feast day of St Benedict in 1901.

This explains my silence and the kind of whirlwind I am living in, beneath these monastic vaults.

Pax! In my present circumstances, no. Other than at the offices and in the mornings, when with the aid of a lantern one goes off to dawn mass at the monastery, in the black of night.

It is certain that it would be preferable to take the habit in the monastery itself and to live there – things would be quieter – but there is the *book* question, which is the stumbling block. If one wishes to keep one's rights as regards verbs and adjectives, one has to live, as medieval families did, in the environs; I shall be clothed next month, but it is simply a formality, given that I shall not wear it, in the normal course of events.

To sum things up, I retain my literary freedom, while still becoming a son of the patriarch.

I have received your catalogue in which the numbered item interested me. It is a bit dear of course, and a bit of a hotch-potch, but the whole thing is good, and the introduction by the nuns of the congregation of Beuron is excellent. When shall we put on the Benedictine exhibition: embroideries, miniatures, pictures, books?

Here at Ligugé I am preaching these ideas to the master of novices, and *Durendal* is very helpful to us. When I have read it, I take it to the novitiate, where there are a few artistic souls; but it takes time, there are old dodderers there, as everywhere.

Esquirol spoke to you about a photograph of me. It is a proof printed up by a friend. It is a young one, but as it might amuse you, I enclose it with this letter. When the sun shows itself a bit, we shall have a view taken of the Maison Notre-Dame, and I will keep a copy for you.

We have torrential rain here at the moment, storms shaking the cypresses and pine trees. At night it seems as if the Apocalypse is at hand. We live with carter's boots on our feet and hoods over our heads. But the great wind of the psalms dries you out once you are in the old church; the daily marvels of the liturgy have the effect of a powerful tonic. I am really happy in all that. That, I fully believe, is the better part that will not be taken from me.

To sum up, if I did not have all these external disturbances that distract me, I should be living very quietly in this intimate existence of canonical hours and work. The breaking up of the day is really a bit of a problem for work, for the offices cut me off in mid-stream, but I hope I shall get used to it and fit into the mould without it hurting too much.

Help me with your prayers, my dear Father, and think sometimes of your devoted

Huysmans

To PAUL VALÉRY

Ligugé, [27 February 1900]

Your letter announcing the end of a tiresome celibacy did not surprise me excessively, my dear Valéry.[19] This very morning we were celebrating the feast day of a saint special to our order, St Eustochium,[20] and I thought of you, as I listened to the famous epistle of St Paul on marriage, which is part of the office.[21] Basically Villon[22] was a precursor of Schopenhauer when he took as the refrain for a ballad: 'Happy the man who has none of it', but life is so wretched outside of the Church and marriage, that insanity consists perhaps in remaining halfway to being that frightful thing, a concubine. It will give you a bit of (human) intimacy in your life, calm and the chance to work away from sinister meals and funereal rest in chophouses and cheap lodings. I have been through all that, and know all about those abominable places that leave one with a soul that is crumpled, beaten up, a soul served with black butter.

Be happy, far from such turpitude, dear friend.

Cordially yours,

J. K. H.

To FR ARTHUR MUGNIER

Ligugé, [March 1900]

My Dear Father,

The ceremony of oblation took place on 18 March, after the first vespers of St Joseph. It was simple and very intimate. To avoid curious visitors, it took place in the chapel of the novitiate, where not even a priest may venture. Imagine a small chapel, at the end of a corridor, the size of a pocket handkerchief, the colour of dried roses. There on the altar, in a silver gilt dish, the Benedictine habit lies folded, covered with violets and anemones.

The well-known historian Dom François Chamard, prior of the abbey, officiated, and it was he who put the habit on me, after some very beautiful liturgical prayers that precede the ceremony, with the words:

Induat te Dominus novum hominen etc.[23]

Then the great relic of St Benedict was removed from a bank of candle flames and given me to kiss.

Finally, after matins the following morning, Fr Bluté, the novice master, said mass in the same chapel, and I received communion with the novices.

There, my dear Father, is a succinct account of this ceremony at which, apart from the monks, no-one was permitted to be present.

Yours,

J. K. Huysmans

To ADOLPHE BERTHET

Ligugé, 1 May 1900

Dear Sir,

Through one thing leading to another, you have got to know the people I knew in Lyons. Breton must be the legal clerk that I knew at Boullan's in Lyons. They were two rival pontiffs. Laura is not worth bothering about. Boullan was very good to her, I speak from personal experience here, and she behaved like a real wretch towards him, accusing him in open court when he was charged with practising medicine illegally. She is a cunning little vixen, beaten black and blue by the husband she took to herself, and is very mediocre as a voyante. I saw Boullan use her on a number of occasions. She was not good for much. As for the unions, I rather doubt that they were material; after Boullan's death, I took possession of a document which was the list of proposed unions for certain days. Now amongst the males reserved for the women listed was Raymond Lully and a load of people who are dead. This love play was with succubi, as in the monasteries, which I also got to know about after his death from a voluminous correspondence. I cannot really see Mother Thibault fornicating with old Misme, in whose house Boullan lived. There were a lot of old people for whom this game would have been imprudent and lacking in charm. Guaïta's book is full of errors on this point. And there has been some unworthy underhand dealing on the part of himself and Oswald Wirth that he does not mention, of course. The Gays are decent people,[24] and I find it hard to believe that these girls, whom I know and who live respectably with their parents, were the shameless hussies they were made out to be. It is especially the mystic phraseology of these people that has led to misunderstandings, I think.

Boullan was a Satanist, that is for sure, and Guaïta was another. Only they both pretended to be men of God. And they both lied; as for those involved with Boullan, they were very much small fry. Old Misme, if he had not got sidetracked by heresies, would have been a saint, for no one was better nor more charitable. As for Mother Thibault, she was mad, in the power of the Devil through an insane pride, but she also was devoted and a good woman. On this point, there is no question of giving the young man an address, because she did not want to give it, even to her Paris friends.

Basically, Vintras's heresy is the old gnosis story all over again.

As far as the story of the mirror is conerned, it is true.[25] That was Guaïta's doing, but what I do not remember is whether Boulland warned me of the day it would happen. He had told me to be on my guard, and that was all, I think.

There was also in Lyons, in the same milieu, quite a curious woman, Mme Lyonne-Maupré, who read horoscopes in the Arab manner with salt and broad beans. She was better than little Laura. I don't know what has become of her.

What one must not forget about all these people is that they are possessed, that they are more or less aware of the fact, and that, at some point, you will inevitably see an outburst against Catholicism.

Nothing new here. I spent the day yesterday with Le Cardonnel. He too is glad that Lent is over. Nowadays I have the impression that mortification is a springboard for sin. Everyone becomes irritable: the lack of meat kills charity. That is the most obvious result I see of the imposition of abstinence on people who are temperamentally incapable of coping with it. The nervous system immediately loses its equilibrium. The novices end up giving each other black looks. And I felt myself becoming unreasonable. For me the matter is settled, I will not repeat the experience.

You see, dear sir, I was right to point out the good lass in Lyons as a signpost to heresy. The cause needs to be established, and the whys and wherefores stated. It would be interesting.

Stock's affairs are not any better. I am very worried on that front. He is stupid into the bargain, asking too much and will get nothing at all.

Best wishes, dear sir,

J. K. Huysmans

To MME THÉOPHILE HUC

Ligugé, 16 August 1900

Dear Madam,

The little crate has arrived, and for people used to eating the peaches of Poitou, that are simply turnips with the ends rounded off, and given a bit of colour, it is quite stupefying to see and to savour such succulent spheres, loaded with an incomparable liquid of exquisite and fragrant freshness.

But with my greed satisfied, oh Madam Temptress, let me add that the friendly thought is valued even more highly, and for that, my best thanks.

I have seen our petulant priest.[26] Imagine, he came here to make his retreat, and was sent to the Maison Notre-Dame, which is obviously considered to be an annexe of the monastery; but the monster in question, who was supposed to stay here for a few days after his retreat in the monastery itself, took advantage of the situation to kill two birds with one stone, and upped and off to Ostend, once the statutory three days were up!!!

We have to admit that he is an exquisite priest, but a bird of passage! The silent direction you once spoke of in a letter seems singularly exact.

Here we are caught up in the struggle between the monastery and a priest appointed in place of a monk who served the parish. It is not what one might call a stimulating or edifying spectacle, but that is life. The problem for people perched between hammer and anvil is to strike the right balance. Oh Lord, I think we are managing, but all this is far removed from mysticism; and it is very necessary to detach oneself in spirit from all of this, if one wants a quiet life.

It is also good, I think, to invoke the great St Michael to deflect the ambushes of the enemy, and any kind of 'extras' in the way of prayer are not without their use in this part of the world. I like priests well enough, and like monks a lot, yet that awful Fr Mugnier, who has always reproached me with this partiality in my affections, cried out in dismay when he discovered the antagonism here in Ligugé. So you can see what it is like!

Thank you again, dear madam, for thinking of me in such a delicious way, and be assured of my respect and devotion.

G. Huÿsmans

O quam bonum . . . if only you knew the irony of that!!!

To FR CAMILLE BROUSSOLLE

Ligugé, 24 November 1900

My Dear Friend,

The preface will be passed on to Fr Potvin after vespers this evening,[27] and I laugh, because reading your book makes certain points clear: the impossibility for a priest, for a man who has not known amorous adventure, to understand what lies hidden behind the eye and the mouth of a Madonna by Perugino or Botticelli.

The Renaissance is basically pure theatre, actresses dressed up as the Virgin.

It is along these lines that the preface should have been written, but that would have ruined your and Oudin's chances. What is better for the Catholic reading public is a syrup of sweet nothings in a journalistic style. And as a reward for having done the work for them already, the column writers will quietly take note, and it will bring in many articles, which is the main thing.

For the secret of having the press in one's pocket is this: to provide the journalists, who are always short of subjects, with the material for an article and the means of doing it quickly and effortlessly. By writing the preface in the form of an article, I was taking into account their way of looking at things; that is the most prudent and shrewd approach, I believe.

It is drizzling, rainy and windy; Ligugé is a lake of mud; my soul is purulent amidst this fetid nature. That is not mysticism, but what can one do?

Affectionately yours,

Huysmans

To MOTHER BÉNIE DE JÉSUS

Ligugé, [December 1900]

Dearest Mother,

Thank you for such an affectionate letter, and for the good wishes for the twentieth century that it contained. May Our Lord bring them to fruition, for this era is not beginning with an unclouded horizon for French Catholics. Here we are very much under threat, and as soon as the Law on Association is passed, that will be the end of Ligugé, there will be nothing for the poor monastery to do but to go into exile in Spain, where they have a house. As for me, I do not know . . . It will be whatever the Blessed Virgin wants. Now one can always hope that disaster is not at hand, that Heaven will intervene, but we have deserved punishment, to be honest.

In Algeria, these torments will not come to anything I hope, and you, fortunately, do not have to prepare for a cataclysm; in France, anything can happen, but all the monasteries are praying to avert the blow, and that is a powerful force. And then the Carmelites, whose role it is to be the lightning conductors of society, will, I think, wrench mercy from Heaven; what you tell me about the luminosity of your monastery delights me and comforts me – how useful you will be! Support the old edifice that is crumbling under attack from the Freemasons; our prayers are too weak to shore up the old walls.

I have just finished the life of St Lydwina; there only remains to copy it out and send it to the printer's. I am not very pleased with it. Besides the fact that the fabric is only anecdotal, and there was no means of doing it any other way, since the Bollandists[28] do not provide anything else, it is mediocre from an artistic point of view, for there is nothing to lift it off the ground. If it has any merit, it will come only from the mystical theories on which it is constructed; but I foresee serious difficulties again; the Catholics will be exasperated by the life of this expiatory victim, a saint who substituted herself for others in order to suffer pain for sin and sickness; they will find this brand of Catholicism antisocial and take fright, all the more so as I explain that she has left descendants even into our own times, and I quote them, amongst those who are stigmatized; in short, I have no illusions, there will be an outcry.

In order to avoid trouble with Rome, I am having the book checked here in the monastery by theologians.

But if Catholicism based on suffering and self-sacrifice is not that, then the Carmelites, Benedictines of Our Lady of Calvary, the Poor Clares have no *raison d'être*; but nobody understands what these orders are about. I have heard a lot of pious ladies say: 'I understand the Little Sisters of the Poor, but what is the point of the contemplative orders?' It is frightful to see such a lack of understanding, but that is the way things are.

Still, the Good Lord will sort it all out. It will be as usual: after the newspapers have had a good scream, the book will go quietly on its way, whether the enemies like it or not. I think it can do some good, console the sick, give a more virile image of religion, show the mystic soul to those who are ignorant of its very existence; I have gone to a lot of trouble over this book, which I thought would turn out better than it has; but I hope that good Lydwina will intervene in my favour. Except in Holland, in the little town of Schiedam where I went to seek her out, she has so few friends, she is so forgotten, that she will surely help her poor biographer.

You speak, dearest Mother, of Mme de Ste Foix, who causes you some concern as regards the future. The fact is that personally I have tried, I must admit, to dissuade her as much as possible from settling in Paris. Besides the very great difficulty of establishing oneself there, I have always been afraid for her on account of her adventurous character, that she might not fall into some wasps' nest, and let herself be either exploited or tricked. I have since warned her about one or two dangerous characters she had become involved with, but since she is quite determined not to leave town, I thought there was no point in making her discouraged, she will have enough disappointments, poor woman! This religious operetta business is not serious, it is a bit of amusement that will lead to nothing, but it is all she has, it is better to encourage her, while begging her to act with prudence. That was the line that good Fr Dauzon and I had agreed on when he came to see me at Ligugé.

But there is no future for her in all this, as far as the theatre is concerned; she is only storing up disappointment for herself, but she is still as if intoxicated with the atmosphere in Paris, and there is nothing to be done but let her calm her nerves a bit. You alone can keep her steady from a religious point of view, which is difficult, in the hurly-burly of such a life; what she needs is to find a good spiritual director in Paris, but nothing is more difficult, unless the Blessed Virgin takes a hand. I never write to her without repeating that when she has difficulties she should go to Notre-Dame des Victoires: that is where, in prayer, she will get the best advice. Does she do so? Perhaps she does not have time in her hectic life.

As for me, I do not know if I shall end my days at Ligugé, since it will depend on whether the monks stay or go, but in the meantime I thank Heaven for the offices. This Advent and Christmas, it has been so moving and magnificent! Vespers in the evening in the old, dark church are exquisite. One feels so strongly the need to sing the divine praise. How many times, harassed by the day's work, my head stuffed with sentences, have I not felt my burden of tiredness removed, and become joyful as soon as the organ began the *Deus in adjutorium*... intoned by the hebdomarian.[29] These are joys that the world cannot give. It is now over a year that I have been leading this life of daily mass and offices. I have at most benumbed my former self, I have not managed to kill him off, and yet I have found peace and much liturgical joy, having reached a degree of resignation that I did not have before.

The Lord is indeed truly good to take pains over souls that have, after all, only caused Him trouble!

Let me wish you, my dear Mother, for the coming century, all that is closest to your heart, that is, is it not, the growth in virtue of your daughters, and the spiritual prosperity of your community. I also wish you the good health necessary for the completion of your work, and beg you to be assured of my respect and devotion in Our Lord.

G. Huÿsmans

To JEAN-LOUIS FORAIN

Ligugé, [8 January 1901]

My Dear Friend,

I very well understand your hesitations and moments of blindness that come on with the realization that, with the poor means at one's disposal, one needs to tackle a new form of art. I have been through it, wondering how to use the tool in my hand to write pages that were poles apart from those I had written before. For one has to retain the tool, make it sharper or blunter as circumstances demand, but one has to hang on to it, otherwise nothing is possible. Basically it all becomes clearer with the help of prayer. Personally I have been helped a great deal in poor churches at twilight, when there are only very humble people praying there. There one finds an experience of simplicity and lively faith that can be a real help. Basically, what is called beauty does not exist in the sense we have understood for so long. Once in my life have I seen radiant beauty, divine beauty, the only true kind. It was a quite ugly woman who came to my house one evening. I saw her for ten minutes, and have never seen her since, as, the following day, she entered a convent of the strict observance, with grilles.

Through a priest, I became involved for an instant in the life of this amazing creature. My dear, in my house she spoke of the joy of sacrifice, of happiness in suffering, and this woman who was so ugly was bathed in light. Her eyes became incomparable, how can one convey that! True beauty is not to be found in form or feature, for an impulse from the soul can change them; religion ennobles everything. I have sometimes seen the heaving shoulders of women weeping at Notre-Dame des Victoires. Nothing is more moving. What pictural dramas can equal this movement of grief imploring the Virgin?

One needs patience ... Wait; good Le Cardonnel, with whom I have spoken again about the matter, is praying for this intention at his mass. You can be sure of one thing, that is, if God has brought you back to Himself, as He has done for me, it is in order to be useful to Him, as far as our feebleness will allow; so He will provide you with the means, as He has me. We can be any use to Him only in the field of art, consequently He will help us, and render us capable of accomplishing our work of gratitude and expiation.

Think of art as a lever, precisely the force that is lacking in the Church; whether her sad children understand or not does not matter. It is a force; it brings about conversions more easily than preaching from the pulpit. Do we know for sure, for our own part, what seeds of faith were sown in us by certain Primitive paintings? But, you will say, none of that points to the path I must take. Well no, that is beyond our domain. Pray and you will be helped! The formula will not come to you through human agency. It is most certain that as a precaution against the evil times we are going through, and perhaps worse to come, God is unleashing a wind that blows conversions; He is preparing his defences. And not in order to abandon them.

This thought alone should give you courage.

Nothing new here, other than a magnificent feast of the Epiphany, when I dined in the monastery, to partake of the traditional cake that had received a pontifical blessing at mass. The feast was somewhat spoilt by terrible and incredible cold. I went down in darkness in the morning beneath a sky full of stars, but how cold they were!

I am working like a mad thing from six in the morning until nine o'clock at night, just taking out the time for meals and the offices. Ligugé is empty. Fr Besse is in Paris, perhaps you have already seen him? The Leclaires are still at Vincennes. I am living in the most total solitude. It reminds me a bit of the best time of my life, at the Trappist monastery, although I suffered martyrdom there.

Farewell, dear friend, take courage, pray for me, as I am praying for you.

Affectionately,

Huysmans

To GEORGES LANDRY

Ligugé, 22 March 1901[30]

My Dear Friend,

I am writing to you immersed in printer's proofs,[31] and fighting a losing battle with domestic staff, for it is no mean undertaking to find any in this part of the world, and there is nothing on the horizon; add to that neuralgia, telegrams from Stock demanding the go-ahead for final printing, and you will see how much fun I am having.

Everything is going from bad to worse here. Le Cardonnel, weary of the life they are leading him, is interested only in leaving. Only he would like to leave with military honours, that is that they should turn him down on the grounds of poor health. To have given himself so much trouble, to have endured so much to arrive at such a result! It makes me frightfully sad, especially as I am more than cross with Fr Besse, who on such occasions, and on others, indulges in double dealing and really lacks honesty. The truth is that the novitiate is a den of sneaks, that that numbskill Le Cardonnel mistook it for friendship and then was betrayed; and this with the connivance of Fr Besse. It is obviously a different form of morality from ours, but the evangelical dimension of theirs escapes me. In short, I have no doubt now that Le Cardonnel will not stay here! It is the final routing, but even admitting that there was a lot of wrong on his side, what an environment! And between you and me, what a wretched place this monastery is, with no intellectuals and, what is worse, with no saints!

But let's leave all that. It is obviously an advance taste of purgatory, and if disaster befalls them, they will have deserved it!

Little Buet will be better off if he can enter the seminary at Nice. That is better: as you say, everything considered, poor Buet left them a sad inheritance.

As for Bloy, I have received from some sublieutenant a letter, obviously written by Bloy, begging me to send him a *large* sum, not as a former friend, but as a Christian. Basically, if it is to be well celebrated, the liturgy of Lent demands almsgiving, and fundamentally I am not cross with him over the insults,[32] which I don't give a damn about, and after all, it is only too clear that he is unhappy, so I sent it to a man at Hachette's, who is collecting subscriptions. Much good may it do him! It will only serve to fuel his hatred, but I don't care, that's his business.

I have Xavier Rousselot's book, don't buy it. Just send me the French clergy yearbook, although all that seems destined to return to Paris with me one day or another.

As Stock told you, he took two express trains to spend two hours with me at the station buffet at Poitiers. We settled all our business. He is leaving tomorrow for Hamburg, where he is going to have *St Lydwina* printed in Gothic characters. I am sick of that book! There is no end to it, my life consists in going down to mass in the morning and coming back to work without respite afterwards.

I heard from Stock about the scene at Descaves' and the departure of his grandmother. It would seem that life had become unbearable in that house. They might have known. It would have taken more than Christian charity to insulate one from such an existence, and it ended in war. Descaves said nothing about it to me, so don't mention it. It seems that his friend Fr Lefrançais has had a stroke and gone childish; I am telling you that because I know you know him.

You say you are adrift. Ah! Don't lose heart. We all are in one way or another at the moment. I spend my life trying to overcome anger that seizes hold of me when I see what I see, and all that, inspired by monastic life, is not very divine, and not very salutary for the soul. We must hope for mercy, pity, without which nothing would be possible. The sad truth is that one does not manage to kill off one's old self, one makes it numb and that is all. The image of the old serpent in the Book of Genesis is very accurate. We have a boa constrictor in our soul. We manage to stifle it with woollen blankets, but it does not take much to wake it up and set the monster whistling.

We have black coldness here: an icy sky, tipping down buckets of melancholy. Leclaire has been quite poorly, his wife is better. They are waiting to get a maid, and then will be off to Paris.

Greetings to Girard and Orsat.

Yours, dear friend,

J. K. Huysmans

To ADOLPHE BERTHET

Ligugé, 3 July 1901

Dear Sir,

I am writing to you rather on the off chance, not really knowing whether this leter will reach you in Paris where you are perhaps no longer!

Have you seen Stock? If not, go and see him; I spoke to him about your book when I was in Paris, and he is expecting it.

I have been to Dijon to make notes for *L'Oblat*, and came back very pleased with that town, whose pious places I have thoroughly explored; and I am not sorry to return to the tranquillity of my garden and the offices here, while I wait to be obliged to clear off, on account of the abominable act that has been voted through.

I will admit that writing *St Lydwina* was an act of penance for me. There were so few opportunities for the artistic dimension to take off; it is the literary equivalent of fasting; still, it is finished; I hope to have more fun with *L'Oblat*, where I shall be no longer confined to crushing texts, but free to spread myself.

I was interested in Lydwina only on account of the mystical theories which basically complement those of *En Route*.

Stock wrote that the book is not selling too badly, although times are not exactly favourable for book sales, but I doubt if that one will have the success of *En Route* and *La Cathédrale*.

It is too specialized, and I keep coming back to it, from an artistic point of view, it is very inferior to the other two and, consequently, not very attractive to my usual customers.

For the moment we are drowning here, but I am not complaining; I prefer these downpours to the dazzle of that lout the sun who has roasted me so much over the last few months. And your book? Is it on its way to those happy words: The End?

I must go, as time for mass is ringing, but not without first sending you, dear sir, a good shake of the hand.

Huysmans

To JULES BOIS

Ligugé, 18 July 1901

My Dear Friend,

You will find this bit of a note when you get back from Ipremont, where I hope the correspondence will provide material for some interesting pages. I shall not budge from Ligugé; consequently you can be sure of finding me here, as soon as you are free. Try to manage at least a week between two expeditions, so that you will at least have a little time to rest here.

Soury's article is indeed stupefying. There's one who won't die without a priest, if, that is, he doesn't make up his mind to take the plunge beforehand. He has a very pious mother, who will have been upset by his books. Whether she is dead or alive, she must have prayed a lot for him, and we are seeing the first results of it.

This diabolical Dreyfus affair will at least have allowed some people to get to know their own souls. It has separated the sheep from the goats.

The heat is quite unkind here, but the evenings in the garden are more or less cool. I am working and ruminating on the plants for the real and liturgical seasons in *L'Oblat*, which I should like to make some headway with; this is no little undertaking, for nothing fits easily into place. Still, between correcting the proofs for my volume *De Tout* for October, it keeps me busy and keeps me happy.[33]

The monks will leave in October, and doubtless me too; for without them, life would be too mediocre here; from which it emerges that it is just about impossible to sit down in this life, and that the Divine carpenter no longer produces chairs that are really solid. They all come unstuck, as soon as you touch them; still, I will have had two years in one place, vaguely resting, far from Paris; and doubtless I shall have to take to the road again, only with age one's legs are shaky. May God's will be done! All the same, how ignominous that law is, upsetting the only decent things left in France!

Come as soon as you can, dear friend.
Yours

                                      J. K. Huysmans

To HENRY CÉARD

                                    18 November 1901

My Dear Friend,

Thank you for your affectionate letter and your friendly solicitude. I left Ligugé without too many regrets. Once the monks had gone, there was nothing to keep me there; the countryside in itself, without the monastery, never filled me with joy.

You talk about the ignominy of the Breton soul, what about that of the natives of Poitou, then! A submissive and sullen race, full of cupidity and ungraciousness. The people of Ligugé have behaved abominably towards those monks to whom they owe so much; the thought that I shall not see that riffraff any more has compensated for the sadness at this change of direction in my life. What will it produce? I do not know. I neither expect nor desire anything good in this life.

I have found a haven with the good Benedictine sisters of the Blessed Sacrament, whom I spoke of in *En Route*. They have offered me lodgings in the convent itself on generous terms. It is more provincial here than in Poitou, and I am leading a truly monastic life, really cut off from crass idiots. The government of louts that we have will doubtless try to pick a quarrel with us; then the only thing to do will be to lock oneself up in a Belgian monastery. The thought of all this no longer terrifies me. I am so perfectly disgusted with the age I live in that the best thing would be to be in the place where one no longer heard human speech.

The Dreyfus affair has worn itself out, I think; what interest is there in human stupidity and roguery? There remains only the spectacle of bankruptcy and final defeat. I do not know whether, with the necessary distance of a century, there will emerge a historian of the calibre of Michelet[34] to depict a panorama of our times; it would be very fine, as an example of contemptibility. Zola's inventions in *L'Argent* are nothing compared to people like Herz and Reinach and Jewish bankers.[35] How pitiful!

I am pleased to see that, for your part, you are working at a calm mooring. Do not get upset about the locals, they could be worse elsewhere; wherever one is in the provinces, things are squalid, and Paris is hardly any better, but one does come across some exceptional people, and that is an invigorating consolation.

Affectionately yours, dear friend.

                                      J. K. Huijsmans

To ABBESS CÉCILE OF SOLESMES

20 November 1901

Dear Madam,

It is quite a long time since I wrote to you, but I knew you were so busy looking for a home,[36] and with the tribulations of moving house, that I did not want to add another letter to the pile you must have received; and then I myself had plenty of problems, with all the upheaval of the removal from Ligugé to Paris.

Now you are settled in, and I, for my part, have just about found somewhere to sit down. I am taking advantage of the feast day of St Cecilia to prove that silence is not synonymous with forgetfulness, and to wish you great and holy peace, far from this country of France, whose inhabitants are not to be envied at the present time.

Once the exodus of the monks from Ligugé was over, I found myself in a singularly sad situation in the village of Ligugé that is rotten with Freemasonry. No offices, a parish priest hostile to the monastery and its friends, an ungrateful and triumphant population; it was really too much, and I spent days of deadly boredom, not knowing what to do, for the idea of looking for lodgings in Paris, far from my monastery, did not really appeal. That is the way things were when the prioress of the rue Monsieur offered me, through Fr Chamard, who stayed there on his way back from Belgium, an apartment in the monastery on generous terms.

And here I am, in a suite of irregular-shaped rooms, but still big enough for me to fit in all my books. All in all, I am leading a more monastic existence than in Ligugé, and it is more provincial than the provinces. I take advantage of the fact that the front door is locked at nine o'clock in the evening to turn down all offers of dinner in town, which is a genuine advantage! The offices are very decent, sung better even than at Ligugé, where Fr Andoyer spoilt everything; I am also in a completely monastic atmosphere, because nearly all Benedictines who pass through Paris come and stay here, and so I see all my old friends.

And what beats everything is that there is an excellent confessor, who has a cell above me, Fr Du Bourg, former prior of the Benedictines in the rue de la Source in Paris. He is an old man, very well behaved, which one does not come across every day, and, what is more, he is a monk through and through, living the spiritual life, which is not very common either. In short, from a religious point of view, I think I shall be better off in Paris than in Ligugé.

This is the positive aspect; the other side of the coin is the lack of ceremonial that I had got used to in a male community; it is the sadness of the house, the lack of sun, the icy cold in the rooms that nothing manages to warm up. I cannot but at times miss the spacious life at Ligugé, the freedom from inconvenient visits, the fragrance of the garden, the splendour of the offices, although low-key in comparison with Solesmes. But still, we have to expect to have to put up with something; but it is hard at first!

All that should be nothing, would be nothing, if one were exclusively possessed by God; the misery is being aware at all of these trials and to feel affected by them. Alas, for me the day is nowhere near dawning when I can feel joy or sadness only through the liturgy, when that would be the only barometer of my soul!

To console myself, I tell myself that this awareness of my weakness and impotence is perhaps useful as a foil to vanity, which would otherwise show itself; but all the same, how sad these changes of course and new stages in one's existence are!

De Tout is an abridged collection of my articles in *L'Écho de Paris* in a revised version; a kind of assorted platter, as they say in the cooked meat trade. There is something for everyone, even, I rather hope, to suit monastic tastes.

I wish you a happy feast day of St Cecilia for many years to come, and I ask you once again to pray for me, dear Mother.

J. K. Huysmans

To THE DIRECTOR OF *L'AUBE*

16 March 1902

Dear Sir,

You are good enough to ask my opinion on the service the magazine *L'Aube* can render to religious art.

Although my opinion does not seem to me to be indispensable, here it is, quite baldly:

I believe that this magazine, which should, I think, be aimed especially at Catholic youth, would do well in the first place to try and inculcate into them a taste for liturgy and a love of plainchant.

In fact, do you not consider that if Catholic piety has drifted off into spineless and sentimental devotions, it is precisely because there is an ignorance of the offices of the Church, and people pray using formulae invented by goodness knows who, formulae that are bombastic and mild at one and the same time, such as are found at the beginning and end of so many manuals!

Do not these prayers have a debilitating effect, something approximating to a weak herbal brew for the soul, whereas the real liturgical prayers are, on the contrary, the most potent cordials? And yet how many Catholics bother about them, how many of those who go to mass on Sunday take a rosary out of their pockets and then take any notice of what is going on at the alter only so as to know when to kneel or sit down?

One would need to convince these people that it is an excellent thing to say the rosary before or after, but not during; that there is a time for everything; that, for the most part, masses are wonders of piety and art, and that the Christian's duty is to follow what is going on. One would need to get them interested in vespers, compline, persuade them that the psalms contain everything, our adoration and our joy, our limitations and our raptures, that it is only through the liturgy that we speak to God in His own language, that it corresponds to all our thoughts, all our needs, that it purifies our poor desires and complaints through its own expressive medium, that it functions virtually autonomously, supplying what is lacking in us, reminding Our Lord of the very phrases that He, who is prefigured in the Old Testament, used Himself.

It is, in a word, the mainstay of the soul. That having been said, the inspired word acquires even greater stature and strength, if such is possible, when it is multiplied by many voices, as it is launched forth from our hidden depths in the waves of neums of plainchant.

Gregorian chant is the inseparable companion of the liturgical text. It complements it, dissolves into it, making a single unit, and suggests to us a vague glimpse of what the choirs of angels sing up there in the clouds even more perfectly.

But one must get things straight. When I talk about Gregorian chant, I do not at all mean those cartloads of gravel that are emptied on to sanctuary pavements by overflowing choristers, I mean the plainchant of Solesmes, restored by Dom Pothier and Dom Mocquereau, I mean the only true Church music, and not the odious counterfeit commodity that so many choirmasters are satisfied with.

Now, sir, you must admit that if one succeeds in inculcating an understanding and love of the liturgy into the elite of the Catholic party, the rest will happen of its own accord. Any one who is delighted by the impenetrable beauty of the psalms, responses and hymns will not be far from grasping and loving, in the field of art, the Primitive painters and Catholic literature, ancient and modern. The essential is to guarantee solid spiritual foundations, and I wish you every success in it.

I assure you, sir, of my respect and devotion in Our Lord.

Huysmans

To PAUL MORISSE

29 March 1902

My Dear Friend,

I wrote to the Italian that if he wants to get hold of the Latin edition of Ruysbroeck,[37] which is by Surius if I am not mistaken, he should contact you, but I doubt very much if you will be able to get hold of it for him. I remember having seen it once at Durnerin's, who was selling it for about fifty francs, I think. I have not seen it since in any catalogue.

Here Holy Week has been magnificent: pontifical offices every day, with the abbot of Silos and an army of monks on leave from the Belgian monasteries for the occasion. It was just as beautiful and better sung than in the heyday of Ligugé. The rue Monsieur is the last refuge for Benedictines at the moment.

You speak about the oblates again. I respect your illusions, but do not in any way share them. In my opinion, there is nothing to be done in Ligugé, where there are no monks, no offices, no suitable land. I left that hole with no thoughts of return, and no desire ever to set foot there again. For anyone who has to work, it is a depressing place, with the effect of a wet blanket. I realize that one can work much better in Paris, and I would add that from the point of view of piety one is also infinitely better off, with the exquisite churches and prayer-filled chapels that are to be found here.

Oh no! I have no regrets about Ligugé, and am only amazed at one thing, that I stayed there as long as I did.

My work is in full swing, which will explain the brevity of this epistle.

Greetings to Fr Guyot, whom I shall be very pleased to see if he comes to Paris, also to the good Bourbon,[38] and to you dear friend.

Huysmans

To ARIJ PRINS

17 May 1902

Dear Friend,

It is a long time since I wrote to you, but I have had so much trouble with my toothache, compacted molars that had to be extracted, that I was as if completely annihilated, and found it absolutely impossible to take an interest in anything at all.

Still, I think that there is a monastic connection in this painful neuralgia: the old damp and cold buildings that I live in. It is annoying, because apart from that I am fine here, and the thought of moving house yet again appals me.

The good Leclaires, whom I saw yesterday, are still caught between two stools. They do not want to return to Ligugé, and, on the other hand, they have not found anything that suits them close to Paris.

It is true to say that dear Mme Leclaire does not know what she wants.

I am trying out housekeepers; I have had to retire my old maid and take another, and it is very bothersome to live with people one does not know.

Nothing new. I am harnessed to my book *L'Oblat*, but it is going very slowly. The subject is so specialized that I wonder who the devil it can interest, apart from a few monks. It is true that all my books have been like that for years now, and yet there is a market interested in them, many, I think, out of disgust at the state of this unfortunate country of France, and hatred of the persecutors and sectarians.

His Lordship Bloy lives, it would seem, at Sagny, a few miles from Paris. What the devil can he be up to there?

What you tell me about the Rembrandt left in a portfolio by your family is good. Genuine Rembrandts are becoming rare now! Thirty-five thousand francs to a collector, you cannot complain, damn it all!

Greetings to your wife, dear friend, and all the best to you.

G. Huijsmans

The Rothschilds have donated to the Louvre, where it is on show, the most marvellous collection of medieval religious objects (goldsmiths' work). It is worth seeing.

To HENRY CÉARD

5 October 1902

My Dear Friend,

Thank you for your kind letter. I assure you that it is very good to feel an affectionate and close contact amidst the ignoble array of frightful people around us.

I did not get any more warning of the death than you did.[39] Yesterday evening, the day before the funeral, I simply received an envelope without a stamp (it cost me six sous) containing no letter, no card, no message, just a piece of paper marked: 'Funeral of Émile Zola – Pass'. Can you imagine anything more vulgar!

But I expected as much. As you said so well, his circle hated us basically, anyone decent had distanced himself from him; of course I did not go and mingle with that mob.

I preferred to go and pray for the poor man in a quiet corner.

This shameful funeral stopped at nothing. The writer chosen to speak in the name of literature was Anatole France, who, having dragged him through the mud, is now licking his boots, because he wrote that article *J'accuse*!

Ah, yes! We are invaded by crassness, good old Flaubert saw it all right! I wonder what abuse he would yell out if faced with such things!

Basically, it is a long time since we lost the Zola to whom we turned; heaven was kind to him, taking him when his situation was becoming frightful, for he would certainly have known poverty, given his lifestyle and the total discredit into which his books had fallen.

His wife and the other one and the children are protected by his insurance policies. How many good people die far worse off!

Nevertheless, these deaths stir up the old ashes and, when I think about it, I am seized by an immense sadness and a horror of our times that is becoming more acute. I do not know if our generation was very brilliant, but at least we loved art in a disinterested sort of way, and we were not like them, all the same.

This new twenty-year-old generation that plays about with and drives cars, and does not even spend its money on women, seems truly hideous to me. Evidently I am becoming an old man, for I am not with it any more. The mediocre exploits of Maupassant seem to me to be of an exalted taste, compared with the racing that the newspapers are full of. Long live pigs, they are better than these people, even from a divine point of view, for they are dominated by the lure of lucre and have a taste only for base desires! I met Fleury, who was himself disgusted with this *dreyfusard* funeral. He told me that Zola, covered in pink spots, looked hideous in his coffin.

Have not seen Hennique. I think he is at Ribemont. He certainly would not have come for the funeral.

Affectionately yours, dear friend,

J. K. Huysmans

You heard about poor Daniel's death. But no, I think the family did not have your address. He died on holiday in the Pyrenees, from a chill caught after a bicycle ride. We buried him a week ago. How the list of departed friends grows longer!

To ADOLPHE BERTHET

13 December 1902

My Dear Friend,

L'Oblat is finished. I am mending the sentences that have holes in before giving it, in a few days' time, to the melancholy Stock, so that it can come out in March. I am afraid that next year will be the same as this, a dead loss as far as books are concerned. And reviews! But, my dear, one can have them only when there is nothing happening. For the Humberts and Boulaines of this world,[40] the kidnapping of young girls, religious orders, crimes, take up all the space. And then who is interested? The authors, and that is all.

Commit a serious crime, and your book will be talked about. If you shrink at such a prospect, you can get lost! Embrace the spirit of the age, or do not expect a single line in print.

Nothing new here. Life is still calm, but it is likely to be spoilt, for my good Benedictine sisters will have to clear off.

Fr Du Bourg, the former prior of Paris, with whom I lived in the rue Monsieur, has already gone; it is the final routing. And it bothers me, for he was my confessor, and so here I am, wandering from confessional to confessional, as one tries out restaurants, like in *A Vau l'Eau*.

The little bird is troublesome too.[41] It has flown away from its château and has been perched in the rue de Babylone[42] for the last three days. It whistles and hops, showing off its pretty clothes. What does it all add up to? Whilst being perfectly innocent, she seems to me to be giving herself a foretaste of evil, preparing alibis for a family in the Faubourg St Germain, supposedly going out in the afternoon to tea, where she stays for five minutes, and then comes straight to my place.

It is awkward and not very respectable, and would be singularly perilous for her, if she happened on anyone other than me! This little luxury bird worries me and is a problem.

I see that your military service was not too distressing. So much the better, as beforehand, it looked as if it might be a dull time to get through.

I leave you, as I have people here at the moment, but not without sending you a good shake of the hand.

Huysmans

I have read *Le Succubat* by that funny little character;[43] there is not a single word of his own in it. He got it all from an old article in the *Mercure de France*, which was written under a psuedonym by a follower of Canon Van Haecke, a Dr Lemaunier. He has a cheek, that little priestling!

To ARIJ PRINS

29 December 1902

My Dear Friend,

I received your letter. Another year collapsing about our ears. Here in France each new one is to be feared, with the departure of all the friends I numbered in the monasteries. The one about to begin looks no less black and I fear that my friends the Benedictine sisters in Paris will in their turn pack their bags; it is really disgusting to be so oppressed by a handful of sectarians, but the Catholics here are so cowardly and stupid.

I have finished my book and it has gone to the printer. I hope it will be out in the first few months of the new year. I expect a general uproar with this one, for I have got it in for everybody, the Pope and Loubet.[44] I shall be lucky to avoid being on Rome's Index this time, I narrowly missed it with *La Cathédrale*.

I am weary. *L'Oblat*, which is a thick volume, caused me an enormous amount of research; I wanted to deal with the question of recluses, that is people who, in the Middle Ages, had themselves confined in a walled-up cell, and with Benedictine oblates. No one had done it, and you can imagine the patient research it cost me.

Some days I tell myself that it is a fool's game to write a book conscientiously for two or three years on end, while a bunch of swine write any old novel in a couple of months and satisfy to perfection the taste of the reading public.

But one cannot change one's nature. Novels such as Zola's that you mention make he heave.[45] It is written any old how, the research is even worse. What interest can it have?

It is true that it [Zola's death] was timely. He was becoming greatly discredited in France and he died at a good moment, for with his lifestyle he would have known poverty. With his two households he needed 100,000 francs a year. He could no longer earn that.

So in a way providence was very kind to him, removing him before his irremediable decadence, which was close at hand.

The prices you give me for Mauve's and Maris's pictures are really crazy.[46] For such a sum I would prefer to buy Primitives!

The Leclaires are still in Lourdes, where they are happier than at Ligugé! The wife is in bed with flu, but nothing serious. Fr Besse is in Paris at the moment and is even dining with me this evening.

To tell you the truth, there is a constant coming and going of monks at my house. Many pass through Paris on monastic business, so that I perhaps see more of them than at Ligugé, where there was only one abbey.

A Happy New Year for your health and your work; good health to your family, and yours affectionately,

G. Huijsmans

To JEAN DE CALDAIN

Lourdes, 18 March 1903

My Dear Friend,

Here I am, settled in Lourdes, in a villa adjoining the Leclaires', and I have a view of the mountains, the basilica and the grotto. From my bed, I can see it all lit up at night, for this is the land of water and fire. The grotto is permanently ablaze; I am seeing Lourdes without the pilgrimages and the crowds; it is very charming and very curious like that. I am half living in the Carmelite convent, which is next door to us. The Leclaires saved their convent and help them, so they are at home there; and the portresses are good and kind and are as much in our house as in their own. They are not at all like the Benedictine ones!

The prioress, without knowing of the trouble I had previously with her mother, knew that I was interested in the little novice whose photograph you have seen at my place.[47] And in the parlour she had the shutters opened, and I had a very strange feeling.

When the little lass came in, a white outline, I saw the mother whom she resembles so much, but young and angelic. This child's soul is of an extraordinary openness and piety. She told me some things about myself, quite strange, confirming in quite a resolute tone that I would receive many graces in Lourdes, and insisting that I am to glorify the Virgin of this place.

The offices in the basilica are strange. There are vespers in Solesmes plainchant, with superb men's and boys' voices, but that is all, the masses have songs that are independent of any liturgy. The priest in charge of the music, whom I know, likes plainchant, however. But here, people think that apart from the office of the apparitions, which is very fine and is frequently repeated, this is not the right setting for the liturgy. It is something different. It is evidently something special. On the one hand a simple heart-to-heart, and ostentatious pomp on the other. Hence these enormous errors and a taste for Palestrina are understandable. It must be the same in Rome.

The most infamous thing is the sentimental bad taste of the statues and mosaics. They inspire in me some very particular ideas concerning the Virgin, which I shall write about one day. But the grotto is the charm of the place, baked and mellowed by the constant burning of candles. It is sweet and welcoming, very intimate at the moment, with Lourdes empty of visitors.

As for being an oblate, things are still black, as black as the soot on the rocks.

Stock writes that he is reprinting another five thousand copies of *L'Oblat*, and that consequently we have reached twenty thousand at present; he maintains that he is confident of forty thousand within a year. May his predictions be fulfilled.

Thank you for sending the articles. Can you get any sillier than that Déchamp?[48]

No need to tell you, I am sure, that I have not forgotten you, nor Nugues,[49] nor the good d'Etchebers[50] at the grotto. As the Virgin seems more open-handed here than elsewhere, perhaps there is a chance that our requests will be better answered. I wish so for all of us. Good Fr Séméraire will not be forgotten either,[51] The Grotto Fathers, who are in charge of everything here, are very kind to me. I go to confession with one of them who is a good fellow, and very well disposed towards my books. A curious thing: they speak of Zola in favourable terms, keeping their disgust for Lasserre.[52]

We get on very well.

The good Leclaires spoil me, the Carmelites also; it is not a very penitential stay, as you see.

Regards to Nugues. I will write to him as soon as I have a minute. Greetings to all, and affectionately yours, dear friend.

Huysmans

To HENRY CÉARD

Lourdes, 19 March 1903

My Dear Friend,

Your letter has caught up with me at Lourdes, where I have been resting at the house of friends for the last two weeks.

What you say about the poverty of Breton peasants does not surprise me at all, for I had an idea that they were having us on, in trying to fill us with pity for the fate of those brutes.

Ah yes, peasants are an infamous race, whether they be from Brie, Poitou, Brittany, or, as here, from the Béarn. In Lourdes, these latter add to their fundamental swinishness a hypocritical devotion, which is curious to see. These people, who were all quarrymen, have given up work to sell sausage and rosaries and bleed the pilgrims dry. And I admire Zola, who spent in all three days in Lourdes, and in his book leapt to the defence of these local louts, and of the very mysterious old town, and it takes a lot of time really to understand its secrets. I am starting to fathom it out a bit, and my first conclusion is that Zola has simply taken sides against that famous justice he was always drumming into us.

Poor man! I wanted to read his last volume.[53] I came away from it overwhelmed by the smug optimism that emerges from it, under the guise of socialism. I am not talking about the language; that no longer bears any relationship to what we knew. It no longer has anything to do with art, but the folly of ideas!

The best thing is that all the old cast-offs from his house, well whipped up by the auctioneers, brought in a large sum, and I am pleased for his wife, to whom he left almost nothing I have been told, except the income from his books, which can only get less, year by year.

We have to admit, dear friend, that in our mature years we are witnessing a most surprising spectacle. Good old Flaubert's Homais has become king, and is reigning over this illustrious anticlerical rabble and these pious fools. What you tell me of your campaign in the independent press that saved some sisters and brought down the wrath of the Catholics on you does not surprise me. That is what they are like in the Church party! I am their particular *bête noire*, and so I know something about it. I am constantly being denounced to Rome and threatened with the Index. They cannot at all accept anyone independent who tells them a few home truths. At the present time *L'Oblat* is creating explosions of fury in that wretched camp!

As time goes by, the worse foolishness and cowardice become. There is the consolation of saying what one thinks about everyone; but all the same, things are pretty black.

Affectionately yours, dear friend,

J. K. Huysmans

To MME ALFRED VALLETTE [pseudonym Rachilde]

3 April 1903

Dear Madam,
On returning from a journey, I have just read your kind and most curious article on *L'Oblat*, and I find in it that so delicate and agile Rachilde, who is so devoted to all her friends.

These pages are so far the first to have been written on *L'Oblat* that are worth meditating over. One of them spurs me on to examine my conscience, as they say in ecclesiastical circles, in order to ascertain whether or not it is true: the one where you say that Durtal gives you the impression of having been sucked into a marriage of convenience, when he thought he was making a love match.

I think that is only the impression it gives. It is in fact very true that in religion one eats the white bread first. The love match takes place first. The convert is cosseted until he is steady on his feet, then once he has got to that stage, the sweet support disappears; the time of purification, of dryness begins, and ends one knows not when, sometimes never. All mystics have recorded it. It is bread made from straw, siege rations, but one knows about it in advance, and so it is no surprise; it is necessary and just, if not much fun. That does not prevent the love match from surviving. It is less of a honeymoon, that is all. As you see, it is the same with relations with the beyond as it is with relations in this life.

Humanly speaking, one could answer that familiarity takes the edge off sensibility; yes, but there is something else, all the same; only it becomes more sensitive and less explainable, and is, I admit, incomprehensible when one has not thought about it.

And here I am, getting on my mystical hobbyhorse, and sounding like someone giving a lecture. God knows that is not my wish, but rather to tell you in all simplicity that I was very pleased with your article, and I thank you for it sincerely.

Please accept, dear madam, this expression of my gratitude and my respectful devotion.

Huysmans

To ADOLPHE BERTHET

16 April 1903

Dear Friend,
You have to smile! The city of Dijon is exasperated by *L'Oblat*, and the abbot of Ligugé is protesting, and has declared that I have made his monks look ridiculous!! But what would he have said if I had portrayed them as they really are??

The pride of these people is immense, and they will never forgive me for having said in *L'Oblat* that I found more holiness amongst the Trappists than amongst the Benedictines.

Fortunately old Bourigaud's protest has not got into the press,[54] otherwise I would have been put in the position of having to answer him with some painful things.

What a world we live in, all the same! And what an amalgam of intelligence and pride! I still have loads of errands to run and problems with the Goncourt business,[55] but it has all been settled, I am wasting my time with that.

I have still not got a subject for a book; my series has, in fact, come to an end; and I need to set off on a new tack. The thing is to find it.

The Catholic press is maintaining a deathly silence on *L'Oblat*. Fortunately the book is doing well without them. But in the other camp, on the contrary, it is an amusing shower of insults.

Holy Week was good at St-Sulpice. Good old Vigourel, whom I saw yesterday, had brought the seminarians in to give the choir a rest, so we had some plainchant. And then the Easter vespers are full of interest. Parisian liturgy is rather curious. As there was no visiting abbot at the Benedictine sisters', it was no good there.

I pity you having to move house, it is a hard time to get through! But still, it does pass. And if one is prepared to pay, one can get very good service in that domain.

Yes, Vicomte d'Hennezel is very nice; he likes liturgy, which is the true expression of the Church. And that is rare amongst lay people.

I know the article in *L'Orgue*!

Affectionately yours,

Huysmans

The painter De Caldain has left to be a novice with the Benedictines at Baronville. Will he stick it??

To ARIJ PRINS

21 April 1903

My Dear Friend,

I shall most surely be in Paris in the first two weeks in August; in the second two, I do not know; I am supposed to be going back to Lourdes to see the big pilgrimages, but there is a good chance that, between now and then, Lourdes will be closed down by government order.

It all depends on what is going to happen. I see you are changing your partner. I am pleased, since that will give you a little peace of mind, for you must be weary with these business affairs and exhausted from always having your nose to the grindstone.

Here all fury has been unleashed against *L'Oblat*. Especially by the Catholics, exasperated that one of their own ranks has told them a few home truths. As for the Benedictines, they are not very flattered, and are protesting against the book. Who can put into words the pride and lack of understanding of these people!

And so the full force of their attack is still turned on me. I do not care. I write books in order to tell the truth, to say what I think; my allegiance is not pledged to any party, and never will be. Let them shout!

Nothing new apart from that, other than the imminent closure of some chapels in Paris, those where there was still some flavour of the Middle Ages.

There will be nothing left but parish churches, and how mediocre they are.

There is a war of religion in France – how stupid can you get! But no one, neither Catholic, Protestant nor Jew, will agree to liberty for all. That word has been eliminated from French vocabulary.

What a country of idiots and blackguards this fine France of ours is.

I am getting used to the idea of living in an age with which I no longer have anything in common. I feel myself as far removed from the ideas of the priests as those of the non-believers. What funny times we live in!

The Leclaires are still in Lourdes, where they await events. As at Ligugé, they are going to witness the departure of the religious orders, only it might be worse there.

Greetings to all, dear friend, and affectionately yours,

G. Huijsmans

To ARIJ PRINS

[4 October 1903]

My Dear Friend,

I found your letter on my return. I am exhausted, but delighted. Saw Strasbourg: an amazing pink cathedral, and Colmar, where there are some stupefying Grünewalds. They are unheard of; I shall go back there, they are beyond all preconceived ideas about art. He anticipated the Japanese and the Impressionists and everybody else. In this man there are things that exceed everything that has been tried in mysticism. He is greater than I thought. Then Basle – disappointment – some very ordinary Holbeins; nothing; Freiburg-im-Breisgau: exquisite cathedral; Mainz: Romanesque on a gigantic scale; Frankfurt, where there are two paintings finer than any. A Virgin by the Master of Flémalle that beats all the Van der Weydens and Memlings. And a Veneziano, a girl possessed by the devil which is extraordinary. This centre of high finance is luxuriant with heavy and eccentrically palatial buildings. Finally Cologne: unworthy. Brussels and Antwerp. Ah!

I have come back exhausted and with the flu, but delighted with so many fine things. Colmar is really the place to go, where there are paintings that are quite different from all that we are familiar with.

The Leclaires are in Paris. The little bird has written to me again from her château – damn! Landry is all smug and sorry not to be able to come to dinner. That is the beginning! My stomach is obstructed from all this revelry and I am weary of hotels with lifts and electric flowers, and dubious Rhine wines. I am delighted to be drinking my Burgundy again, in which I have more confidence. And so there is an accurate report on the last few days.

Affectionately yours,

G. Huijsmans

To VICOMTE D'HENNEZEL

19 December 1903

Well yes, dear Sir! You have gratified yourself with procreational prowess of an uncommon variety![56] Ah, but if soft old Esquirol had to submit to such shocks, he would cry out!

But still, the important thing is that everything went well, and I congratulate you on it.

Nothing new here. I have prepared a volume containing all Verlaine's mystical poetry, with a preface that will perhaps not win me admiration from the Catholics. And a substantial piece of work for the magazine *Le Mois* on the paintings of Grünewald in the museum of Colmar.

I am still vaguely thinking about a novel, although I am increasingly disgusted with this form. Decidedly, we need to find something else!

I have read so many of them over the last few months for the Goncourt prize that they are oozing out of my every pore.

Still, while we wait for something better, we must carry on using this old tool. But it is annoying to think about one's work with so little enthusiasm!

Yes, try to come after the New Year, so that we can have a bit of a chat.

I am still at the mercy of the dentist, I am always there!!! How many instruments will have entered my unfortunate mouth. There is an element of the Vaudeville in it!

All for now, then, dear sir, yours,

Huysmans

To JEAN DE CALDAIN

25 December 1903

Dearest Brother,

I was quite touched that you remembered me, and be assured that I was thinking of you, especially on Christmas Eve. We missed you at dinner. As you said, there was Landry, Forain and Fr Du Bourg, and afterwards the guests went into the next room to have what passes for the soul stripped with glasspaper and sanded down.[57]

Then, to be very honest, the rue Monsieur is getting worse. The chapel is ultra-crowded, there is a jostle for communion, people come out of curiosity, despite the issuing of cards; in short, I shall end up going back to Chartres as I used to for that night. It is less and less intimate. The singing is not improving; it is very wearisome not to be able to be recollected amidst all the din. It is my fault, I gave too much publicity to that chapel, and now I am paying for the damage. The shepherds and the magi found the child Jesus easily enough, but we can no longer find him in Paris. They have put him in their drawing rooms! And greeting him has become a parade, like at a ball at the Elysée, as you catch a glimpse of him and then pass by. The nativity at the princess de Sagan's! I would rather have the stable and poor people.

In February I will send you the collection of Verlaine's mystical poetry that I am putting together and prefacing, defending the poor man's life, which, through poverty, was not much different from what he has been so much reproached with. The volume is uneven, but still it is the only book of truly religious poetry since the Middle Ages. I assure you that one can really use it for meditation.

Nothing new. Life flows on, dull and sterile. The weather is worthy of London here, which does not exactly put one in a mood for work. One becomes a prisoner of one's fireside, sitting reading.

And sleep gets the upper hand. One says the prayer of St Peter softly, when one is not obliged to go out to the dentist's; which is the ultimate in human misfortune, and, I hope, in divine testing. It is frightful how many more or less expert hands have plunged into the dark cubbyhole which I have in place of a mouth. They do a load of not very kind, and in fact rather painful, things with their phenol. And what is the point of it? Nothing at all. They always have to begin all over again.

I managed to get my candidate the five thousand francs of the Goncourt prize.[58] A bit of justice for once; he is unknown and I do not know him at all; it was a struggle between him and an awful little Jew, who had gone to great pains to get the prize. That means another load of hatred piled up against me. But . . .

I was grieved to hear of the death of good Fr Legeay;[59] but it is true that I am not very anxious on his account; he was one of the good old monks of the Solesmes school and a very learned man; it is a real loss for the congregation. I think we shall have a mass for him at the Benedictines.

Nugues is supposed to be writing to you. He is surrounded by builders!

Convey my respectful homage, dear brother, to the Reverendissime, to the prior, to Frs Renaudin and Guerry, and to Fr Bourigaud if he is within your walls, to everyone, and affectionately yours, *In Christo*.

J. K. Huysmans

I have not seen Mme d'Etchebers since I wrote to you. So I cannot send you any news of her, as I would like to. Pray for me, as I pray for you.

To HENRI ALLAIS

27 December 1903

Dear Friend,

That's it. We have broken through the literary ranks of those Yids, but it was not without difficulty.[60]

You are right, the old criteria that are constantly being thrown at us are ready for demolition, but it cannot be done overnight.

Ah, yes, the Louvre! What a lot one could say about that. All the Primitives sacrificed for the sake of that tripe-merchant Rubens, who sets up his stall amidst a sea of gold; and what about their French Primitives, who have never existed and are quite simply Flemish, when they are not Germans, like one of their recent acquisitions labelled 'French School' when there is an almost identical subject in the museum at Antwerp, where I happened to come across it in a painting by the Dunwege brothers, Germans.

And the Botticelli frescoes completely repainted!!! I saw them while the paint was still wet.

But basically, no one is interested except the Jews, who run all the museums, and who are doing a good trade.

I have still got the flu and am fed up. I hope you are in better shape and wish that 1904 will at least see you freed from your bland milk diet!

And that really and truly.

Cordially yours, dear friend,

Huysmans

To MME THÉOPHILE HUC

1 January 1904

Dear Madam,

In reply to your kind greetings, I can only wish you the arrangement you desire and a little good health. One thing is certain and established from experience: that God bypasses His priests for this job, and takes charge Himself. So one does not have to be upset at having more or less indifferent or ignorant priests. God remedies their stupidity on the day of confession, and that suffices.

So Loisy has been condemned.[61] I am resolutely hostile to his ideas, but it would be better to refute them than to strike a blow. I find intolerable the heavy machinery of the Index, set in motion by so many denunciations and so much hatred. I do not remember seeing in the Gospels that Christ ever persecuted anyone. It would be so simple just to produce a note warning the faithful not to trust such and such a book for such and such a reason; and it all has such a deplorable effect.

We ask for liberty for ourselves, and we have only one aim, to smother those who don't think the same way as we do. Our demands are ridiculous in such circumstances. We make ourselves hateful to everyone. As Loisy said quite ironically: 'I will submit, Galileo submitted . . . but it did not stop the earth going round.'

What can I tell you; I am ending the year with the flu, that chapel in the rue Monsieur is so cold! I am going to give it up for a while and go to the Ladies of St Thomas de Villeneuve, where it is at least slightly warmer.

I have the good Father to dinner tonight. Today is a sad day for those like him who find themselves alone. I shall try to cheer him up with a good bottle of something and some mutual friends.

Good health to you, to the platonic lover of that rascally Néron and all your dear ones. May the Lord give you His peace, which He is not handing out very liberally these days.

Very respectfully, your devoted servant in Our Lord,

G. Huijsmans

To ARIJ PRINS

Lourdes, [September 1904]

My Dear Friend,

Your letter caught up with me in Lourdes, where I am staying with the Leclaires for another two weeks, I think. I am living amidst an incredibly cosmopolitan hubbub. Imagine forty thousand pilgrims, bedding down anywhere, in the churches, as in the Middle Ages; fantastic processions, with people from every country in the world, and day and night, unceasingly. I am somewhat exhausted by the din, but I am witnessing some very curious things at the medical assessment office, where I have installed myself alongside the doctors. Cases of lupus and leprosy, all the diseases of the Middle Ages are here, and some are cured just like that, after the Blessed Sacrament has passed by. Evidently only in Lourdes can one get an impression of what pilgrimages used to be like in former times. Unfortunately the décor, a poor imitation, is unspeakable. There is such a proliferation of devotional objects.

But one cannot have everything.

I will return the manuscript to you,[62] as soon as I get back, in two weeks' time I think. I want to see the Dutch pilgrimage which is bringing sick people this year, and they will not be here for another two weeks.

The more I think about your book, the more I realize what it is. I felt it between the lines in the translation, but the French evidently cut short the accentuation of the sentences. You are as untranslatable into French as I am into Dutch or German. That is the problem of stylists.

The Leclaires ask to be remembered to you.

With friendly greetings, dear friend,

G. Huijsmans

To ARIJ PRINS

26 December 1904

My Dear Friend,

I was still expecting you, but I see that your ill-fated business has taken a hand in matters, and that there is no longer any hope of seeing you in Paris, except some time in 1905.

Still, thank you for your New Year's greetings. The year is coming to an end with a lot of bother for me; besides the fact that I treated myself to three weeks of bronchitis and neuralgia of the throat that confined me to my room, I am in a frightful amorous mess.

You know about my little bird. For a long time I have suspected that she was well and truly in love (we have been seeing each other for four years now, or rather she escapes from her château once or twice a month to come and spend a day here). As a result of circumstances that were in no way of my making, the little lass blurted it all out. Once the family knew, they wanted to send her away to England to some relatives in order to change her mind. It got worse. I was receiving demented letters. She came back and I had to tell her, as decently as possible, in what lovemaking consisted, given the way things were going. I hoped she would be disgusted. She confined herself to answering that she was mine, that she was only my little bird.

I was really embarrassed, as you can imagine. I declared that I would not marry her, that I was nearly fifty-seven and she was twenty-four! That it was ridiculous. Thereupon she became indignant, telling me that she did not care about age, that she loved me just as I was; in short, if nothing happened, it was because I exerted a certain willpower. Her mother came; I could only say: 'What do you want me to do? I have done nothing to attract her here, I have never even courted her, and I did not take advantage of her when she offered herself.'

Damn it all, virginity at fifty-seven!

Things are still the same: I receive letters from her every morning; she is coming to Paris on the sixth, then I shall have to start exercising my virtue again. All the same, it is not funny. She is a solitary romantic and unaware of her sensuality. The worst thing, as her mother admits, would be to treat her harshly, she would be capable of doing anything.

Apart from that, she is most charming and very intelligent; and the most curious thing is that she is talented without being aware of it. I have in a letter a little prose poem by her which is a gem!

She is evidently the victim of a mirage. She is mad about my books and sees Durtal in me. How will it all end?

I don't see this new year being much fun. Added to that, the frightening situation of France, in the hands of bandits. Books are not selling at all, and I am very worried as regards my publisher, who owes me a lot of money. It is no joke!

Still, providence has always extricated me from the worst situations, and I hope it will continue to do so.

The Leclaires are ill at Menton; I will write to you at length about these poor unfortunates: he has a weak chest, I think; she is neurotic to a degree that is hard to believe. What wretchedness!

Happy New Year, dear friend, may the new beginning you are going to make at Schiedam be favourable to you, and good health to your wife and children. Health is so precious.

Affectionately yours,

G. Huijsmans

To ADOLPHE BERTHET

25 March 1905

My Dear Friend,

Don't send any manuscripts for the moment, as I am up to my eyeballs! Besides other manuscripts that are piling up on the sofa – and in vain, what is more, for Stock won't take any of them – I am busy with studies on Paris. I have handed in a 'St Germain l'Auxerrois,' I have just finished 'Symbolisme de la cathédrale de Paris.' I am working on a 'Cour de Rouen' and 'Passage du Commerce' for the *Tour de France* and *La Revue bleue*, and I find it absorbing. I have no time to do anything else.

Stock is opulently set up, it is the finest bookshop in Paris. All he needs now is to do some business!!

And to earn the formidable rent he has to pay in such a fine situation!

Nothing special; I have barely got over my flu, which has degenerated into a sore throat and lumbago. It has made me lose an awful lot of time, being unable to go out and take notes for the works mentioned above.

Fortunately I can now venture out of doors.

And yet it is raining, the weather is filthy. I cheer myself up at table with an exquisite rosé wine of which I have been able to sequester a few cases. That puts a little sunshine into my mess of pottage. Basically, given that religion forbids amorous frolics, which were nevertheless not without a certain grace, greediness is the only thing left and it ends up becoming an easy habit.

It is not very elevating, and *coïtus* was certainly more noble, but the Church has made such a fuss about amorous adventures that she has thrown us all back on to the stomach instead of the lower regions.

One can only bow in assent... whilst awaiting for her to accept more liberal ideas, less stupid and less shady!

Work in peace, call down damnation on motorcars and bicycles, which are preventing the sale of books; keep cool and enjoy life!

Cordially yours,

Huysmans

To RENÉ DUMESNIL

25 June 1905

Dear Sir,

It was really kind of you to send me your book on Flaubert.[63] I have read it, and I really admire the extent to which you have succeeded in penetrating the writer and the man, and have expressed with sagacity the dual nature – romantic and realist – that was his. As far as his style is concerned, what always amazed me was the timid aspect, fearful almost, for a man who showed heroism with words that are not to be found in any official dictionary, and, alongside the excessive pruning of certain phrases, too many *whiches* and *thats*, the anger that certain adjectives, such as 'picturesque', provoked in him, and complete oblivion of 'as' which recurs constantly in his sentences, when synonyms to avoid it exist. I think the Goncourts assessed the situation correctly in their *Journal*. But what one has to admit is that if one stops to think about it, all writers are in the same boat. He who manages to avoid certain repetitions is blind to others. It is even strange! What is certain is that with a limited vocabulary, if one compares him with the Goncourts and Gautier, Flaubert was a wonderful writer; he was also the decent man of letters *par excellence*, a generous heart.

You have shown all that; and all those who knew and loved old Flaubert are most sincerely grateful to you. I beg to be included amongst them.

Thank you again, sir. Very cordially yours,

Huysmans

To MME THÉOPHILE HUC

Issy, 17 August 1906

Dear Madam and Friend,

Here is good news at last – the liberation of your eyes! That consoles me for all the trouble you will have in store. As for me, I am still in the same state, suffering from neuralgia and not really getting my strength back. I think I shall very likely leave Issy as I came.[64]

You have read this pope's mad encyclical.[65] It is the de-Christianization of our country. He will have done more than the Freemasons to kill us off. He finds that religious associations are not schismatic in Switzerland and in Germany, but that they are in France! All churches will be closed on 11 December. What an imbecilic sovereign, pope though he may be, and far removed is the Holy Spirit from the page where he asks Catholics to be 'firm' (about what?) but not 'violent'. What then?

My heart is crucified at the thought of all the sanctuaries of the Virgin being closed, of Lourdes being dead, and Protestants taking over most of our churches. To console oneself, one has to tell oneself that God will make a clean sweep in His Church and this load of bureaucratic priests, but . . . but . . .

Father is very upset. I send you, dear madam and friend, every assurance of my respectful devotion.

G. Huysmans

To VICOMTE D'HENNEZEL

Issy, 26 August 1906

My Dear Friend,

Since the beginning of the month, I have been settled in this place which is a couple of miles from Paris, while being only five minutes away by the railway. We are lost amongst the trees, and there is an enormous library of exegetical studies. I have dipped into it, and the ineptitude of Catholic exegetes is frightful! Ah – they are even lower than I thought.

And what can one say about the Pope, caught in the act of lying in his encyclical where he says that the majority of bishops were opposed to associations, when it was the exact opposite. That's the truth! How lucky we are, to have such clowns!

I am not very well and am not getting back into my stride. But still, I am getting some fresh air and am trying to convince myself that it is doing me good, and I am trying to be patient until October when I go back to Paris, to immerse myself in life once again.

Caldain sends you his greetings. He also has toothache. For the

punishment of our old sins, we use a steel masticator, which takes all the taste away from our food!!! Damn it!
Cordially yours. Greetings from Caldain.

Huysmans

Basically I find the country boring. Long live Paris.

To DOM MICHEAU

Issy, 16 September 1906

My Dear Father,

Thank you for your affectionate letter that reached me here, where I am trying to get a bit of strength back, beneath the trees. Unfortunately, on the 26th, I am going to have to go back to Paris, where business calls, back to the rue St Placide for another year.[66]

My health is still very mediocre, but I believe that On High they will continue to lead me along a path that I would not have chosen, through lack of courage.

God knows very well what He is about, and one needs only to answer *Amen*; the unfortunate thing is that one does not say it very willingly when one is in too much pain.

It is true that we have the right to groan, as the terrifying God of the Book of Genesis did not reproach the holy man Job for it!

That is some consolation!

I see from your letter that you too, my dear Father, have been tried in your flesh; but you are one of God's own hard nuts, whereas I am an old wet hen, from which the Lord could not make a very tasty soul stew – ah, no!!!

Things are going very badly in France, and I envy you being abroad, in a haven where you can say mass in peace. I wonder if we shall have any masses at all soon.

I do not have a copy of *L'Oblat* here, but as soon as I am back in Paris, I will see about sending you one.

Kind regards to Fr George. I hope he will come to Paris. If you could come with him, what good biblical chat we should have!

Would you be kind enough to offer my respectful greetings to the Reverendissime, if he is with you, and be assured, dear Father, of my affection.

J. K. Huysmans

To ADOLPHE RETTÉ

7 November 1906

My Dear Friend,

So you are in solitude, and I hope that he whom the good Curé d'Ars referred to as 'the claw' is leaving you in peace.[67] I pray for that intention every morning and evening. In any case, have confidence, refuse to have any dealings with him, and even if prayers to the Virgin seem empty sounds, say them all the same. These moreover are the ones that are the most acceptable to God, prayers said without joy, almost without hope, because they cost an effort. The others are easy, and consequently have less merit.

Tell yourself also that suffering is the hallmark of divine love. There is not a single one of the saints that He did not put through the mill. Remember Jesus's answer to St Teresa when she was crushed with pain and finally complained to Him about this harsh treatment: 'My daughter, that is the way I treat those I love.' See, He treats us converts, us good-for-nothings, as His real friends!

As I told you, it is a very good sign. But that does not stop it being frightful. I have had experience of it, and continue to do so, not being in an exactly happy state, either spiritually or physically. But I tell myself that it is doubtless so much less to suffer in purgatory, and that consoles me.

Keep in mind also that the Lord is rather crafty. He is often closest to us when we think He is farthest away. He lets the Prince of Fools take a hand, and he purifies us against his own wishes. For all things considered, that is the outcome of all his ridiculous persecutions.

So be pleased: the Blessed Virgin has taken you under Her wing. Despite the bumpy road, everything is going very well.

Huysmans

To MYRIAM HARRY

5 January 1907

My Dear and Good Myrrhiam [sic],

How good you are to have remembered a quite pathetic man who lives henceforth as a sort of recluse, cut off from the world of the living!

Ah, yes! Since you saw me half blind in my bed, things have almost gone from bad to worse, or at least, it is a different kind of torture. I have had a recurrence of shingles on the jaw, it was a firework display of incredible pain! A month ago, I was in a clinic where a dextrous surgeon cut open my neck as if he were slicing fruit. Now I am back in the rue St Placide, but threatened with another operation, as I have a cheek that is blown up like a balloon, but which won't fly away, alas!

And basically nothing is more dangerous than rejoicing in pain, and I am paying for, with no regrets, the pages of *St Lydwina* and *Les Foules de Lourdes*. 'You have only bizarre pains', I was told by the Princes of Science, who were consulted in my case; that means that they are at a loss as to what to do!

But let us leave all this moaning.

I am living in great pain, but with my books, whenever I have a moment of respite between my four walls. And that suffices, if one resigns oneself in prayer to accepting life, however mediocre it might be.

And I assure you that in these conditions one thinks more affectionately, I believe, of one's friends than when one's mind wanders about, full of good health, and that is why your letter cheered me up, because I can picture you in your surroundings of sunny silence, dreaming under the Moorish arcades of some palace, then at work, polishing up artistic sentences, full of nuance and fragrance. I should like to breathe in some of that Harry cinnamon! Yes, if your impressions of Tunis have come out, send them to me to read. As I am more or less incapable of working, I could console myself with them.

Moreover, I can see that I shall have nothing but mysticism and literature left to occupy myself with, for I have a vague intuition that henceforward I shall be led away from literary paths, along the paths of reparation and suffering until my end. The trouble is not feeling one has a particular vocation for this kind of life; but I shall most certainly get used to it in the long run; but all the same, I hope that amidst the melancholy monotony of these tortures, they will leave me a little artistic dessert! And you will help to provide it for me, won't you?

As for the poor little creature you mention, nothing has been done. The family is resolutely opposed to her going, and she has lacked the courage to break off the connection.[68]

She has managed to be even more unhappy than ever with my catastrophic health. The day of the operation, as I was taken away unexpectedly, she ran all over Paris from one clinic to another, trying to find me, even my maid did not know the address of the place where I was. And she did not catch up with me until the evening.

All that adds not a little to my problems, although I have limited her visits and the tone of our relationship has completely changed.

Basically, how much better a life with God would have been for her, instead of all this! At least I will have done all I can to lead her to it.

What else can I tell you? Nothing! I live apart, such a sleepy life, when the pain does not wake me up! I know nothing and see nothing, and am moreover so disgusted at what I read in the newspapers about the Catholics and their persecutors that I almost feel like giving up any interest in the one or the other.

All that is so basically human that one can find no comfort in it.

Work hard, my dear Myriam, think sometimes of the old and feeble one who sends you every assurance of his very affectionate devotion.

Huysmans

You are right about the Gothic style. It certainly contains memories brought back from the Crusades. Moreover, what are quite striking are the great stained-glass windows at Chartres, which have borders designed and painted exactly like oriental carpets. There is no doubt that the great glass-makers of the thirteenth century had some of these textiles to hand. Other considerations apart, the Crusades were certainly a great event for Western art.

You must have seen Bauer, who lives in Tunis, I was told?

To ARIJ PRINS

1 February 1907

My Dear Friend,

Every calamity has happened to me since we last wrote to each other. By way of a holiday, I was taken off to a rest home and operated on for a tumorous swelling in the neck, then once back home things were no better. I was operated on again, a few days ago, but I am still suffering atrociously. I can harbour no illusions: my health is finished and I have reached an age where one can no longer spring back and get the upper hand. The future is one of suffering behind closed doors.

Meanwhile, as a comic interlude, the present government, comprised of men of letters who are enthusiastic about my books, despite their Catholic dimension, wanted to promote me in the Légion d'Honneur and announce that I was an officer of the order. Thereupon the press was enraged, the socialists declaring that it was shameful to honour a clerical, and the Catholics cross at this elegant gesture and non-sectarian spirit on the part of Clemenceau and Briand.[69] In the end it was all dropped . . .

I must leave you, for writing is painful.

Affectionately,

G. Huijsmans

Mme Leclaire is in bed in Pau with an abscess on her leg. We are nothing but suffering. May God grant you health!

To LÉON LECLAIRE

11 March 1907

My Dear Friend,

Just a few lines in answer, as writing kills me and you are the only one for whom I won't use my secretary.

Blessed be little Sr Teresa of Jesus,[70] may the Virgin reward her for her devotion to me!

Life goes on – with flu added to all the rest. I do not sleep, I do not eat, I manufacture abscesses, accompanied by never-ending toothache.

Anyone who was not a believer and lacking courage would already have blown his brains out. But I am not unhappy. The day I said 'Fiat' God gave me an unbelievable strength and admirable peace in my soul. I am not unhappy. I do not want to get better, but to continue to be purged, so that the Virgin may carry me off On High. My dream would be that He should take me at Easter, like the repentant thief, but I am not worthy, alas.

I embrace you.

Huysmans

What about the general? Let me have news of him.

Notes on the Correspondents

ALBERDINGKTHIJM Catharina Ludovica Maria; daughter of a famous Dutch writer, she was born in the same year as Huysmans. A novelist and dramatist in her own right, she gave up her literary career in 1895 in order to found an institution for homeless women and children in Amsterdam. She addressed her first letter to Huysmans c/o The Blessed Virgin, Chartres cathedral.[3]

ALEXIS Paul (1847–1901); a minor naturalist writer whom Baldick describes as 'Zola's devoted but untalented Boswell'. Huysmans met him in Zola's circle in 1876; it was he who introduced Huysmans to Guy de Maupassant.[3]

ALLAIS Henry, a lawyer from Rouen whom Huysmans met while on a retreat at the Abbey of Saint-Wandrille in Normandy. He was the author of a number of short stories.[3]

BÉNIE DE JÉSUS, Mère, Jeanne de Bibesco (1858–1943), was the third daughter of Prince Nicholas Bibesco of Romania. She entered the Carmelite convent at Meyerling, near Vienna, and then at the age of twenty-one founded the Carmelite Priory in Algiers. Other members of the Bibesco family were prominent on the Parisian social scene.[3]

BERNARD Émile (1868–1941), poet, critic and important post-Impressionist painter, acknowledged to be the father of French Symbolist painting; he had a significant influence on Gauguin. He was a fervent Catholic and religious subjects feature prominently in his work, especially the crucifixion.[2]

BERTHET Adolphe (pseudonym Joseph Esquirol), a novelist and native of Lyons; at the time of his correspondence with Huysmans, he was researching for his book *Cherchons l'hérétique*, a study of the heresies of Lyons, published by Stock, Huysmans' own publisher, in 1903.[2]

BESSE, Dom Jean-Martial (1861–1920), a monk of the Abbey of Ligugé, who was delegated to refound the Abbey of Saint-Wandrille in 1894; he was in Spain from 1895 to 1897, and then occupied a number of posts at Ligugé. Huysmans was impressed by his scholarship and had taken seriously his encouragement to become an oblate of Saint-Wandrille.[1] (Except for the letter of 12 May 1894, which is published for the first time here.)

BLOY Léon (1846–1917), became a Catholic under the influence of Barbey d'Aurevilly. His embittered character, lacking in moderation, is reflected in a violent streak in his work. He knew desperate poverty; Huysmans met him in the spring of 1884, but Bloy quarrelled easily with people and by 1890 his friendship with Huysmans was at an end. They lost touch after Bloy's marriage.[1]

BOIS Jules; Huysmans met him in 1889; he had been very impressed with the obituary he wrote on Villiers de l'Isle-Adam. They had a common interest in the occult, as Bois was preparing his book *Le Satanisme et la magie*.[3]

BOUCHER Gustave, a bookseller on the quai Voltaire whom Huysmans met in 1890; he introduced the novelist into the den of cut-throats and prostitutes at the Château-Rouge, but at the same time accompanied him on his first tentative visits to Paris churches. It was he who led Huysmans to Ligugé, where he had become editor of a local paper. He too became a Benedictine oblate, but later renounced it; Huysmans broke off all connection with him in the latter part of his life.[2]

BROUSSOLLE, Fr Camille; a young priest and art historian who admired Huysmans' *La Cathédrale*. Huysmans prefaced his book on Italian Renaissance art, and had considered him a potential candidate for the oblate community at Ligugé.[2]

BRUN Charles, a journalist from Lyons.[3]

BRUYÈRE, Mme l'Abbesse Cécile (1845–1909); her parents owned a house near the monastery of Solesmes, and as a child she had known its founder, Dom Guéranger. He received her vow of virginity on her sixteenth birthday. It was her mother's wish that Dom Guéranger should make a Benedictine foundation for women. The first nuns began their religious life at Solesmes in 1867 with the twenty-two-year-old Cécile as superior. She died in exile on the Isle of Wight.[1]

CALDAIN Jean de; Huysmans described him as a 'young man who imitates Redon' but, before turning to art, he had tried to earn a living as a circus trainer; he was also described as charming but unscrupulous. He had an unsuccessful attempt at religious life as a Benedictine monk, and later married.[3]

CAZALS F. A., a graphic artist; Huysmans wrote a preface to his book *Paul Verlaine, ses portraits* in 1896, the year of Verlaine's death.[2]

CÉARD Henry was one of Huysmans' oldest literary friends; a minor naturalist writer, he was one of the contributors to the *Soirées de Médan* stories. He was one of the regular visitors at Huysmans' home in the rue de Sèvres.[3]

DESCAVES Lucien (1861–1949), novelist, dramatist and critic; he had been a disciple of Zola, but was one of the group of five who broke away and signed a manifesto against him in 1887. He had known Huysmans since the early 1880s, but the relationship was not close until Huysmans' last years, when he became his secretary and eventually his literary executor. Fr Mugnier became a great influence in his life.[3]

DESTRÉE Jules (1863–1935); Huysmans knew this Belgian art critic, barrister and politician through Théodore Hannon. They corresponded frequently between 1884 and 1896.[1]

DUMESNIL René, a young doctor who showed great kindness to Huysmans in his last illness, calling regularly to change his dressings; he was also a Flaubert scholar of considerable repute.[2]

EDWARDS Émile, a journalist living in the Middle East.[3]

FERRET, Fr Gabriel-Eugène (1853–97), a curate at Saint-Sulpice, who became Huysmans' confessor and spiritual guide. Huysmans found this relationship very supportive, and Fr Ferret's premature death from stomach cancer was a great blow to him.[1]

FLEURY, Dr Maurice de; Huysmans met him in the early 1880s while he was still a medical student; later relations became rather strained, as de Fleury tended to side with Zola against Huysmans.[3]

FORAIN Jean-Louis, an Impressionist painter who exhibited at the 'Exposition des Indépendants'. He was an old friend of Huysmans and illustrated some of his books. They kept in touch over the years, and Forain visited him at Ligugé.[2]

GEFFROY Gustave, art critic, one of the few to appreciate and review favourably Huysmans' *L'Art moderne*. Later he was a fellow-academician with him in the Académie Goncourt.[3]

GIDE André (1869–1951) novelist, critic and essayist; his early works, all of which he sent to Huysmans, reflect many of the preoccupations of the Symbolist generation, and in particular a concern with the 'self' and a somewhat self-conscious aestheticism. In Gide's mature work a more critical and ironical strain emerges, but 'self-realization' remained a central preoccupation.[2]

GIRARD Henri (1865–1923), a faithful friend to Huysmans over many years; an actor who played bit parts in small productions, he was a man of modest means and indifferent talent.[3]

GOFFIN Arnold (1863–1934), Belgian critic and essayist, he specialized in religious art and had translated the *Little Flowers* of St Francis. He admired Huysmans and sent him a copy of his own first book in 1885.[2]

GONCOURT Edmond de (1822–96); since he was twenty-six years older than Huysmans, they were essentially of different generations and different schools; although Huysmans admitted to finding de Goncourt's Salon boring, he took pains to keep in touch and remained respectful in his letters. The novels of the Goncourts were undoubtedly an influence on Huysmans' naturalist beginnings, and it seems that he valued the contribution to social and literary history made by the volumes of the *Journal*.[1]

GOURMONT Remy de (1858–1915); essayist, critic and novelist, he worked as a librarian at the Bibliothèque Nationale. Huysmans met him in 1889, through Berthe Courrière, who was his mistress. The friendship was quite close for some three years, but then they drifted apart.[2]

HANNON Théodore, Belgian painter and poet, the author of collections of licentious verse. Huysmans met him in Brussels in the summer of 1876. He directed the magazine *L'Artiste* from 1877 to 1879; this review took a boldly pro-naturalist stand, and Huysmans was amongst its contributors. He prefaced Hannon's *Rimes de Joie* in 1881 and the friendship remained close until 1886, but then their paths diverged.[1]

HARRY Myriam (1875–1958), daughter of a Russian Jew and a German deaconess; a young writer who, in 1901, had sent Huysmans a novel she had written about life in China. They met in 1902 and she included her impressions of him in her memoirs.[2]

HENNEQUINN Émile (1859–88), a young friend of Huysmans and a promising literary critic; his *Études de critique scientifique* were published in 1888. He died accidentally the same year, whilst out bathing with Odilon Redon.[2]

HENNEZEL, Vicomte Henri d'; a friend of Adolphe Berthet, he was planning a work on the liturgy of Lyons. He was curator of the Musée des Tissus in that town, and author of five novels. After Huysmans' death, he edited a collection of prayers and reflections by him.[3]

HUC, Mme Théophile, widow of a judge and sister-in-law of a missionary in China; Huysmans described her as 'a charming old lady, full of calm and common sense'. He knew her through Fr Mugnier.[3]

HURET Jules, a journalist; in 1891 he conducted his famous enquiry into the state of French literature for *L'Écho de Paris*; his interview with Huysmans was published on 6 April 1891. He later interviewed him in Ligugé in January 1900.[2]

KISTEMAECKERS Henri; a Belgian publisher, specializing in erotic literature; he had bought up the remaindered stock of Huysmans' first novel, *Marthe*. He later published his *A Vau l'Eau* in 1882.[2]

KLEIN, Fr Félix; priest and journalist, he had defended Huysmans in an article in *Le Monde* of 12 March 1895, expressing his belief in the novelist's sincerity and orthodoxy.[2]

LAFORGUE Jules (1860–87); Symbolist poet born in Montevideo, he came to Paris in 1876. He lived on very scanty means. He innovated with 'vers libre' and a conversational style that appealed to Huysmans. He was a master of irony, and showed great skill in transcending the banal.[2]

LANDRY Georges; long-standing friend of Huysmans and faithful visitor to the rue de Sèvres. At one time he had been secretary to Barbey d'Aurevilly, then worked for years as accountant in a shirt factory, until Huysmans got him a job with Savine, the publisher.[3]

LAUZET Auguste, a painter and engraver from Marseilles; his mistress was one of the models for Mme Chantelouve in *Là-Bas*.[2]

LECLAIRE Léon, b. 1862. His family owned the Leclaire quarries in Montmartre, but on his marriage he left the family business to run his wife's shop; they were a perfectly ordinary couple, but of great moral integrity.[3]

LEMONNIER Camille (1845–1913), Belgian art critic and novelist with Symbolist tendencies; he was involved in the revival of Belgian literature centred on the review *La Jeune Belgique*.[1]

LORRAIN Jean (pseudonym of Paul Duval: 1856–1906), a minor but fervent Symbolist poet and novelist; also a literary journalist whose homosexual tendencies were no secret.[3]

MAILLAT Henriette, *née* Picot; she had a passionate interest in literature, mysticism and men of letters. Besides Huysmans, her lovers included Sâr Péladan, Bloy, Maupassant and d'Aurevilly. Although no longer attracted to her, Huysmans helped her financially when she fell on hard times.[3]

MALLARMÉ Stéphane (1842–98), like Huysmans, a close friend of Villiers de l'Isle-Adam; *A Rebours* brought them together and cemented their mutual admiration. There was some estrangement after Huysmans' conversion, but they were reconciled before Mallarmé's death.[2]

MAUPASSANT Guy de (1850–93); together with Huysmans, he was one of the five young writers who met regularly at Zola's on Thursday evenings in the late 1870s. In later years Huysmans was rather dismissive of his work, considering it to be without substance.[3]

MICHEAU, Dom Ernest-Hilaire (1853–1931), a secular priest who entered the Abbey of Saint-Wandrille as a postulant in 1894. He remained there for the rest of his life, and was in charge of relics for many years.[1]

MOELLER, Fr Henry, Belgian priest and magazine editor; *Durendal*, a review of religious art much admired by Huysmans, was his creation. After Huysmans' death, he published the hundred-odd letters he had received from him in *Durendal*.[2]

MORICE Charles; a literary scholar who attempted to work out a theoretical approach to Symbolism.[2]

MORISSE Paul; minor writer, Benedictine oblate, and prospective member of the artistic community at Ligugé. He opened a bookshop in Poitiers and later worked for the *Mercure de France*.[3]

MUGNIER, Fr Arthur (1853–1944); he finished his studies for the priesthood at the seminary at Saint-Sulpice; he taught for a while and was then curate in a number of Parisian parishes; he was appointed to St Thomas d'Aquin, where he met Huysmans, in 1881. He kept a diary regularly from 1879, and this is a valuable document for the study of the moral and intellectual climate of *fin-de-siècle* Paris. His love of literature and genuinely attractive personality ensured him enormous success as confessor and confidant. Society hostesses vied with each other to have this humble cleric at their dinner tables. His ecclesiastical career was less brilliant than Huysmans had predicted, but the archbishop of Paris made him a canon in 1924.[2]

PACHEU, Fr Jules, Jesuit priest and literary critic who was a neighbour of Huysmans in the rue de Sèvres. He said of him: 'He is a very pleasant and very intelligent priest, and it was a great surprise to me to find a Jesuit who held such ideas.'[2]

POL DEMADE, Dr; Belgian doctor and literary critic, a friend of Fr Moeller. He wrote several articles on Huysmans' novels for Belgian magazines.[3]

PONTAVICE DE HEUSSEY Robert du; second cousin and friend of Villiers de l'Isle-Adam, and his first biographer: *Villiers de l'Isle-Adam*, Paris, 1893.[1]

PRINS Arij (1860–1922), industrialist and amateur of literature and the arts, who sought to introduce naturalism into Holland. He wrote an article on Huysmans' *En Ménage* in 1885, and this marked the beginning of their long correspondence. Huysmans was clearly flattered by his attentiveness. He also provided financial help for Villiers de l'Isle-Adam, and Léon Bloy, as well as for Huysmans himself.[1]

RAFFAËLLI Jean-François (1850–1924); Huysmans was one of the first to discern the talent of this Impressionist painter; he admired the melancholy of his suburban landscapes at the Exhibition of 1879. He illustrated Huysmans' *Croquis parisiens* in 1880.[3]

RAFFALOVICH, Dr Marc-André; sent Huysmans a copy of his book on sexual deviation.[3]

RAMAEKERS G.; a young Belgian Catholic writer.[2]

REDON Odilon (1840–1916); he has become quite well-known for his Impressionist-style paintings of vases of flowers, but his more serious work, and that which attracted Huysmans, was Symbolist. He worked on a large scale, attempting highly imaginative subjects with a dream quality. Huysmans was one of his earliest champions; they met in 1880.[2]

RETTÉ Adolphe (1863–1930), Symbolist poet and editor of two pioneer Symbolist reviews; he wrote much about the theory of Symbolism and 'vers libre'; a convert to Catholicism.[3]

RIVIÈRE Charles; a retired businessman from Rheims, who settled at the Cistercian monastery at Igny as an oblate. Huysmans met him on his first retreat there in 1892. He later visited Huysmans in Paris and in Ligugé, and the latter hoped that he might join his own proposed oblate community. Huysmans portrays him as M. Bruno in *En Route*.[3]

ROBERT Louis de; a prolific writer who began his career as a novelist in the 1890s.[2]

SÉRIEUX, Dr Paul; a psychiatrist at the mental asylum at Villejuif; Huysmans met him through the hospitalization of Anna Meunier there in the spring of 1893.[3]

THIBAULT Julie, a peasant woman from Champagne who had left her husband and been drawn into occult circles; she was consecrated as a 'high priestess' in 1873. She travelled on extensive pilgrimages throughout France before settling in Lyons with Boullan in 1883. On the death of Pascal Misme, who provided accommodation for the sect, Huysmans took her in as his housekeeper, but the arrangement did not suit him for long.[3]

THOMASSON, Dom de Gournay; a Benedictine monk of Solesmes, who helped Huysmans with *La Cathédrale* by collecting material for him in the abbey library.[3]

VALERIO Edith, *née* Huybers; she spent several years in Paris in the late 1880s as correspondent for Quilter's *Universal Review*; Huysmans rather fell for her, but he never managed to communicate his feelings to 'la petite Anglaise'.[3]

VALÉRY Paul-Ambroise (1871–1945), poet, critic and essayist, he was influenced as a young man by the Symbolists, especially Mallarmé. He worked for the Havas news agency at the time he wrote to Huysmans; he admired his work and considered *Là-Bas* to be a landmark in the novel form.

Letter of 14 September 1898[1]
Letters of 10 March 1898 and 27 February 1900[3]

VALLETTE, Mme Alfred (pseudonym Rachilde 1860–1953), wife of the founder of the *Mercure de France*. Her own work as a novelist centred on studies of exceptional psychological cases.[3]

VERHAEREN Emile (1855–1916), Belgian symbolist poet who made frequent visits to Paris; he became a close friend of Léon Bloy, whose works he defended and promoted in the Belgian press.[2]

VERLAINE Paul (1844–96) wrote some of the most lyrical poetry in the French language. Huysmans met him in the summer of 1884 and greatly admired his talent. He was a heavy drinker, and Huysmans often helped him financially. He experienced a religious conversion while serving a prison sentence for shooting (but not killing) his lover, the poet Rimbaud. In 1904 Huysmans edited and prefaced Verlaine's *Poésies religieuses*.[1]

WIRTH Oswald; famous occultist, involved with the Rosicrucians. He offered to help Huysmans with his research for *Là-Bas* and warned him of the danger of certain contacts. Huysmans visited him in the winter of 1890; according to his notes Wirth 'believed in a religion of free love and wanted to be pope'.[1]

ZOLA Émile (1840–1902); a writer of immense vigour whose enormous output has rather dwarfed all other achievements in the novel form in France in the last quarter of the nineteenth century. He was at the height of his powers with *Germinal* of 1885. In the latter part of his life he became a political figure, able to influence public opinion, as his involvement with the Dreyfus case shows. Huysmans was mistaken in his view that Zola's works would fall into obscurity; however, from the early 1890s onwards, there had been a marked decline in the quality of his work, and a turning away of critical opinion.[1]

Notes

1. These letters have been previously published in French in volume form. (See bibliography for details.)
2. These letters have been previously published in French in a newspaper or journal.
3. No trace of a previous publication of these letters has been found.

Notes on the Text

Introduction

1 Details of these are given in the Bibliography.
2 Details are given in the Notes on the Correspondents.
3 *En Route*, ed. P. Cogny, 1985; *La Cathédrale*, ed. P. Cogny, 1986; *L'Oblat* is in preparation.
4 Letter of 5 September 1877.
5 Letter of 17 February 1877, quoted from *J. K. Huysmans, Lettres à Théodore Hannon*, 1985, p. 40.
6 Baldick, Robert, *The Life of J. K. Huysmans*, 1955, p. 70.
7 Hippolyte Taine (1828–93), philosopher and historian; much influenced by positivism, he sought to apply scientific principles to the study of literature, history and art.
8 J. K. Huysmans, 'Émile Zola et l'Assommoir', in *L'Actualité*, Brussels, 1880.
9 J. H. Rosny, collective pseudonym of the Rosny brothers, novelists who usually collaborated; they were amongst the signatories of the manifesto against Zola published in *Le Figaro* of 18 August 1887.
10 Matthias Grünewald (1455–1528), Bavarian painter, noted for altarpieces; few details of his life are known, and he was not famous in his own day, but he has since been acknowledged as one of the most outstanding of the German Primitives.
11 Sr Anne Catherine Emmerich (1774–1824) wrote vivid accounts of her visions of the Passion of Christ.
12 McManners, John, *Church and State in France 1870–1914*, 1972, p. 124.
13 Quoted from McManners, *op. cit.*, p. 132.

I 1876–84 Naturalism and Decadence

1 Works of J. K. Huysmans published in this period:
   Marthe, histoire d'une fille, 1876
   Les Sœurs Vatard, 1879
   'Sac au dos', in *Les Soirées de Médan*, 1880
   Croquis parisiens, 1880
   En Ménage, 1881
   A Vau l'Eau, 1882
   L'Art moderne, 1883
   A Rebours, 1884
2 Alexandre Dumas the elder (1802–70), highly successful writer of historical romantic dramas and novels.

3 Théophile Gautier (1811–72), Romantic poet, whose cult of beauty made him a leader of the 'art for art's sake' movement.
4 François Ponsard (1814–67), one of the leaders of the 'school of good sense' in the theatre, a reaction against the exaggerations of Romantic drama; his verse dramas are considered to be very slight.
5 *L'Assommoir*, Zola's vivid portrayal of alcoholism, poverty and brutality, began serial publication in 1877.
6 Carolus Duran (1837–1917) was a fashionable portrait painter.
7 Vollon, a painter whom Huysmans found particularly antipathetic, describing his work as 'unhealthy and dull'.
8 Jean-Paul Laurens (1838–1921), a history painter.
9 Georges Sauvage, painter of portraits and historical subjects; awarded a medal for his painting in 1879.
10 Hector Malot (1830–1907), remembered mainly for his children's stories; Catulle Mendès (1842–1909), poet, playwright and founder of various literary reviews; T. Réveillon was a journalist hostile to Huysmans' circle.
11 The Parnassians were a group of poets who reacted against Romanticism, approaching poetry in a more 'scientific' manner, aiming at objective and precise representation of nature, thus eliminating personal emotion.
12 Alexandre Cabanel (1823–89), a traditionalist painter described by Huysmans in *L'Art moderne* as 'this over-famous pastrycook of fine art'.
13 *Les Sœurs Vatard*.
14 Henry Céard (1851–1924), naturalist novelist, civil servant and friend of Huysmans from the mid-1870s onwards.
15 Huysmans and his dining companions had been ridiculed in the Parisian press by hostile journalists who published an imaginary menu for this meal, based on the titles of their works.
16 Émile Bergerat (1845–1923), married to Théophile Gautier's daughter Estelle and director of *La Vie Moderne*, in which Huysmans had articles published.
17 Although Flaubert was always best known for his realist novel of French provincial life, *Madam Bovary*, his personal preference remained for *La Tentation de Saint Antoine*, a long and diffuse work which explores metaphysical anguish in a style independent of any literary movement.
18 Victor Marie Hugo (1802–85) was very much the doyen of French literary life in the 1870s and 80s. *La Légende des siècles*, his last major work, was a series of epic poems portraying the intellectual and spiritual aspirations of man throughout the ages.
19 *Le Drageoir aux épices*, Huysmans' first published work of 1874.
20 Félicien Rops (1833–98), Belgian engraver and libertine. Huysmans met him in Brussels in 1876.
21 Flaubert's *Trois Contes* of 1877.
22 Gérôme was another painter whose style was abhorrent to Huysmans; he described it as 'fermenting'.
23 Arthur Stevens (1825–90), Belgian art critic and champion of modernism, worked as a journalist in Paris for *Le Figaro*.
24 Pierre Zaccone and Fortuné Du Boisgobey were prolific writers of popular novels; in the 1870s their works ran to many editions.
25 Paul Féval had been a collaborator of Zaccone; Assolent was a writer of similar calibre.
26 Ivan Turgenev (1818–83), Russian novelist who lived in Paris for a number of years and was a close friend of Flaubert.

27 *Salammbô* of 1862, a novel full of exoticism, set in ancient Carthage.
28 *L'Éducation sentimentale* of 1869 was Flaubert's second attempt to render nineteenth-century reality in the novel; this work, set against the background of the 1848 revolution, enjoyed little success in the lifetime of its author.
29 Bachelin-Deflorenne was the publisher of the art review *Musée des Deux Mondes*.
30 In the *coup d'état* of 16 May 1877, President MacMahon forced the moderate government of Jules Simon into resignation; the new ministers were largely Legitimists and Bonapartists.
31 Huysmans published an article in *L'Artiste* on Manet's painting *Nana*, which had been refused for the 1877 Salon.
32 *Marcelle*, a poem by Maurice du Seigneur, was published in *L'Artiste* on 3 June 1877.
33 A poem by Victor Hugo.
34 Fourcaud was literary critic on *Le Gaulois*, a supporter of Zola and naturalism.
35 These brochures were offprints of Huysmans' article 'Emile Zola et l'Assommoir'.
36 A reference to an article by Huysmans on landscapes and paintings of military subjects in his series 'Notes sur le Salon de 1877'.
37 Hippolyte Babou had written an article entitled 'La Fin des Impressionnistes' which appeared in *L'Actualité* in June 1877.
38 Jules Barbey d'Aurevilly (1808–89) became doyen for a group of young writers; he was a flamboyant character, militantly Royalist and Catholic.
39 Léon Hennique (1851–1935), naturalist novelist and dramatist, born in Guadeloupe; one of Zola's circle of young admirers; Paul Alexis (1847–1901), novelist and dramatist, responsible for the dramatization of some of de Goncourt's novels; Octave Mirbeau (1848–1917), best known for his *Journal d'une femme de chambre*, later to be a member of the Académie Goncourt with Huysmans.
40 Alphonse Daudet's *Le Nabob* of 1877 was a story of successful fortune-making in the colonies under the Second Empire.
41 In *La Curée* of 1872, Zola had portrayed decadence and vice in Second Empire society.
42 The rue de Rennes, not far from where Huysmans lived in the rue de Sèvres, housed many antique and bric-à-brac dealers. Huysmans was an inveterate collector.
43 Raton was one of Zola's pet dogs.
44 A reference to two editions of the review *L'Artiste*, of which Hannon had been director since 1877.
45 Félix Callewaert was a Brussels printer.
46 *Le Ventre de Paris* of 1873 was the third volume of Zola's Rougon-Macquart cycle of novels and was set in the central wholesale market of Paris.
47 Camille Lemonnier, *Gustave Courbet et son œuvre*, Paris, 1878.
48 A. E. Michallon (1796–1822), landscape and history painter.
49 A collection of short stories by Lemonnier, published in 1873.
50 A reference to *La Faim*, Huysmans' first novel in terms of idea and conception. Although he returned to this project several times, he never in fact finished it.
51 Lemonnier never actually published a collection under this title, but he had previously written articles on Rubens in *Le Bien public*.
52 Pyotr Boborykin (1836–1921), Russian naturalist novelist in exile in France.
53 Through the good offices of Turgenev, Zola had become a regular contributor to the St Petersburg literary journal *Vestnik Evropy*.
54 Zola was working on his novel of prostitution, sequel to *L'Assommoir*, at this time.
55 Probably a further reference to *La Faim*.

56 Lebarre was an employee of Charpentier, the publisher.
57 Judith Gautier, daughter of Théophile Gautier, had published a collection of poems from the Chinese, *Le Livre de jade*, in 1867, hence Huysmans' reference, but the book in question here is her *Les Peuples étranges*.
58 A volume of three plays by Zola, published by Charpentier in 1878.
59 This adaptation of Zola's novel of 1867 had been first performed in 1873.
60 *Les Héritiers Rabourdin*, a three-act comedy, was first performed in 1874.
61 *Bouton de rose*, first produced in 1878, was not a success; it was to serve as Zola's admission ticket to the 'dinners for heckled playwrights' frequented also by Flaubert, Turgenev and Daudet.
62 Hannon had been suffering from a nervous disorder.
63 Léon Carton de Wiart was one of Hannon's collaborators on *L'Artiste*.
64 Camille Etiévant was general secretary to the editorial board of *Le Voltaire*.
65 Jules Lafitte had taken over as director of *Le Voltaire* in July 1878. R. F. is a reference to *La République Française*, a daily newspaper.
66 Elémir Bourges had sought Zola's patronage; the novel in question here is *Sous la Hache*, which was not to be published until 1883.
67 Charles Marpon had been in partnership with the publisher Flammarion and had run *Le Voltaire* for a while.
68 A comic drama by Auguste Vacquerie.
69 Jean-Baptiste-Antoine Guillemet (1842–1918) began as a landscape painter as a disciple of Corot and later adopted the Impressionist style; his work was praised by Huysmans in his *Salons*.
70 Journalists who had led the attack on Huysmans' *Les Sœurs Vatard*, accusing him of misrepresenting French working-class life, in *La Revue politique et littéraire*.
71 Edmond de Goncourt's last novel, published in 1879, was an impressionistic story of circus life.
72 Goncourt's novel of 1869 was a study of religious mania.
73 *La Fille Elisa* of 1877, which had certain affinities with Huysmans' own work *Marthe*, was a novel of prostitution and murder in which Goncourt sought to denounce prison conditions in France.
74 This letter is redated here; on its first publication in the *Bulletin de la Société des Amis de J. K. Huysmans*, vol. XII, No. 64, it was dated early October 1876, but the reference here is clearly to the later, French edition of *Marthe*, not the original Belgian one. What is more, Alexis's story 'Lucie Pellegrin' did not appear until 1879.
75 There was a certain vogue for stories of prostitution in the late 1870s in France, and so Huysmans now successfully tried to have *Marthe* published there; three years earlier, it had been seized by the Customs and Excise.
76 One of a collection of short stories recently published by Paul Alexis.
77 Huysmans and Alexis had been to a fancy-dress ball together on that evening.
78 Zola's *Nana* was still being published in serial form.
79 Huysmans' *Croquis parisiens* of 1880 contained a prose poem, 'Le Gousset' ('The Armpit'), somewhat reminiscent of Baudelaire, inspired by the various odours exuded from female armpits. Critical reaction was almost universally indignant.
80 Guy de Maupassant was a civil servant at the Ministère de la Marine.
81 *Le Rappel* was a paper that supported Victor Hugo.
82 *Un Mâle* by Camille Lemonnier was published in Belgium in 1881.
83 A reference to *A Vau l'Eau*.

84 This is Goncourt's two-volume work *La Maison d'un artiste au XIXe siècle*, a catalogue of the art treasures in his own home.
85 *Les Charniers* was published in Paris in 1881.
86 The work had been previously published under the title *Sédan*, site of a crushing French defeat during the Franco-Prussian war.
87 Léon Cladel, Romantic novelist from Quercy and friend of Huysmans; he had written a preface to the new edition of Lemonnier's work.
88 Alexis Bouvier (1836–1892), popular playwright and songwriter.
89 *En Ménage*.
90 V. Cherbuliez was a popular writer of sentimental stories; in *A Vau l'Eau*, Huysmans describes his work as 'veal broth'.
91 Untranslatable pseudonyms of Parisian journalists.
92 Charles Potvin (1818–1902) was a prolific Belgian writer; in 1875 he had won the national drama prize in Belgium for his *La Mère de Rubens*.
93 The woman in question here is Anna Meunier. Huysmans frequently referred to her simply as 'ma femme', which is the way husbands refer to their wives, but it can simply mean 'my woman'.
94 Huysmans made his first visit to the village of Jutigny in the Seine-et-Marne in 1882; the ruined Château de Lourps was to provide him with inspiration for *A Rebours*.
95 We see here the beginnings of the notion of the purely imaginary journey which is to be fully developed through Des Esseintes in *A Rebours*.
96 The *Treize Sonnets du doigt dedans* by a certain 'Monsieur de la Braguette' was a collection of obscene verse in private circulation.
97 A reference to *A Rebours*.
98 Orientius was a fifth-century Gallic Latin poet; his principal work was the *Commonitorium*, an exhortation to virtue; Baudonivia, a monk, wrote a life of the sixth-century St Radegonde; Veranius of Le Gévaudan was probably the son of St Eucherius, a fifth-century bishop of Lyons.
99 Edouard-Joachim Corbière, self-styled Tristan (1845–75), was a Breton poet admired by Verlaine; he wrote mostly about marine subjects; his work is tinged with a certain irony.
100 This is the work that later inspired the composer Debussy.
101 Mallarmé's prose poem of 1864, 'Le Démon de l'analogie', was not published until 1874, and then under the title 'La Pénultième'.
102 This poem that Huysmans greatly admired was in three parts: *Ouverture, Scène, Cantique de St Jean*.
103 Gustave Moreau (1826–98), painted mythological and biblical subjects, combining fantasy with realistic detail.
104 François Coppée (1842–1902), a Catholic poet and dramatist who took as his subject the banal pathos in the lives of humble people.
105 Mallarmé wrote this prose poem in 1864; it was published in 1868 in the *Revue des Lettres et des Arts*, which was under Villiers de l'Isle-Adam's direction at the time.
106 Léon-Lucien Goupil (1834–90), a portrait painter who exhibited at the Salon.
107 Homais was a character in Flaubert's *Madame Bovary* who came to be synonymous with provincial materialism and narrow-mindedness.
108 See note 101 above.
109 Verhaeren's *Les Flamandes* of 1883 were poems of peasant life in Flanders, in which he sought to reproduce the realistic manner of the old masters.

110 Teniers and Ostade were seventeenth-century Flemish painters who specialized in scenes of peasant life.
111 A volume of poems by Théodore Hannon, published under the pseudonym of 'Frère Cupidon'.
112 Huysmans greatly admired this macabre collection of stories, published in February 1883.
113 A reference to Huysmans himself; while writing *Les Sœurs Vatard* he frequently referred to his character Désirée as his daughter.
114 Huysmans' *L'Art moderne* of 1883.
115 J. J. Henner, an influential painter.
116 H. Gervex and J. Bastien Le Page were painters whom Huysmans described as being 'at the opposite pole to Degas'.
117 *Au Pays de Mannekin Pis* was the alternative title of Hannon's collection of verse *Le Mirliton priapique*.
118 The *Contes de la Bécasse* were a small collection of stories published by Maupassant in 1883.
119 Le Tréport is a small seaside resort in Normandy.
120 Georges Clemenceau (1841–1929), the left-wing politician who was to reach pre-eminence during the First World War. His portrait was also painted by Manet.
121 William Bouguereau (1825–1905), a French painter considered by Huysmans to be mediocre.
122 Michet was presumably a journalist.
123 Marius Vachon had been one of Huysmans' fellow-contributors to *L'Exposition des Beaux-Arts*, on the Salon of 1880.
124 Georges Ohnet (1848–1918), a writer of sentimental novels that were best sellers in their day; much despised by Huysmans.
125 An abbreviation of Kistemaeckers, the Belgian publisher.
126 This was the twelfth volume of Zola's Rougon-Macquart cycle, a portrayal of country life.
127 *The Imitation of Jesus Christ* is one of the best-known classics of devotional literature, generally attributed to Thomas à Kempis (1379–1471); it is permeated with the ideal of serving and imitating Christ, deepening the inner life of faith. It opens the way to an understanding of medieval piety, to which Huysmans was to be more and more drawn.
128 Jean Bourdeau (1848–1928), philosopher and translator; he published Schopenhauer's *Pensées et fragments* in 1880.
129 E. Bouchut, *Du Névrosisme aigu et chronique et des maladies nerveuses*, 1860; Axenfeld, *Traité des névroses*, 1883.
130 Robert, Comte de Montesquiou (1855–1921), aesthete and man of letters, was well-known in fashionable circles for his life of luxury and decadence; he was partially the model for Des Esseintes, and was later to serve also as inspiration for Marcel Proust's character Charlus.
131 This series of oppositions takes two works each by Flaubert, Goncourt and Zola, setting a romantic or lyrical work against a realistic or documentary one. In each case Huysmans' own preference was for the second of the pair.
132 The sincerity of Huysmans' sentiments here is to be doubted. From other letters, we know that he did admire Mallarmé greatly. He would appear to be humouring Zola here, not yet ready to break completely with his earlier master.
133 Leconte de Lisle (1818–94), leader of the Parnassian poets, who aimed for formal perfection and visual beauty in his work.

134 *En Rade* was originally conceived as a short story, but it expanded to novel dimensions in composition.
135 Huysmans' unfinished novel, set in Paris at the time of the Franco–Prussian War of 1870–1.
136 This was the title of Léon Bloy's review of *A Rebours*.
137 As hiatus can also mean 'orifice' in French, there is a possible homosexual double entendre here.
138 This collection of poems written by Verlaine after his religious conversion was greatly admired by Huysmans.
139 For the bookbinding business in the rue de Sèvres.
140 There had been talk of Zola receiving the Légion d'Honneur at this time, but in fact he was not decorated until 1888.
141 A reference to Zola's work on his novel *Germinal*, set in a mining village in the north of France.
142 This letter is redated here; in his edition Vanwelkenhuyzen dates it 'early 1885', but as the letter of thanks to Jules Destrée was in fact written on 22 November 1884, and this clearly precedes it, the previous dating would seem inaccurate.
143 Camille Lemonnier's novel *L'Hystérique* was serialized in *Le National belge* from 30 August 1884.
144 Humility is a character in Lemonnier's novel.
145 In a famous trial of 1731 the Jesuit J. B. Girard was accused, but acquitted, of seducing the mystic Catherine Cadière; a reference to the famous 'devils of Loudun' case: the young priest Urbain Grandier was burnt at the stake for having led the nuns of Loudun into demonic possession.
146 Louise Lateau was a nineteenth-century Belgian stigmatist.
147 Works by Barbey d'Aurevilly: *L'Ensorcelée* of 1854 is a novel of jealous passion and murder, the victim of which is a parish priest; *Les Diaboliques* of 1874 are short stories that reflect a late-Romantic fascination with satanism.

II 1885–92 Carbolic for the Soul
1 Works of J. K. Huysmans published in this period:
En Rade, 1887
Certains, 1889 (a collection of articles on art and architecture)
La Bièvre, 1890 (evocations of Paris's second river)
Là-Bas, 1891
2 In a letter to louis de Robert of November 1891.
3 *Ibid.*
4 Zola's novel *Germinal* was published in 1885.
5 Le Voreux is the name given to the mine in *Germinal*.
6 In Hebrew 'My God, why have you forsaken me', Psalm 21, quoted by Christ at his crucifixion.
7 A reference to Zola's *Le Ventre de Paris*.
8 It is difficult to identify this accurately; possibly J. Luyken's *Histoires les plus remarquables de l'Ancien et du Nouveau Testament*.
9 Jan Luyken (1649–1712), an engraver of Amsterdam, turned to religious subjects after the death of his five children. His lugubrious works were a favourite of Des Esseintes, who had them on the walls of his boudoir.
10 Victor Hugo died on 22 May 1885; his funeral was a grandiose affair.

11 Huysmans exaggerates somewhat here; Flaubert's funeral, although not in Paris, was well attended.
12 Pierre Puvis de Chavannes (1824–98). The visiting card image comes from Destrée's article on the Salon: an ironical comment, as this painter usually worked on a monumental scale, but had sent only one very small picture to this Salon.
13 Bouguereau, a professor at the Académie des Beaux-Arts, had produced over a thousand paintings of religious and allegorical subjects.
14 *La Revue indépendante*, a monthly journal, first appeared in May 1884, with Félix Fénéon as editor; Huysmans worked for it regularly for a year until May 1885.
15 Robert Caze (1853–86), naturalist novelist and friend of Huysmans.
16 The Pel trial caught the popular imagination during the summer of 1885; he was accused of poisoning a woman.
17 Veuve Lebel-Bouasse was a firm producing pious pictures in the rue St-Sulpice; Bloy, who was skilled at calligraphy and illumination, worked for them for a while.
18 Georges Landry worked for a Jewish shirt manufacturer.
19 Miss Louise Read was Barbey d'Aurevilly's secretary and companion.
20 A reference to Anna Meunier and her two daughters.
21 *Le Journal d'André*, a recently published work by Goffin.
22 Paul Déroulède (1846–1914), a veteran of the Franco–Prussian War, whose patriotic verse enjoyed great popularity.
23 Comte de Lautréamont was the pseudonym of Isidore Ducasse (1846–70); in 1868 he published a collection of lyrical fragments in prose centred on a demonic figure, *Les Chants de Maldoror*.
24 A reference to Chapter II, verse 13 of *Les Chants de Maldoror*.
25 In *Les Complaintes* of 1885, Laforgue had sought to rejuvenate French poetry with inspiration from barrel-organ and other popular songs, with verbal inventiveness and acrobatic rhyming.
26 Léon Vanier was Laforgue's publisher.
27 Jules Claretie (1818–1913), a prolific journalist and man of letters, but of mediocre talent. He wrote twenty volumes of memoirs, *La Vie á Paris*.
28 From 1881 to 1886, through the good offices of the novelist Paul Bourget, Laforgue was French reader to the Empress Augusta of Germany.
29 A light-hearted collection of verse, expressing a cult of the moon seen as a symbol of sterility; the work reflects a Schopenhauerian brand of pessimism.
30 Caze died as the result of an illegal duel fought with C. Vignier in February 1886.
31 W. Kloos was the editor of *De Nieuwe Gids*, which published Huysmans' *La Bièvre*.
32 Totor was the pet-name of Villiers' illegitimate son Victor; Huysmans took particular trouble to ensure the boy's future at the time of his father's death.
33 Thomas Rowlandson (1756–1827), English caricaturist and engraver.
34 Eugène Chevreul was the inventor of stearic candles; this was not a very tactful remark on Huysmans' part, given that Prins himself made his living from the manufacture of candles.
35 The dedication read 'A monsieur Ary Prins, Hollandais. Le diable est de tous les pays.'
36 A reference to *En Rade*.
37 This was Bloy's major novel *Le Désespéré*, an anguished, autobiographical work, full of attacks on literary figures.
38 The family of the king of Mycenae was cursed because of its history of incest and child murder.

39 The technique of these pointillist painters was to use blobs of primary colours to produce brighter secondaries; for example, dots of blue and yellow mix *in the eye* to produce green from a distance.
40 This work was the sequel to Villiers' *Claire Lenoir*, which had appeared in 1867. *Tribulat Bonhomet* was published by Stock in May 1887.
41 Serial publication of Zola's *La Terre* had begun before the manuscript was completed.
42 The agricultural province where *La Terre* is set.
43 Huysmans' neologism.
44 Ferdinand Brunetière (1849–1906), the prestigious literary editor of *La Revue des Deux Mondes*, accused Baudelaire of 'illustrious mystification', and believed that he would fall into complete obscurity.
45 A five-act play based on Zola's *La Curée*.
46 Verlaine's *Romances sans Paroles* found their inspiration in the vagabond life he had led with the poet Rimbaud in London and in Belgium. *Sagesse*, the poetic fruit of Verlaine's conversion whilst in prison for shooting Rimbaud, is generally acknowledged to be amongst his finest work; these poems are the humble prayer of a repentant sinner amazed at God's grace.
47 A monthly art and literary magazine.
48 Huysmans' neologism.
49 This was to be *Là-Bas*, but the scope of the novel changed considerably during the three years that Huysmans worked on it; in the final version, most of the Naundorff material was dropped.
50 César Matteï (1809–96) practised a kind of herbal homeopathy.
51 Paul Bourget's novel, published in 1887.
52 The five who signed the manifesto attacking Zola were: P. Bonnetain, J. Rosny, L. Descaves, P. Margueritte, G. Guiches.
53 Huysmans is here deliberately confusing two titles of works by Daudet, in order to poke fun at their author. Tartarin was the hero of numerous stories by Daudet, notably *Tartarin de Tarascon* of 1872, and *Tartarin sur les Alpes* of 1885.
54 A further reference to Alphonse Daudet.
55 Jules Grévy, President of the Republic, had been involved in a scandal over deals done with people who hoped to obtain the Légion d'Honneur decoration.
56 Georges Boulanger (1837–91), general and a former Minister of War; he became very popular in the 1880s, and although he did not stand for election, he received a large number of votes in a by-election. He was exiled to Clermont-Ferrand, from where his supporters tried to push him into a *coup d'état*. He refused, but on news of his imminent arrest he fled to Belgium in April 1889.
57 De Fleury was about to get married.
58 Ste Périne was a Paris nursing home where de Fleury was a medical student.
59 Léon Bloy lived at 127 rue Blomet. Le Toboso (birthplace of Don Quixote's Dulcinea) was the nickname of Eugénie Pasdeloup, mistress of Bloy, by whom he had a child.
60 Huysmans' friendship with Gustave Guiches dates back to the early 1880s; he had written a novel while very young, and was to remain a close and faithful friend; Louis-Henry May was a director of the publishing house of Quantin, which was to publish Villiers' *Axël* in 1890.
61 Huysmans has inverted the names of Edgar Poe and Adolphe Thiers for comic effect. The historian Thiers was the first president of the Third Republic; he died in 1877.

62 Paul Hervieu was a novelist who worked for *La Revue indépendante* at the same time as Huysmans and Villiers.
63 The hospital in which Verlaine was a patient at this time.
64 *Amours* is perhaps the least well-known of Verlaine's collections of verse.
65 There was a certain amount of suspicion surrounding this subscription for the penniless Verlaine; not all the money destined for the poet reached him.
66 Albert Savine was a publisher and friend of Verlaine; he also published Bloy's works.
67 A reference to Arij Prins.
68 A novel by Alphonse Daudet, published in 1888.
69 A. A. Baron (pseudonym Ernouf de Verclives: 1817–89), minor historian and friend of Léon Bloy.
70 Gustave Kahn, poet, novelist and editor of *La Revue indépendante*.
71 Edouard Dujardin, playwright and novelist, one of the founders of *La Revue indépendante*.
72 Prins's landlady, whose maternal qualities had impressed Huysmans on his visit to Hamburg.
73 Alexis Orsat, alias the Professor, old friend and fellow-civil servant, with whom Huysmans frequently lunched.
74 A reference to Henriette Maillat, *née* Picot; previously mistress of Sâr Péladan and Léon Bloy, she was passionately interested in mysticism, and 'collected' men of letters.
75 Possibly Benjamin Hawkins, an English painter and lithographer who exhibited at the Royal Academy in the 1840s.
76 Bloy's *Un Brelan d'Excommuniés*.
77 Ernest Hello (1828–85), Catholic mystic writer; Bloy had considered him one of his literary masters.
78 A reference to Maurice de Fleury.
79 This is the subscription fund for Villiers de l'Isle-Adam, set up by his friends.
80 Edmond de Goncourt's play.
81 Victorien Sardou (1831–1908); his comedies with complicated plots enjoyed a fair measure of success.
82 Goncourt's novel *Germinie Lacerteux* had also been adapted for the stage.
83 This letter is an example of Huysmans' particular skill at combining insult and compliment.
84 Pierre Loti (1850–1922), naval officer and novelist, who tried – unsuccessfully in Huysmans' view – to use Impressionist techniques in his works, which frequently reflect his taste for exotic landscapes and civilizations.
85 Albert Trachsel (1863–1929), Swiss painter and illustrator; Huysmans was enthusiastic about his work in the early 1890s. Jean Court, a poet, was one of the founders of the *Mercure de France*.
86 Théodore de Banville (1823–91), a poet of great creative imagination, who took immense pains over his versification.
87 Albert Robin was a friend of Mallarmé and Bloy, a doctor and literary enthusiast, he had already treated Barbey d'Aurevilly.
88 Marie Bregeras, *née* Dantine; this illiterate widow had been Villiers' maid for some time; she became his mistress and had a child by him in 1881; Villiers liked to recount that the child was a foundling, the son of a beautiful princess.
89 Henry Roujon was a friend of Mallarmé and brother-in-law of Jean Marras, one of Villiers' closest friends; he worked on *La République des lettres*.

Notes on the Text 255

90 This letter is taken out of sequence: it is such a vivid narrative account of the death of Villiers de l'Isle-Adam – which occurred at this time – and its impact on Huysmans that it highlights his feelings at this critical stage of his journey towards conversion, in which the circumstances of this death were unquestionably an influence.
91 Mme Méry Laurent was the companion of Stéphane Mallarmé's later years.
92 Léon Dierx (1838–1912), parnassian poet and friend of Villiers.
93 Gilles de Rais (c. 1396–1440), marshal of France, who fought alongside Joan of Arc against the English; he later indulged in necromancy, kidnapping children and murdering them.
94 Ganymede, a Trojan prince mentioned by Homer, has traditionally been associated with homosexuality, but the legend according to which he was carried up to heaven on the back of a dung beetle has given rise to interpretations representing the soul's ascent to the absolute.
95 Because of his poor health and impoverished state, Verlaine spent periods in various institutions.
96 Canon Roca was a priest with socialist tendencies and an interest in the occult. He was editor of *L'Anticlérical* and had received Boullan's confidences in 1886, but later broke with him and the Lyons sect. He tried to warn off Huysmans, telling him of the dangers of the black arts.
97 A reference to *Là-Bas*.
98 Succubi are female demons who visit sleeping men and have sexual intercourse with them.
99 Prins had written to Huysmans of a young man he had seen out ice skating, whom he found attractive.
100 A collection of engravings by F. Rops.
101 Edmond Bailly was a publisher and bookseller, who published some of Villiers' work.
102 Friedrich Ebeling was Prins's business partner.
103 A reference to Caroline-Louise-Victoire (Berthe) Courrière.
104 Maurice Barrès (1862–1923), novelist and politician from Lorraine; a 'sceptical aesthete', impatient for new sensations. His work had a strong regional character.
105 In May 1890 Léon Bloy married Johanna Molbech, daughter of the Danish poet Christian Molbech.
106 The Carnavalet museum of the history of Paris.
107 Jacob van Santen Kolff (1848–96) was the first enthusiast and propagator of naturalism in the Netherlands, an unequivocal admirer of Zola. Isaac Israëls (1865–1934) lived and worked in The Hague as an Impressionist painter. Jean-François Millet (1814–75) was the son of a peasant who reflected the labouring life of the peasantry in his painting; his choice of subject matter led to accusations of socialism.
108 The woman in question is Julie Thibault, a peasant woman who dabbled in mysticism; she was later to be Huysmans' housekeeper.
109 Joachim of Fiore (1130–1201), an Italian Cistercian mystic whose entire doctrine is reducible to his teaching on the unity of the Trinity.
110 Volume IV of the *Journal des Goncourt*.
111 Théophile Gautier, *Tableaux de Siège, Paris 1870–71*, 1871.
112 Louis Blanc (1811–82); Goncourt rather makes fun of this extreme left-wing politician, who had been a seminarian in his youth.

113 Ernest Renan (1823–92) had been educated for the priesthood, but he abandoned his studies as a result of a crisis of faith. He spent the rest of his life trying to apply 'scientific' method to sacred history; he spent twenty-five years writing a *Vie de Jésus* and twenty years on *Les Origines du Christianisme*. His works caused a sensation in their day.
114 Zola's novel *L'Argent*, eighteenth in the Rougon-Macquart cycle, began serial publication on 30 November 1890.
115 Painters of the Primitive school admired by Huysmans.
116 A reference to the place Maubert.
117 Mémèche, also known as Antoinette, was a young thief of seventeen.
118 Saint-Séverin was the church where Huysmans had been baptized as a baby; he revisited the area in 1890 to collect material for his series of articles on 'Les Vieux quartiers de Paris'. *O Salutaris hostia* is a hymn sung at Benediction of the Blessed Sacrament.
119 Fr Milleriot had been Barbey d'Aurevilly's spiritual director.
120 Gide published this work anonymously in 1891; it is presented as the posthumous work of a young man who died of cerebral fever.
121 In the first part of the *Cahiers*, the 'Cahier Blanc', Gide reflects a struggle between spirit and flesh; the hero aspires to transcend the flesh and enter into a soul-to-soul communion with Emmanuelle. The passage referred to by Huysmans deals with the possible relationship between food and religious experience, the possibility of artificial ecstasy, given that the flesh is an inevitable partner.
122 The character in *Là-Bas* who was largely inspired by Boullan.
123 Pascal Misme, an architect and disciple of Vintras, gave a home to Boullan and Julie Thibault.
124 Lyons was an active and important centre in the early Church; St Irenaeus, Bishop of Lyons, was one of the most important theologians of the second century; he wrote against the heresy of the Gnostics; St Pothinus, also Bishop of Lyons, was martyred in the year 177.
125 *Mme Mœuriot* is a rather slight novel by Paul Alexis.
126 Guy de Maupassant's play *Musotte* had its first performance at the Gymnase theatre on 4 March 1891. The play was dedicated to Alexander Dumas the younger.
127 Louis Nicolardot (1824–88), an ultra-conservative pamphleteer, had been portrayed satirically by Léon Bloy in his novel *Le Désespéré*.
128 Alfred Vallette was, with Remy de Gourmont, editor and co-founder of the *Mercure de France*.
129 Jean-Martin Charcot (1825–93), a doctor specializing in nervous illnesses; he was attacked by Berthe Courrière in her pamphlet 'Néron, prince de la Science'.
130 St Teresa of Avila (1515–82), a Spanish Carmelite nun with a great reforming zeal, whose writings have become classics on the life of prayer; Sr Maria d'Agreida (1602–65), also a Spanish nun, whose work *Mistica Ciudad de Dios y Vida de la Virgen por ella misma manifestada* of 1670 did not receive the approval of the Church.
131 Huysmans was to visit the famous Carthusian monastery in the French Alps that summer, in the company of Boullan.
132 A reference to Léon Bloy.
133 Presumably a dig at Bloy, who had written about La Chartreuse with great enthusiasm.
134 The foothills of the Vosges.
135 A battle won by Napoleon in 1809.

136 *The Interior Castle*, written by St Teresa of Avila in 1577, is one of the most celebrated books of all time on mystical prayer. Fr Jean-Jacques Olier (1608–57) was the founder of the seminary and Society of Saint-Sulpice, acknowledged as leader of the French school of spirituality.
137 Alcide Guérin was a civil servant, occasional journalist and faithful friend to Léon Bloy; this Jacquemin is presumably the husband of Jeanne Jacquemin, mistress of Huysmans' artist friend Auguste Lauzet.
138 This was to be *En Route*.
139 At this time Zola was working on *La Débâcle*, a vast historical fresco dealing with the Franco–Prussian War.
140 Oscar Méténier (1859–1913) was a dramatist who collaborated with Paul Alexis.
141 A reference to Fr Mugnier, who did not in fact accompany Huysmans on his retreat.
142 The model for Canon Docre was Fr Louis van Haecke (1829–1912), chaplain of the chapel of the Precious Blood in Bruges; Huysmans probably obtained details of his sacrilegious practices from Berthe Courrière, who had been found by the police wandering half naked though the streets of Bruges.
143 There had been four explosions in Paris, attributed to the anarchist Ravachol.
144 Fr Mugnier had advised Huysmans to take a supply of chocolate to Igny with him, on account of the rigours of the Trappist diet.
145 The unfortunate woman was Anna Meunier, now in her last illness.
146 A reference to Berthe Courrière.
147 It has been impossible to identify either the author or the book in question here.
148 Fr Tardif de Moidrey, priest and biblical scholar who had a great influence on Léon Bloy, who felt that he had learnt from him a kind of 'universal algebra' for interpreting the Scriptures.
149 '*Sans-culottes*' was originally a contemptuous label applied to the revolutionaries of 1793, but it later became synonymous with patriotism.

III 1893–98 The Call of the Cloister

1 Works published by J. K. Huysmans in this period:
En Route, 1895
La Cathédrale, 1898
La Bièvre et Saint-Séverin, 1898
2 In a letter to Charles Brun of 13 April 1898.
3 L'Abbé Mugnier, *Journal 1879–1939*, p. 103.
4 *Ibid.*, p. 123.
5 *Ibid.*, p. 85.
6 Dom Besse wrote to the Vatican on Huysmans' behalf on 18 November 1898; a copy of the letter is conserved in the monastic archives at Ligugé.
7 A reference to Prins's future wife, Nelly Goudkade, a nurse.
8 A reference to the sudden death of Prins's brother.
9 Nelly Goudkade had turned down Prins's first proposal of marriage.
10 The Cabinet resigned on 30 March 1893 after a period of financial scandal centred on the liquidation of de Lesseps' Panama Canal Company.
11 *En Route*.
12 The confessor in question was Boullan.
13 This mixture of narrative and dialogue was the last of the 'early' works of Gide.
14 *Le Voyage d'Urien* was illustrated by Maurice Denis.

15 Huysmans was made a Chevalier de la Légion d'Honneur on 3 September 1893, after twenty-seven years' loyal service to the Ministry.
16 *La Tentative amoureuse* by Gide was published in 1893.
17 This was an earlier work by Gide, published in 1891.
18 The photograph was of Prins's fiancée.
19 Daniel Wilson, son-in-law of Grévy, former President of the Republic, had been implicated in a scandal concerning a trade in Légion d'Honneur decorations.
20 Dom J. M. Besse, *Le Moine Bénédictin*, Ligugé, 1892.
21 Blessed (not Saint) Angela of Foligno (1248–1309), a mystic, who was married and lived a worldly life until the age of forty, when she underwent a sudden conversion. She became a Franciscan tertiary; her writings trace twenty steps of penance and seven steps of the mystical life.
22 St Gertrude (1256–1302), Benedictine nun, who entered the convent at the age of five; she committed herself completely to the contemplative life, after a vision of Christ at the age of twenty-five; her life was a succession of intense spiritual experiences.
23 'Uffizi' is a chapter in *Italie d'hier. Notes de voyages (1855–56)* by E. and J. de Goncourt, 1894.
24 Théophile Gautier, *Italia*, 1852.
25 Hippolyte Taine, *Voyage en Italie*, 1866.
26 Count Pellegrino Rossi, politician and president of the constitutional government, was assassinated in Rome in 1848.
27 Dom François Chamard (1828–1907); his monastic career took him to a number of the monasteries frequented by Huysmans in the 1890s: Ligugé, Saint-Wandrille and Saint-Maur.
28 A reference to Psalm 129, which is associated with the liturgy for the dead.
29 Little is known of this early convert: he heard St Paul preach, and is mentioned in the Acts of the Apostles.
30 This hymn to the Blessed Virgin is sung every evening after compline in monastic communities.
31 As Huysmans' forthcoming book was known to be a counterpart to *Là-Bas*, which means 'down below', journalists had assumed that its title would be *Là-Haut*, 'up above'.
32 Huysmans probably based this character in *Là-Bas* on both Berthe Courrière and Henriette Maillat.
33 St John of the Cross (1542–91), great Spanish Carmelite mystic, author of supremely beautiful poems on the mystery of divine love. St Mary Magdalene de Pazzi (1566–1607) was also a Carmelite mystic; she had been extremely pious as a child, and made a vow of virginity at the age of ten. She was known as the Ecstatic Saint; her extraordinary experiences were documented by her community.
34 Charles Buet (1846–97), Catholic writer and journalist, friend of Léon Bloy; he was the model for Chantelouve, the Catholic historian in Huysmans' *Là-Bas*.
35 The attacks on the secular clergy in *En Route*.
36 A recently published work by Fr Klein.
37 Anatole France (1844–1924), novelist and critic; his anticlerical, socialist and pro-Dreyfus stance made him antipathetic to Huysmans.
38 'Man is nothing but a stinking seed, a bag of excrement, a mass of sexual appetite.' St Bernard (1090–1153) was a founder of the Cistercian order of monks.
39 The doctrine of Cornelius Jansen, a seventeenth-century Flemish bishop, which reduced the role of human will, seeing predestination as the supreme manifestation of divine grace.
40 *The Little Flowers* of St Francis of Assisi.

Notes on the Text 259

41 Jules Lemaître (1853–1914), a brilliant and ironical literary critic.
42 Odo of Cluny (879–942), abbot and monastic reformer.
43 Knowing that Huysmans was a misogynist, Catharina Alberdingkthijm had concealed the fact that she was a woman when writing to him. He discovered the truth after a while, but kept up the pretence.
44 Published by Gide in 1896, *Paludes* is a satire on literary conventionalism.
45 A reference to Volume VIII of the *Journal des Goncourt*.
46 It was for this Exhibition of 1889 that the Eiffel Tower had been erected; Huysmans was always particularly irritated by its presence on the Paris skyline.
47 Beuron is a Benedictine monastery in Germany.
48 This convent, near Valence, was founded by Mère Célestine de la Croix; she wrote Huysmans a very flattering letter in 1895, saying that she planned to found an order for artists, in order to renew ecclesiastical art.
49 Saint Lydwina (1380–1433) lived a life of constant pain and suffering from her early youth onwards; this she used as a means of purification and lived largely without food or sleep; canonized in 1892.
50 Huysmans saw some parallel between this work by Pol Demade and something planned, but never actually written, by Barbey d'Aurevilly.
51 St Hildegarde (1098–1179), German Benedictine nun, had a gift of prophecy and corresponded with many notable personages of her day, including Henry II of England. St Catherine of Siena (1347–80), Dominican tertiary, a mystic who spent long periods in prayer and rapture; she showed great concern for the integrity of the papacy.
52 A reference to Catharina Alberdingkthijm.
53 The idea of founding a colony of Christian artists at Fiancey.
54 Alongside her artistic plans, the enterprising Mère Célestine had founded a hydrotherapy establishment under the direction of the dubious Sebastian Kneipp; the enterprise failed financially, and all the nuns left Financey.
55 Fr Parisot was a Benedictine monk at Ligugé.
56 A reference to Arnaud, an orphan protégé of Fr Ferret; he was to enter Solesmes as a novice in 1896.
57 In fact *La Cathédrale* was finished in less than three years.
58 A character in Huysmans' novels; Durtal's spiritual guide, who incorporates elements of both Fr Mugnier and Boullan.
59 Probably Henry Bauer, who worked for *L'Écho de Paris* and had been instrumental in arranging the serialization of *Là-Bas* in that paper.
60 Louis Le Cardonnel had given up his life as a poet to train for the priesthood; he was ordained and later had an unsuccessful attempt at monastic life at Ligugé, during Huysmans' time there.
61 Edouard Dubus, poet, morphine addict and dabbler in magic; he had supplied Huysmans with evidence of black masses.
62 Jeanne Jacquemin was Lauzet's mistress.
63 M. A. Raffalovich, *Uranisme et unisexualité*.
64 A reference to Jean Lorrain (pseudonym of Paul Duval: 1856–1906), minor Symbolist poet and novelist, well known in homosexual circles.
65 Julie de Lespinasse (1732–76) ran a brilliant salon frequented by the encyclopaedists.
66 *Le Moine Bénédictin* of 1892 was originally conceived as the first in a series of monastic biographies, but the plan was not carried through.
67 Monastic discretion still requires that these monks not be identified.

68 The choirmaster at the seminary at Saint-Sulpice.
69 The composer Charles-Marie Widor (1844–1937) was organist at Saint-Sulpice at this time.
70 Dom Pothier, a monk of Saint-Wandrille who did much to restore the art of Gregorian chant in the monastic liturgy.
71 'Let women be silent in church'; Epistle of St Paul to Timothy: I, 2; 11.
72 St Leu was archbishop of Sens in the seventh century.
73 St Soter, pope and martyr in the second century.
74 Verlaine undertook a lecture tour of England in 1893; he had previously worked as a teacher in this country in the 1870s.
75 Zola's *Rome* of 1896 was the second volume of his trilogy *Les Trois Villes*. The other two were *Lourdes* (1894) and *Paris* (1898).
76 A reference to *La Vie spirituelle et l'oraison* by Mme Cécile Bruyère, abbess of Solesmes.
77 A reference to the suggestion that Huysmans should renounce his earlier works. He was prepared, however, to retract the unfavourable remarks he had made about the abbess's own book in *En Route*.
78 In April 1892, two troublemaking monks had sent a memorandum to the Holy Office in which they accused Dom Delatte, abbot of Solesmes, of heresy and immoral conduct with Abbess Cécile; she had been his spiritual daughter, and was appointed abbess very young.
79 Fr Pacheu had planned to call his work *De Dante à Huysmans*.
80 Fr Pacheu accepted Huysmans' suggestion and the work was published with this title.
81 There had been articles in the Parisian press questioning the sincerity of Huysmans' conversion.
82 St Albert the Great (1206–80), Dominican scholar and patron saint of students of the natural sciences; Durand de Mende (1230–96), bishop and canon lawyer, wrote important works on liturgy; Walafried Strabo, a scholar monk of the early ninth century, wrote lives of saints; Macer Florius, latin poet of the twelfth century, author of a long work on the properties of plants.
83 Judges 9: 14. 'Then all the trees said to the thorn bush: Come now, you be our king.'
84 St Melito of Sardes was a second-century theologian and exegete who lived in great seclusion.
85 Harry Quilter, a London barrister and amateur of the arts, had launched *The Universal Review* in the late 1880s. He had sent Miss Huybers to Paris to prospect for articles.
86 'Huysmans intime' by Julien de Narfon in *Le Figaro* of 29 January 1898.
87 It has not been possible to identify this article by Valéry.
88 A reference to the Countess de Galoez, who was madly in love with Huysmans at this time.
89 This woman was an old friend of Anna Meunier; she did become Huysmans' maid.
90 One of Huysmans' expressions for going to confession. This confession to the sub-prior of Saint-Maur was to be decisive: it determined him not to enter religious life, but to become an oblate instead.
91 The friend in question is Gustave Boucher.
92 Dom Besse had had extremely ambitious plans for an artistic revival at Saint-Wandrille; these came to an end when he was sent to the order's house at Silos in Spain for a number of years.
93 M. Cartier was an oblate of the monastery of Solesmes.
94 Mallarmé died on 9 September 1898. His funeral was well attended by men of letters and artists.

IV 1898–1907 Ligugé and the Last Years

1 Works of J. K. Huysmans published in this period:
   Ste Lydwine, 1901
   De Tout, 1902
   L'Oblat, 1903
   Trois Primitifs, 1905
   Les Foules de Lourdes, 1906
2 In a letter to Lucien Descaves, 3 July 1900.
3 In a letter to Arij Prins, 21 April 1903.
4 A fine Romanesque church in the centre of Poitiers.
5 Edouard Drumont (1844–1917), a polemical and anti-Semitic journalist; Huysmans agreed with his ideas on mystical substitution and suffering.
6 The Marquise de Ste Foix was a pious woman sympathetic to Huysmans' cause; she had lived in Algiers, and was material in persuading the Carmelite prioress to intercede with the Vatican on his behalf.
7 'Make me know the way I should walk', Psalm 142.
8 Charles-Marie Dulac (d. 1898); Huysmans said of him: 'Of all our pious painters, young Dulac is the only one with any talent.'
9 Although the institution of Benedictine oblation had flourished in the Middle Ages, it had fallen into disuse; this document by Leo XIII was influential in fostering its revival.
10 A Belgian Catholic journal edited by Fr Moeller.
11 Two of these saints have local associations for Ligugé: the great fourth-century St Martin is associated with the foundation of the monastery; St Radegonde was a former queen, abbess-foundress of a Benedictine monastery in Poitiers in the sixth century.
12 St Frances of Rome (1384–1440) is patron of Benedictine oblates.
13 'The just will flourish like the palm tree', Psalm 91.
14 Fr Louis Van Haecke.
15 Mme Godefroid was also a Benedictine oblate; Huysmans became quite friendly with her during his years at Ligugé, describing her as 'a gay little woman, endowed with the enormous appetite and sweet nature of an unspoilt child'. He immortalized her as Mlle de Garambois in *L'Oblat*.
16 A reference to Paray le Monial, shrine of St Margaret Mary, associated with devotion to the Sacred Heart of Jesus. The Hiéron museum of sacred art still exists.
17 A reference to the *Rule of St Benedict*.
18 The journalist in question is Jules Huret.
19 Valéry married a Mlle Gobillaud in 1900.
20 Blessed Eustochium, virgin, d. 1484; she refused two suitors, preferring to become a bride of Christ, and entered the order of St Clare at Messina.
21 St Paul's first epistle to the Corinthians: 6, 1–11.
22 François Villon, fifteenth-century French poet, whose work was frequently marked by a tone of melancholy and amorous disappointment. Huysmans misquotes from the *Double Ballade* here.
23 'May the Lord clothe you as a new man', an antiphon used at Benedictine clothing ceremonies.
24 Claudine and Joséphine Gay were two young Lyons dressmakers, disciples of Boullan.

25 In 1891, Huysmans had felt himself to be under 'attack' from his occultist opponents; Boullan supplied him with exorcistic paste to keep them at bay. One day when he decided not to go to the Ministry, he learnt that a heavy gilt-framed mirror had fallen on to the place where he would have been sitting.
26 A reference to Fr Mugnier.
27 A monk of Ligugé.
28 The Bollandists were a small group of Jesuits in Antwerp, organized by Jean Bolland in the seventeenth century for the critical study and publication of the lives of the saints.
29 'Oh God, come to my aid', the opening words of each monastic office, intoned by the monk appointed to that function for the week.
30 Although this letter was written the day after Huysmans' ceremony of oblation, he makes no reference to it, and in fact speaks of Ligugé in uncomplimentary terms.
31 The proofs of his life of St Lydwina.
32 Bloy's difficult character meant that he quarrelled with Huysmans, as with most of his other friends; he was constantly reproaching his friends for their lack of financial generosity towards himself.
33 Huysmans' volume *De Tout* was a collection of miscellaneous articles; it had originally been commissioned by a sort of book club, but when that went bankrupt, Stock, his usual publisher, brought it out.
34 Jules Michelet (1798–1874), an outstanding historian with a 'romantic narrative' approach, who made a history of France his life's work.
35 Baron Jacques de Reinach and Cornelius Herz had been implicated in the Panama scandal of 1891.
36 The Solesmes community went into exile on the Isle of Wight in 1901. Their monastic foundations there still survive.
37 Jan van Ruysbroeck (1293–1381), one of Huysmans' earliest favourites amongst spiritual writers, a Flemish mystic who lived a life of great austerity and study. His writings stress the essential role of the mass and the sacraments.
38 Antonin Bourbon, painter, pupil of Gustave Moreau, lived at Ligugé for a while.
39 Émile Zola died accidentally on 29 September 1902; his funeral took place on 5 October.
40 The Humbert affair was a sensational case of fraud and impersonation that had tenuous links with the Dreyfus case.
41 A reference to Henriette du Fresnel, Huysmans' youthful admirer.
42 Huysmans left the convent in the rue Monsieur for a flat in the rue de Babylone in the summer of 1902, both because he found his apartment there cold and damp, and because he knew the Benedictines would have to leave sooner or later.
43 A reference to a pamphlet entitled *Des Esseintes, méthode pratique pour l'Incubat et le Succubat*, Gaillac, 1902.
44 Émile Loubet was President of the Republic from 1899 to 1906.
45 Possibly a reference to Zola's uncompleted series of novels based on his four gospels of Maternity, Truth, Work and Justice. *Fécondité* had appeared in 1899 and *Travail* in 1901.
46 Prins had pictures by both A. Mauve and Jacob Maris in his private collection.
47 The Countess of Galoez's daughter had entered a convent at Lourdes; Huysmans was present at her profession as Sr Thérèse de Jésus on 25 March 1903; they corresponded until his death.
48 Gaston Déchamp was the rather unimaginitve literary critic of *Le Temps*.

49 Emile Nugues was a close friend of Huysmans' last years; he was a teacher at the Catholic École Centrale, and had been introduced to him by his confessor Fr Du Bourg in 1902.
50 Mme d'Etchebers was Jean de Caldain's future mother-in-law.
51 Fr Louis-Marie Séméraire of the church of St François de Sales had died on 13 July 1903.
52 Henri Lasserre, author of *Notre-Dame de Lourdes*; almost a caricature of the popular religious writer, he has been described as 'a commercial traveller in piety'. His family considered legal action against Huysmans for the outspoken opinions he expressed in *Les Foules de Lourdes*.
53 Zola's *Vérité* was published posthumously in 1903.
54 Dom Joseph Bourigaud, abbot of Ligugé, criticized *L'Oblat* in the April 1903 issue of the *Bulletin de Saint-Martin*, reproaching Huysmans with grotesque caricatures of the monks.
55 A reference to the Académie Goncourt and its work of selecting a novel to receive its annual prize.
56 The Vicomte's wife had given birth to twins.
57 One of Huysmans' picturesque ways of referring to confession before midnight mass.
58 The first Prix Goncourt was in fact awarded to Huysmans' protégé, J. A. Nau, for his novel *Force Ennemie*.
59 Dom Georges Legeay, a monk of Saint-Maur, author of a work on Symbolism.
60 Huysmans' anti-Semitism is here directed against the unsuccessful contender for the Prix Goncourt.
61 Alfred Loisy (1857–1940), biblical scholar in favour of a non-literal interpretation of the Scriptures; he was excommunicated.
62 Prins's work *Een Koning* had been translated into French by Georges Khnopff; he had hoped that Huysmans would place it with a Paris publisher, but Huysmans seems to have been less than enthusiastic about the work.
63 René Dumesnil, *Gustave Flaubert, l'homme et l'œuvre*, remains one of the standard biographies of Flaubert; Dumesnil, who was medically qualified, was very attentive to Huysmans during his last illness.
64 The house at Issy was lent to Huysmans by Fr Broussolle.
65 A reference to Pope Pius X's *Gravissimo* of 14 August 1906.
66 Huysmans had moved house yet again: in the rue de Babylone his neighbours all seem to have been eccentric musicians, and he found no peace there.
67 St Jean-Marie Vianney, Curé d'Ars (1786–1859), parish priest and confessor extraordinary; a man of great personal holiness, he suffered frequent physical attack from the Devil.
68 Henriette du Fresnel's family was opposed to her entering a convent.
69 Aristide Briand and Georges Clemenceau were both ministers in the radical coalition government of 1906–9.
70 A reference to the Countess Galoez's daughter.

Bibliography

Editions of the Correspondence of J. K. Huysmans
J. K. Huysmans et Cécile, abbesse de Ste Cécile de Solesmes, *Correspondence*, ed. René Rancœur, 1950.
J. K. Huysmans, *Lettres inédites à Jules Destrée*, 1966.
J. K. Huysmans, *Lettres inédites à Edmond de Goncourt*, 1956.
J. K. Huysmans, *Lettres à Théodore Hannon*, 1985.
J. K. Huysmans, *Lettres inédites à Camille Lemonnier*, 1957.
J. K. Huysmans, *Lettres inédites à Arij Prins*, 1977.
J. K. Huysmans, *Lettres inédites à Émile Zola*, 1953.
Léon Bloy, J. K. Huysmans, Villiers de l'Isle-Adam, *Lettres, Correspondance a trois*, 1980.
Une étape de la vie de J. K. Huysmans, Lettres inédites de J. K. Huysmans à l'Abbé Ferret, ed. E. Bourget Besnier, 1973.

Works Consulted in the Preparation of this Edition
Baldick, Robert, *The Life of J. K. Huysmans*, 1955.
Daoust, Joseph, *Les Débuts bénédictins de J. K. Huysmans*, 1950.
Johnson, Douglas, *France and the Dreyfus Affair*, 1966.
Laver, James, *The First Decadent*, 1954.
McManners, John, *Church and State in France 1870–1914*, 1972.
Mugnier, L'Abbé, *Journal 1879–1939*, 1985.

Index

Alberdingkthijm, Catharina *148, 150*, 152, 237
Alexis, Paul, 27, 34, *36*, 39, 89, 109, 237
  Lucie Pellegrin, 36
  Mme Moeuriot, 109
Allais, Henri, *170, 225*, 237
Andoyer, Fr, 210
Angela of Foligno, Blessed, 136, 143, 152
Arnaud, Br. 154, 172–3, 174
Artiste, L', 16, 19, 24, 29, 33
Aube, L', 211

Babou, Hippolyte, 26
Bachelin, Henri, 23, 26
Bailly, Edmond, 101
Balzac, Honoré de, 6, 16
Banville, Théodore de, 92
Barbey d'Aurevilly, Jules, 27, 61, 63, 70, 74, 78, 90, 94, 96, 146, 151, 166, 176, 183
  L'Ensorcelée, 61
  Les Diaboliques, 61, 78
Barrès, Maurice, 102, 125, 145
Bastien-Lepage, J., 4, 48, 89
Baudelaire, Charles, 13, 44, 67, 82, 92
Benedict, St, 192, 199
  Order of, 9, 11, 128, 135, 138, 143, 172, 177, 179, 186, 197, 216, 221
  Rule of, 196, 197
Bénie de Jésus, Prioress, née Princess Jeanne Bibesco, 178, *184, 185, 188, 195, 202*, 237
Bergerat, Emile, 20
Bernard, Emile, *188*, 237
Bernard, St, 146, 147, 152
Berthet, Adolphe, *alias* Esquirol, 183, *194*, 197, *199, 207, 215, 220*, 223, *228*, 237
Besse, Dom Jean-Martial, 127, 135, *138*, *158*, 173, 175, 179, 181, 190, 191, 205, 206, 217, 237
Blanc, Louis, 104
Bloy, Léon, *56, 68*, 69–70, 76–77, 78, 81, 85, 86, *88*, 90, 102, 111, 206, 213, 237–8
  Le Désespéré, 79
  Un Brelan d'excommuniés, 90
  Johanna, née Molbech, 102
Boborykin, P., 31, 33, 38, 75
Bois, Jules, 153, 194, 238
Bollandists, The, 202
Botticelli, 138, 201, 225
Boucher, Gustave, 106, *106, 113, 117*, 123, 154, 156, 159, 175, 177,184, 238
Bouguereau, Adolphe William, 51, 68
Boulanger, Georges, 85
Boullan, Joseph-Antoine, 63, 64, 65, 100, 103, 104, 108, 112, 113, 114, 121, 122–3, 127, 137, 194, 199, 200
Bourdeau, Jean, 53
Bourges, Elémir, 34
Bourget, Paul, 84, 103, 104, 105, 109, 116, 125, 145, 146
Bourigaud, Dom Joseph, 221, 225
Bouvier, Alexis, 41
Breughel the Elder, 83
Briand, Aristide, 234
Brothers of St John of God, The, 95, 96, 97, 186
Broussolle, Fr Camille, *201*, 238
Brun, Charles, *171*, 238
Brunetière, Ferdinand, 82
Bruyère, Mme Cécile, Abbess, 128, *163, 173, 182*, 184–8, *191, 210*, 238
  Treatise on Prayer, 164, 188–9, 191
Buet, Charles, 144, 206
Bunyan, John, 146

Cabanel, Alexandre, 18, 21, 50

Index

Cadière, Catherine, 60
Caldain, Jean de, *217*, 221, *224*, 230, 238
Callewaert, Félix, 28
Carnavalet, Musée, 102
Carton de Wiart, Léon, 33
Catherine of Siena, St, 152
Cazals, F.-A., *160*, 238
Caze, Robert, 68, 75, 77, 161, 176
Céard, Henry, 3, 18, 19, 20, 22, 26, 27, 31, 33, 34, 39, 50, 58, 59, *209*, *214*, *218*, 238
Célestine de la Croix, Mère, Abbess, 154
Chamard, Dom François, 138, 139, 173, 199, 210
Charcot, Jean-Martin, 111
Chardin, Jean-Baptiste, 40
Charpentier, Georges, 18, 23, 29, 30, 31, 39, 48, 52, 58, 75
Chat noir, Le, 56, 84
Chevalier, Sr Adèle, 63
Chevreul, Eugène, 77
Church, The Catholic, 9–11, 53, 64, 116, 125, 127, 137, 144, 145, 146, 147, 151–2, 172, 177–8, 184–5, 186–8, 188, 200, 203, 205, 219, 226
Cistercians, The (Trappists), 120–1, 133, 140, 141–2, 143, 144, 185, 221
Cladel, Léon, 41
Claretie, Jules, 73
Clemenceau, Georges, 50, 234
Combes, Emile, 10, 11
Comédie humaine, La, 38–9, 41
Corbière, Tristan, 44, 72
Coppée, François, 45, 95
Courrière, Berthe, 65, 101, 102
Cot, Pierre-Auguste, 51
Courbet, Gustave, 29, 52

Dantine, Marie, later Comtesse de Villiers de l'Isle-Adam, 93, 96–7, 101, 169
Daudet, Alphonse, 22, 23, 28, 84–5, 86, 90, 105, 125, 180
  The Nabob, 28
  Tartarin de Tarascon, 84
  Tartarin sur les Alpes, 84
  L'Immortel, 87, 88
Dauzon, Fr, 203
Decadence, 8, 13, 15, 44
Degas, Edgar, 5, 26, 48, 51

Delatte, Dom Paul, 128, 162, 165, 174
Delfour, Fr, 127, 166
Delpit, Albert, 70
Denis, St, 141
Denis, Maurice, 132
Dentu, E., 21, 30
Déroulède, Paul, 70
Descaves, Lucien, *52*, 95, 128, 137, 171, 180, 207, 238
Destrée, Jules, 59–60, *60*, *67*, *68*, *71*, *73*, *84*, *105*, 238
Dickens, Charles, 43
Dierx, Léon, 96, 97
Dostoevsky, Fyodr, 7, 70
Dreyfus, Alfred, 3, 10, 178, 209, 215
Drumont, Edouard, 184
Du Boisgobey, Fortuné, 21
Dubois, Martial, 80
Du Bourg, Fr, 210, 215, 224
Dubus, Edouard, 156
Dujardin, Edouard, 89
Dulac, Charles, 186, 187
Dumas, Alexandre, the Elder, 16
Dumesnil, René, *229*, 238
Duran, Charles, 17
Durendal, 191, 197
Durtal*, 6, 7, 9, 125, 142–3, 148, 156, 165, 171, 179, 228

Ebeling, Friedrich, 101, 111, 137
Echo de Paris, L', 111, 171, 211
Edwards, Emile, *110*, 238
Emmerich, Sr Anne Catherine, 8, 60, 167
Ernouf de Verclives, Baron (A. A. Baron, *pseud.*), 89
Esseintes, Duc Jean des*, 2, 8, 9, 15, 44, 55, 61, 70, 72, 158
Etchebers, Mme d', 218, 225
Etiévant, Camille, 34

Ferret, Fr Gabriel-Eugène, 127, *139*, *141*, *154*, 159, 169, 173–4, 177, 184, 192, 239
Figaro, Le, 82, 87, 97, 103, 121, *123*, 123, 170, 197
Flaubert, Gustave, 3, 6, 7, 14, 16, 18, 20, 22, 24, 25, 42, 67, 92, 214, 219, 229
  Mme Bovary, 3, 20, 22, 25

Salammbô, 22
L'Education sentimentale, 22, 55, 116, 117
La Tentation de Saint Antoine, 20, 22, 55
Trois contes, 20, 21, 25
Fleury, Maurice de, *85*, 90, 103, 215, 239
Fleury, Rohaut, 167
Forain, Jean-Louis, *204*, 224, 239
Fra Angelico, 156
France, Anatole, 145, 146, 214
Frances of Rome, St, 192
Franco-Prussian War, The, 9
Freemasonry, 10, 127, 137, 159, 193, 195, 202, 230
Fresnel, Henriette du, 180, 215, 223, 227–8, 233

Galoez, Comtesse de, *alias* La Sol, 126, 172, 173, 175, 181, 183, 191, 192–3
Gauguin, Paul, 5
Gaulois, Le, 19, 25, 38, 45
Gautier, Judith, 31
Gautier, Théophile, 16, 20, 29, 36, 55, 229
  Tableaux de siège, 104
  Italia, 138
Gavarni, Sulpice-Guillaume, 40, 45
Gay, Claudine and Joséphine, 199
Geffroy, Gustave, *51*, 239
Gérôme, 21
Gertrude, St, 136
Gervex, Henri, 48
Gide, André, 2, *107*, 125, *132, 133*, 145, *148*, 190–1, 239
  Les Cahiers d'André Walter, 107–8
  La Tentative amoureuse, 133
  Voyage d'Urien, 132, 133
  Traité du Narcisse, 133, 145
  Paludes, 148
Gil Blas, Le, 42, 79, 82, 105, 109, *159*
Girard, Henri, 106, *106*, 113, 114, 123, 191, 207, 239
Godefroid, Mme, 193
Goffin, Arnold, *70*, 239
  Le Journal d'André, 70–1
Goncourt, Académie, 1, 180
Goncourt, Edmond de, 1, 2, 7, 16, 18, 20, 21, 22, 29, 35, *40*, 50, 78, 82, 84, 90, *91, 104, 112*, 112, *137, 149*, 180, 239
  La Faustin, 44, 55
  La Fille Elisa, 36
  Les Frères Zemganno, 35–6
  La Maison d'un artiste, 40
  Patrie en danger, 91
Goncourt, Edmond and Jules de, 6, 14, 117, 229
  Germinie Lacerteux, 55, 91
  Mme Gervaisais, 35
  Italie d'hier, 137–8
  Journal, vol. VIII, 149
Goncourt Prize, The, 180, 223, 224
Gourmont, Remy de, 65, *94*, 101, 239
Grandier, Urbain, 60
Grévy, Jules, 85
Grünewald, Matthias, 7–8, 105, 180, 222, 223
Guaïta, Stanislas de, 63, 199, 200
Guérin, Alcide, 114
Guerry, Dom Georges, 225
Guiches, Gustave, 86, 89, 93, 96, 97
Guillemet, Jean-Baptiste, 34
Guyot, Fr, 213

Hannon, Théodore, 3, 14, *16, 17, 18, 19*, 23, 26, *28*, 30, *33*, 41, *43*, 44, *47, 48*, 239
  Au Pays de Manneken Pis, 47, 49
Harry, Myriam, *232*, 239
Hello, Ernest, 90
Hennequin, Emile, 54, *57*, 240
Henner, J. J., 48, 51
Hennezel, Vicomte Henri d', 221, 223, *230*, 240
Hennique, Léon, 27, 31, 34, 35, 39, 48, 50, 75, 215
Hervieu, Paul, 86, 89
Hildegarde, St, 152
Hokusaï, 40
Huc, Mme Théophile, 180, *200, 225, 230*, 240
Hugo, Victor-Marie, 20, 22, 23, 24, 33, 34, 55, 67, 68, 92
  Les Misérables, 67
  Les Travailleurs de la mer, 67, 98
  La Légende des siècles, 20, 24
Huret, Jules, *142*, 240

Huysmans, Joris-Karl, *works*
  Le Drageoir aux épices, 13, 20, 21, 85
  Marthe, 8, 14, 16, 19, 25, 27, 29, 36, 74, 178
  Les Soeurs Vatard, 8, 14, 18, 19, 21, 26, 31, 33, 116, 129
  Croquis parisiens, 38, 46, 57
  En Ménage, 8, 14, 39, 41, 116, 117, 119, 129
  A Vau l'Eau, 8, 14, 42, 80, 116, 117, 215
  L'Art moderne, 15, 48, 50, 51, 55, 73
  A Rebours, 1, 2, 8, 9, 15, 44, 46, 47–8, 50, 52, 54–5, 60, 71, 72, 73, 78, 81, 89, 94, 110, 116, 118, 121, 166
  En Rade, 8, 62, 78, 79, 80, 81
  Certains, 118
  La Bièvre, 76, 102, 103
  Là-Bas, 6, 9, 63, 64, 105, 109, 110, 111, 116, 117, 118, 121, 131, 137, 144, 145, 149, 153, 193, 194
  En Route, 65, 125, 127, 137, 142–3, 144, 146, 155, 156, 159, 163, 165, 171, 177, 184, 187, 207, 208, 209
  La Cathédrale, 8, 9, 125, 155–6, 162–3, 165, 169, 170, 171, 178, 185, 187, 189, 208, 216
  Sainte Lydwine, 197, 202, 206, 207, 233
  De Tout, 208, 211
  Pages catholiques, 186, 194
  L'Oblat, 2, 8, 9, 179, 207, 208, 213, 215, 216, 219, 220, 221, 222, 231
  Trois primitifs, 180
  Les Foules de Lourdes, 179, 233

Imitation of Jesus Christ, The, 53
Impressionists, The, 4–5, 6, 15, 17, 19, 26, 80, 222
Index Prohibitorum, 177, 186, 187–8, 216, 219
Irenaeus, St, 108

Jacquemin, Jeanne, 156
Jansenism, 146
Jeune Belgique, La, 68
Joachim of Fiore, 103
John of the Cross, St, 143
Joseph, St, 192

Joyce, James, 9

Kahn, Gustave, 89
Kistemaeckers, Henri, *43*, 48, 49, 52, 240
Klein, Fr Félix, *144*, *145*, 240
Kloos, W., 76
Kneipp, Sebastian, 154

Lafitte, Jules, 34, 35
Laforgue, Jules, 62, *72*, 92, 125, 240
  Les Complaintes, 72–3
  L'Imitation de Notre-Dame de la Lune, 73
Lambert, Pierre, 1
Landry, Georges, *68*, *104*, 106, *107*, *112*, *122*, 128, 140, 179, *183*, *190*, *206*, 223, 224, 240
Lasserre, Henri, 218
Laurens, J.-P., 17, 51
Laurent, Mme Méry, 95, 96
Lautréamont, Comte de (Isidore Ducasse, *pseud.*), 71
Lauzet, Auguste, *155*, 240
Lebel-Bouasse, veuve, 69
Le Cardonnel, Fr Louis, 156, 200, 205, 206
Leclair, Léon, *172*, 177, 179, 181, 191, 192, 205, 217, 218, 222, 223, 226, 228, *234*, 240
  Mme Marguerite, 173, 177, 179, 181, 190, 191, 192, 205, 213, 234
Leconte de Lisle, 55
Legeay, Dom Georges, 224
Lemonnier, Camille, 4, 14, 16, 17, *22*, 24, *25*, 29, 38, *41*, 49, *59*, *79*, 240
  Contes flamands et wallons, 29
  Le Mâle, 39
  Le Mort, 79
  Les Charniers, 41
  L'Hystérique, 60
Leo XIII, Pope, 10
Lespinasse, Mlle de, 157
Lesseps, Ferdinand de, 125
Leu, St, 160
Liturgy, 125, 160, 164, 166–7, 178, 185, 186, 189, 190, 198, 204, 211–2, 221
Loisy, Alfred, 226
Logerot, Dom Athanase, 172, 174, 175, 182

Index

Lorrain, Jean (Paul Duval, *pseud.*), *109*, 156, 240
Loti, Pierre, 92
Lourdes, 170, 179, 217–8, 219, 221, 226–7, 230
Louvre, Musée du, 5, 30, 74, 99, 214, 225
Lully, Raymond, 199
Luyken, Jan, 67, 71
Lydwina, St, 151, 169, 175, 178, 181, 192, 193, 196, 203

Maillat, Henriette, 89, *120*, 240
Mallarmé, Stéphane, 1, 14, *44, 45, 46*, 55–7, *58*, 62, 72, 73, 78, 84, 91, *93*, 94, 95, 96, 97, 101, 176, 241
  Eglogus, 44
  L'Après-midi d'un faune, 44, 45
  L'Hérodiade, 45
  La Pipe, 45
  Le Démon de l'Analogie, 46
Malot, Hector, 17
Manet, Edouard, 5, 52
Maria, d'Agreida, Sr, 111
Marpon, Charles, 34, 39
Marras, Jean, 94
Martin, St, 192
Mary, The Blessed Virgin, 145, 148, 154–5, 170, 172, 182, 184, 186, 189, 191, 192, 196, 203, 218, 232
Matteï, César, 84
Maupassant, Guy de, 27, 29, 31, 38, 39, *42, 49*, 51, 88, 90, 103, 105, 215, 241
  Contes de la Bécasse, 49
  Musotte, 109
Melito, St, 167
Memmi, Filippo di, 138
Mendès, Catulle, 17, 18, 20, 23, 44, 94
Mercure de France, 168
Merry del Val, Cardinal, 11
Méténier, Oscar, 116
Metsys, Jan, 105
Meunier, Anna, 62, 70, 79, 89, 112, 120, 125, 130
Michallon, A. E., 29
Micheau, Dom Ernest Hilaire, *169, 231*, 241
Michelet, Jules, 209
Milleriot, Fr, 107

Mirbeau, Octave, 27, 86
Misme, Pascal, 108, 113, 114, 141, 156, 199, 200
Moeller, Fr Henry, *144, 197*, 241
Monastic Life, 126–7, 133, 135, 159, 165, 169–70, 172, 174, 181, 182, 189, 197, 203, 207
Monet, Claude, 5, 75, 80
Mocquereau, Dom, 164, 168, 212
Montesquiou, Comte Robert de, 55
Montrosier, Eugène, 21, 23, 26
Moreau, Gustave, 5, 45, 55, 57
Morice, Charles, *92*, 241
Morisse, Paul, *212*, 241
Mugnier, Fr Arthur, 65, 112, 113, *119, 120*, 123, 126, 156, 165, 167, 173, 180, 181, 186, *198*, 201, 226, 230, 241
Musée des Deux-Mondes, Le, 21, 23, 26

Narfon, Julien de, 171
Naturalism, 5, 6, 7, 8, 13, 16, 20, 25, 60–1, 62, 69, 74, 78, 100, 116
Naundorff, Louis-Charles, 63, 84
Novel, The, 8–9, 116–7, 125, 223, 225
Nugues, Emile, 218

Odo of Cluny, St, 147
Og, Jules, 13
Ohnet, Georges, 52, 61, 70, 72, 73, 88
Olier, Fr Jean-Jacques, 114
Orsat, Alexis, 101, 113, 123, 191, 207
Ostade, Adriaen van, 46

Pacheu, Fr Jules, *146, 165, 166*, 241
Paray-le-Monial, 140, 194
Parisot, Fr, 154
Parnassians, The, 17, 18, 20, 22, 23, 25
Péladan, Sâr Joséphin, 63, 194
Perugino, 201
Pinard, Albert, 57
Pissarro, Camille, 5, 80
Pius X, Pope, 11, 230
Poe, Edgar Allen, 44, 68, 70, 92
Poictevin, Francis, 95, 100, 103
Pol Demade, Dr, *151, 152*, 241
Pointillists, The, 80
Ponsard, François, 16
Pontavice de Heussey, Robert du, *94*, 241

272 *Index*

Pothier, Dom Joseph, 159, 212
Pothinus, St, 108
Potvin, Charles, 43
Potvin, Fr, 201
Primitives, The, 7, 88, 105, 118, 152, 156, 180, 205, 212, 217, 225
Prins, Arij, 2, 12, 62, *74*, 75, *76*, *77*, *78*, *80*, 88, *89*, *100*, *101*, *102*, *110*, *115*, *117*, *121*, *128*, *129*, *130*, *133*, *134*, *136*, *187*, *213*, *216*, *221*, *222*, *226*, *227*, *234*, 241
Proust, Marcel, 9, 65
Puvis de Chavannes, Pierre, 4, 68

Quilter, Harry, 168

Rachilde (Mme Alfred Vallette, *pseud*.), *220*, 242
Rafaëlli, Jean-Francois, 5, *50*, 51, 74, 75, 241
Raffalovich, Marc-André, *157*, 242
Rais, Gilles de, *alias* Bluebeard, 98, 101, 110
Ramaekers, G., *153*, 242
Rappel, Le, 24, 39
Read, Louise, 70, 183
Redon, Odilon, 2, 5, 45, 71, 73, 74, *75*, 79, *98*, 105, 118, 242
Réforme, La, 41, 68
Reiskiold, Waldemar de, 185
Rembrandt van Rijn, 214
Renan, Ernest, 104, 146
Renoir, Auguste, 80
République française, La, 34
République des Lettres, La, 23, 44, 84
Retté, Adolphe, *232*, 242
Revue des Deux Mondes, La, 68, 168
Revue indépendante, La, 68, 78, 79, 80, 81, 168
Richard, Cardinal Archbishop, 159–60
Rivière, Charles, *124*, 141, *162*, 242
Robert, Louis de, 6, *116*, 242
Robin, Albert, 93, 95
Roca, Canon, 100
Rops, Félicien, 20, 26, 41
  Les Sataniques, 101
Rosicrucians, The, 63, 103
Rosny, J. H., 7, 82
Rossi, Count Pellegrino, 138

Roujon, Henry, 93
Rowlandson, Thomas, 77
Rubens, Peter Paul, 26, 31, 46, 225
Ruysbroeck, Jan van, 212

Sade, Marquis de, 71
Sainte-Foix, Marquise de, 185, 203
Salette, La, 112, 113–4, 115, 120
Sand, George, 7, 112
Santen Kolff, Jacob van, 103, 115
Sartre, Jean-Paul, 14
Sauvage, Georges, 17
Savine, Albert, 87, 90
Schopenhauer, Arthur, 2, 14, 53, 55, 63, 116, 198
Séméraire, Fr Louis-Marie, 218
Sérieux, Paul, *131*, 242
Seurat, Georges, 80
Signac, Paul, 80
Soter, St, 160
Stevens, Arthur, 21
Stock, Pierre-Victor, 74, 76, 79, 80, 111, 117, 136–7, 140, 142, 171, 200, 206, 207, 228
Symbolists, The, 3, 15, 62, 72, 92

Taine, Hippolyte, 6, 44
  Voyage en Italie, 138
Tardif de Moidrey, Fr, 123
Teniers, David, 46
Teresa of Avila, St, 111, 136, 143, 192, 195, 196, 232
  The Interior Castle, 114
Teresa of Jesus, Sr, 217, 234
Thibault, Julie, 103, 111, 112, 114, 123, *140*, 155, 156, 172, 183, 194, 195, 199, 200, 242
Third Republic, The, 3, 9–11, 64, 125
Thomasson, Dom de Gournay, *164*, *166*, 176, 242
Trachsel, 118
Turgenev, Ivan Sergeevich, 22, 75

Ulbach, Louis, 35

Valerio, Edith, née Huybers, *168*, 242
Valéry, Paul-Ambroise, 2, *171*, *176*, *198*, 242
Vallette, Alfred, 110

Vanier, Léon, 72, 73
Van der Weyden, Rogier, 105, 222
Van Haecke, Fr Louis, 118, 193, 216
Vannutelli, Cardinal Vicenzo, 184
Verhaeren, Emile, 4, *46*, 242
  Les Flamandes, 46
Verlaine, Paul, 1, 14, 44, 57–8, 62, 70, 72, 73, *82*, 84, *86*, 87, 90, 99, 125, 147, 160–1, 166, 176, 223, 224, 243
  Romances sans paroles, 82
  Amours, 86
  Sagesse, 58, 82, 147, 161
Vianney, St Jean-Marie, curé d'Ars, 232
Vigourel, Fr, 159, 221
Villiers de l'Isle-Adam, Comte Jean-Marie-Mathias-Philippe-Auguste de, 14, 45, 47, 74, 76–7, 78, 79, 84–5, 86, 90, 91, 93, 94–8, 125, 151, 176
  Axël, 94, 95, 101
  Contes cruels, 47
  Tribulat Bonhomet, 81
Villiers de l'Isle-Adam, Victor-Philippe-Auguste de, *alias* Totor, 77, 93, 94, 101, 168–9
Villon, François, 198
Vintras, Eugène, 63, 123, 194, 200
Voltaire, Le, 34
Vollon, 4, 17

Wagner, Richard, 95
Waldeck-Rousseau, René, 10, 11
Wallonie, La, 84
Watteau, Antoine, 40
Widor, Charles-Marie, 159
Wilde, Oscar, 2
Wilson, Daniel, 134

Wirth, Oswald, 63, *100*, 199, 243

Zaccone, Pierre, 21
Zola, Emile, 1, 2, 5, 6, 8, 13, 16, *16*, 17, 18, 20, 21, 22, 23, *27*, 29, 30, *31*, 33, *34*, 37, 37, *38*, 38, 43, 50, 52, *53*, *54*, 54, *58*, 61, 62, *66*, 74, 78, *81*, *83*, 84, 86, *87*, 88, 100, 102, 103, 104, 105, 109, 111, 115, 116, 117, 122, 125, *161*, 178, 180, 214–5, 216–7, 218, 219, 243
  The Rougon-Macquart novels, 6, 13, 53
  L'Argent, 105, 209
  L'Assommoir, 6, 16, 17, 20, 28, 55, 61, 105
  La Bête Humaine, 105
  Bouton de rose, 32
  La Curée, 28, 162
  La Débâcle, 115
  La Faute de l'Abbé Mouret, 55
  Germinal, 59, 66
  Les Héritiers Rabourdin, 32
  J'accuse, 178, 214
  La Joie de vivre, 53
  Nana, 31, 32, 37–8
  Renée, 82
  Le Rêve, 105
  Les Soirées de Médan, 13
  La Terre, 82, 83, 84
  Thérèse Raquin, 31, 32
  Le Ventre de Paris, 29, 53, 66, 158
  Les Trois Villes, 161–2

NOTE
Numbers in italics indicate addressees of letters.
* indicates fictional characters.